LEWIS MORRIS

A History of the

Honourable Society of Cymmrodorion

and of the

Gwyneddigion and Cymreigyddion Societies

(1751—1951)

By

R. T. JENKINS

and

HELEN M. RAMAGE

Y Cymmrodor

Vol. L.

LONDON

The Honourable Society of Cymmrodorion

20 Bedford Square

—

1951

PREFACE

IN 1939, Miss Helen Myfanwy Jones (now Mrs. Ramage), "Lloyd George" Research Student in Welsh History at the University College of North Wales, was awarded the degree of M.A. for a dissertation on the history of the Society of Cymmrodorion. The Society had at first intended to print this piece of research work as it stood ; but war and other obstacles cut across the intention. By the time the possibility of printing the work returned, the celebration of the Society's Bi-centenary loomed ahead, and the Council was led to contemplate a somewhat different scheme, namely the publication of a volume destined for the general reader rather than for the academic student. Mrs. Ramage's work was necessarily somewhat more austere in treatment than would be expected in a book of that kind, and in particular its copious footnotes and bibliography might have seemed out of place in a volume whose readers would not feel impelled to refer constantly to the original sources. I am glad to say that Mrs. Ramage herself, in the second and third numbers of *Llên Cymru*, has now printed an annotated digest of her work as far as the history of the First Cymmrodorion Society is concerned—and I may add that, as is customary in such cases, the whole of her dissertation is available for consultation in the National Library of Wales and in the Library of her own College at Bangor.

The Council felt that the account of the First Cymmrodorion Society should be expanded so as to include a fuller account of the more prominent of the earlier Cymmrodorion, and an amplified treatment of the social and cultural background which conditioned their work. Further, they wished the book to include an account of the Gwyneddigion and Cymreigyddion Societies, deeming (most rightly, if I may presume to say so) that the continuity of London-Welsh cultural life should be emphasised—Mrs. Ramage, limited as she was by her terms of reference to the Cymmrodorion proper, had confined herself to a short "linkage" connecting the First with the Second Cymmrodorion, although, as is shown by her paper on the Cymreigyddion in *Y Llenor* (1938), she was in fact perfectly familiar with the history of these "intermediate" Societies.

iii

I have myself written the chapters dealing with the earlier societies. I-III are based on Mrs. Ramage's work, but I have worked over the whole of the sources, including Mrs. Ramage's transcripts of MS. material in the British Museum, the National Library of Wales, and other libraries, and I have to thank her for saving me much time and trouble by her readiness to lend me her transcripts. She has also lent me MS. material bearing upon the subject of my fourth chapter ; but here I have leaned rather more on modern printed studies, e.g., those by Sir William Ll. Davies, Mr. G. T. Roberts of Llanrug, Mr. J. Hubert Morgan, Mr. Robert Owen of Croesor, and above all Professor G. J. Williams, whose long and valuable series of papers in *Y Llenor* (and elsewhere) on the London-Welsh literati will be so familiar to all readers of Welsh. I ought, further, to make it clear that all comments or other expressions of opinion in my chapters are my own, and that Mrs. Ramage is not in the slightest degree to be blamed for any of them.

The fifth and sixth chapters are as they stood in Mrs. Ramage's dissertation. I have " edited " them to the extent of transposing a few dates from her footnotes into her text, and making the necessary alterations when the death or resignation of officials of the Society since she wrote (in 1939) had to be recorded.

The illustrations have been selected by the Hon. Secretary and the Hon. Editor of the Society. I feel that I owe them both my very sincere apologies for my very long delay in completing this book, and can only hope that their wrath will be mitigated by remembering that I have been simultaneously occupied on another piece of business on the Honourable Society's behalf.

R. T. JENKINS

University College of North Wales,

Bangor,

April 21st 1951.

CONTENTS

LIST OF ILLUSTRATIONS

Frontispiece: LEWIS MORRIS

1. THE WELSH SCHOOL AT CLERKENWELL

   By courtesy of the St. Pancras Borough Council : from a water-colour in the Heal Bequest

2. THE BANNER OF THE 1751 SOCIETY

   In the possession of the Honourable Society : formerly preserved at the Welsh Girls School, Ashford

3. WILLIAM VAUGHAN OF CORS-Y-GEDOL, FIRST CHIEF PRESIDENT

   By courtesy of the Right. Hon. Lord Mostyn, owner of the original painting

4. OWEN JONES (OWAIN MYFYR)

   From Leathart's *Origin and Progress of the Gwyneddigion Society;* the protrait was made by John Vaughan

5. SIR HUGH OWEN

   By courtesy of the National Library of Wales

6. THE CYMMRODORION MEDAL

7. SIR EVAN VINCENT EVANS

8. REV. DR. GRIFFITH HARTWELL JONES

NOTE ON THE SOURCES

The chief MS. sources used by Mrs. Ramage were :

1. The " Cymmrodorion " and " Myvyrian " MSS. in the British Museum (see pp. 36 and 166-7); more specifically :

    B.M. Add. MSS. 14,927 ; 14,929 ; 14,949; 15,015 ; 15,021 ; 15,022 ; 15,029 ; 15,030 ; 15,060 ; 15,089.

2. MSS. in the National Library of Wales, more specifically :

    Crosswood MSS. (the papers of Gwallter Mechain) 97 ; 1737; 1804-8 ; 1860 ; 1894-5.

    Panton MS. 74.

    Mysefin MSS. (W. O. Pughe).

    N.L.W. MS. 244.

    Minute-book of the Cymreigyddion Society (formerly kept at Ashford).

3. MSS. in the Cardiff City Library : the Tonn correspondence (for Chapter 5 of this book).

4. MSS. 652 and 1,001 in the Library of the University College of North Wales.

5. Minutes (from 1873) of the Council of the Hon. Society of Cymmrodorion.

The main *printed* source, down to 1787, is of course the correspondence of the Morrises and their friends, as contained in *The Morris Letters*, ed. J. H. Davies, 2 vols., 1906-9 (copious indexes by Hugh Owen, in the *Transactions of the Anglesey Antiquarian Society*, 1942 and 1944—also issued separately in three parts by that Society), and the *Additional Morris Letters* transcribed and indexed by Hugh Owen and forming Vol. 49 (in two parts) of *Y Cymmrodor*. In the present book, the term " Morris Letters " is used for the *entire* corpus ; the form "Letter" or "Letters" marks a definite citation, while "letter(s)" is of more general reference. It should be added that in this book the Welsh portions of the letters have been rendered into English. Other printed sources which have been used are *Llythyrau at Ddafydd Jones o Drefriw* transcribed and annotated by G. J. Williams in the *National Library of Wales Journal Supplement* Series 3, No. 2 ; and *Llawysgrif Richard Morris o Gerddi* ed. T. H. Parry-Williams (1931). W. D. Leathart's *Origin and Progress of the Gwyneddigion Society* (1831), though not technically a " source," has the value of a source for the history of that Society.

As has been explained in the Preface, the exclusion of footnotes and internal references from this work makes it quite pointless to add a list (which would have been very long) of secondary books and papers consulted by the writers.

A History *of* The Cymmrodorion

I.—"ANTIENT BRITONS"

THE Council of the Honourable Society of Cymmrodorion, when it decided to publish this bi-centenary memorial, was far from wishing to confine its compilers to a bare historical account of the Society itself. Rather, it instructed them to relate the history to its background—to sketch, as far as space permitted and materials were available, the story of Welshmen in London during the past two centuries, and of the links connecting them with their native land. Obviously, there would have been no Cymmrodorion Society at all had it not been, firstly, for the presence in London of a relatively large number of exiles from Wales, and next, for the desire of influential members of the London-Welsh community to create and maintain some form of corporate life and activity. The history of the Cymmrodorion Society proper is discontinuous ; three Societies in succession have borne that name. But the essential features have been uninterruptedly present : the influx of Welsh people into London and the nostalgia which has impelled them (or at least a number of them) to cling together in that Babylon—admittedly a Babylon in which on the whole they found life agreeable and indeed profitable—to revive memories of the homeland. It is noteworthy that even when the First Cymmrodorion Society suffered eclipse, there yet arose other London-Welsh societies which kept the flag flying ; and the compilers have been instructed to include an account of these as well. In the long interval between the Second and Third Cymmrodorion, the circumstances had become rather different. London Welshmen were considerably more numerous, and their interests were therefore more widely dispersed, less easy to focus. Again, the vast improvement of communications between London and Wales made London less of an exile, and contact with home easier and more frequent. Few

London Welshmen in 1873 were like Richard Morris of Anglesey, who left his Welsh home in 1721 or 1722 and died in 1779 without once revisiting it. Yet the old ideal of a home from home had not perished, and in that year the present Honourable Society was established to realise it.

Nostalgia, however, or home-sickness, is far too often a faith without works. Natural (indeed inevitable) as it is, it must needs quickly fade if it be not combined with something more positive. A very great number of Welsh (as also of Scots or Irish) who have settled in England throughout the centuries have sunk into the surrounding Englishry, retaining nothing but their surnames to betray their origin. At a very early date in the annals of Anglo-Welshry, the epigrammatist John Owen had laughed at a compatriot who boasted that he came of " the London Davises," and had nought to do with Wales. Said John Owen in 1606, in a Latin epigram which may be Englished thus :—

> Why talk of " London Davises " ? I cannot understand
> Your boast that you have nought to do with Wales, your father's land ;
> You do not see, poor fool, that you thereby have cast away
> A noble ancestry, to claim descent from baser clay ;
> Still, on one point your father's land and you do well concur—
> For Wales has full as much contempt of you, as you of her.

Like Boswell in one of his more obsequious moods, such men might have excused themselves in the words " Mr. Johnson, indeed I come from [Wales], but I cannot help it." And to them, too, Johnson might have replied, " Sir, that, I find, is what a very great number of your countrymen cannot help." But indeed, who shall blame such folk ? for once their home-sickness was past, they had no other " Welshness " left, so why bother about it ?

Others, again, have made themselves slightly ridiculous by a recurring but purely sentimental nostalgia, paraded only on state occasions. Which of us has not listened to a prosperous compatriot, upon a S. David's Day, recounting with a catch in his voice how, in his penurious childhood in far-off Llŷn or Cardiganshire, he ate his supper of oatmeal in the dim rush-light —and sighing for " those good old days " ? His sighs were echoed by a sympathetic audience, which, however, knew perfectly well that if the excellent man had that day been offered *llymru* for breakfast, there would have been a grave domestic crisis at "The Lindens."

But the London Cymmrodorion or Gwyneddigion or Cymreigyddion wore their leeks "with a difference." To be sure, there was sentimentalism there too ; to be sure, there was even misunderstanding of the Wales which they had left behind them, lack of appreciation of far-reaching changes which were transforming it. But there was also a conscious and deliberate effort to confer positive benefits upon Wales ; the nostalgia of these men was a faith which issued in works, however ill-judged their efforts might have seemed to various people for various reasons. It may seem odd to an outsider, to-day, who scans the printed " constitutions " of the University of Wales, and of other Welsh public institutions, to find that this "London" Society has official representation on their governing bodies, and a statutory meeting at every National Eisteddfod. But there is a perfectly sound reason for that ; this hitherto unchartered association of London Welshmen has played a leading part in the establishment of all these institutions. Throughout their long history, the Cymmrodorion and their congeners have looked out beyond the city in which they were pent, upon the land which they had left behind them ; not content with remembering Jerusalem they have striven according to their lights to rebuild it.

* * * *

It was to a Scotsman, as we remember, that Samuel Johnson, brushing aside that patriot's praises of the " fine wild prospects " of his native land, grimly replied that the finest " prospect " a Scotsman ever saw was the high road to England. But the Doctor could equally well have trumped a Welshman's ace with the same remark. For Wales, like Scotland, though thinly populated, was over-populated for its resources in food. There had always, even in the Middle Ages, been immigration to England—and specifically to London. But the crucial date is that of the battle of Bosworth, 1485, which opened an era during which the trickle of Welshmen became a flood ; the flood, indeed, had subsided in a measure by 1660, but a pretty sizeable stream still ran. The accession of the Tudor dynasty, and the political and economic results of that accession, opened England wide to the Welshman. " Careers," high and

3

low, became accessible to him. From the political standpoint, the "high" careers no doubt seemed the more important— the careers at Court, on Bench and at Bar, in the upper walks of the Church, in the higher ranks of commerce in which a Clough or a Middleton found himself at home. But in a consideration of the history of Welsh life in London, the opportunities afforded to the lower-middle and even to the poorer Welshman loom even more large. The rank and file of the later Welsh Societies in London were composed of such folk, and their influence upon their home-keeping relations has from time to time been demonstrably important.

Before we come to the London-Welshman proper, it may be as well to say a few words about what we may call seasonal influxes of Welsh people into the capital. For the most part, such invaders would only by accident become domiciled in Town ; they would usually go home when their immediate purpose was achieved. But they were a not inconsiderable factor in London life, and they were a very considerable factor in the life of Wales ; standards of life and of manners, fashions, ideas and literary influences, ballads and chap-books and tunes for the humbler folk, were smuggled as it were in their saddle-bags, to be grafted upon the main Welsh tradition of life. At the top end, there are the visits of the Welsh gentry to London, either for the short sessions of Parliament or for mere pleasure. Below the gentry (if indeed one should say "below," for the practice of entering young men of good family at an Inn of Court persisted even down to a recent epoch) came the students at the Inns ; nor should we forget the hospitals. Next in importance came the cattle-drovers ; the droving of cattle (and later, of sheep), already in evidence in the fourteenth century, had assumed vast proportions under the *pax Britannica* of the Tudors, and had by 1640 become, in the words of Archbishop John Williams, "The Plate Fleet of Wales." Thousands of Welsh cattle and sheep were driven eastwards in two great annual tides, spring and autumn ; and each of the little units which made up a drove had its half-dozen men and boys. Much, though not all, of this traffic was focussed upon London ; much indeed reached its goal in London, at Smith-field ; while another part passed through to Essex or Kent or Sussex. And whether goal or merely halting-place, London left its mark on the drovers—as indeed, one fears, they left

4

their mark upon it at times. A hint has already been given of the miscellaneous freight which a drover would carry home with him. And if a sober-sided Welshman to-day should feel inclined to bewail, with the satirist Twm o'r Nant (Thomas Edwards) the riotous and extravagant theatre-going (and worse) of Welsh drovers in Town, let him also bethink him that Isaac Watts's hymns were translated and brought to Wales by a drover, and that at least one drover (who had dropped into an Evangelical church in London) became a prominent Welsh preacher.

A poorer relation of the drover was the " hosier "—the seller of stockings. Of the tripod on which the economy of the older Welsh countryside was somewhat precariously supported in pre-industrial ages, agriculture proper was one leg, livestock the second (and more dependable), and wool the third. Welsh " webs " and " flannels " do not concern us here, for they were marketed by English middle-men. But *knitted* ware was a different matter ; here the whole process, from sheep to retail, was domestic. Welsh hosiers (women even more than men) travelled enormous distances on foot (and bare-footed) with their stock slung over their shoulders. They were known in London Town, where some of them indeed settled down, rose above peddling, and became solid tradesmen ; the first Treasurer of the Cymmrodorion Society was a hosier from Montgomeryshire.

Even poorer than the " hosier-women " were the *weeders*, who begin to appear in London in the eighteenth century. In 1700, the City of London proper had a population which was less than that of Cardiff to-day ; a radius of 12-15 miles from Charing Cross even then had an estimated population of 675,000 —probably, again, not more that that of the comparable area around Cardiff at present. Even so, this was more than a tenth of the estimated population of England and Wales at that time. Yet, a glance at the map of London in Gibson's 1695 edition of Camden is apt to surprise those of us whose conception of a large town is that of 1951. The *nuclei* of the older London—the City, Westminster, and the straggling link connecting the two—are dense enough on the map. But the London area as a whole was much more open—it was not a continent of bricks-and-mortar, but an archipelago, so to speak, of many little hamlets, each isolated in green fields. Of course, we are throughout the eighteenth century moving on towards the built-up area of 1801 (when Greater London had 832,000 inhabitants) ; but the process was gradual. Richard Morris the Cymmrodor, it is true, can tell his brother Lewis in 1763 that London " now stretches as far as Marybone, and along the Park wall and Tyburn Highway to Piccadilly— Hyde Park Corner, I ought to have said—and is expanding on both sides of the River." Yet Richard himself could in 1761 still speak of " that walk across the fields from the Tower to Stepney," still remaining in his day as it was marked on Gibson's map ; in 1770 he took " summer lodgings " for his ailing wife, " on Clapham Common," even as a London-Welsh bookbinder (no Cymmrodor) in 1766 sent his wife " to Islington for her health." Grosvenor, Cavendish, and Hanover Squares date only from George II's reign ; Portman and Belgrave Squares were later still. The saddle-horse and the chaise for the middling and wealthy, stout boots for the less fortunate, were needed for visits to one's fellow-Welshmen in the outskirts ; Richard Morris's rides to Hampstead, Ham, Deptford, Sheerness (for sea-bathing and " drinking syllabub in a farm house ") seem almost adventures, in his telling of them.

London, in short, was still in a measure rural. And its parks, its new squares, its private gardens, its large market-gardens serving the growing population, all called for considerable weeding. Among the multitudes of poor folk who flocked to London to earn a few pence at this work, in slack seasons on the farms, were whole companies of Welshwomen, especially from Cardiganshire and Carmarthenshire. It was a nineteenth century Cardiganshire poet, " Daniel Ddu " (the Rev. Daniel Evans) who burst forth into a song of sorts which may be rendered :—

> Oh, had I the wings of a dove,
> I should perch on Saint-Paul's at my ease,
> Beholding the gardens below,
> Where the Welshwomen weed on their knees ;

though what pleasure that could have given to the reverend Fellow of Jesus College, it is hard to say—surely chivalry might have impelled him to lend a helping finger-and-thumb. The weeders were very numerous, and they even brought their children with them—we read that philanthropists established a Sunday-school for the poor little wretches.

These great tides of Welsh-people were, to be sure, *tides*—not, in principle, *migrations*. Yet there is ample evidence that their recession was not complete—a remnant, however small, became true Londoners. We are told, for instance, that some drovers' helpers, beginning by disposing of the milk of their employers' kine in transit, blossomed into milk-vending as a permanent occupation ; these were the heralds of the vast tribe of London-Welsh dairymen. Again, weeding-women did not all return to their " starved fields " in West Wales. Many stayed on as domestic servants. One of them may be singled out : Jane Evans of Caeo, born about 1803, who came up to London in 1842 to weed in the gardens of Hammersmith, and settled down there. This staunch Welshwoman would walk the five miles to Jewin Welsh Methodist chapel every Sunday morning for the nine o'clock service ; she afterwards became a charwoman in Wilton Square, with occasional spells of nursing. In 1855 she went out to nurse in the Crimea, like the very much better-known Elizabeth Davis (Cadwaladr) of Bala. Less domineering than her compatriot, Jane Evans would burrow through snowdrifts to milk the cows for her hospital. Returning to London, she spent the rest of her days in poverty and increasing blindness, though charitable relations and a pension from the Clothworkers' Company alleviated her distress at the end.

Jane Evans and the more colourful Elizabeth Davis must here stand for a very large (though less romantic) army of Welshwomen who have left no name behind them, but have toiled in a humble way in London. There was, of course, no place for women (and indeed, in any case, no congenial atmosphere for women) in the London-Welsh Societies with which we are concerned in this book—at least before the establishment of the Second Cymmrodorion Society, which had a few " lady subscribers." But they were an important element in the London-Welsh churches and chapels which came into being in the early nineteenth century. Even in the eighteenth century, for that matter, Welshpeople in London were not wholly without ministrations in their native tongue, however " irregular " or " fanatical " those might seem in the eyes of stout Anglican Cymmrodorion and their like. Howel Harris, on his frequent visits to Town, preached in Welsh there, and there was a Welsh Methodist Society in Lambeth, at which Harris and Daniel Rowland were familiar figures. At Fetter-Lane chapel, too (which soon became definitely Moravian), Harris in 1739 "discoursed in Welsh." The Moravians themselves (three of the foundation-members of their Congregation were Welsh—one a woman, a squire's daughter) provided Welsh services ; in 1745 they proposed "having preaching in the Welch language, there being a good many of that nation in town at present," and in 1749 are found so doing. John Parry, the famous "blind harpist" (afterwards a Cymmrodor) dallied awhile with Moravianism ; David Williams, the book-binder already mentioned, was a Moravian ; so was Robert Lewis, the poor bankrupt coach-builder, born in the same parish as the three Morrises.

But it is time to deal more systematically with the London-Welshman proper, the man who deliberately came up to Town to live there. According to Mr. Robert Owen of Croesor (who has most generously allowed us to utilise his unpublished research-work on this subject), the initial migrations, roughly those of the sixteenth century, were chiefly of upper-class and well-to-do folk, while the advent of craftsmen and traders in proportionately large numbers is later—more characteristic of the seventeenth century. Of the hundreds of sixteenth century London Welshmen whose names Mr. Owen has ex-tracted from his documents, a very high proportion were servants at Court and holders of Government posts—Tudor gratitude for Bosworth had not yet faded. The gentry and their servants form the next largest class ; we have already reminded ourselves that these are "visitors" rather than migrants proper, yet it should be remembered that their stay was often prolonged (and this is even more true of the inordinately large number of young Welshmen at the Inns of Court) ; one of them, Thomas Prys of Plas Iolyn (d. 1632) has depicted the none too orderly life which they led while in Town, in such poems as "A cywydd showing how a man lost his money by drabbing and dicing in London," and "A cywydd showing that London is Hell." But even in the early sixteenth century there were Welsh newcomers in other walks of life. Remem-bering the only-recently-ended Welsh dominance along Oxford Street, we note with interest Mr. Owen's seventeen pre-1540 "tailors and merchant-tailors," and his twelve "clothiers." There are "vintners and beer-sellers" too, ten of them before

1540 ; and the eighteenth and nineteenth century " Antient Briton " or Cymmrodor, as we shall see, found it easy to forgather in a tavern or a coffee-house kept by a compatriot— there were, says Mr. Owen, at least twenty-nine Welsh taverns in the second half of the eighteenth century ; and during its first half there were fourteen Welsh coffee-houses—a change of fashion had reduced these to six by 1800.

A more detailed analysis of the occupations of London-Welshmen in the middle of the eighteenth century must be deferred until we come to the Cymmrodorion Society's Lists of members—being careful, however, to bear in mind that the Society cannot at any time have included more than a tiny fraction of the London-Welsh colony. At the moment, it is better to turn back to the pre-1750 period, and inquire of Mr. Owen what seem to have been the favourite occupations of our countrymen in the capital. There were, for example, thirty-two goldsmiths in the period 1500-1700 ; some of these were in effect bankers, such as Sir Thomas Middleton, or again John Williams of Hafod Lwyfog (Beddgelert), goldsmith to James I, money-lender to his kinsmen of Gwydir, benefactor to his native parish. Then there were the grocers ; in the two centuries mentioned, thirty-seven members of the Worshipful Company of Grocers were Welshmen. We may observe in passing that another City Company, the Glovers', entertained Richard Morris to dinner on more than one occasion, and that in 1762 he remarks that there were " abundance of Cymry in this Company," whose Master, David Davies, was a Welshman. To return to Mr. Owen : one of the most interesting of his discoveries is the frequency of Welsh printers in London ; in 1500-1700 there were as many as 345—the term in those days included booksellers and publishers. It is not of course, pretended that these were printers only of *Welsh* books, though for that matter, in the whole period 1500-1800, London printed more Welsh books (521) than any other town. Welsh harpists and other musicians, relatively numerous in eighteenth century London, elude exact enumeration before that time. Actors and actresses, again, among whom " Welsh " *surnames* are very common (there are seventeen in the Drury-Lane casts of 1768), can rarely be definitely identified as Welsh—but in any case, they would not be very likely to belong to the old Cymmrodorion !

Let us pass on to the manifestations of Welsh patriotism in London. The earliest of these, one is not surprised to learn, was the celebration of S. David's Day. State Papers of Henry VIII show that Welshmen in the King's Guard were on that day given extra pay and additional good cheer. The wearing of the leek on the Day became usual ; Shakespeare was obviously familiar with the custom—and with the incidents which it was apt to provoke. A slight effusion of blood (Cymric and Saxon) tended to accompany our national festival—it was more than slight in 1640, when an irate Welshman, " provoked" on S. David's Day, resented the provocation so strongly that he had to be indicted for manslaughter. Again, in March, 1670, Lady (Sarah) Wynn of Gwydir writes to her husband, Sir Richard, then at Westminster, that she " hopes he has passed S. David's Day well, and that none of the enemies of Taffy have lost an ear for lack of reverence." Indeed, in the Stuart period, when Welshmen no longer basked quite so freely in the favour of their sovereigns, broadsides and pamphlets ranging between genial leg-pulling and downright hostility testify to the heat engendered on the first of March. An amusing pamphlet, "*The Welshman's Jubilee* with an excellent merry sonnet annexed unto it, composed by T. Morgan, gent.," of ca.1642, though its author adjures us to " think not that I speak this in a ludibrious jeer or abuse of the country, for I speak altogether in praise and commendation of it," deals merrily with the " Mythologie of the Leek " and the Welsh affection for " green cheese." One verse of the " sonnet " is worth quoting for its broad hint that Welshmen were doing well in London—far too well, as it seemed to the envious Englishry of London Town :

> This is a good week, when we wear a Leek,
>   And carouse in Bacchus's fountains—
> We had better be here than in poor small beer,
>   Or in our country mountains.

The less articulate Saxonry expressed its feelings by burning Welshmen in effigy. Pepys, under March 1st, 1666-7, records : " Back again to my office, and in the streets, in Mark Lane, I do observe, it being S. David's Day, the picture of a man dressed like a Welshman, hanging by the neck upon one of the poles that stand out at the top of one of the merchants' houses, in full proportion, and very handsomely done "—Pepys's editor Wheatley adds, on the strength of *Poor Richard's Almanack* for 1757, that " in former times a Welshman was burned in effigy on this anniversary," and further quotes W. Carey Hazlitt : " the practice to which Pepys refers was very common at one time ; and till very lately bakers made gingerbread Welshmen called *Taffies* on S. David's Day, which were made to represent a man, skewered." This quaint (and indeed fortuitous) amalgam of Saturnalianism, ritual magic, and chauvinism, is more proper matter for the anthropologist. But the wearing of the leek, by high and low alike, and indeed not by Welshmen only, is attested in the fourth of the prints in Hogarth's *Rake's Progress* (1735), where the Rake's downward career is regarded, with sardonic detachment (in S. James's), by a fashionably-attired gentleman with his hands tucked into a muff, wearing in his cocked hat a truly gigantic leek.

Hogarth's print is significant ; it belongs to a period in which S. David's Day had, as it were, risen in the social scale. Broken noses and burnt effigies are after all but individual happenings ; and we are now on the threshold of a more corporate manifestation on the part of Welshmen *in partibus infidelium*. The accession of the House of Hanover, in 1714, brought things to a point. In the first place, the new regime had some grounds for fearing that Wales, like Scotland, was Jacobite. The situation in this matter is far from clear even to-day, for conspiratorial wariness on the one hand and politic (and in the event well-rewarded) tact on the other have hushed matters up. But it is a fact that a Welsh bishop (Lloyd of Norwich) was a non-juror (and for that matter that a non-juring Welsh cleric, Lawrence Howell, was imprisoned at Newgate and died there in 1720) ; that there was a " White Rose Circle " in North Wales, a stout Jacobite squire at Gogerddan in Cardiganshire, and a body of " Sea-sergeants " in West Wales ; that the Morrises of Anglesey, very much later on, speak of Anglesey " Jacobites," whatever they may have meant by that term, and hint very broadly that the Bulkeleys of Baron Hill (like the more famous Sir Watkin Williams Wynn of Wynnstay) were for the Pretender ; that quite certainly a Jacobite landing in Wales was contemplated in 1717. It is quite on the cards that the more important of our countrymen in London felt some concern about the safety of their persons and property, should it happen that the suspicion and active disfavour of the government fell upon them.

Secondly, a more disinterested motive comes to light. The age, in England and Wales alike, was an age of organised charity, and especially of attempts to provide a measure of elementary education for the children of the poor, and a provision for apprenticing them in industry. And there were many poor Welsh children in London by 1714. We have hitherto dwelt, perhaps overmuch, on wealthy goldsmiths, prosperous merchants, established shopkeepers ; it is now right to remind ourselves that not all Welshmen who came up to Town " found their America " there, as Carlyle puts it. For example, not in 1714 but in the 1760's and in the Morris Letters, we hear of a neighbour of their own, Robert Lewis of Plas Llanfihangel, scion of a landed family, one of whose members was high sheriff of Anglesey in 1764. Robert Lewis (not a Cymmrodor, by the way), had hopefully set up in London as a coach-builder ; but he never made good (there is no hint of dissoluteness, and the man was a member of the Moravian congregation), and died " in the workhouse, deaf and stupefied." There must have been many such Welshmen in Town, and their children must have been in bad case. And their wealthier Welsh fellow-townsmen had come to feel concern about them.

This dual desire, of safeguarding the more prosperous London-Welshry from imputation of disloyalty, and of assisting Welsh children in London, led in 1715 to the foundation of the " Honourable and Loyal Society of Antient Britons." The Antient Britons never formally merged into the subsequent Cymmrodorion Society—indeed, even to-day they maintain their separate existence, after a fashion. But the affairs of both societies were closely intertwined from 1751 to 1787, and the Antient British Society has some claim to be regarded as the parent of the Cymmrodorion. It is most unfortunate that although the *name* of its founder is perfectly well known to us, his identity can still not be regarded as quite certain, and his history and ancestry elude us. He was the " Thomas Jones, of Lincoln's Inn, J.P., Registrar of Memorials relating to the Estates of the County of Middlesex," who died on January 11th, 1731, " at his house in Boswel Court." Examination of the printed Admissions to Lincoln's Inn, within the relevant chronological limits, reveals only two Thomas Joneses, one of whom, Thomas Jones of Carreg-Hwfa, Chief Justice of Common Pleas, died in 1692, while the other, admitted to the Inn on

February 17th, 1707-8, is described as " Thomas Jones, of Chancery Lane, gent." But turning to the printed Admissions to *Gray's* Inn, we find : " November 20th, 1713, Thomas Jones, of Newcastle, co. Glam., gent. (Admitted to Lincoln's Inn, February 10th, 1707, by certificate of John Hungerford, Treasurer)." " Newcastle " will be more familiar to the reader under the name Bridgend. It is difficult not to feel that this is our man, despite the week's discrepancy in the date of admission to Lincoln's Inn, and despite our wonder why, after admission to Gray's in 1713, he should continue to describe himself as " of Lincoln's Inn." If he is indeed the Bridgend man, perhaps some Glamorgan Cymmrodor can trace his ancestry for us.

Thomas Jones, whoever he was, printed and circulated in 1717 a pamphlet, *The Rise and Progress of the Most Honourable and Loyal Society of Antient Britons, in a Letter to his Countrymen of the Principality of Wales* (frequently reprinted in part in the Society's periodical reports), which gives an account of the founding of the Society. It so happened that Caroline of Anspach, the Princess of Wales, whose almoner was the bishop of Bangor, had been born on the first of March. This providential coincidence led a number of Welshmen, headed by the Earl of Lisburne (who counted City magnates among his ancestors, and who was chief of the " Whig " interest in Cardiganshire), but with Thomas Jones as the active agent, to form the Society and to seek for it the official patronage of the Prince and Princess of Wales ; Thomas Jones became its " Treasurer and Secretary." On February 12th, 1714 (our 1715) the *London Gazette* advertised that " on Tuesday the 1st of March next, being S. David's Day, there will be Prayers and a sermon preached in the Antient British Language, by the Rev. Mr. George Lewis, a Native of the Principality of Wales " ; 4,000 copies of the sermon were printed and distributed. On April 5th, the *Gazette* announces that the Stewards of the Society had on March 29th been introduced to their Royal Highnesses, and that the Prince had consented to become their President ; on September 29th, that on September 23rd it presented an address to the King himself, who was " at the same time pleased to confer the honour of Knighthood on Thomas Jones, of Lincoln's Inn, Barrister at Law, Treasurer and Secretary of the said Society." The " address," by the way, was evoked by thickening rumours of disaffection in the provinces during the summer, and it was signed not only by London Welshmen but by two hundred gentry in Wales—an interesting anticipation of the later view held by the London Societies : that their functions were to be not merely associations of London Welshmen but also channels of a two-way traffic of ideas and influences between London and Wales.

Thus began the annual S. David's Day sermon in London, which is still with us in a much-changed world. Unfortunately, it was not always to be preached " in the Antient British Language " ; indeed, not only was the sermon English at times but courtly English bishops of Welsh sees even went out of their way, while preaching to " Antient Britons," to deplore the survival of the Welsh language, thereby arousing the wrath of leading Welshmen like the Morrises. But to go on : the Day was also—need one say ?—marked by a dinner, another precedent religiously followed by the Cymmrodorion and other Societies. Notwithstanding the fact that Sir Thomas Jones in his pamphlet speaks of the perpetuation of " the Memory of our *abstemious* Saint " (they are his italics), " who lived a rigid Eremitick Life, feeding only on Herbs (of which perhaps *Leeks* were a principal Part), and drinking nothing but Water," the 1715 Antient Britons felt no compunction in " dining with Viscount Lisburne (etc.) at Haberdashers' Hall, in decent order," after the sermon—not, one fears, upon " herbs " and water. On February 14th, 1716-17, the *Gazette* speaks of " the " dinner, again " at Haberdashers' Hall in Maiden Lane," at 10s.6d. a head. At these celebrations (so we learn from an account of the 1715-16 festivities, at which " the Rev. Mr. Phillips, Vicar of Devynnock," preached), the Antient Britons wore " favours, of good silver ribbon, with the motto *Caroline and S. David* "—the order of precedence seems rather odd—and the stewards bore green staves " with the arms of the Principality painted on top." The solemn list of addresses read, toasts drunk, songs sung, and " poems " recited, is given in awesome detail by Sir Thomas, who indeed has to interrupt himself with " But whither am I going ? Where can I stop in this long and pleasant way ? "

Sermon and dinner done with, we turn to the third—the charitable—activity of the Antient Britons. The collections in church, and the profits of the dinner, were to be vested in the Stewards and the Prince of Wales's almoner (the bishop of Bangor), " for the benefit of the *Welch* Nation in general." In May, 1716, it was resolved " that two Welch boys be put out Apprentices to Trades " ; £10 each was to be spent on them. After the dinner of 1717, the scheme was extended : boys other than the two apprentices had come under the Society's observation, and the upshot was the founding of a school " for the benefit of children of Welch parents living within the City of London and the Liberties of Westminster." Already, indeed, the Stewards had rented a room in Sheer-lane (Clerkenwell), and were paying the Rev. Thomas Williams for instructing ten boys. But it seems that it was not till the end of 1718 that " the Welch School " was officially instituted ; the children were to be clothed (at £1 a head) and the Master paid £1 for each pupil, with coals and candles for his own use. The School, to-day known as " The Welsh *Girls'* School," and to-day situated at Ashford in Middlesex, has recently (1950) had its history written by Miss Rachel Leighton. It moved from Sheer Lane to the " Aylesbury Chapel " in Clerkenwell Street, thence (1738) to a new building on Clerkenwell Green, and finally (as far as its sojourn in London is concerned) to Gray's-Inn Lane, in 1772. Girls had been admitted to the school in 1768 ; it was removed to Ashford in 1857, and boys were not admitted after 1882.

The support of the Welsh Charity-School appears to have been the only continuous activity of the Antient Britons. The stewards were to hold monthly meetings, but the *Society*, as a body, met only on March 1st. The Cymmrodorion, on the other hand, met (as we shall see) every month, regularly. There is some evidence of an ebb in the energies and resources of the Antient Britons by 1751, and the newly-founded Cymmrodorion Society, as its printed Constitutions show, quite clearly regarded itself as concerned, in part at least, with reviving the older foundation. Though the two Societies never amalgamated, the personnel at the head of both, from 1751 to 1787, tended to be the same—Richard Morris, for example, had himself been a Steward of the Antient Britons as early as 1728.

II.—THE MORRISES OF ANGLESEY

THE three brothers Lewis, Richard, and William Morris of Anglesey would no doubt have left a name behind them, and Lewis Morris a considerable name, even if the Cymmrodorion Society had never come into being. But there would never have been a Cymmrodorion Society but for the Morrises. It was but fitting that the piety of the Third Cymmrodorion, in June, 1945, should have undertaken the restoration of the Morris monument set up in 1910 near Pentrerianell. And the present chapter will be devoted to giving an account of this remarkable family, and of their activities up to 1751, the year in which Richard Morris, the only London-Welshman among them, founded the Cymmrodorion Society.

Anglesey, " the mother of Wales " (and more particularly the northern part of it), seems on the map very remote from London, and it might seem reasonable to suppose that its ancient Welsh way of life had been very little affected, at the dawn of the eighteenth century, by outside influences. To some extent, indeed, the supposition would be correct—needless to say, the deposit of old Welsh tradition there will explain a great deal of the Morrises' characteristics and interests. But merely looking at a map may be deceptive. In actual fact, Anglesey in 1750 was far less primitive than, say, the Western coasts of Merionethshire. From the standpoint of the older Welsh tradition, it was a dangerous thing to dwell on or near a great highway. . The post-road to Holyhead, carrying as it did a very considerable volume of traffic between London and Ireland, was a much more potent Anglicising factor, and for that matter a greater stimulus to general social changes, than any outside influence which impinged upon Ardudwy, nearer though the latter is to London in actual mileage. A cursory inspection of William Morris's letters reveals how constantly, in virtue of his office, he came into close contact with " foreigners," even of high degree, who passed through the port of Holyhead. The gentry of the island were early affected by the contagion of Englishry, and indeed not a few of them *were* English or Irish, as their names show, notably the great Bulkeley family of Baron Hill (Beaumaris)—though we should be careful to notice that cadet branches of these families (as with similar families on the Denbighshire border) in many cases " went native " as time rolled on. An angry outburst of William Morris's, in 1760, is worth noting. Speaking of some lawlessness in the island, he says : " here's a poor young fellow murdered at Cleifiog the other day, and nobody bothers about it. Blast 'em !—what does it matter to Irish Lloyd of Hirdre-Faig, or Irish Nangle of Llwydiarth, or English Briscoe of Beaumaris, or English Sparrow of Plas Coch, or Irish Bayly of Plas Newydd, if we Welsh kill one another off, so long as *they* can keep their estates ? "

Over and over again, in the Morris Letters, the passing of the older Welsh world is observed—sometimes in a vein of satire, as in 1757, when William Morris speaks of " hitting a man when he is down, as they used to do in Llannerch-y-medd Fair—that martial spirit is quite laid, but not everywhere, I hope " ; or earlier (1755) : "*follow up your blows at once*, as Griff Huws the blacksmith used to tell his three sons when they fought at Llannerch-y-medd Fair long ago ; that praiseworthy custom of knocking one another about in fairs has long since perished ; nowadays you may see *lambs* from Llanfihangel Tre'r Beirdd and Penrhoslligwy and Llanfechell drinking together without a single snappy word or so much as a *Keep off !* much less breaking pates and arms like true Britons."

To be sure, the Letters from time to time show that there was still no little " martial spirit " left in Anglesey ; and it is only fair to add that its diminution, as indeed William Morris tells us more than once, was due not only to Anglicisation *per se* but to other causes, among which we may mention the labours of William's stern pastor and friend Parson Ellis of Holyhead, who had succeeded in dissociating patronal festivals (*gwyliau mabsant*) in his district from the Lord's Day, and celebrating them on a week-day, when people were too busy to riot. Yet even the fairs, as we saw, had lost their pristine liveliness. Indeed, Mrs. Nesta Evans, in a recent study of social life in Anglesey, has been impelled to the conclusion that a kind of anaemia, so to speak, had overcome the islanders in the early eighteenth century, and that this created a vacuum in their lives, in which the Methodist Revival found its opportunity.

In the introductory paragraphs of this book, the word
" nostalgia " has occurred more than once. And nostalgia—
a *double* nostalgia, of space, in separation from Anglesey, and of
time, in a sorrow at the passing of an old way of life which they
loved—was a marked element in the characters of the two
exiles Lewis and Richard Morris ; we shall have to make the
same observation when we come to speak of the Denbighshire
men who dominated the London Gwyneddigion Society. Their
younger brother William plays up to it in his letters to them
from the homeland ; a few set pieces seem almost deliberately
written to draw tears from an exiled brother's eyes, notably
the oft-quoted passage from his New Year's Day Letter of
1752, and another in 1758 ; he lovingly rides along from
homestead to homestead, where sons and grandsons of old
playmates had become " old married men "—past the church
" where you and I were made Christians at the font "—
along " the lane which led to our grandmother's house " ;
the place-names are made to ring like bells ; how remote all
this old life was from the dusty ledgers of the Navy Office or the
squabbles of the Cardiganshire lead-miners, or even William's
own pleasant revenue-collecting and botanising at Holyhead !
It seems almost unkind to record that hard-headed Lewis, and
Richard too, despite their tears, never once returned to their
ancient home.

But it was this nostalgia that lay at the root of the three
brothers' attempts to do something for Wales. In a sense,
they were indeed culpably parochial. There was no place like
Anglesey. Yet, they admitted, there were five other shires in
North Wales, whose people, though to be sure not Anglesey
folk *pur sang*, were still within the covenant, spoke the same
language, had held to the same ancient ways. South Wales
was another matter ; *there* dwelt a lesser breed ; and the
Morrises' contempt for South-Walians in general was most
marked—they could do nothing right—they didn't know Welsh
—they couldn't 'spell—" I question whether there is a man in
South Wales that can write a tolerable *cywydd*," etc., etc.
It need hardly be said that this presumptuousness of theirs was
ridiculous : Tivy-side (to name only one Southern region) had
as rich a native culture in the early eighteenth century as any
region in North Wales. The disdain is quite inexcusable in
Lewis especially, who not only lived in South Wales but had

travelled extensively there. This arrogance was to be amply revenged. Iolo Morganwg, in 1805, in his wrath with Lewis Morris, roundly accused him of all sorts of literary malpractices, and asserted that his Welsh was "little better than that of a Hottentot"; even Goronwy Owen, nay, even the Cardigan-shire Evan Evans, were found wanting by the Glamorgan seer; and the gap in the Morrises' knowledge of South Wales was filled by the production of a whole corpus of supposititious Glamorgan poetry and history.

But parochial though they might be, what the three brothers felt was that the old Wales of their boyhood was slipping away, and its language and literature with it. Sion Prichard Prys of Llangadwaladr, poet, genealogist, and antiquary (not that the Morrises rated him highly, though Lewis in 1725 calls him "the incomparable poet"), bewailed in 1721 the "late" decline of bardic technique, due (so he held) to its neglect by the gentry; in a burst of rhetoric the old bard paints a picture of its "decrepitude, plunging into destruction." Lewis Morris in 1736, after a contemptuous snort at Welshmen "in a foreign country, forgetting where they came from," or again, "quarrelling with things because they have not a genius to comprehend them," addresses himself to the more serious argument put forward by "uneasy men," that the survival of Welsh created "discord between the subjects of . . . . Great Britain," and maintains that "congruency of opinion" rather than "that mistaken tye of unity in language" is the real unifying force in a state. Let "none of my countrymen," therefore "spend so much useless breath upon this point hereafter." The "defence and illustration" (if we may use Joachim du Bellay's words) of the Welsh language and of the tradition of which it is the vehicle became the over-riding aim of Lewis and his brothers. True, they were too narrow in their conception of this task. They found it hard to grasp the fact that rustic versifiers—whose work they were quite capable of enjoying, to do them justice—and interlude-writers and almanack-makers all over Wales were at the time doing more (and doing it more directly) to keep the Welsh language and its literature alive than a coterie of *illuminati* could do; and indeed that but for the instinctive efforts of the former, the work of the latter might have become mere dilettantism "without hope of posterity." Still less did it occur to them that Methodism, which they all three hated so cordially, was to bring healing in its wings—to give the language a new and a long lease of life—to multiply the Welsh reading public to such a point that when the initial and exclusively religious phase of the Revival was spent, and when the Circulating Schools of Griffith Jones and the Sunday Schools had taught the Welsh masses to read and to *think*, their reading could (and did) embrace not only the Tudor Bible but also the popular poetry and even (in cheap reprints and at a later date) the "classical" poetry of the Morrisian circle itself. Ultimately, many Welshmen, thus disciplined, became capable of appreciating the still older poetry which the Morrises and their like had rescued from oblivion ; and their periodicals would argue points of orthography and grammar with a vigour, indeed an acrimony, worthy of the Morrises themselves.

The Morrises, despite what has been said about the impact of external influences upon Anglesey and the weakening of the older culture in the island, were personally fortunate in their early environment. In their corner of Anglesey, there were still substantial remnants of the older world. Not all the minor gentry—certainly not, for example, William Bulkeley of Brynddu in Llanfechell, their father's kinsman and friend— had lost their Welsh. Not all the practitioners of the technical Welsh art of poetry (as distinguished from homespun versification) had perished ; indeed, their neighbour Hugh Hughes (1693-1776) of Llwydiarth Esgob (between Llandyfrydog and Llannerch-y-medd), "y Bardd Coch," a competent *cywyddwr* to whom two of Goronwy Owen's *cywyddau* were to be dedicated, outlived his friends Lewis and William Morris and died only three years before Richard. More : even the peasantry of the north-east of Anglesey had not completely lost contact with ancient tradition. Some of them indeed still retained pride of *ancestry*. To quote Professor W. J. Gruffydd : "as the families of the petty squires became more numerous, it was necessary for many of their members to work with their own hands, and by 1700 many of them had become weavers, carpenters, tailors, coopers, and small farmers. They still remembered that the blood of the *uchelwyr*, the aristocracy, flowed in their veins, and for that reason they endeavoured to keep up a connection with the ancient culture." To put it in another way : not every "Durberville" in north-east Anglesey had fallen the *whole* gamut down to " Durbeyfield " by 1700. And the Morrises, both by heredity and by environment, were racy of their soil ; the *hauteur*—the snobbery—which has so often been found in them (and especially in Lewis) was to some extent a matter of " blood."

Their father, Morris Prichard (Morris ap Richard), born probably in 1674, was a carpenter and cooper, and later a farmer and corn-dealer, of " lower-middle " economic status— he had a parliamentary vote, and lived not unprosperously, keeping (as his son William's letters show) a shrewd eye on his income. Yet, on his mother's side he was of the Bulkeley clan. And his wife Margaret, born about 1671 and married in June 1700, daughter of Morris Owen of Bodafon-y-glyn in Llanfihangel Tre'r Beirdd, could boast of a *bonedd* (a " gentle " pedigree) derived in unbroken descent from a mediaeval " lord " of the commote of Twrcelyn. And Margaret Morris (she died in 1752) retained a sense of the " obligation " which *noblesse* proverbially entails ; she was " generous " in the Latin and in the English meaning of that word. We may be tempted to extenuate Goronwy Owen's praises of her boundless charity, as expressions of mere personal gratitude. But we cannot dismiss a casual flashback in her son William's Christmastide Letter of 1762 ; " here we are, as happy as the beggars used to be in Pentrerianell barn long ago "—few are the farmers' wives who welcome tramps. Her generosity descended to her second son Richard ; it is no idle flourish to say that the Society of Cymmrodorion owes its foundation, in large measure, to that uncalculating love of his fellows which Richard Morris inherited from his mother. The newly-married couple at first lived apart in their respective homes, Tyddyn-melys and Bodafon-y-glyn (both in Llanfihangel) ; later, they set up house at Y Fferem in the same parish ; and later still, settled at Pentre-rianell in Penrhoslligwy. Richard and William, on their own statements, were born at Y Fferem.

Morris Prichard is clearly delineated in his sons' letters. Lewis and Richard kept up correspondence with him (he would testily complain that their letters were few and far between) and invariably showed great affection for him. William was not so far off, and father and son exchanged frequent visits. We get the impression of a hale and hearty old fellow, troubled

21

though he was by bronchitis and asthma (his sons inherited these) and minor complaints—and towards the close by failing eyesight and hearing. " He will outlive us all," says one of his sons, and indeed he very nearly did outlive William and Lewis, dying at 89, while his three elder sons died at 65, 76, and 62 respectively. Like many other healthy men, when he was ill he was very ill, and William would anxiously prepare his brothers for the worst. But the very next thing William would see would be the old gentleman cheerfully arriving at Holyhead, on horseback, " without taking foot out of stirrup " in the whole twenty miles of foul roads—" and I," says William ruefully, " haven't been on a horse for ever so long." The sons, repentantly remembering a plenteous crop of wild oats sown in their youth, would from time to time murmur : " Oh, the blessing, the inestimable blessing, of *temperance !* " when they spoke of their father. But an ascetic reader should be warned that " temperance " is a relative term. In 1746, Morris and his son William paid a visit to Bodorgan (the seat of the Meyricks), and there found foolish young Lord Londonderry, who must needs amuse himself by trying to "make my father drunk "—but as William records with grim satisfaction, it was the peer " who fell in the field of battle." Morris Prichard, though not as fine-textured as his wife, was not without parts. " His memory," says William in 1762 (when the old man was 88), " is astounding ; there is probably not a man in all Anglesey who is a surer genealogist ; and it is wonderful to hear him recount hundreds of events which have befallen since his boyhood." Here was the *old* world, and we cannot doubt that much of his sons' store of information about it came from their father.

And he was no unlettered wiseacre ; he could read Welsh, and write it (we have several of his letters) ; he could scent a MS. afar off, and put William on its track. He was a devout Anglican, and when William revisited the home he would be dragged off to church on Sunday (" on foot," as he grumbles, " though the paddock was full of horses ") to witness the curiosity with which the parish regarded his father's ear-trumpet. He eagerly subscribed for a copy of the new Bible and Prayer-Book which Richard Morris had edited, and acted as a receiver of subscriptions for this and other books like Thomas Richards's Welsh Dictionary. After his wife's death, he took his grand-daughter Margaret Owen (his daughter's daughter) to keep house for him. But he was an uneasy house-fellow. More than once, he contemplated re-marrying, and his sons' letters betray their own and their sister's comical dismay at the thought that some unsuitable female might get hold of him—to be sure, the two elder sons were qualified by experience to speak on that matter. Eventually, he insisted on removing to lodgings at Llannerch-y-medd (more alarm on his sons' part) ; there he was perfectly happy ; even when failing eyesight compelled him to employ a reader and an amanuensis, he could still beguile the time with basket-making—dutiful William sent him bales of osiers and reeds. A likeable old fellow—more likeable than his son Lewis who inherited his canniness and love of money ; according to Lewis, what *Richard* got from the old man was unteachableness.

Morris and Margaret Prichard had four sons and a daughter. The youngest son, John (who was in London with his brother Richard in 1735) joined the Navy, was mate of the *Torbay*, and died at thirty-four in the expedition against Cartagena (1740) ; he seems to have been genial, and his extant letters show that he made a good fourth in this remarkable family. The daughter, Ellen, married Owen Dafydd or Davies (he succeeded Lewis Morris as " waiter and searcher " at Holyhead and Beaumaris in 1743), and had a long family. Her daughter Margaret Owen, already mentioned, kept house for old Morris Prichard and remained at Pentrerianell when he left it ; she seems to have kept a school there ; she could play the harp ; and her letters (written, like her uncles', in Welsh interlarded with English) show that she was no fool. One of Ellen Davies's sons, John (" Sion ") Owen, figures largely in the Morris Letters ; he shared his uncles' love of poetry and music, was employed by his uncle Lewis in 1750 as book-keeper in Cardiganshire, but afterwards broke with him, and after a spell of unemployment in London (1758-9) became a purser on a man-of-war, and died at Gibraltar in 1759. His letters are most interesting—not least so for his pungent (indeed ribald) comments on his uncle Lewis and his affairs.

Lewis Morris, the eldest of the three famous brothers, was christened at Llanfihangel Tre'r Beirdd on March 2nd, 1700-1, but passed his boyhood at Pentrerianell ; he and his brothers (as William remembered) " ran about naked " and happy on

Dulas sands. Like his brothers, he was taught his father's craft, in which they all became proficient—there is much talk, in their letters, of the making of cabinets to preserve their collections of shells and fossils and what not, and there are drawings in illustration. Tradition alleges that Lewis could " build a boat and sail it, construct a harp and play on it " ; Richard, again, in a note written when he was only fifteen, takes great pride in the number of wooden articles "done at the shop " by himself. In such respects, Lewis in particular reminds us of a brother poet in South Wales, Lewis Hopkin (1708-71) of Llandyfodwg in Glamorgan : carpenter, mason, stone-carver, builder, land-surveyor, farmer, and considerable man of letters, well read in Welsh and in English literature, and indeed resembling Lewis Morris too in admiring Dafydd ap Gwilym of whose poems he is said to have made copies. It seems a pity that the two men never met—it might have abated a little of Lewis Morris's conceit. He *was* personally acquainted with Hopkin's contemporary and friend John Bradford, the Glamorgan antiquary and poet, but (as was his wont), didn't think much of him. What formal education the brothers received is not known. Lewis's own account of it, in letters to Edward Richard of Ystrad Meurig (1759) and Samuel Pegge (1761) is : " what little stock of knowledge I have attained to was in a manner by dint of nature ; my education as to languages was not regular, and my masters were chiefly sycamore and ash trees." Is this statement, possibly, too deprecating ? One cannot help observing that all three brothers wrote an excellent hand, and were competent accountants, that not only their Welsh but their English is sound, that Lewis's earliest extant letter (1725) speaks of " Zoilus and Momus " (clichés, but *literary* clichés), and that later on he showed a little Latinity, and assumed in his letters that his brothers too understood it. Can self-instruction (diligent as that no doubt was) be a complete explanation of all this ?

During his early manhood, Lewis Morris seems to have lived at home and practised as a surveyor—a letter of Richard's to him in 1728 is addressed " to Mr. Lewis Morris, Land Surveyor, at Penrhos Lligwy." In 1729, he was appointed " waiter and searcher " at the custom-houses of Beaumaris and Holyhead, a post which he retained till 1743. But he still kept on his private practice as a surveyor, and as early as 1737, apparently through the influence of the Meyricks of Bodorgan on Thomas Corbett, an Admiralty official, he was employed on a survey of the coasts of Wales. This survey was abandoned for a while, but was resumed in 1741 ; the results were not published till 1748 (a revised edition by his son William appeared in 1801), though individual charts seem to have been in circulation before 1748. A letter of his brother William's in 1742 shows that Lewis was then at Aberystwyth and " had taken a mining lease " ; and according to J. H. Davies he was commissioned in 1744 to survey the Crown manor of Perfedd (between Clarach and Rheidol rivers) ; in the same year he was Collector of Customs at Aberdovey. But in 1746 William Corbett (brother of Thomas) became Steward of the Crown Manors in Cardiganshire, and appointed Lewis Morris to be his Deputy-steward.

Thus began what was to prove a calamitous chapter in Lewis Morris's history. In his official capacity, he became involved in ceaseless litigation between the Crown grantees of lead-mining rights and the local gentry—he himself had entered into partnership with one group of these concession-holders. The disputes were attended by riots and *force majeure* ; Lewis himself was haled off to prison at Cardigan for a short time in 1753. For many years he lived in unresting anxiety, not lessened by his own unpunctuality in rendering accounts to the Crown officials, his eagerness to make money, and the recurring disappointments caused by over-sanguine prospecting on his own account. Four long visits to London (1753 ; 1754 ; 1755 ; 1756-8) to battle with enemies in Cardiganshire and supine (or even hostile) Crown officials in Town were distractions redeemed only in small part by work at the British Museum—we should add here that these visits alone brought him into *personal* contact with the Cymmrodorion Society. His legal troubles (which incidentally had in 1756 cost him his Collectorship at Aberdovey) ceased (apparently by settlement out of court) in 1760. But he lost a lot of money over them ; nor, though made a J.P. for Cardiganshire in 1760, was he even afterwards free from pecuniary troubles arising out of his own private mining-ventures.

The effect of all this upon him was disastrous. Never a man of sunny nature, he became increasingly embittered and touchy ; his ever-ready sneer became a snarl ; and his brother Richard had more than once to complain hotly of the tone of his letters. His health, too, broke down ; he had always been asthmatic, and now a whole platoon of other ailments descended upon him. He fell into hypochondria (the *three* brothers were prone to this, and their letters at times read like so many pages of the *British Pharmacopoeia*), caught at every conceivable physick, regime, or diet (pestering his brother Richard for tips from the Cymmrodor Dr. Henry Owen), and from 1752 took the " waters " (though as he tells us, not those waters alone !) at Llandrindod—he and Edward Richard were perhaps the earliest Welsh men of letters to visit the place. It is right that his increasing waspishness should be extenuated by remembering his constant ill-health. Said he in 1759 to Edward Richard : " my pain is now very great while I write this, and I would advise satyrical writers to have always a deep wound on their leg, which would certainly make them shine " ; and he wonders " whether all ill-natured critics have not ulcers in some part or other." The odd thing, however, is that his literary correspondence in these bad times with men like Edward Richard exhibits a poise—one might almost say a serenity—which the letters of his earlier and less troubled years do not show.

Lewis Morris succumbed, on April 11th, 1765, to a combination of ailments including gout and paralysis ; he was buried within Llanbadarn-fawr church near Aberystwyth. One fears that " Llewelyn Ddu " was always ill to live with—a tall, ruddy, stout man (" y Tew," as his brothers called him, or, to his nephew John, " the Fat Man "), arrogant, quick to take offence, hard, secretive, selfish. When his brother Richard, in an *englyn* of 1734, describes him as " a jealous Jew, of angry countenance," we may perhaps discount it, remembering that poor Richard was then well-nigh down-and-out. But says William to Richard in 1753 ; " a bit of a trial at times is [Lewis] . . . with his schemes ; . . . he always or pretty generally leaves me in the dark." Again, when Lewis had taunted Richard in 1759 with " living at ease, with nothing to do but fiddle with pen and paper," Richard blazes out : " it's cruel in you, who rowl (*sic*) in money (bags full of thousands), to say [this] . . . ; if any one but a brother had told me so, I would have told him that he insulted me." Lewis's niece

Margaret Owen dryly comments on his " everlasting boasting."
And her brother John Owen is even less mealy-mouthed ;
when he came up to London to live with his uncle Richard,
he averred that never could two brothers have been more
unlike ; " Lord ! who would have thought that the same man
sired them both ? "—and again (1758) : " I remember the
time when he used to be a great lover of music and poetry, and
an encourager of everybody that were that way inclined, but
of late the getting and spending of money have drove (sic) all
these good qualifications out of his noddle." Long as John
had been in his employ, Lewis " never showed me the difference
between a *cywydd* and an *englyn*." To be sure, the lad was
over-censorious—even in Cardiganshire, Lewis Morris would
pick up promising poets ; and he not only discovered Edward
Richard but stoutly maintained his high opinion of him against
Richard Morris.

To go on : on Lewis's visit to London of 1756-8, Richard
put his house at his brother's disposal, meekly going out into
lodgings with his nephew John. But, says the disrespectful
John (whom Lewis, by the way, described as " a thoughtless
vain lad, God help him ! "), " you wouldn't believe how glad
the family will be to get rid of him ; he has been nothing but a
nuisance to them ever since he came to Town, snapping at the
maids, who take offence and hourly give notice ; . . . he
makes more trouble and wants more attendance danced upon
him than would half a dozen others." Well, perhaps few of
us are heroes to our nephews. It is fairer to remember the
very real affection which the three Morris brothers bore to one
another, even if we have a sneaking suspicion that separation
made the heart grow fonder where Lewis was concerned. And
about his two brothers' immense admiration for Lewis, we are
never left in the very slightest doubt.

Lewis Morris's disposition can hardly have been sweetened
by his domestic worries. He had in 1729 married a girl of not
quite sixteen, Elizabeth Griffiths of Ty-wriddyn in Rhoscolyn ;
she died before 1741. They had a son, Lewis, born at the very
end of 1729, who died in 1745. And they had two daughters,
Margaret (1731) and Ellen (1732), who are found in 1741
being boarded out at Holyhead. Margaret, " a strapping
lass, like her father " according to William Morris, was indeed
too like her father; she gave him untold trouble, married badly

in insolent defiance of him, and died in misery in 1761. Ellen, to quote her uncle again, was " a ladylike comfort-loving girl, fit to be a lord's wife." No lord married her ; she married Richard Morris of Bathafarn near Cemaes (Mont.), bore him six sons and two daughters, then married an Anglesey parson and had four more children—she was a perfectly normal Morris ! She died at Llangefni in 1823 ; it was probably from her that Gwallter Mechain (who met her in 1793) obtained the MS. of the second part of her father's *Celtic Remains*.

Ellen, unlike her more attractive but unhappy sister, managed to rub along quite well with a stepmother. For on October 20th, 1749, Lewis Morris, then living at Gallt Fadog not far from Aberystwyth, had married Anne Lloyd, a young woman of about 25, heiress of the small estate of Penbryn in the Melindwr (Goginan) valley ; later on (1757), the household was able to move to Penbryn itself, where Lewis, an enthusiastic gardener (like his brother William) and a typical eighteenth century " improver," dug and walled and planted, and waged unceasing war upon pests—not human, this time. Perhaps it was injudicious in a man of 49, whose financial prospects were more than a trifle speculative, to start a new family of ten children (six sons and four daughters), of whom six survived him. Richard and William and their niece Margaret Owen exchanged chuckles over this neck-and-neck race between Anne Morris and her stepdaughter Ellen—John Owen (need it be said ?) made most outrageous remarks. The new wife visited William Morris at Holyhead, and he evidently liked her, though he makes fun of her South-Wales Welsh. And Richard and his wife showed her a good-will which she reciprocated— Richard, for that matter, went expressly down to Penbryn on Lewis's death to straighten her affairs. But John Owen simply loathed " the Captain," as he calls her, and his editor is reduced to helpless dots when he prints John's comments on his aunt-by-marriage. Lewis himself keeps his counsel, apart from tart remarks (such as have in all ages been addressed by " any husband to any wife ") on her " spendthrift " habits— to be sure, she might well have retorted that a man who sinks his wife's money in unremunerative lead-mines has not much right to grouse when the wife and her step-daughter amicably " waste " money on trifles in Machynlleth Fair. Still, it is evident that life was not smooth for Lewis Morris. Yet it must not be supposed that he died poor, though a rumour to that effect reached Goronwy Owen in distant Virginia—and though the inventory of his personal property was only £66. In his own words in 1763, he was "neither in want nor in great plenty," and his anxiety was mainly for his "small children"; how much of his sunken capital was ever retrieved does not seem to be known. His widow later (1772) married William Jones of Gwynfryn in Llancynfelin and thus became step-ancestress, so to speak, of William Basil Jones, bishop of S. David's from 1874 to 1897, and an antiquary of repute. She died in 1785. Of her children by Lewis Morris, one alone is immediately interesting to us, the fourth son, William, who republished his father's survey of the Welsh coasts; *his* eldest son, Lewis, became the father of the Victorian poet Sir Lewis Morris.

Richard Morris, the second of the brothers, was born, according to his own statement, at Y Fferem, on February 2nd, 1702-3. As he was the "Father of the Cymmrodorion," a Londoner in a very real sense, it would have been proper in this book to give a pretty detailed account of his career. But unfortunately we know very much less about him than we do about his brothers; his letters form but a very small part of the corpus of Morris Letters, and even so they belong mostly to the short period 1759-63. According to statements of his own, he came up to London in 1721 or 1722. It would not be literally true to say that he never left London during the last fifty-seven years of his life; for official duties compelled him to visit Portsmouth and other naval stations. Once only, however, did he return to Wales—in 1766, when he went down to Penbryn to see his widowed sister-in-law; "I had never before seen South Wales, or indeed seen Wales at all for forty-four years."

We have already caught a glimpse of Richard Morris at fifteen, working in the carpenter's shop. But it is quite clear that he came up to Town as a book-keeper and accountant. In his earliest extant letter (March, 1728), we find him contemplating a "place" of £100 a year with a Captain Jones (to whom he was already "bound" till Christmas or Lady-day following) in Town; another possibility was a better "place" abroad. He was also busy "settling" the accounts of a bankrupt "Mr. Edwards"; further, he talks of possibly getting into the Customs. Characteristically, he was even then " a secretary to near a score of my countrymen." In 1728, again, he was evidently of sufficient standing to be " pricked " as one of the Stewards of the Antient Britons at the S. David's Day feast of 1729; in 1729, too, he married. His brother William visited him in Town in the early '30's, attending the S. David's Day dinner and being asked out with him to dine at Woolwich. Thus, up to that time Richard appears to have jogged on fairly comfortably. Then adversity befell him. Even in 1734, a set of *englynion* shows that for some reason his elder brothers (so he says) would have nothing to do with him, and " were ashamed to own him "—John alone, who was up with him in 1735, was " a kindly brother." Richard indeed spent 1734 or 1735 (or parts of both amounting to twelve months) in the Fleet prison—a " lament," and a *cywydd*, both now in the British Museum and both dated 1735, tell us all about it ; he had been rash enough to stand surety for a defaulting debtor. Another set of verses, of 1735, represents him and his brother John (perhaps more or less fancifully) as " starving for food and drink." In February, 1738-9, Richard writes to his parents ; he was in sore straits, and had been so for two years, indeed for *four* years, though he had not liked to tell them ; his sufferings had been greater than they could imagine. At the moment, he had a three months' job of Parliamentary clerical work (a dated poem shows also that in May, 1739, he acted as interpreter for Welsh witnesses in an Exchequer case) ; but though Mr. Meyrick of Bodorgan had lent him two guineas and promised to do something for him, he had no clothes—would the old people send him some cloth, and also a pot of butter and a cheese ? and would they prepay the carriage ? " for mostly I have not a penny in my pocket." He is " again " over head and shoulders in debt, though things are now looking more promising.

In 1742, the Rev. Thomas Ellis of Holyhead got the bishop of Bangor to give Richard Morris work as corrector of Welsh pamphlets to be printed in London ; and in 1744 he was appointed corrector of the new S.P.C.K. edition of the Welsh Bible with Prayer-book (1746 ; reissued in 1752). But auditing, accountancy, and interpreting in the Courts must have been his main resources. In a letter written in 1770, looking back over his life in London, he names a whole string of

" noblemen's agents " who employed him to examine their stewards' accounts ; unfortunately no dates are given, other than " in the last age, when the present big men were little boys." More definitely attested is his employment (by the influence of Meyrick of Bodorgan) to clean up the accounts of the Lord Londonderry who had died in 1729. J. H. Davies would seem to have believed that this job began in 1729 ; that looks improbable, in view of Richard's bad luck in the next ten years, and William Morris's letters show that Richard was at the work from about 1742 to 1747, that the foolish young heir had to be repeatedly pressed by the Meyricks to make payments to Richard for his services, and that there was a vague promise to employ him permanently as accountant to the Londonderry estates.

Things were better by 1747 ; two sympathetic letters of William's express the hope that Richard's hard times are now past. For in that year, Richard Morris (again we may con-jecture that the Meyrick-Corbett influence had been at work) was appointed to a clerkship in the Navy Office ; by 1757 he was " Chief Clerk for Foreign Accounts to the Controller of the Navy," with a salary of £100 a year, which in those days was not too bad ; and to his brother William's amusement, he could now be addressed as " Esquire "—what was perhaps more to the point, in the eyes of his letter-writing brothers, was that letters to and from him (if not too bulky) paid no postage. Despite his open-handed habits, he must now have been a less worried man, especially as we learn in 1760 that he had also " my private agency affairs, which take up all my time out of office hours." Let us pause, by the way, to remind ourselves that all three brothers were never at any time afraid of *work*—they might, and indeed two of them did at times, make a mess of things, but that was certainly not for lack of industry.

Yet we are by no means to suppose that the free-and-easy life, the love of wine and song, the uncalculating generosity, which had led Richard Morris into such dire straits in the 1730's, ceased when better days came. In the very year 1757, his censorious brother Lewis reports that Cymmrodorion meetings (not so sedate as they are to-day) kept Richard up till one, two, three or four in the morning, after which he would stagger home and sleep on his doorstep till the watch (" the policeman," to us) woke him, " and afterwards cough for a month "—in later days, the President (reformed, as he ruefully confesses, by compulsion rather than by choice) confined himself to a single pint. A more pronounced weakness (if weakness it was) was his open-handedness. Lewis disgustedly tells William that Richard was " the softest man you ever saw—simple, weak, credulous, and wants common cunning " ; he " loves his country to excess, and for that reason his countrymen, who all impose upon him, . . . there is no Welshman in London hardly but what has been with their common father borrowing money ; he would lend a scoundrel money when his own family was in want ; he hath (or had) a notion that he had no occasion to hoard any money or goods for his children, for that after his death some good people that had a value for him would take care of his family, as he had taken care to assist several helpless children." Richard himself once avowed : " I set great store on a kindly man who freely does a good turn to all men." On one occasion (1762), when some money due to a poor widow was paid through him, he refrained from deducting a sum which her late husband owed him ; he explains : " there was too much misery there to take advantage—unclad children crying out for food, shocking to behold ! I hope *my* children will not have a mouthful less for such an act of humanity." It is pleasant to record that in one instance at least the bread thus cast upon the waters returned after many days. In 1763, Richard was able to tell Lewis that an old friend from Anglesey, a tide-waiter (but at the beginning of their friendship, forty years back, a cheesemonger in Holborn), to whom Richard had shown hospitality in his loneliness, had left him some £200 ; " I have never, God help me, had such luck since I was born."

Small wonder that such a man should have led a nomadic existence, married man and father though he was. His wanderings from lodging to lodging are hard to trace, for we have only casual references in the small body of his letters. It is said that at one time he lived in Cowley Street— presumably when his work lay in Courts or Parliament at Westminster. He was married in 1729 ; the marriage is said to have been " unfortunate." The wife (whose name is unknown) bore him two children at least, Llewelyn and Marian, and seems to have died during his years of adversity—in 1740, says J. E. Griffith. In 1739, Richard was lodging with " Benjamin

Jones, salter, near Union Street, Wapping," and a letter of William Morris's in February shows that the boy Llewelyn was dead. The daughter Marian (sometimes called " Meiran ") figures frequently, but not with approval, in the letters—she was a " handful " (not unnaturally when we consider her upbringing), married (1760) a Yorkshire clothworker named Thomas Whitaker, went to the bad, and is last heard of in the Letters in 1763, but was alive when her father made his last will. Her father had in 1741 taken a second wife, whose name again is unknown, but she died in 1750 (as William again reveals to us) ; there were (says J. E. Griffith) " several children, who died young," but the Letters make no reference to them. Richard and his second wife seem to have lived for a time at Stratford, " in a house with a fine garden," but in 1746 were in another house (locality unknown), from which, on his wife's death, he and Marian moved into lodgings, losing much money (as William tells us) on the sale of the furniture. In 1754, he was still in lodgings—or perhaps " again," for there is a hint that in the meantime he had taken a furnished house.

By that year, he had married for the third time ; and this time, at least, he was lucky. The third Mrs. Morris's Christian name was Elizabeth (" Elsbeth ") ; Richard's will calls her " Betty " ; her surname we do not know, but she came from Worcester, and her people (we gather from hints) were tolerably well off ; she was thirty years younger than her husband. Every reference to her speaks well of her—William Morris with unwonted and indeed excessive courtliness avers that her praises were sung in the uttermost parts of Anglesey ! She behaved well towards her very troublesome stepdaughter, and she was on the kindliest terms with the Penbryn people. Even Lewis felt impelled to do her one good turn. Elizabeth had at first had to put up with Richard's quaint ideas of domesticity—*he*, says Lewis, would not leave " a filthy hole which he called his office or chambers," continuing to live there while his wife and children lived " in a loft elsewhere." But Lewis, during that long visit to London which (according to John Owen) caused Mrs. Morris such trouble, put his foot down and insisted on Richard's taking a proper house. Richard objected ; as Lewis says : " people that have used themselves to a hugger-mugger way of life don't know what it is to live comfortably and genteel." But Lewis personally superintended the removal, bought odds and ends for the house, and made book-shelves for Richard, who had " so many books that he did not know what he had." More : he laid out the garden—for Richard, unlike his brothers, was no gardener ; his ignorance on such matters provoked guffaws from them—" he hath no manner of notion of such things, unless the plants grow without help " ; so Lewis, tongue in cheek, laid out the garden with " large foreign *shells* . . . which will be always in bloom " ! This was in August, 1757 ; the house was in Pennington Street, Stepney, very near S. George-in-the-East where Richard was to find his last resting-place. He must have lived in Stepney before, when he was a much younger man ; for among his papers in the British Museum is a set of English verses written in 1728, *The Rarities of Stepney ;* the first verse may surprise a modern Londoner :

> Within two short miles of the Royal Exchange
> There lies a fine village, wherein you may range
> With pleasure abundant, when weather is fair,
> If you go from London to take the cool air.

Now, says Lewis, Richard " begins to like this way of life, and has bought several good pieces of furniture." Alas ! this was too good to last. By 1763, " murders and robberies " at Stepney had frightened Richard out of Pennington Street, and he took a house within the precincts of the Tower, and closer to his work.

Our piety towards the founder of the Cymmrodorion calls for some account of the children of his third marriage. There were ten of them—Richard's will speaks of seven buried at S. George, and three survived him. The Morris Letters allow us to identify seven of the ten, with approximate dates : *Angharad* (b.1754 ?) ; Llewelyn (b. December 31st, 1755, d. June 2nd, 1758) ; *Margaret* (b. 1757 ?) ; Richard (b. August ? 1759, d. September 24th, 1760) ; Elizabeth (b. end of 1760, d. February, 1761) ; *Richard* (b. January 31st, 1762) ; William (b. August, 1767, d. in infancy) ; the other three, perhaps born before 1754 or after 1767, we do not hear of.

Of the three survivors (italicised in the above list), we hear much of the two girls. Angharad, a delicate rickety little girl, was early packed off to a school at Worcester, and afterwards to her cousin Margaret Owen at Pentrerianell, where, says her

uncle William, she soon learned to prattle in broken Welsh ;
" her arm," says William, " is no thicker than my finger."
Margaret, on the other hand, as her father proudly reports,
was " as fat as a porker." What became of them is not known ;
a writer in 1875 speaks of them as " living in London, some years
ago "—even this extremely vague indication seems to point to
a very ripe old age. Their brother Richard was in 1766 sent
off to Penbryn " to be made a Welshman of " under Mrs. Lewis
Morris's aegis, and certainly acquired some of his father's and
his uncles' love of Welsh antiquities ; he contemplated completing Lewis Morris's *Celtic Remains*, and became a member
of the Cymmrodorion and of the Gwyneddigion. He went to
India, becoming a merchant there, and we have a letter of his
to Owain Myfyr, written at " Tumlook " (Tamluk) in Bengal
and speaking of matters Welsh. And in the same year (1785)
he sent over from India the part of his father's library which he
had taken out with him, thus fulfilling his father's bequest of all
his Welsh books to the Welsh Charity-School.

Mrs. Richard Morris died in October 1772 (she had been
ailing " for a long time " says Richard in 1770—he then calls
her " my poor rib "), and was buried at S. George-in-the-East.
Richard married for the fourth time, before November 7th,
1773 (when he executed his will), a widow, Mary Major, whose
maiden name we do not know. She must have survived him,
for Thomas Pennant speaks of remitting to her, in view of her
" narrow circumstances " a sum of £63 which Richard had not
yet paid him in respect of the *British Zoology*. On July 1st,
1776, the minutes of the Welsh Charity-School Trustees speak
of a letter received " from Mr. William Lloyd, giving account
of the indisposition of Richard Morris, Esq., one of the Trustees
of the Charity, and of his signifying his wish to be accommodated
with an apartment in the School for a month or two, to lie in
for the benefit of the air " ; and it was resolved that he should
have " a choice of one or two rooms for one or two months,
or as long as he may think proper." He died " in the Tower "
in December, 1779, and was by his own directions buried with
his third wife and their seven children at S. George-in-the-East.
The will (of 1773) was proved on New Year's Day 1780 ;
the executors named in it were William Parry of the Mint (who
however, as we know, died in 1775), Thomas Parry (unknown
to us), and the widow Mary Morris. The widow was to benefit

by arrangements made by her previous husband John Major (including a leasehold house in Pennington Street; it looks as if Richard and his fourth wife had been old neighbours and friends); the daughter of Richard's first marriage was cut off with a guinea; the two Parrys were each to have a guinea ring. Richard's ordinary books and his "cabinet of shells, fossils, ores, minerals, coins, medals, and other natural curiosities" were to be sold. The residue of the estate (with the exception which we shall note later) goes to the widow—together with the above-mentioned interests derived from her former husband —for the term of her life, and is afterwards (apart from the interests spoken of, which are then to pass to other parties) to go to Angharad, Margaret, and Richard, "share and share alike." But Richard Morris gives "to the Governors and Trustees of the British or Welsh School in Gray's Inn Road my whole valuable collection of ancient British books in print and manuscript, to be deposited in the Library of the said School for the perusal of the curious in British antiquities, and none of them ever suffered to be taken out of the School upon any pretence whatsoever, in hopes that they will be accompanied with the manuscripts of the worthy patriot my honoured friend Sir Watkin Williams Wynne, Baronet, and those of other gentlemen lovers of the original language of Great Britain." There, in fact, the MSS. remained till 1844, when the Trustees very wisely transferred them to the British Museum.

William Morris, born on May 6th, 1705, had neither the genius and irritability of his brother Lewis nor the large generosity of his brother Richard; both in character and in career he was more normal. Chance references show that he, too, was tall; but he was lanky ("he's a lath, like his father," says he of his own son)—when his nephew John calls him "Gwilym Gam," we may perhaps conclude also that he had a pronounced stoop, though it is quite possible that the angry youth meant that his uncle was "morally" crooked. For John had found him stingy (crintach); and we cannot forget that Richard Morris too, in the bad year 1734, had felt that William was hard and not forthcoming—"sour," as he puts it. Still, we know that the careless are apt thus to describe the careful. William was much the most religious of the brothers. It is true that Lewis and Richard were sound Church-men who could not abide Papists and Dissenters. But Lewis at times was cynical enough about religion : " why go to church, to try to deceive God who seeth all things ? "—and in another letter, though he carefully puts the words in another man's mouth, he broadly hints that all religions are much the same. As for Richard, it is pretty clear that he let his wife Betty do most of his church-going for him. But as for William, it was not merely that his formidable neighbour Parson Ellis kept him up to the mark ; he was keenly interested in church music and was for many years choirmaster of his parish church. It has not been proved beyond doubt that he was the author of a very famous Welsh hymn—but to him alone of the three brothers has anyone ever dreamt of attributing a hymn. " Careful " he may have been in money matters ; " sensible " is pre-eminently the adjective which one could apply continuously to him and only at times to his brothers. He was a kindly man ; his letters show genuine concern and sympathy, and his occasional remonstrances are mildly worded. His correspondence with his brothers was most diligent ; of the 705 Letters in J. H. Davies's edition, some two-thirds were written by William.

We are told that William when a young man " spent some considerable time at Liverpool " ; there is proof that he was there in 1726 ; and we have seen that he visited Richard in London in the early 1730's. But on February 24th, 1736-7, he was appointed Collector of Customs at Holyhead ; later, he added to this a variety of smaller jobs (collecting the duties on coal, salt, etc.) ; and finally (1758), he became Comptroller of Customs at Holyhead. He had in 1742 been offered the Chief Clerkship to the Collector at Chester, at £80 a year, but had declined the offer—students of the social history of Anglesey will be eternally grateful to him for this. Thus he remained at Holyhead till his death, carrying out his multifarious duties, practising as an amateur physician, pestering his brother Richard with requests on behalf of Tom and Dick and Harry (for all poor people in Anglesey innocently assumed that Richard Morris " ran " the British Government), keeping a benevolent eye on the Society of Cymmrodorion, hobnobbing with high and low (but, we must confess, leaning somewhat more to the " high "), and above all, cultivating his garden.

For he was a most ardent botanist—indeed, a most ardent naturalist in general. It would appear from Goronwy Owen's elegy on Margaret Morris that William (and presumably Lewis too) had inherited this passion from his mother. Sea-captains (it is wise to make a friend at the Custom-house) brought him offerings of plants and seeds from the ends of the earth ; Richard in London had similar distraint laid upon him (of course, Richard being Richard, the packing was often bad, and the contents spilled, or spoilt by damp) ; high-born ladies on their way to or from Ireland made inspections of William's gardens, which were apt to be accompanied by pilfering his strawberries ; his letters at times read like a seedsman's catalogue. He really was a botanist of repute, and was given to inveighing against the inaccurate naming of plants in Welsh dictionaries. The *Welsh Botanology* (1813) of Hugh Davies of Aber was based on William Morris's researches, and we shall later have to note that Welsh botany and the other branches of Welsh natural history were to be included among the studies proper to the Cymmrodorion Society. It would not be true to say that William Morris never left Holyhead : he knew every corner of Anglesey, now and then went to see a friend on the mainland of North Wales, and visited Ireland. But on the whole, his life moved only " from the blue bed to the brown " ; his letters are a mirror of life in Anglesey in the middle of the eighteenth century.

In 1745, William Morris married Jane, daughter and heiress of Robert Hughes of Llanfugail ; she was some fourteen years his junior. Not only was there a sheriff in her lineage, but William was able to boast that his children were descendants of the twelfth century poet-prince Hywel ab Owain Gwynedd. But Jane Morris died in 1750, and William never married again. Two of their three children survived the mother : Robert (" Robin "), born in March, 1746, and Jane (" Sian "), born in February, 1748-9. Their father, proud of them, was too sensible to over-rate them. Robin, " soft, but as I hope, honest," after being in a commercial school at Liverpool, was for a time (after his father's death) with Richard Morris in London, but afterwards settled down in Holyhead, selling his portion of Llanfugail estate. Jane, quick-witted and well educated, with (as her father averred) a better brain than her brother's, married twice—in both cases " within the craft," for her first husband was an exciseman, and the second a Customs-officer at Beaumaris who seems to have been a (very much older) kinsman of hers. She died on February 21st, 1833. It is to her that we owe the preservation of the letters which Goronwy Owen had sent to her father ; she allowed Robert Hughes ("Robin Ddu"), to copy them, in 1783. William Morris himself died on December 29th, 1763—his very last letter, of November 12th, informs Lewis Morris of their father's death, and adds that he himself was bedridden and unable to attend the funeral.

We pass from a survey of the careers of the three brothers to a consideration of that common fund of ideas which shaped their conception of the purposes of the Cymmrodorion Society— *their* conception, rather than that of the rank and file of the Society's members. A common fund it was, for though Lewis alone had genius and scholarship, yet in kind the brothers' equipment was much the same. For one thing, they were all collectors of local lore and of the rustic verse of their countryside. Richard, for example, at the early age of 15, had made an extensive collection of verse (nearly all in the "free" metres)— this was edited by Professor T. H. Parry-Williams and published in 1931 ; and there are other such collections in the Morris MSS. at the British Museum. It is, by the way, a common mistake to believe that the Morrises held such verse in un-mitigated contempt. Naturally, being "classicists," they ranked it far beneath the more sophisticated, technically "artistic," poetry of the schools ; but they delighted in it none the less. From an early age, they themselves wrote this kind of verse, and some of the Lewis Morris poems printed in *Diddanwch Teuluaidd* (1763)—and obviously passed for publica-tion by Lewis himself in his maturity—are of early date, even earlier than 1723. They are "free" in metre, and indeed "free" in another sense ; a Victorian reprinter felt called upon to "amend" them. One branch of popular poetic art, the harp-verse (*pennill telyn*), Lewis Morris (in this matter well in advance of his time) rated very highly indeed— the collecting of *penillion telyn* was set down in the programme of Cymmrodorion activities. He himself used this verse-form ; ironically enough, the best-remembered poem, to-day, of this stout champion of Welsh "classical" poetry, is *Caniad y Gog i Feirionydd*.

Yet, more characteristic and more important, in a con-sideration of the Morrises' influence on Welsh literature, was their deliberate effort to foster the more " professional " poetic art that had come down from the Middle Ages but had by their day lost much of its vogue and forgotten much of its skill. True, in its simplest and easiest vehicle, the *englyn*, it was still fairly widely practised ; but the *cywydd*, and still more the complicated *awdl*, had suffered eclipse. The Morrises had from the first attempted the " strict " techniques. A *cywydd* of Lewis's (a very rabelaisian *cywydd*) in *Diddanwch Teuluaidd* is dated in his own hand " 1720," in his copy of that book. And J. H. Davies tells us that in 1728 Lewis was one of a team of Anglesey poets which in that year engaged in bardic contest with Caernarvonshire poets—a useful reminder to us that the older bardic craft, though fallen on evil days, was yet not extinct ; the Morrises were after all not alone, though they sometimes talked as if they had been. Recently-published letters show us that Lewis was in early touch with " Sion Rhydderch " (John Roderick; *ca.* 1690-1735), the Cardiganshire printer (at Shrewsbury) whose *Grammar* is held by Professor G. J. Williams to have contributed very greatly, despite its defects, to the revival of " classicism " in all parts of Wales. Then there are letters which passed between Lewis and Michael Prichard (1709-33), the weaver-poet of Llanllyfni, (a disciple of the veteran poet Owen Gruffydd of Llanystumdwy) and between Lewis and Hugh Hughes, " y Bardd Coch," already mentioned. Lewis no doubt liked to pose as a Maecenas ; it is but just to say (as the letters to Prichard and others show) that he *was* a Maecenas, and indeed kept the part up throughout his life, admittedly with much scolding and peevishness.

But the Morrisian " classicism " went beyond a mere instinctive preservation of the bardic tradition as it existed in their own day. They looked further back. To use a phrase which Thomas Jones the almanack-maker had taken as a title for his 1688 Welsh Dictionary, they aimed at restoring Welsh poetry (and poetic diction) " in its effulgence "—*yn ei disgleirdeb*. It is true that, as Mr. Saunders Lewis and Professor Thomas Parry have pointed out, the Morrisian school, as far as the *content* of their verse (be that low or high) is concerned, and indeed as far as their notions of the essence of poetry are concerned, were " Augustan " : Dryden and Pope (with a hark-back to Milton in some cases), Swift and the English essayists, were their mentors ; the title-page of Lewis Morris's first venture in print (1735) is adorned with four lines of Waller. But their standards of form and diction came from the Welsh poets of the golden age of the *cywydd*, and even from the " heroic " poets of the still older " age of the Princes," and their critical care for correctness of diction and of metre is a paramount feature of their work and influence.

They were diligent collectors of the older poetry ; transcripts made by them from MSS. owned by other collectors, lists of known MSS., indexes, notes, fill volume after volume in the British Museum. William Morris especially took pride in his collections ; Lewis again, in 1736, tells us that he has " about 230 of Lewis Glyn Cothi's poems, in fine order." Lewis set up a private printing-press, perhaps as early as 1731 ; only a single number of his miscellany, *Tlysau yr Hen Oesoedd* (1735) appeared, but his correspondence with leading Welsh literati like Edward Samuel shows that at one time he thought of launching out as a printer, and in particular a printer of the older literature ; there is talk of printing the poems of that fine old poet Huw Morys (1622-1709) of the Vale of Ceiriog. What with inadequate support, and Lewis's departure from Holyhead, printing was abandoned. The press was packed away in William's house till William's death ; it seems then to have been removed to Penbryn. After Lewis's death, the *types* passed somehow into the possession of David Jones of Trefriw ; we shall hear of them again.

Long before 1751, the Morrises had been preoccupied by two matters of paramount importance (as it seemed to them) in the rehabilitation of the Welsh language : the standardising of its orthography and inflexions, and the purifying of its vocabulary and idiom. In these two matters, they most interestingly anticipate the work of a distinguished Anglesey man of our own day, the late Sir John Morris-Jones, who resembled them too in his inability to suffer fools gladly, and in the very trenchant language in which he combated them.

There is much talk, in the earlier Morris Letters, of a correct edition of the standard (1620) Welsh Bible. The S.P.C.K. in its 1717 and 1727 reprints of Bible and Prayer-book had employed, as " corrector," Moses Williams, F.R.S., vicar of Devynnock and afterwards of Bridgwater (he preached the " Antient Britons' " sermon in 1717 and 1721), a disciple of

Edward Lhuyd's and a zealous student of older Welsh literature. But Williams (1685-1742) was a Tivy-side man, a fact sufficient in itself to damn him in the eyes of the Morrises. He was, said they, "not an honest man" ; his edition was a piece of "dirty work" ("*hagr weithiau Moesen*"), etc., etc. Their judgment, though unnecessarily vehement, was not wholly unjust. When one is editing an ancient text, one should not silently alter it, even with the highest motives and even if the alterations are real improvements. The head and front of the Cardiganshire scholar's offending was that his Bible had departed from the orthography of that very high authority on Welsh, Dr. John Davies of Mallwyd (the 1620 reviser), and his Prayer-book from that of the classic edition (1710) of Ellis Wynne of Lasynys. We have a well-reasoned handling of the matter by Richard Morris, in a recently-printed letter of 1769. Sir John Morris-Jones, one may add, was in hearty agreement with the Morrises on this point. Naturally, Richard Morris's own (1746, 1752) S.P.C.K. edition reverts to older precedent ; the Letters afford ample evidence of the care which all three brothers bestowed upon this edition, and upon the chronological and other tables which were included in it—not to mention William's special concern with the metrical Psalter and the accompanying tunes.

Another matter which looms large in the early Letters is the need for a new Welsh dictionary. Here again, the pioneer had been Dr. John Davies, whose famous Welsh-Latin dictionary had appeared in 1632. Cheap "popular" dictionaries based on John Davies—that of Thomas Jones, and that of John Roderick—made no pretence of scholarship. But at least as early as 1714, Moses Williams, who had diligently travelled up and down Wales collecting MSS. and scarce printed books of the older period, contemplated a revision of Davies's Dictionary, which was to incorporate the materials at his own disposal. Further John Morgan (1688-1733), vicar of Matchin in Essex, a Welsh prose-writer of great distinction who had preached before the "Antient Britons" in 1728, offered Williams his assistance. John Morgan was regarded with great respect by the Morrises (was he not a good Merioneth man ?), but Moses Williams was a red rag to them ; when he applied to Lewis Morris (about 1733) for help, it was curtly refused : "Mr. Moses Williams desir'd my Collections, whom I refused, knowing him incapable of carrying on ye work " !—Richard Morris, ever the kindlier man, did in 1734 send Williams " a catalogue of Welsh words omitted in Dr. Davies's Dictionary." It should be mentioned that both Lewis and William would have been perfectly ready to assist Edward Samuel (who also toyed with the idea of revising Davies) had they not judged that he was now too old to carry out the work. And in sober fact, Lewis Morris was probably right in deeming that he himself was at the time the only one man fit for the job. His *premisses* were sound and scholarly. No one yielded to him and his brothers in their respect for John Davies. But that fine old scholar's book rested on too narrow a lexical basis—the MSS. of the older literature which were at his disposal were limited in number ; his book, says Lewis Morris, " doth not contain above half the body of our language " ; further, as William Morris grumbles, he was weak in natural history—to quote Lewis again : " he knew no animals except his own cattle and fowls ; . . . . published in the infancy of natural philosophy, his book is like a child born in the sixth month." Another hero of the Morrises' was Edward Lhuyd, " inferior to no man in natural history, and had a prodigious knack of languages." But *his* weakness was that " his knowledge of Welsh poetry was none at all," so that he could not grapple with the immense wealth of words used by the mediaeval Welsh poets. These criticisms (1761) are sound and discriminating. Unfortunately Lewis Morris's projected dictionary was drowned in the sea of his troubles ; and not till our own day, and with the help of a regiment of collaborators, has the University of Wales come within sight of his goal.

Lesser men tried their hand. William Gambold, rector of Puncheston, father of the Moravian bishop John Gambold who makes a fleeting appearance in Richard Morris's letters, had compiled an English-Welsh dictionary (the MS. is to-day in the National Library) which Lewis Morris examined and found wanting. Then Thomas Richards, curate of Coychurch, near Bridgend, ventured in 1753 to publish a substantial Welsh Dictionary, having previously had much correspondence with the Morrises. Their attitude towards this work is amusing. They thought little of it. Their letters to each other treat it with contempt, and in 1761, Lewis tells Samuel Pegge : " Richards was not equal to the task ; he has taken in even the faults of Dr. Davies and added many of his own ; . . laborious, but very ignorant.'' Yet here, as later with David Jones of Trefriw and Hugh Jones of Llangwm whom we shall meet in the next chapter, the Morrises' bark, reprehensible enough though it was, was worse than their bite. When it came to promoting the sale of Richards's Dictionary, they did their best for it, collecting names of subscribers and forwarding packages. Good-humoured William even went as far as to say that the book was not so bad—except, of course, the botanology, which was dreadful. And Thomas Richards was one of the very first to be elected a corresponding member of the Cymmrodorion Society.

Enough has now been said to illustrate the interests of these three remarkable brothers—interests which were to be reflected in the official programme of work of the 1751 Cymmrodorion Society, however little of that programme was actually fulfilled, and however rightly we may deem that in hard fact the Gwyneddigion and the later Cymmrodorion Societies have done far more than the First to realise it. Another point worth noting is the ascendancy already won by Lewis Morris, in all parts of Wales, as an authority and consultant on matters appertaining to the Welsh language and its older literature. In Wales itself, the Cymmrodorion Society of 1751 was regarded as *Lewis Morris's* society, and its prestige and leadership there came from its association with his name—to the London Welshman, on the other hand, the name of power was that of his brother Richard.

III.—THE FIRST CYMMRODORION SOCIETY

THE Morrises were not the only lads from Llanfihangel Tre'r Beirdd who have left a name behind them. From that parish, too, came William Jones (1675-1749), F.R.S., an eminent mathematician, editor of some of Isaac Newton's works, and father of the very famous philologist Sir William Jones. We are all of us prone to belittle our fellow-parishioners, and the Morrises seem to have felt little sense of awe when they referred to their quondam neighbour, " born," says William Morris in 1746, " within a quarter-mile of Y Fferem " (his birthplace was Merddyn) ; they call him " old Wil Siôn Siors " (presumably his father's name was John George), or " Pabo," or " yr Ustus " (he was a J.P.). Richard alone seems to have known William Jones personally. He had drawn maps for Richard's 1746 Bible—they are duly described there as " a gift of William Jones, F.R.S., to the Welsh people." Further, Richard had catalogued and indexed the Welsh MSS. which William Jones had purchased from the widow of his friend Moses Williams of whom we have already heard. It will be convenient to add here that William Jones, on his death, bequeathed these MSS. to the Earl of Macclesfield, his patron, and that the Earl rather churlishly refused Richard Morris further access to them. The Morrises' wrath with the Earl was unbounded : " Welsh books in Saxon hands are as a jewel of gold in a swine's snout—so goodbye to [the MSS.]." Fortunately for us, that princely benefactor Sir John Williams purchased the " Shirburn " Library in 1899, and Moses Williams's MSS., with Richard Morris's indexes and notes, are to-day safe in the National Library of Wales.

Richard Morris had evidently suggested to William Jones that he might use his influence to get Lewis Morris elected into the Royal Society—he had already proposed Moses Williams and Dr. Henry Owen (of whom we shall hear again) ; says William Morris to Richard in 1747 : " so you and old Justice Pabo have a mind to get F.R.S. added to Lewis's name ? " and there are other references to " the three letters." William Jones died in 1749, and we hear nothing of the matter afterwards.

It has been widely believed that pique at this disappointment led Lewis Morris to set up the Cymmrodorion as a rival society in which his own paramountcy would be undisputed.

A modern reader, accustomed to think of the " Royal Society of Science " as an austere body concerned only with atoms or bacilli, may regard Lewis Morris's aspirations as presumptuous. They were not—it is simply that our ideas of " science " have contracted. When Gray spoke of Eton College as a place

> Where grateful Science still adores
> Her holy Henry's shade,

he was not thinking of chemistry or physics. " Science " was just *Learning* ; Moses Williams, to name only one example, was quite innocent of " science " in the modern sense. But it is right to add that the early eighteenth century conception of " science " or learning was polymathic, not specialised— Edward Lhuyd, F.R.S., for example, that great philologist and antiquary, was learned also in biology and geology ; Henry Owen, F.R.S. (a very much lesser man) was not only a physician but also a theologian and a classical scholar. And Lhuyd was in this sense the " father " of Lewis and of William Morris (even Richard, as we saw, dabbled in " natural curiosities ") ; Lewis Morris would in sober fact have made a very presentable Fellow of the Royal Society in his own day.

But it is a great leap in argument to hold that this disappointment of Lewis's impelled him at that time to found the Cymmrodorion. There is nothing to show that he could not have become F.R.S. at some later date. Even if not, there were still other learned societies, if he had merely wanted " letters after his name." And indeed, membership of the Cymmrodorion did not confer (and never has conferred) " letters "—it was only an occasional very worthy country bard in Wales who with harmless vanity styled himself " C.C.C." —*Cyfaill Cymdeithas y Cymmrodorion*. Though Lewis Morris did indeed at first talk of the Society as if it had been a "learned society," though he hopefully loaded its printed " statement of aims " with all sorts of learned projects, though at first he seems to have regarded the Society as an instrument for carrying out his very laudable designs—at first, for later on he betrays much disappointment—yet the *founder* of the Society was not Lewis, but *Richard* Morris. And though Richard quite certainly was (fortunately for posterity) an enthusiastic supporter of his brother's projects, these formed in his intention only part of the purposes (and indeed appear in print only as part of the purposes) of the foundation of the Society. We must remember that the Society was primarily an association of *London* Welshmen, designed to subserve the social needs of Welshmen in Town, who alone could be " full " members of it. William Morris, writing to Richard in November, 1752, thanks him for " the account of that excellent society there ; may you have God-speed in achieving your kindly purposes." The word to note here is " *kindly* "—and a few lines later William uses the word " *club* " in a context which implies that this was his con-ception of the Cymmrodorion. In this book, we shall necess-arily have very much to say of the literary and antiquarian sides of the work of all three Cymmrodorion Societies and of their congeners, the Gwyneddigion and Cymreigyddion ; but we shall be doing the First Cymmrodorion an injustice if we dwell overmuch on their comparative failure under his head. They had other objects in view—and *those* objects (perhaps less obviously important to us) they did pursue with what seemed to them a good measure of success.

The " Antient Britons," as a *society*, assembled only once a year, at the S. David's Day festivities. And the School founded by that Society, so we understand, was not being adequately supported in 1750, especially when we consider that the Society had since 1738 incurred the expense of a new school building, on Clerkenwell Green, and was admitting a greater number of boys into the school. Its Treasurer from 1733 to 1747, Ynyr Lloyd, a clothier, had indeed remedied " a certain dullness " which (says Miss Leighton) had fallen upon the " Antient Britons " after 1725. He died in 1747, and was succeeded by David Humphreys (of whom we shall hear again) who remained in office till 1775 ; Humphreys (again to quote Miss Leighton) " was not satisfied with the financial side of the Charity," and even when " a special effort " was made on S. David's Day, 1749, the collection amounted to less than £39—there was also complaint of " slackness " in admitting boys improperly into the School. What all this has to do with the foundation of the Cymmrodorion becomes apparent when we turn to the 1755 *Constitutions*, which refer to the need for

47

"the better regulating and conducting" of the "Antient Britons'" festival, "in order to retrieve the credit and dignity of that honourable and charitable institution," and observe "with the utmost regret" that the older Society "cannot carry on their charitable design without the further assistance of the well-disposed." We shall have occasion later to note that the foundation of the Cymmrodorion resulted in a substantial improvement of the finances of the Welsh School ; the point at the moment is one which is often forgotten by those of us who are primarily concerned with Welsh literature—that this was one of the *main* purposes for which the Cymmrodorion Society was founded.

But a mere annual splash, it seemed to Richard Morris, was hardly an adequate means of maintaining "unity and fraternity" (*undeb a brawdgarwch*) among London Welshmen. The age, as is well known, was in London a *social* age ; clubs and societies abounded, and the taverns and coffee-houses furnished ample provision for their meetings. Good-fellowship, conviviality, was at all times the common denominator of these gatherings ; over and above this, one club might be political, another literary, another mercantile, another a gambling-club. To the London Welshman, the First Cymmrodorion Society was primarily *social* ; it provided regular monthly opportunities for meeting one's fellow-countrymen and for hearing and speaking one's own language. These exiles had no thought of hanging their harps on willows beside Thomes—rather, they brought them forth on such occasions to accompany the songs of their Zion.

We may now venture to set forth, in a kind of hierarchy, the various aims which were present to the founders of the First Cymmrodorion. The *basis* is sheer sociability. On this is superimposed the philanthropic motive—the support of the Welsh Charity-School is one, but not the only, example of this. Then comes, in the intention of some at least of the founders, the literary and antiquarian interest which we associate primarily with Lewis Morris but which was equally dear to his brother Richard. To complete the tale of aspirations : there was a quite definite feeling—it had been in the air ever since 1715, as we have had occasion to observe—that London Welshmen ought to represent, and to *lead*, their countrymen in Wales. Wales was a country which had (and still has) no Edinburgh, no central point of convergence or focus of diffusion. In Wales itself, as the Morrises felt (luckily, events beyond their purview were to belie their fears), even the Welsh language was in decay : " Good Lord," said Richard, " what if we find our own countrymen the greatest strangers to it ? I blush even to think of it, but I am afraid the reflection will be found too just of Cambria's ungrateful undutiful sons " ; and again : " they, the residents of the country, shame to them (if they can feel ashamed), reject and despise not only their native country but also their praiseworthy native language."

It was not unnatural that Lewis Morris on his part should feel that " the want of a Society or body of people to encourage and promote knowledge amongst themselves hath been a great occasion of our indolence and indifference." This point is of great importance. The assumption of leadership by London Welshmen, and (what is more) the general acceptance of that leadership in Wales itself, is the common thread which runs through the history of all the London-Welsh Societies with which this book is concerned. In the eighteenth century, when there was no University of Wales, no National Library, no National Museum, no National Eisteddfod—and not even any nation-wide Governing Body or Union or Assembly in the religious field—London was the only possible home of Welsh national leadership. Even in the nineteenth century, as we shall see, the *demand* for the revival of the Cymmrodorion Society, in 1820 and in 1873 alike, came *from Wales*. Only at the end of that century and in the early twentieth did most of the newer agencies mentioned above begin to operate— and even so, most of them were in no small measure indebted to the Third Cymmrodorion Society for stimulating their very foundation.

Like other London societies or clubs, the first Society of Cymmrodorion, though it used the Welsh Charity-School as a business address, and kept its library and museum there, held its regular meetings in taverns, for obvious reasons of convenience and conviviality—one sometimes feels tempted to wonder, by the way, what proportion of its members even the " large room " of any tavern could have accommodated in comfort at any given meeting. The place of meeting was to be " some convenient House near the centre of the City." In April, 1753, the Society was meeting at the " London Stone Tavern " in Cannon Street ; on March 14th, 1951, the Council of the present Society felt itself entitled to assume that this had been the 1751 meeting-place, and accordingly held a bi-centenary dinner in this ancient (but transformed) hostelry. Our 1753 forefathers, however, felt that the house was " very inconvenient to resort to, especially in the winter months, being at one end of Town and away from the principal streets " ; in any case, a month later, the (Welsh) landlord moved to the " Salutation " in Bridge Street. The Society declined to follow him, and took up with the " Castle " in Paternoster-row, on the advice of the Chief President, William Vaughan. But this tavern soon closed down, and a little bother ensued, for some of the members wished to return to their old host, now at the " Salutation." The majority, led by Richard Morris (whom his brother William credits with " ruling the Society as Pelham [the Prime Minister] rules Parliament "), decided for the " Half Moon " in Cheapside ; there, says Lewis Morris, " in the great room," was set up " the grand costly chair for the President, bearing the arms of the Principality." The minority objected, partly from partiality to their former host and fellow-member, partly because the " Half Moon " served wine only—not even then, it would seem, a poor man's drink ! Richard Morris rode the storm ; conciliated the rebels by enacting that *punch* should also be provided—and later on got a rule passed " that no innkeeper shall be admitted member of the Society." The Society was certainly at the " Half-Moon " when the *Constitutions* were finally approved in 1755 ; indeed, it was still meeting there in 1762. But by September 1767, a letter of Richard Morris's to the poet Evan Evans (" Ieuan Fardd ") shows that John Parry the " blind harpist " was to play before the Society at the " Queen's Arms " in St. Paul's Churchyard (the " Queen " was Anne, whose statue was hard by), which is described in another source as " a good tavern for gentlemen, and has a spacious room for parties." There, in 1787 (when the landlord's name was Baker), the First Cymmrodorion Society came to its end. It is, by the way, curious to find, in Miss Leighton's book, that the Trustees of the " Antient Britons " used a completely different set of taverns and coffee-houses.

No early records of the First Cymmrodorion Society seem to have survived, and it is only on the title-page of its

Constitutions that we are told that the Society was " begun in the month of September, 1751." It was in full working order before August, 1752, when Richard Morris is found consulting his brother Lewis about a suitable name for it. Reading between the lines of the introductory letter prefixed to the 1755 *Constitutions*, we may conjecture that the original intention had been to call it "*Cymdeithas o Hen Frutaniaid*," i.e., " Society of Ancient Britons " ; and Lewis in his reply to Richard Morris speaks of it as " the British Society." Did Richard, one wonders, conceive of it as just a rejuvenation of the " Antient Britons," with more frequent meetings and wider activities ? And did the " Antient Britons " refuse to immolate themselves in this way—cling to their separate existence ? We do not know ; at any rate Lewis Morris had to find a new name. He began with the curious designation *Yr Hen Drigolion*, " the Old Inhabitants "—of Britain, one presumes. But " on second thoughts," he discarded this quite impracticable title, which " may admit of some bad, as if they grumbled because there are *trigolion newydd* "—Lewis had no desire to offend the new-comers of A.D. 449 ! Finally, he fell upon *Y Cymmrodorion*, which he explains as " *y cyn-frodorion*," i.e., exactly the same thing, but " throwing a sort of disguise over it " ; this is what Gibbon in an immortal footnote calls " the decent obscurity of a learned language " ! The " *mm*," which modern Welsh orthography abhors, has clung to the Cymmrodorion ever since, just as our Fusiliers are still " Welch "—after all, are we not an antiquarian Society ?

" Cymmrodorion," however we spell it, is seemly enough. That can hardly be said of Lewis's rendering of *Constitutions*, namely *Gosodedigaethau*, " a monstrous long word," as his brother William very rightly judged ; it must have been difficult to pronounce in the later stages of a First Cymmrodorion meeting. The Rules were adopted in April, 1753, the printed, partly bilingual, *Constitutions* not till May, 1755 ; the Welsh version was done by Goronwy Owen (who received five guineas for his work), and the *Constitutions* conclude with an *awdl* by him " to the honourable Society of Cymmrodorion in London, and to the ancient and splendid Welsh language." The reader will perhaps recollect that Lewis Morris was in Town at both these times ; there can be no doubt that much of the wording of the elaborate *Constitutions* is his. They were to have been re-issued at the end of 1766, but in August of that year Richard Morris complains that he has " no leisure to edit them." There was, indeed, no new edition till 1778 (author-ised in 1777) ; the changes in this are of no great moment, but we shall later have to comment on the much ampler space given in the 1778 booklet to the affairs of the Welsh Charity-School.

The 1755 *Constitutions* were printed by John Oliver (" Siôn Olfyr " to Richard Morris), whose press was at Bartholomew Close from 1740 to 1775, and who printed for the S.P.C.K. and for Griffith Jones of Llanddowror—he was not, by the way, a Cymmrodor. The 1762 List of Members was printed by " William Roberts, Printiwr y Gymdeithas," of Abchurch Lane ; the 1778 *Constitutions* bears no printer's name. All three publications show the armorial bearings of the Society, these are also emblazoned on its banner, which is still in existence. The shield is that of Llewelyn ap Gruffydd ("y llyw olaf "), Prince of Wales ; it is surmounted by the Prince of Wales's feathers and motto—for the Prince was Patron of the Society, which, like the " Antient Britons " before it, was loyally Hanoverian and Protestant. The " supporters " are a bishop (S. David) and a druid, each with a leek at his foot. The motto should be noted : it is *Undeb a Brawdgarwch* (Unity and Fraternity), a useful reminder to us of the predominantly *social* and *philanthropic* aims of the First Society—the motto of the Second and Third Cymmrodorion is deliberately *anti-quarian*. The arms had been discussed at length between Richard and William Morris—William appears to have been regarded as the family expert on heraldry ; he wanted a lion as crest—red or yellow (red would be better), holding the feathers in one hand and a leek in the other " (which seems rather odd heraldry !) ; but he heartily approved of the motto (" in Welsh—none of your beastly Latin "), and to add force to it, he thought (bethinking him probably of Isaiah) the supporters should be " a lion and a lamb." On the whole, one is glad that less fanciful men in London had their way this time.

The President (*Llywydd*) of the Society, down to his death in 1779, was Richard Morris ; he was succeeded by Sir Watkin Lewes (known to Richard as " Wat Lewis "), a Pembrokeshire man whose family is in later times better known as " of Tŷ-glyn Aeron " ; he was a barrister of the Inner Temple, and lived in King's Road. This famous London Welshman was from 1781 to 1796 M.P. for the City, and was Lord Mayor in 1780 ; he was an active supporter of John Wilkes. Like other leading Cymmrodorion, he was a pillar among the " Antient Britons," and from 1775 to 1795 (following David Humphreys) was Treasurer of the School, which was near his house. The second President saw the First Cymmrodorion out. In later years, he fell into adverse circumstances, dying at 85, in 1821, " within the Rules of the Fleet."

The Society had also an honorific " Chief President " (*Penllywydd*). The first of these was William Vaughan (1707-75) of Cors-y-gedol in Ardudwy, M.P. for Merioneth in five Parliaments between 1734 and 1748, Lord Lieutenant of his shire in 1762. The choice was probably a suggestion of Lewis Morris's, who had long known Vaughan and as early as 1738 refers to him as " my dear and respected friend " ; but Richard knew him too—Vaughan seems to have helped him to some clerical work in Parliament in his struggling days. In any case, no better choice could possibly have been made. William Vaughan, owner of Cors-y-gedol, had by marriage become owner also of Nannau near Dolgelley (Lewis Morris calls him " *Y Brawd Du o'r Nannau*," thereby resurrecting a sobriquet applied to a thirteenth century bishop of S. Asaph), already in previous generations connected with Cors-y-gedol. Vaughan himself wrote an interesting account of his family, which will be found printed in the 1875 volume of *Archaeologia Cambrensis*. An ancestor of his had built the fine house of Cors-y-gedol in Jacobean days ; William's great-grandfather William, a man of wide culture and a friend of Ben Jonson's and of James Howell's, had employed Inigo Jones on the building of the beautiful gateway there. But along with this cosmopolitan culture, the Vaughans had been steadfast patrons of Welsh poetry. It has already been observed, early in the preceding chapter, that the gentry of Ardudwy (and indeed of West Merioneth in general) had clung to their Welsh speech and tradition down to a much later period than many of their compeers in other parts of Wales. Readers of Pennant will recall his vivid description of old Evan Lloyd of Cwmbychan in Ardudwy, who even in 1776 dressed and ate and drank, and lived in general, exactly as the old Welsh gentry had comported themselves two centuries before that date. The region was indeed a stronghold of things Welsh—could it not boast, in three successive generations, of those masters of Welsh, Edmund Prys and Morgan Llwyd and Ellis Wynne, not to speak of lesser, yet noteworthy, men of letters ?

And although the Vaughans of Cors-y-gedol, and for that matter the Nanneys of Nannau with whom they inter-married, were not so primitive as the Lloyds of Cwmbychan, they all honoured the old Welsh " gentle " tradition of " maintaining poetry." Parallel with the succession of ardent Royalist squires of Cors-y-gedol runs the succession of their bardic proteges, " Phylipiaid Ardudwy "—from old Siôn Phylip (1543-1620), bardic graduate of the Caerwys Eisteddfod of 1568, down to Phylip Siôn Phylip who died in 1678—while at Nannau, Siôn Dafydd Las, who died about 1694, was the last " household bard " in North Wales. Even in the 1770's William Owen Pughe as a boy breathed an atmosphere of vigorous poetical and musical culture under the aegis of the great houses of that countryside. And the gentry not only patronised these arts ; a minor landowner, Rhys Jones (1713-1801) of Blaenau near Nannau, was himself a poet of repute, having also a knowledge of ancient Welsh poetry which even Lewis Morris neither could nor did despise.

Our William Vaughan, to be sure, had moved with the times. Schooled in Chester and near London, he was in 1726 a fellow-commoner of S. John's at Cambridge—he did not graduate. Tory though he was, he was a " Hanoverian " Tory, one of the group which in Parliament followed Sir William Windham in forswearing Jacobitism and rallying to the new dynasty—after 1760, he attached himself to Bute. Further, he dabbled in commerce—his ship, the *Harlech Castle*, was in 1752 seized by a Liverpool mob who thought no Tory could be a loyalist, to the amusement of Lewis Morris who turned out humorous verse on the incident. But he clung to his Welsh, and to its literature. Richard Morris invariably writes to him in Welsh ; Lewis, writing in English, apologises for doing so. Says Lewis to Richard in 1738, when Richard wished to solicit Vaughan's help in getting employment : " when you go to see him, don't forget to take two or three *englynion* with you." We have two *cywyddau*, and two *awdlau*, of Lewis Morris's to him, all in 1741. In 1755, we find the squire translating Lewis's *Caniad Hanes Henaint* into English, and in 1762, his more famous *Caniad y Gog*. In 1753, Vaughan, on a visit to Liverpool, called on Goronwy Owen at Walton, " and swore a mighty oath that he should not be there another year " ; at another time, he pronounces Goronwy's *Cywydd y Farn* to be far above the poem on the same subject by William Wynn, though he himself had in 1763 translated Wynn's *cywydd*. Ieuan Fardd, again, was welcomed at Cors-y-gedol, and dedicated his *Dissertatio de Bardis* to Vaughan and to the Cymmrodorion.

William Vaughan himself is described by his neighbour Rhys Jones of Blaenau as *bardd celfydd rhydd*, a skilled and ready poet. He is said to have written English verse—he most certainly wrote satirical verse in Welsh, notably, for instance, in 1761 when his fellow-M.P., Bayly of Anglesey, " blotted his copybook "—Lewis Morris, too, wrote lively *englynion* on that occasion. The freedom of these effusions reminds us that Vaughan's own morals were not impeccable ; the Morris Letters have more than one dig at his aberrations ; and indeed William Morris, when he first met him, thought him (at 42) prematurely aged, " though genial and unpretentious." When William Vaughan had to present an address to George III, Lewis Morris amused himself by sending Richard an imaginary dialogue between the Chief President and his sovereign— Vaughan chaffs the King on his black mourning garb, and His Majesty improbably retorts : " well, come to that, you're pretty fond of black yourself, especially black-eyed lasses ! " Richard promptly showed the squib to Vaughan " in the great chair of the Cymmrodorion " ; and the Chief President, without a moment's delay, rapped out five lines of Welsh verse in which the tables were turned, not too delicately, upon the absent Lewis himself. In fact, the squire of Cors-y-gedol, with all his modernity and for all the " Age of Reason " in which he lived, was a throw-back. His virtues, and his foibles too, were those of a Welsh *uchelwr* of the colourful days of Bosworth Field. Small wonder that William Morris should have exclaimed : " oh, that we had his like in the Isle of Anglesey ! " as he thought of the Anglo-Hibernian magnates of his native island.

William Vaughan took his Chief Presidency of the Cymmro-dorion quite seriously ; Richard Morris's letters show that he often attended meetings. After 1768, when he retired

from Parliament, his attendance naturally became less frequent :
" when," writes Richard to him in 1769, " are you coming up
again to preside over us ? we drink your health every month."
As late as November, 1770, Richard refers to him as " *Penllywydd*," and even in 1773 the subscription-list in the
" Trefdraeth case " styles him " Chief President." He died
on April 12th, 1775 ; his daughter had died, childless, before
him ; and on the death in 1791 of his brother Evan Lloyd (a
Cymmrodor in 1778) the estates passed on to the allied Vaughans
of Hengwrt. Some who would have sung William Vaughan's
praises had died before him—Goronwy Owen, Lewis Morris ;
Richard Morris was old and broken. But Ieuan Fardd, in an
elegiac *cywydd*, mourned the loss of a Welsh landowner " whose
honour had never allowed him to raise a tenant's rent," a
Welsh gentleman who stood out in contrast with " the
Judases " (as the poet puts it) who had turned their backs on
their native language and literature.

William Vaughan's successor as Chief President was in
some ways a more resplendent personage : Sir Watkin Williams
Wynn (1749-89) of Wynnstay, fourth baronet, but second
Wynn. Sir Watkin's pedigree was a jig-saw puzzle to which
almost every landed family in North Wales had contributed
bits. The " Wynn," first assumed by his father the famous
Jacobite, was that of Gwydir (in the female line) ; the
" Williams " was that of Llanforda (but of Anglesey origin) ;
our Chief President's great-grandfather Sir Watkin Williams
(first baronet) had been Speaker of the House of Commons.
From 1716 till the great Liberal triumph of 1886, a Williams
or a Williams Wynn in almost unbroken succession represented
Denbighshire in Parliament ; in Montgomeryshire, too, the
family had a quasi-monopoly down to the election of 1880.
Whether in wealth, or in the breadth of his acres, or in political
influence, " Sir Watkin " (*any* Sir Watkin) was not inaptly
styled " Prince in Wales."

Sir Watkin, according to the 1778 List of Members, had
become Chief President before his predecessor's death—" on
resignation of William Vaughan, Esq." Richard Morris knew
him at least as far back as 1767, when he thought him a " sensible,
clever young man," and it looks (from another of Richard's
letters) as if he were being " groomed " for his coming elevation

as early as 1770. He was Vice-President of the "Antient Britons," and gave £100 a year to the Welsh School—he had also given £100 to the Trefdraeth fund. It is not over-cynical to suppose that these generous habits had much to do with his elevation to our Chief Presidency. For it could not be expected that Wynn, brought up on Offa's Dyke itself by a most admirable but wholly English mother (he was only five months old when his father died), would much resemble William Vaughan ; one can hardly imagine him smacking his lips over an *englyn* (however naughty !), and indeed the only old Welsh custom which survived at Wynnstay was that of keeping a harpist. What Sir Watkin *could* do for the Society was no doubt generously done ; an old member in 1819 recollected seeing him in the Chair " some five or six times "—no doubt that " handsome piece of furniture, mahogany, excellently carved," which Sir Watkin himself had presented to the Society, and which in 1787 passed to the Gwyneddigion. It must not be supposed that Sir Watkin (though " of a retiring disposition ") was without parts. He was a friend of Sir Joshua Reynolds, belonged (1775) to the " Dilettanti Society " and figures in Reynolds's picture of that society, was an accomplished 'cellist and a zealous promoter of oratorios. But above all, he was an ardent patron of the drama, and loved taking part in amateur theatricals. Possibly we are not greatly edified when we read that at 20 he appeared as " a Druid " in a masquerade, and that in 1773 " the jolly Sir Watkin produced great effect . . . by riding in as S. David, mounted on a Welsh goat." It was unkind of caricaturists to depict him with a goat's face—and indeed, on a somewhat higher dramatic plane he was a friend of Garrick's, and his private theatre at Wynnstay from 1780 on, stage-managed by the elder Coleman, attracted numbers of fashionable guests from Town. Yet we can hardly feel that he was a very appropriate successor to the fine old Welsh squire of Cors-y-gedol.

The Society had eight Vice-Presidents ; as they seem to have been changed annually, there is no point in naming the occupants of the office known to us. Its first Treasurer was David Humphreys. Little is known of him but that he was a Montgomeryshire man who was in business as a hosier in St. Martin's-le-grand. It seems reasonably certain that he was the David Humphreys who was Treasurer of the " Antient

Britons " from 1747 to 1775—he had ceased so to act, and was not even a Trustee of the School, in 1775. Nor was he Treasurer of the Cymmrodorion in 1777 ; possibly he had quit this office too in 1775. The only references to him in the Morris Letters refer to three small freeholds of his in Dark Gate, Aberystwyth. His successor as Cymmrodorion Treasurer was David Thomas. A David Thomas was senior Vice-President in 1751, a Flintshire man, a " stocking-presser " in Rope-makers' Alley, Moorfields, and his name appears in all four Lists of Members, invariably with the asterisk which denotes membership of the Council (of 16 plus officers) ; it is certain that this was the man. We have definite proof that David Thomas was Treasurer almost to the last. But in 1787, the Treasurer was David Jones—possibly the David Jones who was Secretary from 1777 at latest to 1781—who took over the office of Treasurer to wind up the Society's affairs.

The first Secretary of the Cymmrodorion was Daniel Venables of Princess Street, a Flintshire man and an accountant ; but he died before the 1755 *Constitutions* appeared. His successor, appointed in 1755, is well known to readers of the Morris Letters. He was William Parry. We do not know nearly enough about him ; even in the Letters, only by careful scrutiny of the context can we always distinguish him from another " Will Parry," who was a sailor. He was an Anglesey man, and if we took the words " *y câr* " in their literal sense, we might think him related to the Morrises—so indeed he may have been, but the poet Hugh Hughes too hails Parry as " *fy nghâr*." In 1766, it seems to have occurred to Parry (now an " esquire ") that he ought to have armorial bearings, and Richard Morris writes on his behalf to the old bard of Llwydiarth Esgob for Parry's pedigree. If Richard did not know it, it seems doubtful whether the two men were of very near kin— and Hugh Hughes (it seems) didn't know it either, dryly commenting " it's a pity someone can't get this giddiness out of his light head ! " He *did* know the name of William Parry's *great-grandfather*, William Parri Owen of Mynydd Parys near Amlwch, and of his great-grandmother, Marged verch Evan— which helped Parry (and helps us) very little. According to J. E. Griffith, Parry was one of the Pendref (Rhodogeidio) family. We do know from another source that he had a sister living at Beaumaris in 1768 ; and Griffith has " Richard Jones, curate of Beaumaris," as her husband. The date of Parry's death is not quite certainly known ; Griffith says " October 23rd, 1755 "—clearly a misprint for 1775. He is named in Richard Morris's last will (1773), but was dead by 1777 (on the evidence of the *Constitutions* of 1778), and the dropping of his name out of the *Court and City Register* of 1775 is significant. As to the date of his birth, Griffith gives it as 1719 ; a letter of Richard Morris's in 1770 to Hugh Hughes speaks of Parry as " getting on in years."

Whether or not he was related to the Morrises, his career, as soon as we begin to have continuous knowledge of it, is clearly bound up with Richard Morris's. It would seem that he was at the Navy Office with Richard from 1747. In 1753, Lewis Morris believes that Parry " will have a place in the Ordnance Office in the Tower " ; he was at any rate in a position to expedite the grant of a commission to William Morris early in 1754, and William in March commiserates with Richard on " losing Gwilym Parri—let us hope you'll see him back soon " ; further, we learn in August that Parry was then " at Woolwich." In 1755, Lewis speaks of him as being at the Mint, and William in 1756 refers to him as " my brother Comptroller " ; later in that year, he had had some promotion, unidentified but clearly at the Mint. But by 1757, he had returned to the Navy Office, and from 1757 to 1775 was " Under Clerk for Foreign Accounts to the Comptroller of the Navy," i.e., he was the immediate subordinate of Richard Morris there—curiously enough, Lewis Morris at the end of 1757 thinks it likely that Parry will be transferred to the Exchequer. Richard tells us in 1767 that he could not be away from Town " as Parry has gone to Anglesey for six weeks." Yet Parry, as the Cymmrodorion Lists of 1759 and 1762 show (not to speak of *the Court and City Register*), still remained " Comptroller's Deputy and Clerk " at the Royal Mint.

On all the evidence we have, our second Secretary was an amiable and popular man. Lewis Morris thought him " the most honest man in the world," and William found him " ever ready to do anyone a good turn." Richard took him out to dine with him at the Town lodgings of the Meyricks of Bodorgan and at other houses. A visit paid to the Rev. Thomas Ellis (formerly of Holyhead) at Nutfield Rectory provoked a comical incident—Parry went out fishing on the Sunday, and the rector (a strict Sabbatarian, who had once *excommunicated* a Holyhead parishioner for so doing) dressed him down so severely that " Parry swears he will never go there again." Parry was repeatedly pressed to visit Goronwy Owen at Northolt—indeed, the poet indited a whole poem (*Cywydd y Gwahawdd*, 1755) of invitation ; " having no work to do at your office," writes Goronwy to Richard Morris, "Parry can stay here a month, or even two " ; it may be added that Parry showed the poet much kindness, which one regrets to say was ill-requited, and further that he did his best to smooth matters between Goronwy and the justly-incensed Richard Morris. Goronwy, in his last letter (1767) from America to Richard, desires to be remembered to " my friend Parry of the Mint." In 1761, Parry was a bachelor, paying court to a wealthy corn-factor's daughter—unsuccessfully, for in 1772-3, Richard Morris's last letter to Goronwy Owen (already dead) says that Parry has now married a " *hen forwyn* "— whether " an old maid " or " a former maidservant " we are left to conjecture.

The Society's next Secretary was " David Jones, Esq." There are four men of this not very uncommon name in the 1778 List, but the only one called " Esq.", a Montgomeryshire man living in Markham Street, was a recently-elected member. The one " David Jones " who is in all four lists, and was further " Second Vice-President " in 1751, was a Cardiganshire man, a linen-draper in the Borough. This much may be said : the 1751 man would probably be an elderly man by 1775, and it *may* be significant that in 1777 we have an " Assistant Secretary, Mr. Owen Jones "—this was " Owain Myfyr," of whom much will be said in the next chapter. The Secretary's responsibilities were further lightened by the appointment of two Librarians : Robert Hughes (" Robin Ddu o Fôn ") , with whom again the next chapter will deal, and the famous Pembrokeshire antiquary Richard Fenton (1747-1821), then at the Custom-House in London. David Jones was succeeded as Secretary in 1781 by a John Evans—there is a " John Evans, Esq." in the 1778 List, but his " place of abode " was Oswestry, so we are left guessing.

It was not expected of the Hon. Secretary that he should do all the little office-jobs. In fact, though the *Constitutions* call him " Secretary " in English, the Welsh version has *Cofiadur*, " Recorder " ; he was also (till 1777) Librarian and Keeper of the Museum. But there was also a " Clerk," called in the Welsh version *Ysgrifen[n]ydd*. The Master of the Welsh School was to be " perpetual clerk " ; he was to call the roll, take minutes, call the reckoning, direct circulars (and send them out by his boys), insert advertisements, notify members of the " funerals of deceased brethren," etc.—for this, he was exempt from entrance-fee and all other payments, and was further to be given " a compliment at Christmas yearly." Other non-commissioned officers, so to speak, were the " messenger " (inside the room door), and the " doorkeeper " (outside it)—the latter was to " take particular care that none but brethren enter the room." Each of these was paid a shilling a night, plus a " gratuity " (not a " compliment " !) at Christmas.

Admission of members was by proposal and ballot ; three (later, five) adverse votes barred election ; there was no limit of numbers. The proposer paid 10/6d. entrance-fee (presumably getting it out of the postulant first)—it was returned if there was no election. It seems clear, both from the *Constitutions* and from Lewis Morris's statement in *Diddanwch Teuluaidd*, that this 10/6d., once for all, was the *only* payment made by a member—other than the " shot " at meetings (reckoned by Lewis at 1/6d.) and the quarterly minimum of sixpence for the poor-box. By 1777, however, (and most probably for the first time *in* 1777), the new member had immediately to hand over *another* 10/6d., and to repeat this payment in January of each year. A letter (1777) of Owen Jones's shows that this new annual levy was ear-marked " for the support of Welsh publications." It will be obvious that before this change the Society's funds must have been totally inadequate for any ambitious programme—we should remember this fact when we criticise it for publishing so little. Even the purchase of " every printed book," old and new, in Welsh, for the Society's library, not to mention " as many ancient British MSS. as can be procured at a moderate price," would have swamped the Society's resources. It is clear that the *social* or " club " aspect of the Society predominated, and that a low entrance-fee (with no annual subscription) was deemed essential for the recruiting of members. Richard Morris, it may be, imagined that *publishing* costs might be met, partly by sales and partly by *ad hoc* subscriptions from the more prosperous members.

Three official Lists of Members are extant—those appended to the *Constitutions* of 1755 and 1778, and a List (alone) of 1762 ; the old bibliographer William Rowlands (" Gwilym Lleyn ") printed in *Golud yr Oes* for 1863 a fourth list, which he had found somewhere, of 1759. If we have counted correctly, the membership up to (not *in*) 1755 was 112 ; in 1759 it was 168 ; in 1762, 200 ; in 1778, 228. " Corresponding Members " numbered 12, 40, 183 and 136 in the respective Lists, but the 1762 figure is somewhat artificially swollen by including a whole batch of 70 members of Jesus College, Oxford, and in the 1778 List the " corresponding members " include " members elected but not yet initiated "—though their half-guineas had been prudently extracted beforehand. The 1755 List has two " Honorary Members," but in later lists they are merged in the " correspondents "—on the other hand, some early " correspondents " are later reckoned as resident or full members, even though they did not actually live in or near London. The Lists of 1755 and 1762 tabulate the figures under " counties of birth." Anglesey, curiously enough, does not show up too well : 9 and 12. Montgomery has much the largest number (25) in 1755—David Humphreys's personal efforts ?—and is still ahead in 1762 ; Carmarthen and Glamorgan and Caernarvon come next ; Pembrokeshire is at the bottom.

Some of the members are well-known people. The first List includes John Evans (1702-82), absentee rector of Eglwys Cymyn, " Reading-chaplain at the Chapel Royal at Whitehall," bitter adversary of Methodism and of Griffith Jones of Llanddowror, but good friend of the Welsh School in London. Others were Watkin Lewes the future President ; Sir Richard Glynne of Glynllivon, banker, Lord Mayor of London (1780), another prominent supporter of the Welsh School ; Roderick Richardes of Penglais (Aberystwyth), at the Navy Office ; Noah Thomas, F.R.S., of Neath (knighted in 1775), physician to George III. In 1759 we come across " Thomas Harris, of York Buildings, Tailor." He was Howel Harris's brother, but no Methodist, indeed a distinctly raffish fellow who as we learn from other sources was " given to wine-drinking " and though a bachelor was not without posterity. He had gone bankrupt in 1736 and had fled to France, but had re-established himself and made a fortune out of army contracts. We can hardly suppose him enthusiastic about Welsh poetry—the stage-doors of the theatres were more in his line. He has dropped out of the Society by 1762, having retired to his native county to become a J.P. and the squire of the Tregunter estate, where the famous actress " Perdita " Robinson (wife of one of his illegitimate sons) describes him as a regular attendant at church but a man of most unedifying speech outside it.

The 1762 List includes " the Hon. Thomas Harley, M.P.", brother of the Earl of Oxford, but himself a " wine-merchant and under-writer." Then there was Richard Morris's neighbour, the Rev. Henry Owen, M.D., F.R.S. (1716-95), rector of S. Olave's and later (1775) also vicar of Edmonton, of whom there is much talk in the Letters—a bit of a miser (says Richard), whose servants were forever leaving his house. Henry Owen (of Tanygadair, Dolgelley) was a classical and mathematical scholar, a physician, and a theologian ; according to the *D.N.B.* " his reputation for learning is amply attested by contemporaries." As far as we in Wales are concerned, it may be noted that in 1776 he published a revised edition of Rowlands's *Mona Antiqua*. It was he who was charged with deciding what papers were to be read at Cymmrodorion meetings. But one can hardly afford space to name all the men of social standing who appear in one or other of the Lists—the 1778 List is even more " gentlemanly." Richard Morris, indeed, in April 1770, has a paean on " the remarkably flourishing state of the Cymmrodorion ; many great men are joining us, such as Sir Watkin Williams Wynn, Lord Bulkeley, Lord Grosvenor, Lord Paget, Sir Hugh Williams [M.P. for Beaumaris], John Pugh Pryse of Gogerddan, etc., etc., and if God give me life, I doubt not that I shall see all the aristocrats of Wales among us." A cold-blooded examination of the 1778 List shows that most of these magnates had not even bothered to be formally initiated—and Lewis even in 1761 sardonically tells his brother : " a fine lot of big men you've got in your Cymmrodorion ! but you'll never see their faces except when they *want* something." Still, we shall have to observe later that there was *some* method in Richard Morris's apparent madness.

One name, however, must be singled out from the 1778 List—that of Thomas Llewelyn (1720?-83) of Gelligaer in Glamorgan. He was a Baptist minister, though the List

63

demurely disguises this fact by styling him "Esq., LL.D." We have here perhaps not so much a mitigation of the Society's rooted objection to Dissent as the recognition by Richard Morris of a kindred spirit—a man who had written one book on the Welsh versions of the Bible and another on " The British Tongue." Richard wrote him a courteous letter in appreciation of the former work (with a vicious jab at the " wretched " 1768 Bible of his fellow-Cymmrodor John Evans) ; William Vaughan too was on good terms with him. To do Richard Morris justice, he was becoming increasingly willing to see good where he found it. When in 1770 a Welsh periodical was published, with Dissenting and some Methodist backing, at Carmarthen, it was Richard who " revised " its prospectus and coined its admirable title *Yr Eurgrawn ;* he further sent some ancient *englynion* to be printed in it. To be sure, he found the press-correcting very faulty, but he gives the Carmarthen printers generous praise for their enterprise, and later laments the failure of the magazine. More, when Peter Williams, the Methodist, brought forth his ill-starred annotated Bible, Richard Morris generously sent down 18,000 copies of William Jones's (1746) maps to be bound with the book. One fears that Richard Morris was kinder to Peter Williams (" poor as his Welsh is," says Richard) than were his own fellow-Methodists.

The Lists of 1759 and 1762 give us the occupations of the members, and thereby a most interesting cross-section of London-Welsh society in the mid-eighteenth century. Let us therefore without dwelling further on those members whom, *honoris causa*, we may call " upper-class "—clergymen, men of law, civil servants (a substantial element in the First, as in the Second and Third Cymmrodorion)—turn to the rank and file. Their occupations were in 1759 given in English, and Lewis Morris's snobbishness revolted against the look of the List. To him, we must remember, the Society was to be a *learned* Society, modelled on the Royal Society. He remonstrated with Richard, who tearfully excused himself, " but I *did* try to do it in Welsh, but couldn't manage it." But Lewis got in in time for the 1762 List—in September 1761, he writes " for God's sake, don't put down *weaver, tinker, cooper ;* let their titles be disguised as much as possible, that every English fool may not have room to laugh in his sleeve and say *such a Society, indeed !* '' ; or, as he graphically puts it in another place, '' let us turn the soiled side of the sheet to face the blanket.'' As Matthew Arnold might have said, there were no tinkers beside the Ilissus of the Royal Society. It was clearly, this time, to be the '' decent obscurity '' of an *un*-learned language. So Richard in anxious consultation with the helpful William, went at it—for indeed the invention of Welsh equivalents for some of the technical terms was no easy matter.

Well over forty '' trades '' appear in the Lists ; we shall enumerate most of them, adding the Welsh equivalents when they call for mention or comment : accountant ; apothecary (*poticari,* a good old term now disused) ; bees-man ; brandy-merchant (*masnachwr dwfr poeth !*) ; breeches-maker ; brewer ; bricklayer (*saer priddfaen,* on the sound analogy of *saer maen*) ; cabinet-maker (*saer cist*) ; chinaman (no Oriental, but a seller of crockery, *gwerthwr tsini*) ; chocolate-maker (*cocolatydd !*); coal-merchant ; coffee-man ; cordwainer ; cutler ; distiller (*diferwr*) ; farrier (*march-feddyg*) ; glover ; goldbeater (*aur-ddeilydd*) ; grocer (*siopwr*—rather feeble) ; haberdasher (*gwerthwr mân bethau*); hosier; insurance-broker (*torrwr sicrhad*—what on earth came over Richard here ?) ; japanner (*cabolydd*) ; leather-cutter ; linen-draper ; mason ; merchant ; musician (this, rendered *telynior,* was John Parry, the blind harpist, former harpist to the Jacobite Sir Watkin at Wynnstay, but now harpist to the Prince of Wales) ; oilman ; perfumer ; peruke-maker (*gwalltweydd* in one instance, *gosodwalltwr* in another) ; poulterer ; printer ; sailmaker (this was Wheldon Jones of Anglesey, an old friend of the Morrises whose name occurs frequently and favourably in the Letters) ; scarlet-dyer ; schoolmaster ; soap-maker ; stable-keeper ; stationer (a Tomley of Montgomery—the name still survives in that ancient borough) ; stocking-presser ; tailor ; tobacconist ; toyman (*teganwr*) ; warehouseman ; watchmaker (*awrflychydd* in the printed List, but the man was William Hughes of High Holborn, an Anglesey man whom his friend Robin Ddu invariably calls *aurflychydd*—Robin has an amusing *englyn* on the ticking clocks in Hughes's shop) ; some of the members, by the way, had changed their occupations between 1759 and 1762. The 1778 List has no '' occupations ''—had Richard by then veered round to his brother Lewis's 1761 views ? Here, then, are the First Cymmrodorion ; not in general, it is to be feared, high authorities on Welsh literature and antiquities ; likely enough to be bored by the learned papers sent up by Lewis Morris to be read to them ; but for the most part good " tidy " Welshmen who liked a pot and a pipe and a gossip in the "large room" of the "Half Moon" or the " Queen's Arms." " Some there be which have no memorial, who have perished as though they had not been " ; but without such men, the Cymmrodorion would never have come into being.

The first small batch of " corresponding members " was hand-picked—men like William Morris (Lewis ranked as a resident member), Thomas Pennant of Downing, poor despised Thomas Richards the lexicographer, Thomas Ellis of Holyhead (who in 1759, at Nutfield, became a resident member) ; William Wynn (1710 ?-61) of Llangynhafal, a poet of respectable stature who yet fell short of genius. Genius, on the other hand, and in abundant measure, had been given to two other men in this batch : Goronwy Owen (1723-69) and Evan Evans (1731-88 ; " Ieuan Brydydd Hir"—"the tall bard"—to the Morrises, " Ieuan Fardd " to most writers of to-day) ; their chequered careers, and their remarkable achievements in the fields of poetry and of Welsh literary scholarship respectively, are too well known to call for extended treatment in this book. It is right, however, that something should be said in defence of the Morrises against the charge, so often repeated by Goronwy's champions, that they treated him scurvily. There is ample evidence of their anxiety to get him " settled " somewhere : it was William Morris who got him his curacy at Walton ; Lewis fairly deafened the Earl of Powis with his solicitations on the poet's behalf ; we have a letter of Richard's to the bishop of Bangor, pleading Richard's own " fatiguing labours " on the Welsh Bible as an excuse for begging for a living for Goronwy. The one matter in which they may be held open to criticism in their dealings with him is their over-sanguine invitation to him (May, 1755) to leave Walton and come up to Town as chaplain-elect of the " Welsh Church " which was one of the Society's official projects—Goronwy was also, one gathers, to be Richard Morris's right-hand man in the publishing schemes which Richard and Lewis contemplated. Nothing came of the " Welsh Church " for well-nigh another hundred years. Obviously a Society with so small a budget could not have built, or even rented, a place for worship ; it would seem from the Letters that the idea in 1755 (and indeed in later years) was to induce a London incumbent to take a Welsh curate and allow him the use of his church for Welsh services financially supported by the Cymmrodorion. It may not unfairly be judged that Richard Morris ought to have made sure of his incumbent first, before uprooting Goronwy ; but against this it must be observed that Goronwy had already made Walton too hot to hold him. He did, however, after some months of unemployment in Town, get the extremely comfortable curacy of Northolt outside London, where he was as happy as it was in him to be happy. The sad truth was that the unfortunate man could not be helped, and wore out everybody's patience with his drunkenness and shiftlessness ; not only did moody Lewis Morris consign him to the devil, but the much more placable William lost all patience (who would not ?) when the poet borrowed his most cherished MS. of old poetry, and pawned it in Liverpool ; Richard, too, grew " cool," though in the end he relented, " lent " Goronwy more money, and saw him off on his departure to Virginia, at the end of 1757. Yet the Morrises never at any time faltered in their high opinion of Goronwy as a poet ; it was they, after all, who prepared his poems for press, and backed up their publisher when the poet was thousands of miles away. The ill-feeling on both sides passed away with the years, and letters were exchanged between Goronwy and Richard Morris—one of Richard's last extant letters was written to Goronwy, who, however, was dead before it was written. Even the angry Lewis, on Goronwy's departure to America, said that " the most glorious poet in the Kingdom " had now left it. And the poet, who had once written a *cywydd* " To the Devil," i.e., to Lewis Morris, made amends, when he heard of Lewis Morris's death, with a stately elegiac *awdl*. The Cymmrodorion Society, on January 18th, 1924, placed in Northolt Church a memorial tablet to Goronwy Owen.

Goronwy Owen, admit his misfortunes as we readily may, certainly was his own worst enemy. His successive incumbents, on all the impartial evidence we possess, were kindly and even generous men. It may seem a Philistine comment to point out that his curacy at Northolt, at £50 a year, brought him £10 a year more than what Griffith Jones received as rector of Llanddowror—and that in terms of purchasing power he was at least as well off as the great majority of clergymen and ministers in Wales to-day, who yet somehow manage to rub along without excessive complaint. His friend Evan Evans (Ieuan Fardd) resembled him in habits and vicissitudes, but there were differences. Ieuan, ranking far below Goronwy as a poet, but far higher as a scholar (though Goronwy was indeed a good scholar and an even better critic), was in general much less querulous. Irascible and abusive he might be, in his cups, but he took Richard Morris's stern lectures in good part, never showing resentment. He wandered (he was unmarried) from one short-lived curacy to another, generally in Wales, though there was one almost comical interlude in Kent and Sussex (where a kindly fellow-Cymmrodor had managed to "place" him) —he tells us, by the way, that there were " very many " Welsh curates in those parts, not to mention a Brecknockshire saddler at Rye who befriended him. But wherever he went, Ieuan diligently scoured the neighbourhood for old MSS., and sought permission to copy them. He thus became one of the most learned Welsh scholars of his day, and an important figure in the history of literary tradition. We in Wales know our Goronwy Owen well ; his English contemporaries had not even heard of him. But they *had* heard of Evan Evans before his short and calamitous career came to its end.

Those were the days when English scholars and men of letters were beginning to show a not always well-informed interest in British antiquities and in " Celtic " literature. It was in 1760 that James Macpherson began publishing his " Ossianic " poems—in which, by the way, Lewis Morris believed not a whit, and concerning which he corresponded with Michael Lort (a Pembrokeshire man), Regius Professor of Greek at Cambridge ; Lewis, indeed, gave his brother William a long list of his " correspondents " in those days : " Pegge, Lye, Percy, Hurd, Shenstone, Gray, Mason." To this list we may add others like Thomas Carte, and Thomas Warton the historian of English poetry. Thomas Percy, afterwards bishop of Dromore, was a zealous student of early " Northern " and " Celtic " poetry. With him, Evan Evans (encouraged by Lewis Morris) engaged in a correspondence which by 1767 had gone on " for six years," on Welsh and Icelandic poetry. Percy offered Ieuan a curacy, which he refused, being at the time " happy " in that Sussex curacy which came to an untimely end and was followed by enlistment in the army (from which, like Coleridge in like case, he was rescued by his friends). He has recorded that " all Welsh literati " had assured him that Evan Evans knew more about old Welsh than any other man living. And it was Percy (and Daines Barrington, Justice of the Great Sessions in Wales) who brought Ieuan to the notice of Thomas Gray and of Samuel Johnson.

We are not to suppose that Gray's interest in Welsh poetry was due to this contact, for we have a list of the books on Welsh lore which Gray had read before this time, and indeed *The Bard* was published as early as 1757, and he had taken the (unfounded) story which underlies it from Carte (1750) ; the poem, which had been laid aside uncompleted, was put " in motion again " (to quote Gray's own words) when Gray heard the blind harpist John Parry (the Cymmrodor) playing at Cambridge. It was after *The Bard* had been published that Evan Evans told Gray (through Percy) where Carte had got the story from. There is no evidence that the two men ever met, or ever corresponded except through Percy and Barrington. But when Ieuan had finished his *Dissertatio de Bardis*, intended (1759) for inclusion in the projected Cymmrodorion edition of Goronwy Owen's poems, he offered it to the Society (1761) for separate publication, asking £8 or £10 for it—which the Society could not afford. In the meantime, Ieuan had rendered into English some " specimens " of old Welsh poetry. Barrington showed some of these to Gray, who liked them ; the Justice now suggested that Ieuan should make " a small book " of them—and further borrowed the MS. of the *Dissertatio* to show to Gray ; this is confirmed by a 1760 letter of Gray's. In 1761, Percy offered to interest the publisher Dodsley in the publication of the work, and also to submit some of the " specimens " to Johnson. Ieuan now rightly decided that the *originals* of the " specimens " must accompany the versions, and in 1763 asked Richard Morris to correct the proofs of the Welsh texts, a task which that kindly man readily undertook. The book, *Some Specimens of the Poetry of the Antient Welsh Bards*, appeared in 1764. Its composite origin is betrayed by its triple dedication. The English " specimens " are dedicated to Ieuan's patron Sir Roger Mostyn of Gloddaeth ; the Latin *Dissertatio* to William Vaughan " and the other members of the Society of Cymmrodorion " ; the Welsh texts to Richard, Lewis, and William Morris, though William had died at the end of 1763. The book is of very real importance : not only Gray himself, in subsequent poems, but a whole host of lesser English poets drew upon this new fount of " Celtic " inspiration.

Samuel Johnson has been mentioned. It is curious to note that there is no evidence whatsoever of any awareness of the Cymmrodorion on the Doctor's part, though Johnson was not in the least anti-Welsh. Nor do the leading Cymmrodorion seem to know much about Johnson ; though Lewis Morris " took " *The Idler* in 1760, and had of course heard of Johnson as the author of the *Dictionary*, he did not know in 1761 that " Dictionary Johnson, author of *The Rambler* " (as he puts it) was also responsible for *The Idler*—Richard had to tell him that as a bit of gossip. But Johnson knew of Evan Evans ; we have one solitary reference in proof. In 1774, at Gwaenynog, during the Doctor's tour in North Wales, the talk turned on the preservation of the Welsh language, for which " I offered them a scheme "—he does not tell us what it was, but he somewhat optimistically recommended the reprinting of Siôn Dafydd Rhys's Grammar. Then follows : " poor Evan Evans was mentioned as incorrigibly addicted to drink." Indeed, drink and decline (even in 1760 Lewis Morris had noted a symptom of consumption), and lack of stable employment, eventually compelled Ieuan to return to his small native freehold at Cynhawdref, where he died in 1788. His MSS. (" more than 80 volumes ") went to Paul Panton of Plas Gwyn (Anglesey), who had been paying Ieuan an annuity of £20 for the last few years in return. They were eventually to see the light of day— without explicit acknowledgement that they were Ieuan's— in the *Myvyrian Archaiology*.

The " Corresponding Members " grew more numerous as time went on. In 1759 we have Browne Willis the antiquary ; Paul Panton who has just been mentioned (his collection of MSS. is to-day in the National Library) ; Evan Williams (though he actually lived in London) the harpist from Llangybi in Eifionydd, who had composed 24 psalm-tunes for inclusion in the Prayer-book bound up with Richard Morris's Bible, and had previously collaborated uneasily with the peppery harpist John Parry in the production of *Antient British Music* (1742)— he was also a *cywyddwr* of sorts, and Richard Morris in 1761 speaks of him as " the fittest man to be Secretary of the Society " (possibly William Parry wanted to resign). Then there were Hugh Hughes (" y Bardd Coch ") ; John Bradford the Glamorgan poet ; David Jones of Trefriw and Hugh Jones of Llangwm, who will both come up for further notice. And there was Joseph Harris, Assay-Master of the Mint, brother of Howel and of the somewhat shady Thomas, and author of important books on coinage, on navigation, and on optics. Presumably he was a " correspondent " because, though living in Town, he was too sober a man to attend convivial meetings— and presumably it was his fellow-moneyer William Parry who dragged him into the Society somehow. We have it on record that he gave Goronwy Owen a guinea to speed him to Virginia.

In 1762, we have Edward Richard, the schoolmaster-poet of Ystrad Meurig, Lewis Morris's fairly near neighbour—while the fastidious Lewis (like most of us) rated him very highly, the much more amenable Richard could see nothing to praise in his work. Then there are oddities like Dr. William Stukeley of Druidic fame, and Silvanus Bevan, F.R.S., of Hackney, apothecary-physician and founder (at Plough Court) of the firm of Allen and Hanburys. Bevan came of a Swansea Quaker family whose roots were near Laugharne. He spoke Welsh " very brokenly " says Richard Morris, and " was surprised to hear " that there *were* such things as Welsh MSS.—odd qualifications for membership ! A dilettante, a collector of fossils, curios, paintings, an amateur wood-carver, and enthusiastic gardener, he was " slovenly, and with trembling hands," and his table-manners (like Johnson's) were queer. We round off this tale of corresponding members with a single name from the somewhat over-ornate 1778 List—it is that of Rhys Jones of Tyddyn Mawr, Llanfachreth—" Rhys Jones o'r Blaenau," already mentioned. His election seems inexplicably belated, though perhaps it may go as far back as 1766, when Hugh Hughes of Anglesey put his name forward. If, however, he was elected only in 1777, his election was a tribute to the famous *Gorchestion Beirdd Cymru* which he published in splendid type and format in 1773—the first printed anthology of the poets of the " golden age " between Dafydd ap Gwilym and Tudur Aled ; the book includes also some of the even more ancient poetry. Rhys Jones himself wrote poetry in the strictest and most conservative tradition.

71

The role, and the importance, of these " corresponding " members should not be overlooked. No doubt there are dummies in the Lists. But discarding these, we observe that the correspondents fall into three classes. First, there are eminent English antiquaries—we have named but a few of them. Next, there are the Welsh territorial magnates of whom Richard Morris was so proud. These two categories bear witness to the growing repute of the Society. But the third category is even more significant ; the prominent men of letters *in Wales* who rallied round the Society. And if we except Lewis and Richard Morris and one or two others, the " resident " members of the Society rendered not a tithe of the services to the revival of Welsh literature which were rendered by Goronwy Owen, Ieuan Fardd, William Wynn, Hugh Hughes, Hugh Jones, David Jones, Rhys Jones, Edward Richard, and their like. The triumph of the Morrises was that linking of these men with the Cymmrodorion Society which thus made it an accepted leader of the Welsh renaissance. Nor indeed should we despise Richard Morris's success in getting the aristocracy of Wales to look upon membership of this Society, which had sprung from sufficiently humble beginnings, as an appropriate expression of Welsh patriotism in the sense in which they were able to conceive of it.

The First Cymmrodorion Society held its annual meetings on the first Wednesday in January, " between the hours of eight and nine " ; at this meeting, the officers and Council (to be summoned at the President's discretion) were elected for the year. A modern Cymmrodor may be surprised to find that there was no Annual Dinner—at least, no Annual *Cymmrodorion* Dinner. The reason was that in this matter the Society left the field clear for the " Antient Britons " ; the support of the older Society's Charity-School was one of the principal objects of the very foundation of the Cymmrodorion, and even the first edition of its *Constitutions* has a brief account of the School appended to it. We have already observed that the Master of the School was the Society's " perpetual clerk," and that it was he (or rather, his boys) who delivered its circulars ; further, whenever a Cymmrodor was being buried in London, " the British Charity Boys shall walk before the corps, singing psalms, to the grave " ; it has also been recorded that the Society's library and museum were kept at the School ;

and its effects were to pass to the School on its dissolution. As for the Dinner : the Cymmrodorion are to " make rules and orders for the better regulating and conducting the Annual Feast of the Antient Britons on S. David's Day," and " not any other feast, annual or otherwise, shall be held by the Society, but they shall use their best endeavours for supporting the British Charity School . . . by their own subscriptions thereunto, etc." In fact, the festival was from 1751 to 1787 managed jointly by both Societies, its chief promoters being members of both. Advertisements in the newspapers were inserted by one or the other Society indiscriminately. The financial benefit which accrued to the School from this revival is known to have been " very considerable," and it may be significant that after the demise of the First Cymmrodorion the " Antient British " Dinner became a liability rather than an asset. In 1762, William Morris was astounded to learn from Richard that the collection amounted to £1,200—" my good souls, I had no idea you were so rich ! " In 1760, there had been " about 500 persons " at the Dinner. There are unfortunately but scanty references to the Dinner in the Morris Letters ; usually it is only " met so-and-so at the Dinner." In 1760, Richard Morris (who had been prudently admonished by Lewis in February " not to burst his belly " at the Dinner, and to remember that S. David himself never drank aught but spring-water), reports that he had too bad a cough to attend the Sermon—he *went* to the Dinner, but " had little pleasure, choking in the foul tobacco-smoke, and left an hour before the end " ; at the 1761 Dinner, he had a bout of asthma—" it was almost unavoidable " comments Lewis.

The Society's regular meetings were on the first Wednesday in each month. Most unfortunately, no minute-books appear to have survived, but the *Constitutions* give us the " order of proceedings." When all the members present were seated, the President wielded the " big mallet " thoughtfully provided for him, and the toast *Church and King* was honoured. Next came balloting, proposals of new postulants for the next meeting's ballot, and initiation of new members—this was concluded by the singing of twelve verses composed by Lewis Morris ; three of these verses, patriotically breathing fire and slaughter upon Frenchmen and Spaniards, were to be omitted in times of peace, and in 1757 were replaced by three new

73

verses in praise of our new ally Frederick of Prussia. Then to business, including, one presumes, the reading of the " papers " or " communications " submitted to the Society, on the analogy of all " learned " societies of the period. A portentous list of general heads of " subjects to be occasionally considered . . . in the correspondence of the Society " (obviously Lewis Morris's work) fills five pages of the *Constitutions*. But it is only from chance references in the Morris Letters that we can hazard conjecture on what was actually done at the meetings. " Contributions " might be poetical : in 1753 Goronwy Owen's *Cywydd y Farn* ; in 1757 Hugh Hughes's *Cywydd Gardd y Bugail* and a *cywydd* by David Jones of Trefriw ; in 1759 another *cywydd* of Hugh Hughes's. In 1762, there was a blaze of loyalty, kindled by the birth of a Prince of Wales (August 12th)— Ieuan Fardd and Rhys Jones of Blaenau each sent up a *cywydd* on the occasion, and it was resolved that the Chief President should present Ieuan's poem to the King in person ; in 1764, with William Vaughan in the Chair, Evan Evans's elegy on Robert Davies of Llannerch was read ; and in 1767 a set of verses to the Prince of Wales, composed at the harpist's request by William Lloyd (rector of Cowden in Kent—the man who got Ieuan Fardd a Kentish curacy), was sung to the Cymmrodorion by the " royal harpist," John Parry.

The " papers," of which we catch fitful glimpses in the Letters, may seem to us rather technical. We must remember Lewis Morris's dream of a learned society—and remember too, as has been said earlier, the polymathic tendency of the earlier eighteenth century : not literature and antiquities alone, but . " natural philosophy " as well, beseemed a good Cymmrodor in Lewis's idea—says he : " who is ignorant of the low state of knowledge and learning, even in England and France, before the Royal Society of London and the Royal Academy at Paris were instituted ? and they are not of a hundred years' standing." Why should not the Cymmrodorion, given time, attain a like pre-eminence ? thought he. To tell the sad truth, however, one is left under the strong impression that Lewis was the only man who sent up papers or suggested subjects. In 1754, he sends a communication on " knockers " (a phenomenon well known to miners) ; in 1755, " an abstract of a letter sent to the [Royal] Society by my acquaintance Mr. Henry Baker . . . about his microscopical observations " ; in 1757 a " dissertation on Whales," in which one regrets to find that he derives the Greek and Latin *cête* from the Welsh *ci tew* or *ci teg* ! ; and in the same year Richard worries him for a paper on coins. In 1760, Lewis turns his own ill-health to good account by sending up a paper on the Llandrindod Wells, and further suggests *Meddygon Myddfai* as " quite a good subject." Less " philosophical " were his 1762 paper on Cardiganshire Weddings, and the selection of Edward Richard's letters to him which he sent to be read to the Society in 1764. Lewis Morris's death in 1765 must, one thinks, have considerably abridged the official agenda of Cymmrodorion meetings.

It is to be feared that the humbler members of the Society were not over-enthusiastic when these "too, too solid" offerings were laid before them—and presumably they were read in English, though the Rules laid it down that " the discourse of the Society shall be as much as possible in the *Antient British* language, which they are specially bound to cultivate." Even the Welsh poetry was at times coolly received. Lewis Morris was incensed beyond measure at the Society's reception of Hugh Hughes's *Cywydd y Ardd* in 1757 ; in a letter of June 18th to William (the letter which contains his most vitriolic portrait of Goronwy Owen), he writes : " don't weep when I tell you that among the numerous meeting of A. Br. (some read Ancient Brutes) at the Cymmrodorion meeting when that *cywydd* was read, one, and one only, said he thought the *cywydd* was an allegory, and so all with one voice desired it might be read over again, and explained in English," and much more in the same vein. Yet, allowing for Lewis Morris's natural chagrin with the Cymmrodorion when he discovered that " there are few that anything can be expected of them," let us not be too hard on our forbears. Even to-day, literary enthusiasts are to be found, not in the main pavilion of the National Eisteddfod, but in a small annexe—which for that matter is seldom full. The London-Welshry of 200 years ago were very like us !

But Richard Morris was a humaner man than his more gifted brother. As the preamble to the *Constitutions* remarks, the Society was founded not only for what Lewis Morris thought " the principal end of our meeting here," but also for " imitating those social and generous virtues for which our ancestors were so justly renowned "—or again, to quote from the draft of the Society's unpublished *Memoirs* : " for the promoting of friendship and good understanding among the people of Wales residing in London " ; *undeb a brawdgarwch*, in short. And so, say the Rules, " when the current business is over, they shall drink *Health to the Prince of Wales and Prosperity to the Principality* " ; after which come the comfortable words : " then to mixt conversation."

The Chairman, indeed (who was " to be treated with the greatest respect "), was to see that " due harmony and decorum be kept up ; . . . and if any member shall be guilty of drunkenness, profane cursing or swearing, using any obscene or irreligious expression in his discourse," and especially engaging in " religious and party disputes, the bane of civil society " ; such a member was to be " admonished," and if need be " immediately turned out of the room as a common disturber." This was all very fine on paper ; but as the evening wore on, the President himself (if we believe his brother Lewis) can hardly have been capable of meticulous supervision, however great the " respect " shown to him. A long oration of Richard's own (preserved in the British Museum) is full of reproof : " no one is allowed to speak more than once [in the business meeting, presumably], and that in Welsh, if he can. . . . Some of you think that the whole purpose of our meetings is to carouse—a shocking misconception." The " hours of sitting " were supposed to " expire " reasonably early (the hours were 8—11 in spring and summer, 7—10 in autumn and winter), but in September, 1755, Lewis Morris " staid till 2 in the morning," while in August 1757, he tells us that " they seldom part till 12 or 2 in the morning, all boozy " ; another reference, in the same year, speaking of " four o'clock in the morning " has been quoted in the preceding chapter—it may be an exaggeration, for Lewis was genuinely concerned about his brother's health : " the Cymmrodorion meetings are very bad for him." Lewis himself was the culprit on one occasion, for he " kept them an hour or two " practising the amended Initiation Song. This, by the way, appears to have been the only singing which took place during the *business* part of the meetings. It has often been said that the Gwyneddigion " hived off " from the Cymmrodorion in 1770 principally because there was neither singing nor harp-playing in the more august Society's meetings. We have indeed noted that John Parry played and sang in one meeting in 1767, but that appears

76

to have been a very special occasion. But the " mixt conversation " may possibly at times have included singing—
though William Morris's allusion to chaplain Bevan's singing
will not serve us here, for the reverend man's name is not in
the List unless John Evans is meant.

Certainly, despite the *Constitutions*, there was hard drinking
and turbulent talk. Goronwy Owen, at a meeting in 1755,
was " as muzzy as a moon-calf," says Lewis Morris, " while
other members wrangled ; there will have to be better order
than this, else it will be all up with the Cymmrodorion." But
Goronwy, poor man, was not the only cleric who could
unbend at Cymmrodorion meetings. In 1763, no less a man
than the Rev. Dr. Edward Edwards, of Towyn (Merioneth),
Vice-Principal of Jesus College, Oxford, came up for initiation.
Edwards was a friend and host of Dr. Johnson's, and a man
whose " life of learned leisure, or leisurely learning " (as
the College historian suavely puts it) at Jesus extended over
39 years—he left, by the way, an unfinished edition of Xenophon
which was completed by the Cymmrodor Dr. Henry Owen.
But, says Richard Morris, when the Doctor came to the meeting,
" he was dizzy with drink, and I sweated for him ; the Chief
President was in the Chair, and most uncomfortable about it "—
and neither man, as we know, was very strait-laced. One gets
the impression that the toast *Health to the Chief President and
Success to the Society*, which the Rules ordained to " conclude the
night," must have been a rather confused preliminary to the
unhappy Clerk's " calling over the members," and that the
Treasurer may have had some difficulty in " adjusting the
reckoning." For the cost of drinks was pooled (there was
also included a shilling each for messenger and doorkeeper,
and a shilling for the " drawer," who had most certainly
earned it), and each member paid his shot—the Rules prudently
ordain that " not any liquors called for before the hour of
meeting, or drunk out of the meeting room, nor any eatables,
are to be charged to the general reckoning, each member being
to defray the whole of such expence out of his own pocket."
Nor could you dodge the " reckoning " by leaving early, for on
departure you were to " signify the same to the Chair," and
" lay down thirteen pence at least for the reckoning." Lewis
Morris tells us in 1763 that the " reckoning " usually amounted
to eighteen pence. This small figure might tempt a modern

man to surmise that never did so many get so drunk for so little. But that was two centuries ago, when beer was eightpence a *gallon*, ale two shillings, gin (for punch) from 6/- to 7/6. One could go far on eighteen pence in those days.

It is perhaps time to turn to less frivolous matters. One of the Librarian's duties was " to make extracts from the letters of Correspondents and regularly digest them into a book," and the Council was to select material for this book " to be published under the title of *Memoirs of the Society of Cymmrodorion in London*," further, " the Society also propose to print all the scarce and valuable antient British MSS., with notes critical and explanatory." There is much talk of this in the Letters ; William and Lewis are continually inquiring of Richard when the " Transactions" or "Memoirs" are to appear. Unfortunately, Richard was far too busy, and had nobody to help him— the idea of employing Goronwy Owen had fallen through, and it was only for a few months that he had the help of his nephew John Owen before that lively lad went to sea and to his death. " How can I possibly publish anything as things are ? " complains Richard in 1761, " when I can hardly find time to take a bit of food to keep me alive ; let the Kings of this world first make peace, *then* we may have a chance of . . . printing books." As it is, we have only an undated MS. draft, in the British Museum. The title is *Memoirs of the Cymmrodorion Society* ; the printer was to be John Oliver ; there is a long sub-title and a very long preface. Seemingly it was to contain : " 1. Hen Chwedl Dial y Dwndwr ; 2. Cywydd i yrru'r Falwen at William Bulkeley o'r Brynddu, gan Lewis Morris ; 3. Can Siôn y Swyddog ; 4. Llythyr o'r Brynddu ; 5. Cywydd y Baradwys Ddaearol ; 6. Llythyr Goronwy Owen at Owen Meurig." And as neither this nor any other " number " of *Memoirs* ever appeared in print, it is rather amusing to note that apart from the two *Gosodedigaethau*, the List of 1762, and the pamphlet in the " Trefdraeth Case," the only printed books which carry the official imprint of the First Cymmrodorion are the large-paper Prayer-book of 1770, which was Richard Morris's own publication, and the folio 1766 edition of Pennant's *British Zoology*—neither of which had in fact anything whatsoever to do with the Society as such ! Particularly disappointing to Richard Morris was the failure to publish, " for the honour of the Cymmrodorion," his brother Lewis's *Celtic Remains*, which he had begun as a youth and had finished in 1757 ; even Part I was not published till 1878, and Part II is still in MS. at the National Library.

It will have been observed that the items in the above draft were not at all "antiquarian." This was no contravention of the Society's purposes, for the Morrises were as much concerned with the Welsh language and literature of their own day as with the past. Even in 1753, William Morris talks of their printing Goronwy Owen's poetry. And although Goronwy himself in 1757 issued " proposals " and collected subscriptions, the Morrises grimly opined that the money was more likely to go to the public-house than to the printer—and in fact the poet went off to America with nothing done. Thereupon the Cymmrodorion undertook publication—the texts had already been carefully revised by the Morrises, and were in Richard's keeping. But Richard had no time, and the Society no money. A *pis aller* suggested itself ; why not let one or another of the Welsh book-sellers handle the job, while the Cymmrodorion reaped the honour and glory ?

Two such men were ready to hand. One was Hugh Jones (d. 1782) of Llangwm in Denbighshire, a good representative of the " oatmeal rhymers " whom Goronwy Owen had so heartily despised. He had already (1759) published an anthology, *Dewisol Ganiadau yr Oes Hon*, in the first part of which he included three pieces by Goronwy (including the Cymmrodorion Ode), eight poems by William Wynn (given him by their author), three by Ieuan Fardd, one by Hugh Hughes, and one by Edward Samuel ; the second part was filled by less distinguished bards. The Morrises' wrath fell upon the book ; says Lewis : " Mr. Wynn is fonder of fame than I should be, when got through such mean channels " ; and there are scathing remarks in the Letters upon this " botched " production. But pride comes before a fall, and Lewis himself had to resort to the Llangwm book-pedlar. Hugh Jones (no fool) conceived the notion of publishing a volume of contemporary *Anglesey* poetry ; he got hold of Hugh Hughes, who sent him off to William Morris with a letter of introduction ; William passed him on to Richard, and Richard to Lewis— Hugh Jones clinched the matter by calling in person on Lewis, in 1761. Lewis began to see the good points of the scheme : " if some of my works will be published by Hugh Jones, we

shall make mention of the Cymmrodorion and their intentions."
Hugh Jones would collect subscriptions, distribute the books,
and pay the printer ; the Anglesey poets (Goronwy Owen,
Lewis Morris, Hugh Hughes, and even the youthful Robert
Hughes) would shine in print ; and the Cymmrodorion would
get the credit. The book, *Diddanwch Teuluaidd*, appeared in
1763. Excepting the official badge, it bore all the stigmata
of the Society of Cymmrodorion : it was to have been printed
by John Oliver, and was in fact printed by William Roberts
(who printed the Society's 1762 List) ; the whole of the proof-
reading was done, amid all his distractions, by Richard Morris ;
the unsigned Welsh dedication to William Vaughan, and the
" epistle " to William Parry, were by Lewis Morris. Hugh
Jones himself appears to have done precisely nothing about the
editing. Not unrightly did William Morris feel that the title
should have been *Cymmrodorion Poetry, Part One*—for Hugh
Jones was already talking of a " Part Two," to contain work
by William Wynn, Ieuan Fardd, Rhys Jones, and others. Not
unrightly, again, did Lewis grumble : " yes, no doubt a book
whose authors are all Cymmrodorion is Cymmrodorion Poetry—
but who gets the profit ? Why should Llangwm get it all ? "
Indeed, " Llangwm " *did* get it all, not even paying the printer,
who died bankrupt in the workhouse. But the book is a very
important landmark in the history of Welsh Literature. And
it is in a very real sense a Cymmrodorion book, albeit the
Society's official imprint is lacking.

The second of the homespun literati associated (more
or less) with the Cymmrodorion as publisher was David Jones
(1708-85) of Trefriw ; parish clerk, schoolmaster, publisher
and hawker of books, and finally printer—in 1776, he began
printing, using the types that had belonged to Lewis Morris.
He was a very much more reputable figure than his poor friend
" Llangwm." We have seen that he sent up a *cywydd* of his
own in 1757 to be read to the Society. Lewis Morris suspected
that this was a sprat to catch a mackerel—to get Cymmrodorion
support for a project of David Jones's to print the works of
Huw Morys of Glyn Ceiriog ; and he countered by asking
David Jones to collect material locally for his own *Celtic Remains*.
But he did re-word David Jones's " proposals," and added to
them a statement that he himself and his brother Richard
(" President of the Society of Cymmrodorion ") would receive

subscriptions for the work ; further, he obtained for David Jones estimates from a London printer, and gave him most sensible advice (which he did not take) on simplifying his extremely florid preface. Richard Morris (by the hand of John Owen) warned David Jones to be very careful of his proof-reading, and sent a list of 102 Cymmrodorion subscribers. It should be noticed that neither Lewis nor Richard had *seen* the proposed book. William *had*—and he is far more wary ; says he to John Owen : " confound David Jones for his misprints ! he will do great injury to Huw Morys's carols, and will bring shame to my two brothers "—and later, to Richard : " a fine piece of work you'll find it ! "

The book, *Blodeugerdd Cymry*, printed not in London but at Shrewsbury, appeared in 1759, a stout little volume of some 730 pages, greatly treasured to-day by its possessors. But Lewis and Richard Morris were horrified. What they had expected was a collection of the works of Huw Morys, " that sweet and natural poet." There were, indeed, 46 of his poems in the book, and there were some 30 poems by other well-known poets of the end of the seventeenth century. But not only were these badly edited ; they were swamped by well over a hundred pieces by inferior rhymers—not that we to-day are not very grateful to David Jones for preserving them for us. William Morris complains that David Jones has " mixed up rubbish with excellent poetry " ; Richard curses his " botching of the orthography, which sets one's teeth on edge "—we must remember Richard's constant care for correctness in such matters, of which we have plenty of other evidence. The upshot, unfortunately, was that the book was a failure *in London*, though it sold well in Wales. Yet David Jones himself did not wholly fall out of favour with the Morrises. Though Richard (at the time in Cardiganshire) was not able to push the sale of the *Cydymaith Diddan* (1766), and remonstrated once more with David Jones for the " ugly mistakes " in its ortho-graphy, and though he dissuaded the worthy man from com-piling a grammar (" don't take it unkindly on my part to tell you that you have not sufficient knowledge "), yet Owen Jones the Assistant-Secretary is found in 1777 writing to David Jones and inviting him to send up " proposals " for publishing, on the strength of the new annual levy of 10/6d. a head upon the Cymmrodorion. Whether David Jones did so is not known

—one wonders whether the new and enlarged edition of the *Blodeugerdd* (1779) was helped by the Society. Other publications mooted by Owen Jones at this time are *Brut y Brenhinoedd* with notes by Lewis Morris, an edition of the old Triads and Proverbs by Ieuan Fardd, and possibly also an edition of the " Llywarch Hen " poems, by Richard Thomas of Jesus College, brother of the better-known antiquary John Thomas of Beaumaris. But the whole history of these projects, from 1751 onwards, shows that the rank and file of the Cymmrodorion displayed little zeal in supporting Welsh publications (indeed, many of them defaulted from taking up their subscribers' copies)— not that we need go so far as Lewis Morris did when he said that " hardly one of them can read " !

The folio edition (1766) of Thomas Pennant's *British Zoology*, bearing as it does the imprint of the Society, has traditionally (and very naturally) been regarded as a " Cymmrodorion publication." Pennant was in fact a corresponding member from the start, and was well acquainted with all three Morrises, more especially at first with William, who visited him at Downing and speaks of him with alternate admiration and amusement. The book was advertised as a forthcoming Cymmrodorion publication in 1762 ; and indeed Richard Morris, writing in 1766 to Ieuan Fardd, says : " *The British Zoology* . . . has been published in the name of the Cymmrodorion, price eight and a half guineas in sheets, . . . it was Mr. Pennant of Downing's job for the most part, but I have had a lot of trouble over it during the last four years." The title-page is rather oddly worded : " Published under the auspices of the Cymmrodorion Society, instituted for the promoting useful charities and the knowledge of nature among the descendants of the Ancient Britons " ; the book was " sold for the benefit of the British Charity-School on Clerkenwell Green." The dedication to the King repeats and underlines this implication that the *chief* purpose of the Cymmrodorion Society was charitable —and the dedication comes from " your very loyal and dutiful subjects, the Presidents and Council of the Society of Cymmrodorion."

But Pennant's own words (in his *Literary Life*) are : " about the year 1761 I began my *British Zoology* . . . I dedicated [it] to the benefit of the Welsh School in Gray's Inn Lane, and supported the far greater part of the expense. I lost considerably by it, notwithstanding several gentlemen contributed. My agent was that very honest man Mr. Richard Morris of the Navy Office." It may be stated at this point that no benefit ever accrued to the School from the *sales*, though Pennant afterwards gave it a donation of £100. Richard Morris, it will be noted, is termed " *my agent* " ; it was he who secured royal patronage for the book ; and a sum of money due to Pennant (in respect of sales ?) had still not been paid over in 1779 and was generously remitted to Mrs. Morris by Pennant. And the Morris Letters reveal the amusing " inner history " of this book. It was *Pennant* who published it, under the Society's name, suppressing his own—for the early editions of the book are anonymous—for private and personal reasons. His father, described by Lewis Morris as " a miserly opinionated old man," kept him very short of money. A maternal uncle liberally assisted him, but naturally wanted to call the tune, and would not support the *Zoology*. So Pennant had recourse to subterfuge—to use the uncle's money without his knowledge ; his friends the Morrises lent him the countenance of the Cymmrodorion Society and Richard carried the transaction through ; no doubt the brothers felt also that the book would redound to the glory of the Society. The later editions, even those published in Pennant's lifetime and before the dissolution of the Society, make not the slightest mention of the Cymmrodorion.

Almost at the end of the First Society's life, we have a most interesting anticipation of what was to become a very important practice of the Gwyneddigion and of the Second and Third Cymmrodorion. On the death of Richard Morris, the Society offered a silver medal for the best elegy on its President ; it also offered a gold and a silver medal for a translation of the *Gododin* of Aneirin. Nothing more is heard of the latter, but the former provoked much discussion. Richard Jones of Trefdraeth (Anglesey) sent in an *awdl* in the full panoply of the " twenty-four metres," and Owain Myfyr and Robin Ddu awarded him the medal, which is still preserved by his descendants. But at the next monthly meeting, members demurred with the *principle* of the adjudication, and moved that the medal be given to John Edwards (" Siôn Ceiriog "), who had written in " free " metre. The upshot was the award of *two* medals. Two points emerge : first, this competition was the fore-runner of the Eisteddfodau of the Gwyneddigion, and therefore of the National Eisteddfod ; next, the distinction, in the National Eisteddfod of to-day, between the " Chair " and the " Crown " competitions, derives from this compromise.

We have already referred to the " poor-box " which in 1755 was to receive at least sixpence a quarter from each member —the Morris Letters show that the wealthy dropped substantial sums into it. If Rowland Jones's recollections (1819) are to be trusted, " tradesmen " in later days put 5/- annually into the box, and " gentlemen " 10/6d. or 21/—this may have become an unwritten law, for the 1778 *Constitutions* specify no sum, merely " recommending " members to " remember the poor's box." We have numbers of " applications " in the British Museum, all in Welsh, and proof that help was granted : Goronwy Owen and Ieuan Fardd were helped— and though angry officials refused to read out Goronwy's last application to the Society, he was then given " five gold pieces." A debtor, at another time, was released from the " Fleet " ; a Bangor man who in 1780 had been for some weeks in S. George's Hospital was given unemployment relief ; money was paid " for sending decay'd distressed countrymen . . . by the waggon to their former home."

The " Welsh Church " project has already been mentioned. But an example of Cymmrodorion interest in Church affairs in Wales itself must be noticed at some length, for the Society has in this instance gained credit which to a later generation may seem somewhat excessive. In 1766, an Englishman, Dr. Bowles, who had been headmaster of Beaumaris Grammar School, was presented and instituted to the parishes of Trefdraeth and Llangwyfan in western Anglesey. Bowles was seventy years of age and in bad health ; he knew hardly any Welsh at all, whereas only five of his 500 parishioners understood English at all. The parishioners decided to take legal measures, and in 1770 a suit was instituted in London— a suit which seems to have made legal history, as being the only recorded case in which an incumbent has been arraigned, not by his bishop, but by his parishioners.

Instigated probably by Ieuan Fardd (a bitter critic of the " Anglian " bishops—" *yr esgyb Eingl* " as he called them) and John Thomas, the antiquary, who was then usher at the

Friars School and afterwards acting-headmaster of Beaumaris, the Cymmrodorion Society, whose President was himself an Anglesey man, decided to support the Trefdraeth people. Money amounting to £254 was collected : £5 10s. 0d. from the Society's funds, £20 from the Chief President William Vaughan, £100 from his destined successor Sir Watkin Williams Wynn ; various M.P.s figure in the list, and the Dissenter Dr. Thomas Llewelyn is neatly balanced (£5 each) by the Dean of Bangor. £92 of this money was spent in bringing six witnesses from Trefdraeth up to Town (Richard Morris interpreted for them in court), £10 on printing—the Society in 1776 published *The Depositions, Arguments, and Judgment in the cause of the Churchwardens of Trefdraeth* ; the rest went in barristers' fees. The case was adjourned for two years, then removed (1773) to Llangefni in Anglesey. If a tithe of the plaintiffs' evidence was correct, the reverend gentleman must be accounted lucky in having escaped being jailed for perjury and forgery. Finally, the Dean of Arches found, in effect, that the case against Bowles had been proved ; he further held that both ecclesiastical and civil law required that Welsh-speaking incumbents should be appointed to Welsh-speaking parishes, and that a presentee's ignorance of Welsh was sufficient ground for episcopal refusal to institute him. So far, good. But the Dean felt bound to rule that an institution and an induction which had already taken place could not be invalidated for such ignorance. Thus Dr. Bowles stayed put—not for long, for he died in the same year.

The *moral* victory thus won is a matter on which no Welshman will refuse to congratulate the Trefdraeth people and the Cymmrodorion. It has always been regarded as a feather in the cap of the Society, which had thus, in its own opinion, prevented such presentations as Bowles's being made in future. And indeed, the 1773 judgment did have one or two useful results at the time—results obtained without recourse to law, but pretty clearly in fear that the Dean of Arches's ruling might be invoked in other cases. Cymmrodorion MSS. in the British Museum gleefully record that the presentation of an Englishman to Aber (Caerns.) was *withdrawn*, and that an Englishman presented to Devynnock in 1774 immediately and prudently exchanged that living for a Herefordshire parish whose incumbent was a Welshman. But a little reflection brings some disillusion.

The " resounding example " of Trefdraeth did not " resound "
even as far as Caernarvon, for in 1817 a similar presentation was
made to that important living (Llanbeblig), and the Gwyneddigion Society in London leapt to the fray—but without a single
mention of the " precedent " at Trefdraeth ; here, the vicar
showed his good sense by learning Welsh.   Further, Edward
Copleston, bishop of Llandaff 1828-49, who though no lover
of Welsh tried to do his duty in this matter, was compelled by
threat of proceedings to institute a monoglot Englishman in a
parish where Welsh was occasionally required, and further had
to do battle in the House of Lords with Lord Chancellor
Brougham himself, who had presented a . man who knew no
Welsh to a Crown living in Llandaff diocese ; the Chancellor
eventually gave way as an act of courtesy, but only as an act of
courtesy, refusing to concede the legal point.   As late as 1852,
the Archbishop of Canterbury *over-rode* bishop Ollivant of
Llandaff's refusal to institute a clergyman who knew no Welsh
to a Welsh-speaking parish.   In short, it is highly doubtful
whether the 1773 ruling on this point would have stood in a
higher court, civil or ecclesiastical.

The " aims " of the Cymmrodorion of 1751 included " the
improvement of trade and manufacture in Wales.'' Apparently
nothing was attempted under this head till 1781, when a
circular letter was sent to the magistrates of Wales, offering
the Society's co-operation to this end, suggesting the establishment of County Societies (of which there were already some in
Wales), and promising not only to " send models of every new
or improved machine or implement of husbandry . . . at the
expense of the Society,'' but also to " present gold medals or
bounties '' for the improvement of agriculture, forestry, trade
and commerce.   None of these suggestions was novel ; and
little seems to have been actually done, though some attribute
the foundation of the Cardiganshire Society of Agriculture
(1784) to the impetus thus given by the Cymmrodorion.   One
point, however, should not be overlooked ; these were precisely
the methods applied by " spirited proprietors '' of land, in
various parts of Wales, in promoting the new agriculture and
the new industries.   And it is difficult not to think that the
large influx of public-spirited Welsh gentry into the Society
in its later period had something to do with this project
of turning the Society into a sort of " Welsh Development

Council " in matters economic. It would not have displeased Lewis Morris, if he had lived to see the attempt.

*　　*　　*　　*

We have had more than one indication of a revival, round about 1777, of the energies of the Cymmrodorion : an influx of new members ;　the appointment of new and energetic officers ;　a revision of the *Constitutions :* the new levy in support of publications ;　the entertaining of new and ambitious literary projects such as the printing of the *Celtic Remains ;* the institution of medals for poetry ;　the interest shown in Welsh agriculture and trade ;　and so on.　Yet, the Society in its first form was dissolved in 1787, and would seem to have been languishing for some years previously.

Various explanations have been offered.　As far back as 1780, a writer suggested that the Society had been crippled by " losses " on *British Zoology ;* but it has been shown on a previous page that the *Society* suffered no loss in this respect. W. D. Leathart, in 1831, attributes its demise to " the insolvency of the Treasurer."　A letter of 1819 (at the National Library), by Rowland Jones " of Greenwich," supplies more detail.　Rowland Jones (known to the Gwyneddigion as " Gwybedyn "), a native of Llan-ym-Mawddwy, and a tobacconist, was a nephew of that Morgan Jones of Dinas Mawddwy, " a very ingenious man, and a mountain antiquary " (say Lewis Morris), who figures in the Letters.　Rowland, says he in 1819, was introduced into the Society by Richard Morris, " fifty-nine years since, when I was only seventeen years of age " ;　there is something wrong here, for his name appears for the first time in the 1778 list, and Leathart says that Rowland Jones was " nearly ninety " when he died, in 1829—he would have been seventeen, thus, in 1757, and his name *ought* to have been in the 1759 list, or at least in that of 1762.　But no doubt the old gentleman's memory had been impaired by ill-health— he was " so weak that I can hardly crawl about the house."　He " could not recollect more than three " of the old Cymmro-dorion who were still alive in 1819, namely Sir Watkin Lewes (d. 1821), Lord Bulkeley (d. 1822), and " Matthew Davies of Long Acre," a Cardiganshire man, and apparently a lace-maker, who first appears in the 1778 List.　He gives two reasons for the dissolution of the Society :　Richard Morris's death, and

87

the death, insolvent, of the Treasurer, " Mr. Thomas of Little Moorfields, who had £140 of the Society's money in his hands at the time." The Society, at its dissolution, says he, " consisted of 70 members or more."

That is all the evidence we have. There is no *record* of the dissolution, and indeed it would appear to have been regarded at the time as only a temporary suspension, for when the Presidential Chair was handed over to the Gwyneddigion, " Mr. David Jones, Treasurer of the Cymmrodorion Society " got from them a formal promise to return it again on demand. But there can be little doubt that Richard Morris's death was a fatal blow to the Society. Sir Watkin Lewes was no Richard Morris—and was an even busier man ; Sir Watkin Williams Wynn was no William Vaughan. Their interests, as has been hinted before, were different—Lewes in particular was an active politician. Possibly, in its closing years, the Society had come to be regarded mainly as an agent of the " Antient Britons' " efforts on behalf of the Welsh School—the very much increased space given in the 1778 *Constitutions* booklet to the affairs of the School suggests that. The new officials who seem to have been responsible for the " spurt " of 1777 had already in 1770 established the Gwyneddigion Society, and no man can very easily serve two masters. We may, again, discount Rowland Jones's failing memory when he gives the membership in 1787 as " 70 or more," but at the very best this seems a big drop from the 228 of 1778 ; and this must have seriously affected the Society's finances. £140 may seem to us a small sum, but we must always remember that the Society had throughout been under-capitalised ; 10/6d. a head, paid once for all, could never have amounted to much, and it was naturally a wasting asset ; the poor-box was separately accounted for ; and the yield of the new " publication " fund, of whose disposal we have no information, would automatically shrink with the drop in membership. To a Society run on this extremely inadequate basis, £140 was a very serious loss. It might have survived it, given enthusiasm and energy. But clearly, little of either was left by 1787.

What had the First Cymmrodorion achieved ? It is easy to be hyper-critical—easy to point out that as far as literary and antiquarian matters are concerned, the Society in its corporate capacity published nothing, that the rank and file seem to have shown little interest, that (as has been said by more than one writer) " Richard Morris *was* the Society." Yet the fact remains that the Morrises, *in the name* of the Society, aided the endeavours of humbler men in Wales, and strove hard to keep them on the right path, however disparagingly they might speak of them in their letters ; in this way appeared the first printed selection of Huw Morys's poems, and the first good edition of Goronwy Owen ; the publication of that historic book *Specimens of Antient Welsh Poetry*, again, was most actively encouraged by the men at the head of the *Cymmrodorion*. The whole publishing programme of the Gwyneddigion was consciously inherited from the older Society ; even the Eisteddfodau of the Gwyneddigion can be discerned in embryo in the Cymmrodorion competition of 1780.

We are, again, in danger of forgetting the social and philanthropic motives which in the minds of the founders of the Society loomed fully as large as the intellectual. The Welsh School of the " Antient Britons " had up to 1787 benefited greatly from the support of the Cymmrodorion—it is significant to read that for " some few years before 1795, the expenses of the S. David's Day Festival were not covered by the collections, and the Charity had to make good the deficit." The Society, was, after all, not *primarily* conceived as a group of men of letters, but rather as an association of Welshmen in exile who found in it a common hearth ; its monthly meetings (admittedly they were hardly Rechabite gatherings) must have been oases in the lives of very worthy men dispersed all over the great city. There they found " *undeb, a brawdgarwch* "—and there *alone*, from 1751 to 1770. Indeed, the very fact that from 1770 onwards additional facilities of this sort were available may have made the continuance of the Cymmrodorion seem less essential.

And there is more to say than that, difficult though it may be to put it into concrete terms. It is this : *somehow*, the Cymmrodorion Society had become identified in men's minds with Wales as a whole. There was no centre of corporate— still less of national—life in Wales ; and this Society did something to provide a substitute. We may smile (or even jeer, with Lewis Morris) at Richard Morris's pride in the peers of the realm whom he had cajoled into the Society ; we may be tempted to regard these (or most of them) as mere ornaments,

89

G

and their services to the Society (and to Wales) as mere " lip-service." But one does not pay lip-service without a cause. It *is* significant that the gentry of Wales had come to regard it as their duty (however perfunctorily performed) to associate themselves with the Society of Cymmrodorion ; and it was well-nigh their only manifestation of " Welshness." At the other end of the social scale, all sorts of humble devotees of literature in the Welsh countryside took pride in seeing their names in the printed Lists of the Society's members and associates. The Society *counted*. It had come to be regarded as a leader and organ of opinion in Welsh matters. Such things do not happen without some reason.

IV.—GWYNEDDIGION AND CYMREIGYDDION

WE have noted Richard Morris's pride with the increase of aristocracy among the Cymmrodorion. Possibly a number of the humbler brethren were less elated when " there came into their assembly a man with a gold ring, in goodly apparel." There is no need to suppose that the ordinary Cymmrodor was particularly egalitarian, though it is wise to remember that even in 1770 a sort of " sans-culottism " was prevalent enough in Town, and that in after years some of the more prominent London Welshmen were pretty far " to the left " in politics. But one may surmise that while a high civil servant like Richard Morris or a man-of-the-world lawyer like Watkin Lewes would be comfortable enough among the (no doubt perfectly genial) aristocrats, the good plain shopkeeper or craftsman would have preferred to drink his beer or punch (after listening " with great respect " though in some cases with little comprehension to Mr. Morris's discourse from the Chair) at his ease among men more like himself. We are told also that members wanted more music—in particular, more singing to the harp.

But there was probably something else. When Owen Jones, writing in 1777 to David Jones of Trefriw, tells him that " the greater part of the London Cymreigyddion possessed copies of the *Blodeugerdd* and the *Cydymaith Diddan*," he obviously cannot be referring to the Cymreigyddion *Society*, which in fact was not founded till 1794. He means "London Welshmen "— more specifically the Gwyneddigion, then of seven years' standing. When he wrote, a quarter of a century had elapsed since 1751. Many Welshmen had come up to reinforce the Welsh colony in Town in the meantime. And much had happened in Wales in the meantime ; in particular the ability to read, and the habit of reading, had spread, and the crudely-printed publications of men like Hugh Jones and David Jones— and, though no doubt to a far smaller extent, the fine large-paper 1773 *Gorchestion* of Rhys Jones of Blaenau—had been in circulation. In other words, the Cymmrodorion Society, however indirectly, had been at work. It is not too fanciful to judge that a new stratum of London-Welshmen had come into being. These men, while on the one hand irked, it may be, by the presence among them of "very superior persons," would also be disquieted by the philistinism of the homelier Cymmrodorion of a previous generation, the men whom Lewis Morris had dismissed, with a contemptuous snort, as "illiterate." Ready enough though the newer men (men with a real, however ill-informed, interest in Welsh poetry) were, as the event proved, to continue their membership of the Cymmrodorion Society, they would prefer a less miscellaneous company in which they could follow their own bent without distraction.

Such, it may be believed, were the considerations which led in December, 1770, to the establishment of the "Gwynedd-igion Society"—its active existence began on February 4th, 1771. Its very name suggests a strong North-Wales bias, and indeed the majority of its members hailed from North Wales; its list of annual Presidents down to 1831 includes only five South-Walians, and none between 1775 and 1823.

There was fortunately no need to *revolt* against the Cymmro-dorion Society, to fall into schism. For some of the chief "effective" members of the Cymmrodorion, though enabled by means or education or status not to quail in the presence of "quality," were yet thoroughly democratic in their interests, and shared these with their humbler friends. And so, the Gwyneddigion Society was actually founded by two of the officials of the Cymmrodorion, and (so we are told) "many members of the one Society were also members of the other." The founders were Owen Jones and Robert Hughes, respectively Assistant Secretary and Librarian of the Cymmrodorion. One great name, indeed, is not upon the roll of the new Society— that of Richard Morris. We have absolutely no evidence that he disapproved of the new venture, though we have hints that age and ill-health had made him a bit crotchety ; it seems more probable that he kept out of it because he was old and tired, and was willing to let his two younger colleagues and admirers try their hands. But it is pleasing to note that his former yoke-fellow William Vaughan of Cors-y-gedol, the first Chief President of the Cymmrodorion, was "one of the first members" of the Gwyneddigion, and "their very worthy advocate" ; whether he was ever able to attend meetings is very questionable. And Richard Morris's son Richard became a Gwyneddig in October, 1779—a letter from him (then in India) to Owen Jones in 1785 hopes that " the Cymmrodorion and Gwyneddigion Societies are in a flourishing state."

Owen Jones (1741-1814), " Owain Myfyr," has more than once been called " the Richard Morris of the Gwyneddigion." That is just and right ; it would not be correct to follow the parallel further and to say that he " *was* the Gwyneddigion." for he was fortunate enough to have able and energetic collaborators, though it may truly be said that but for him the results would not have been forthcoming. He was born on September 3rd, 1741, at Tyddyn Tudur in Llanfihangel Glyn Myfyr, Denbighshire—it may be useful to point out here that the name does not mean " S. Michael's in the Vale of Contemplation," as has been romantically believed, but " S. Michael's in the valley of the burial-mound," though whose that legendary tomb (*memoria*) may have been is unknown. His father's name was Hugh Jones, and he himself at first styled himself " Owain ap Huw."

It is believed that he came up to Town in or about 1765 ; his name therefore appears in no Cymmrodorion List before 1778, when he was not only a member but also Assistant-Secretary. He had quickly won Richard Morris's favour, for as early as 1769 he is found excerpting the Morris MSS., and indeed it is obvious that he would not have been made Assistant-Secretary without the old President's support. He entered the employ of a firm of furriers in Upper-Thames Street, becoming later a partner, and eventually owner of the business, which was exceedingly prosperous ; in 1776, he lived at 40, Cannon Street, in 1778, in Duck's-foot Lane. His visits to Wales were extremely infrequent, and seem in any case to have ceased by 1794. He married a certain Hannah Jane Jones ; after his death she married again, economically interred her second husband with her first, and eventually (1838) shared their repose. She was almost thirty years younger than Owen Jones ; they had at least two children : Owen Jones (1809-74), a well-known architect and designer, who wrote a *Grammar of Ornament* and superintended the decoration of the Crystal Palace (sad to say, he was *not* a Gwyneddig) ; and a daughter who lived till 1890—there is said to have been another daughter. Owain Myfyr himself died on September 26th, 1814, and was buried at All Hallows, Thames Street ; two ludicrously mis-carved *englynion* by his protégé Walter Davies (Gwallter Mechain) appear on the tombstone. The stone itself has had its adventures. The church was bombed during the late war ; but when the present Secretary of the Cymmrodorion hurried there to inspect the damage, he found the stone unscathed, alone upright amid the debris. He had it removed to what one would have thought the safety of Nutfield, whose Rectory has had long and pleasant associations with the Cymmrodorion. Unfortunately, Nutfield in its turn was visited by the enemy, and Owain Myfyr's tombstone was slightly damaged. Before these lines appear in print, it will again have been removed—this time, most appropriately, to Llanfihangel Glyn Myfyr church.

It may be as well to finish here with the family. Owain Myfyr had a sister, Jane, who married her next-door neighbour Peter Maurice of Bryn Hir. Bryn Hir, according to Edward Lhuyd's *Parochialia*, belonged in 1700 to " Mr. Peter Morys of Hafod-y-maidd " in Cerrig-y-drudion ; it seems obvious that Owain Myfyr's brother-in-law was of that family—a family with some claims to pedigree, whereas Tyddyn Tudur, as far as can be seen, had none. Jane died in 1810 at Tyddyn Tudur ; her tombstone may be read at Llanfihangel. Her son, Hugh Maurice, comes into our story. He was born at Tyddyn Tudur in 1775 or 1776, and joined his uncle in Town, both in the furriery and in his literary interests ; he lived for a while in Tooley Street, but in 1822 figures as " Hugh Maurice, Esq., of Greenwich "—for a reason which will soon appear. Employed by his uncle to collect or transcribe MSS. for the *Myvyrian Archaiology*, he has been called " the last in the long succession of Welsh scribes " ; he was also an artist, and made (" on a leaf of the records of the Society ") a number of sketches of his fellow-Gwyneddigion, including his uncle " smoking a pipe." His wife was a daughter of that Rowland Jones of Greenwich whose account of the demise of the First Cymmrodorion has appeared on a previous page. Rowland Jones was opposed to the marriage, so the young couple, with the connivance of eminent Gwyneddigion, got married (in S. Olave's, Tooley Street) on the very evening of the Society's dinner in 1800. The unsuspecting tobacconist had left his house for the dinner (at Highbury Barn), and wondered why the officials of the Society were so late—the President (Thomas Roberts), the Vice-President (Hugh Maurice himself), the Secretary (John Jones of Glan-y-gors). When the defaulters turned up, says Leathart, " Mr. Jones, not in the least dreaming of what had been done in his absence, was as merry as the rest, and did not depart till late " ; we are relieved to learn that " shortly after, affairs were satisfactorily explained, and the matter ended amicably "—as we saw, Hugh Maurice was living at Greenwich in 1822. His elder son, Rowland Jones Maurice, translated Nennius ; his second, Dr. Peter Maurice, became chaplain of two Oxford colleges and was vicar of Yarnton, and a hymn-writer ; his daughter Jane wrote hymns. Hugh Maurice returned to Wales. He inherited Tyddyn Tudur (where his daughter was born) ; Owain Myfyr had rebuilt the house, and Owen Jones the architect owned it later on— it is still remembered at Llanfihangel that in his time the parish boundary was slightly altered and part of Tyddyn Tudur land added to Cerrig-y-drudion, whereupon Owen Jones the second made his tenant plant a row of potatoes along the " old " boundary. To return to Hugh Maurice ; he left Tyddyn Tudur and lived successively at Ffestiniog, Tremadoc, and Llanrug, where he died in March, 1825 ; he too was buried at Llanfihangel.

Owain Myfyr has been depicted for us in a waspish article by Dr. John Jones (himself a Gwyneddig, elected in 1809— but expelled in 1815), a Llandybïe man, school-master and afterwards barrister, who in 1824 published a *History of Wales*. According to him, Owain Myfyr " spent his days from 8 to 8 scraping skins in his warehouse," and was during those hours curt and unapproachable. " From 8 till 10 or 12 " he spent at the " Bull " in Walbrook Street, where he was a dictator : a loud " hem ! " heralded his advent ; all made way for him, and he was given three chairs, one to sit upon, the other two to serve as arm-rests. There he consumed " Welch-rabbits, pipes, and porter," among " a heterogeneous company of . . . harpers, fiddlers, and fifers," talking of " the Welch language and customs, and the poet whose works he had last paid for transcribing " ; at the end of the evening, he " discounted a few bills . . . for friendly and deserving Welshmen."

John Jones insinuates further that though Owain Myfyr had not " sufficient learning to comprehend " matters debated in his presence, " it was his pride to be thought the oracle and patron of all that is curious or valuable in the literary remains of the Ancient Britons "—the Doctor's own Welsh, by the way, is described by one writer as that of a man " evidently unacquainted with some of the simplest rules of Welsh construction " ! Again, Iolo Morganwg, when he in his turn had fallen out with Owain Myfyr, speaks of the " Bull " as " a very creditable bawdy house," and of the company there as " very eminent coal-heavers, porters, scavengers, chimney-sweepers, knaves and fools of every class"—which seems rather odd language for a Friend of the People. The engraving of Owain Myfyr (in Leathart's book)—the original portrait was painted in 1802 for the Gwyneddigion by John Vaughan of Conway—shows us a large, heavy, rather lifeless face, with obstinate chin and lips, and a high forehead.

It is indeed easy enough to laugh at Owain Myfyr and his pretensions. It may well be that (though he most certainly loved it) he really understood far less than he imagined of the literature on which he spent so much of his money. Without doubt he was a dictatorial man, and without doubt sycophants pandered to him. He *would* have his way, even in matters on which his opinion was worthless—as when he insisted on awarding Eisteddfodic prizes to his favourites, and even informed them beforehand that they were *going* to get the prize. Again, he had a most violent temper, even if we allow for humorous exaggeration in his friend David Samwel's description of a famous debate at the " Bull " :

Myvyr at length indignant rose
Full five feet from the ground . . .
[And] kicked [the] table to the ground
With one tremendous crash . . .
He upset candles, arguments,
Pint-pots, and all together.

" Money talked " with him, we can hardly doubt.

But our mockery of his self-esteem pales when we consider his enormous services. There have been very many rich men—very many rich Welshmen too—who have spent their gains on far less laudable objects than did Owain Myfyr. That little remark of John Jones's about " discounting bills " must not be overlooked—nor the generosity which, for instance, sent Gwallter Mechain up to Oxford, and aided Iolo Morganwg and

William Owen Pughe. If (to put it at its lowest) it pleased his vanity to parade as " editor " of MSS. which were mostly copied for him, and edited for him, by other men, let it be remembered that he was willing to pay large sums for the copying and the printing. The *Dafydd ap Gwilym* cost him £180 to *print*—in 1789 money. It was he who paid for the transcript of Lewis Morris's *Celtic Remains* which Gwallter Mechain never edited ; he paid £80 for the die for the Gwyneddigion Eisteddfodic medals—and paid for the medals themselves ; he spent more than £1,000 on the printing of the *Myvyrian Archaiology*, smile as we may at its title ; when Gwyneddigion and Cymreigyddion quarrelled over the *Greal*, the angry Myfyr offered to bear the whole cost of that periodical himself rather than give way on what he (quite wrongly) deemed to be right ; copies of Welsh MSS. made at his expense fill a hundred volumes in the British Museum Library ; and students of Welsh literature, from his day to our own, have for the most part had to live on the admittedly imperfect editions of Dafydd ap Gwilym and of the poets of the Age of the Princes which Owain Myfyr's money—and his determination—enabled him to publish. A tenacious man—he clung to his Radical views in politics when some of the more prominent of his fellow-Gwyneddigion wavered under the force of circumstances.

Next among the founders of the Gwyneddigion Society comes Robert Hughes (1744-85), " Robin Ddu," or more fully " Robin Ddu yr Ail o Fôn." Indeed, he was regarded by some in his own day as the prime founder ; but Thomas Jones (" Bardd Cloff ") convinced Leathart that Owain Myfyr took the initiative. He was born at Ceint Bach near Penmynydd. So with him, though most of the leaders of the Gwyneddigion were Denbighshire men, we are back in the Morrises' homeland, and indeed in their circle, for in 1760 William Morris sends up to Lewis a poem by " this fifteen-years-old boy " to be " corrected, . . . he will be grateful." Lewis wanted the lad to be sent to serve him, but his parents declined, as William puts it, to " make a Myrddin or a Taliesin of him " ; Robin's bardic teacher was our old friend Hugh Hughes of Llwydiarth Esgob. After a short visit to Shrewsbury (1760), Robert Hughes started keeping school at Cerrig-Ceinwen, Bodedern, and Amlwch ; then he attached himself to the Stanley family at Penrhos (Holyhead). Stanley got him a clerkship with a firm of solicitors in Manchester, but after six months there he was sent up by the firm to their London office in the Temple, in 1764—it seems to have been a rather important firm, for we find Robin in 1775 drafting the Bill for lighting the streets of London. On his arrival in Town (he lived in King Street, Bloomsbury), he called on Richard Morris—a *cywydd* and two *englynion* of his had already had the honour of being printed, along with the work of the greater Anglesey poets, in *Diddanwch Teuluaidd* (1763).

Robin Ddu actively interested himself in London-Welsh activities ; as we have seen, he appears in the 1778 Cymmro-dorion List as joint Librarian of the Society. A great deal of his correspondence has been preserved in the British Museum, and it is highly interesting ; but "outward events" of his career in Town are not chronicled. Unfortunately, some twenty years of busy life in London ruined his health. In the early summer of 1783 he had to return to Wales ; on his way to Caernarvon he called on various men of letters, including Rhys Jones of Blaenau ; he made a special call on the MS. collector Dr. Griffith Roberts (1737-1808) at Dolgelley, to whom Owain Myfyr had rashly lent a transcript of Dafydd ap Gwilym made as far back as 1768 by Robin himself. Robin tells an amusing tale of the borrower's reluctance, even under threat of proceedings, to return the MS., but in 1784 he triumphantly writes to Owain Myfyr from Caernarvon that "Dafydd is here, safe and sound after his long exile." Another long letter sketches his life at Caernarvon, where he supported himself and his wife by keeping a small school and acting as visiting-master at a boarding-school ; he further amusingly describes a battle-royal between himself ("the black pig") and Ieuan Fardd ("the long hound") in a tavern in the town. Ieuan, "in tattered clothing," hotly attacked North-Walians, from Goronwy Owen downwards, asserting patriotically that South-Walians had done most to preserve the Welsh language and its literature ; while Robin Ddu of course maintained the contrary. Ieuan used language which, says Robin, "would have been a valuable acquisition to Billingsgate," and "asked me if I could handle a sword—I replied that I had never tried, but that I had been a dab at handling a knife and fork." Their terrified friends paid the reckoning and hurried Robin Ddu away. The improvement in his health at Caernarvon was but temporary ;

a letter to Owain Myfyr on January 6th, 1785, had to be finished by his wife, and he died on February 27th. He was buried at Heneglwys, Anglesey, and the Gwyneddigion paid for his tombstone.

Though it is known that not a few members of the old Cymmrodorion were also members of the Gwyneddigion, only a few of them can be definitely named. We may mention Rowland Jones the tobacconist (on Ludgate Hill) ; Griffith Ellis (a Merioneth man who was at Moorfields in 1778 but died at Bishopgate) ; Richard Fenton ; the old poet Rhys Jones of Blaenau (who wrote the " Initiation Song " of the Gwynedd-igion) ; Wheldon Jones the sailmaker ; William Vaughan of Conway (brother of the limner who painted Owain Myfyr's portrait.

It would have been pleasant to include confidently in this group the name of Meredith Jones (President of the Gwyneddigion in 1792), a Merioneth man, known among the Gwyneddigion as " Bedo Jones," " Bedo Oedrain," and " Bedo Beuno," a carpenter who had become an architect's manager. He is unkindly described by Iolo Morganwg as " a mere clown, tolerably well be-cockney'd "—yet it is fair to record that in the preface to the 1789 *Dafydd ap Gwilym* he is thanked for his help. The point about him is this : if Leathart is right in making him a member of the First Cymmrodorion, then Meredith Jones is in some way a historic figure—a member of the First Cymmrodorion, of the Gwyneddigion, and of the Second Cymmrodorion ; he was present at the meeting which founded the latter, and was still alive in 1831. Unfortunately he is not in the 1778 List, and Rowland Jones says that he " never was a member of the Cymmrodorion." The reader, if he wishes, may suppose on the one hand that Meredith Jones had joined the Cymmrodorion after 1777, and on the other that old Rowland Jones's memory was fallible ; still, he knew him well, calls him " a very intelligent man," and adds the endearing touch that he was " to be met with every day at Mr. Jones's, the King's Head, Ludgate Street, where he dines every day "—" Mr. Jones," of course, was John Jones of Glan-y-gors. Rowland Jones himself, Cymmrodor and Gwyn-eddig, was prevented by age and infirmity from joining the Second Cymmrodorion. On the other hand, Richard Edmunds (to whom Rowland Jones's letter was written), though a member alike of the First and of the Second Cymmrodorion (but he died in 1821), never joined the Gwyneddigion. Maybe he disapproved of them, for he was rather an "important" man —a barrister in the Exchequer Office of Pleas, Trustee (and Treasurer, 1818-21) of the Welsh Charity-School ; he came from Montgomeryshire.

One of the most important Gwyneddigion was John Edwards, "Siôn Ceiriog," the year of whose birth is variously given as 1747 and 1751, and who died in 1792. It seems from Leathart that he came in in 1775 ; he is not in the 1778 Cymmrodorion List, but he may well have been a member of that Society in 1780 when (as has been already mentioned) he competed for the Richard Morris memorial medal, defying Robin Ddu's insistence on "strict" metres, and sending in, says David Samwel :

> An ode that rendered Myvyr mad,
> And Robin Ddu declar'd too bad ;
> A monstrous bore in Robin's eyes—
> Against his own it won the prize.
> This Myvyr thought was monstrous wrong
> And damn'd Siôn Ceiriog and his song.

Siôn Ceiriog (also called "Siôn Gwgan"—query *gogan*, satire ?) seems to have been *par excellence* the wit and orator of the Gwyneddigion. David Samwel puts into Siôn's own mouth the lines :

> But all from Wallbrook to George Yard
> Siôn Ceiriog's fame is known ;

and Gwallter Mechain and Glan-y-gors speak most hyperbolically of his eloquence. Thomas Jones ("Bardd Cloff") puts the matter somewhat more dryly, in one of his Minutes as Secretary in 1790 : "tonight Siôn Ceiriog began to preach, but as he forgot his text he soon came to an end"; and Siôn's great admirer John Jones of Glan-y-gors hints very broadly that his eloquence was far above the heads of "moles and bumpkins like myself," as he modestly puts it. Himself a man of great good humour, he "seems to have felt a peculiar delight," says Leathart (drawing here on William Owen Pughe's recollections) in pulling the legs of that irascible pair, Owain Myfyr and David Samwel ; and Samwel himself tells us that Siôn "used to take great delight in roasting the masters of Welsh sloops who frequented the *Seven Stars* near London Bridge, in the Borough ; and those who heard him will allow that he did it with infinite wit and humour." If we are to judge by Glan-y-gors's elegy on him he was a lover of astronomy and music. He died on September 18th, 1792, and was buried at Bishopsgate.

The Society elected Owain Myfyr as its first President (1771). As the officials were in principle, and usually in fact, changed annually, to give a list of them would take undue space ; nor can more than a limited number of the members (" *cyfeillion*," friends) be dwelt upon, for they were very numerous. Since the foundation, says Leathart in 1831, about 1,000 members (including honorary members) had been elected ; an analysis by counties of origin became possible only from 1785 on ; of the 356 elected between 1800 and 1830, 85 hailed from Denbighshire—the other shires furnished quotas ranging from 50 (Flint) to 4 (Radnor). We are told that the list of members had not been kept up to date after 1790 till 1828, when Leathart became Secretary. Leathart's own list of members still living in 1831, on his own admission and on other evidence incomplete, has 177 names, not counting 50 honorary members, 12 " free members," and 5 " philological associates "—and it is a long way from 1831 to 1843. What the effective membership was, in any particular year, is hard to say ; Iolo Morganwg says it was about 40 in 1792 ; attendances recorded at the earliest meetings, and even at the earliest dinners, were small—" 5," " 12," " 23," etc. A more important consideration is this : when in the preceding chapter we had dwelt at fair length upon the small number of " famous " Cymmrodorion, our biographical task was done ; that Society, it must be admitted, had a very long tail of " mute inglorious " members. But the Gwyneddigion had a far larger proportion of members who took an active part ; thus any extended notice of individuals must be confined to a much smaller proportion of the active membership—not all even of those of whom Leathart has something specific to say can figure in the following pages.

The name " Leathart " has already occurred so frequently that it would have been natural to give at this point some account of the industrious Secretary (1828-31) who in 1831 published *The Origin and Progress of the Gwyneddigion Society of London*—it was printed in 1830, but a fire destroyed all the printer's stock except Leathart's own complimentary copy, which was in the post on its way to him, and from which the book had to be set up anew. Most unfortunately, however, we know next to nothing about him. William Leathart, as he calls himself on the title-page of his little book, *Welsh Penillion*, in 1825, William Davies Leathart in 1831, was on his own statement a Bodfari man, and a grandson of a William Davies of Bodfari who was honorary member of the Gwyneddigion in 1790 and died in 1799. But Mr. Edward Davies of Bodfari, who has been good enough to investigate the matter, has failed to find one single " Leathart " in the well-preserved registers of that parish—nor is there any mention of William Davies, the grandfather. All we *know* is that W. D. Leathart was admitted to the Gwyneddigion in 1822, and was at various times Vice-Treasurer, Librarian, and Secretary ; he lived in Goodge Street. The date of his death again, has not been ascertained ; he ceased to be Secretary at the end of 1831, and was succeeded by John Griffiths Jones, an Abergele man who had joined the Society in 1828. A Cuthbert Cadwaladr Leathart (" of Bodfari ") living in Marylebone Lane was a member in 1830 ; a Major John Leathart of Bath was honorary member in 1831 ; and the death in 1833 of a Thomas Leathart of Islington is recorded in the *Cambrian Quarterly Magazine*. Further, our author had a brother, Joseph Davies Leathart, of Shepherd's Bush, like himself a *penillion*-singer (but not a Gwyneddig). The Society was well on in years when Leathart wrote his book, and he naturally had to consult the few survivors of the earlier period. We have memoranda supplied to him by William Owen Pughe, and as Pughe from 1806 lived at Nantglyn, not far from Bodfari, it is perhaps not too fanciful to conjecture that Pughe was responsible for Leathart's introduction to the Society.

William Owen Pughe and Edward Williams were the two men who did most to forward Owain Myfyr's literary enterprises. Pughe (1759-1835) was born plain " William Owen," but added the " Pughe " on succeeding to the estate of a kinsman of that name in 1806 ; it will save much bother if we call him " Pughe " throughout. He was born at Tyn-y-bryn in Llanfihangel y Pennant (Merioneth), but his family removed in his childhood to Egryn near Barmouth, where the boy (as he himself records) was steeped in the vigorous popular culture of Ardudwy and was moreover entranced by the reading of Rhys Jones's *Gorchestion Beirdd Cymru*. Schooled at Altrincham, he went up to London in 1776 to earn his living as writing-master in a girls' boarding-school ; he also did some free-lance writing, and quite certainly (at a later date) much paid transcribing for Owain Myfyr. There is however no definite evidence (apart from his own statement that he attended three or four Cymmrodorion meetings—this must, one thinks, have been in the very last years of that Society) that he was in any very close contact with the London-Welsh literati before 1782, when he " accidentally " met Robin Ddu, who in 1783 brought him into the Gwyneddigion. From that time on, he was one of its pillars. He lived at various times in Panton Street (Pentonville) and in Islington. He did the lion's share of the editorial work on the publications which Owain Myfyr's wealth and good-will brought through the press ; but it must not be forgotten that his own independent work was very considerable, in bulk and in importance—his edition of the " Llywarch Hen " poems (1794—but dated " 1792 ") ; his great *Welsh Dictionary* (1793-1803 ; revised in 1832) ; his *Cambrian Biography* (1803) ; his translation of *Paradise Lost* (1819) ; and so forth. He attained, indeed, an ascendancy in Welsh scholarship (both in the minds of Welshmen and in the opinion of men outside Wales) which can be compared only with that of Lewis Morris ; he was elected Fellow of the Society of Antiquaries, and in June, 1822, received the degree of D.C.L. from the University of Oxford—how happy poor frustrated Lewis Morris would have been with either distinction !

Pughe, over-rated by many in his own day, suffered much detraction even then, and much more in after years—quite apart from the ridicule into which he fell when he espoused the cause of Joanna Southcott. Credulity, for that matter, was his greatest foible. It marred even his great Welsh Dictionary, a massive piece of single-handed work which is still the only completed large-scale dictionary of the language. A queer compatriot, Rowland Jones (1722-74) of Llanbedrog in Llŷn, a barrister relieved of financial cares by a wealthy wife, had put out several crazy books in which (" in a method entirely new," as he very truly said) he analysed language into abstract " roots," of which all languages were permutations and combinations— he was, by the way, not a Cymmrodor (the Morris Letters have a few rather sniffy references to him as a lawyer), though he had a brother, Thomas, who was. Pughe swallowed his ideas, lock, stock, and barrel, and "explained" the etymology of the Welsh vocabulary in their light. Furthermore, he was a "spelling reformer," and rode this hobby, too, very hard, succeeding in persuading some innocent authors and printers in Wales itself to adopt his canons. Pughe yearned, again, to "improve" the Welsh alphabet by abolishing "double letters" and substituting new characters for some of them. As all men know, the fortunate "stupidity" of the public is usually an effective deterrent to such efforts ; no doubt it would be "easier" to write "ovyz" for "ofydd" (or in English, "nolij" for "knowledge")—but people just won't.

When Thomas Charles of Bala innocently employed Pughe, whom he greatly admired, and whose orthography (though not his typography) he adopted at first in some of his own publications, to edit the text of the Welsh Bible published by the Bible Society, there was a most unholy row ; and Pughe's spellings were cleaned away in subsequent editions. Amusingly enough, when Pughe published in 1808 a little manual, *Cadwraeth yr Iaith Gymraeg*, in the full panoply of his typography and orthography, Charles had it reprinted at Bala in "ordinary" Welsh, so to speak, as a text-book for his Sunday-schools. Isolated examples of Pughe's quirks (such as writing *-aw* for *-o*, e.g., "gweithiaw" for "gweithio," though no Welshman for centuries on end has ever *pronounced* the syllable in that way) have survived like flies in amber in the work of conscientious nineteenth century writers of Welsh, to the unbounded wrath of our grammarians. But in our own day, Pughe's general services have come to be more favourably regarded, and his star is now again in the ascendant. So careful and so dispassionate a scholar as the late Sir John Edward Lloyd has felt himself able to say that "in erudition, no student of the Welsh language and literature has ever surpassed him." Withal, Pughe was an amiable and kindly man ; he was known among the Gwyneddigion as "Gwilym Dawel"—and *tawelwch* or quiescence was hardly a normal attribute of the members of that Society. Even after 1806, Pughe, though his home was now at Nantglyn, was frequently at Gwyneddigion meetings. He had married, and had two daughters and a son, Aneurin (1792-1851) who retained the surname Owen ; he joined the Gwyneddigion in

1827, and in 1841 edited the *Laws of Wales* for the Record Commission, "with care and accuracy," to quote Sir John Lloyd once more.

Edward Williams (1746-1826) "Iolo Morganwg," the third of the " Myvyrian " trio, calls for far more copious treatment than can be afforded him here, and it will be wiser (and very much safer) to await Professor G. J. Williams's full study of this extraordinary man and of his equally extraordinary work. In a sense, indeed, the " Bard of Liberty " was hardly a full-blown Gwyneddig, for his years of continuous residence in London ran only from 1771 to 1777, when he worked in Town as a stonemason, and again from 1791 to 1794, when he was in London seeing to the publication of his poems. But in the former period, though he saw much of Owain Myfyr and other individual Gwyneddigion (and indeed in 1776 showed a desire to join the *Cymmrodorion*), there is no mention of him in the Society's early records, and he did not join it till 1785 (in *absentia*, for he was then in Glamorgan ; Leathart makes no mention of his election, though he dwells at some length upon his " singularities ") ; it was in his second London period that he was closely associated with the Society, which after 1805 he so rancorously criticised.

Edward Jones (1752-1825), " Bardd y Brenin," joined the Society in 1783. He was born at Henblas, Llandderfel, and was one of a remarkably musical family—the father and his six sons were skilled instrumentalists and formed a household orchestra. After some years as visiting harpist at such houses as Nannau, Wynnstay, and Powis Castle, Edward Jones came up to London, probably in 1774, and became unpaid assistant to the Keeper of the Robes, a post which he held for 42 years and which had the sole merit of providing him with free quarters in S. James's Palace while he earned his bread elsewhere. His superior was Hugh Rowlands (d. 1831), " Huw Aber " to his fellow-Gwyneddigion—he had, by the way, the odd distinction of being one of Queen Charlotte's executors. Leathart speaks well of Rowlands ; but Edward Jones found him a tyrant, who tried to make him pay rent for his quarters, and eventually (1819) got him dismissed. Jones found work from the beginning as a teacher of music, cherishing meantime his dream of publishing a history of Welsh music and poetry. He played before Dr. Charles Burney at his house—Fanny

H

Burney on that occasion (1775) calls him " a silly young man," but adds that " he played with great neatness and delicacy." In the year of his entry into the Gwyneddigion Society, he was appointed " Harper to the Prince of Wales "—again, there was no salary. And in 1784, he published his *Musical and Poetick Relicks of the Welsh Bards*, of which a greatly augmented edition appeared in 1794. But from about this time, his affairs took a turn for the worse, for his historical researches would seem to have ruined his professional practice. Evicted (as we saw) in 1819 from S. James's, he had to sell much of his large library ; poverty and ill-health drove him into the life of a recluse, at Great Chester Street, Marylebone ; so, says Leathart, though " formerly an active member, he had not latterly frequented the Society." A pension of £50 was voted him by the Royal Society of Music, but it came too late—when John Parry (" Bardd Alaw ") took him the good news, the old musician was too bemused to remember him ; and a few days later (on April 18th, 1825) he died. His MSS. (and one of his harps) are today in the National Library.

John Parry (1776-1851), " Bardd Alaw," a Denbigh man who had been bandmaster in that town, came to London in 1807, and in 1809 began to write songs for the now forgotten concerts in Vauxhall Gardens. In 1809, too, he joined the Gwyneddigion (he was President in 1819) and Leathart has many references to his activity in the Society's concerns ; he further became a prominent Cymmrodor in 1820, and his name will reappear in the next chapter. So will that of another Parry—John Humffreys Parry (1786-1825), of Mold ; indeed, his association with the Cymmrodorion takes precedence ; but the *Cambrian Register*, which he edited from 1820 to 1822, had been planned in 1819 and had the support of the Gwyneddigion, several of whom contributed to its pages. Another prominent Gwyneddig who is best left over for the next chapter was Thomas Jones of Llangollen, " Bard Cloff," who joined the Society in 1789 and was three times President ; he wrote the Society's " jubilee " *awdl*, in 1821.

We next come to three Denbighshire men who were highly picturesque figures. One of the earliest Gwyneddigion (1774) was David Samwel (" Samwell," " Samuel "), grandson of that famous Edward Samuel who was an early correspondent of Lewis Morris's. Born at Nantglyn in 1751, Samwel became

(1775) a naval surgeon. In that capacity, he voyaged to Greenland and afterwards accompanied Captain Cook on his last voyage ; he was an eye-witness of Cook's death and in 1786 published an account of it. At sea, he cherished his pocket copy of Horace ; but he also cherished the poetic tradition of his countryside—we have *englynion* written by him off the Cape of Good Hope in 1776, and in 1777 he patriotically celebrated S. David's Day on the South Seas with a set of verses which incidentally show that he was well acquainted with Owain Myfyr and Siôn Ceiriog. In 1793-4 he was again at sea, and in 1797 was surgeon to the British prisoners-of-war at Versailles. But his long periods ashore enabled him to play a prominent part in the Gwyneddigion Society ; he was Vice-President in 1797, the year before his death.

David Samwel (" Dafydd Ddu Feddyg ") was a colourful man, " tall, stout, black-haired, pock-marked, fierce-looking, wondrous friendly in company, and very fond of the cup," says Edward Charles. Siôn Ceiriog loved to " draw " him, but was prudent enough to work him up only to a certain pitch, says Pughe—" up to a certain point, when he shut one eye, and with the other looked for the pilter(?) pot which was his good missile to batter the skull " of his tormentor ; this " ragging," it should be said, did not take place during a Gwyneddigion meeting, but in a private capacity, so to speak, at the " Bull." Samwel's instinctive reaction to opposition was a challenge to a duel. Thus he fell out with Edward Jones (" Ned Môn "), challenged him, and (says Pughe) " took Iolo Morganwg "—worthy pair !—" from my house to be his second. On coming to the ground, Ned Môn was not there, so the other party marched in battle array to his chambers in the Temple [Edward Jones was a lawyer's clerk] ; there Ned Môn, instead of giving honourable satisfaction, raised his foot against the seat of honour of his foe, and bundled him down-stairs "—Leathart, using this memorandum, demurely con-denses it to " thrust the doctor downstairs." It seems odd that so fiery a warrior should have tamely submitted to this treatment—but as Cicero has it, *cedant arma togae!* Again, when the adjudicators at the Corwen Eisteddfod of 1789 awarded the prize (unjustly, as most of us think) to Gwallter Mechain, over the head of Twm o'r Nant, the doctor (an old friend of Twm's) was so wrath that he " proceeded so far as to demand satisfaction " of one of the adjudicators ; however, " it ended harmlessly," and Samwel presented Twm with a silver pen, characteristically inscribed " to the chief poet of Wales "—the pen is today in the National Museum ; Samwel, by the way, left Twm £10 in his will.

It is little wonder that Leathart, though he never saw David Samwel, speaks of his "clever, whimsical genius," and adds that " in temper he was extremely irascible, but one of those hearty fellows we expect the sailor to have been, 50 or 60 years ago." He died in November, 1798, and was buried at S. Dunstan's in Fleet Street—not at S. Andrew's, Holborn, as Leathart says. His English squib *Padouca Hunt* (from which we have quoted and shall quote again), has footnotes which greatly enhance our knowledge of the Gwyneddigion. But one must not overlook Samwel's very respectable knowledge of Welsh literature. Not only did he help with the 1789 *Dafydd ap Gwilym* ; he was something of an authority on the poet Huw Morys, wrote an essay on him which was afterwards printed in the *Cambrian Register*, and assisted Gwallter Mechain who was later to edit Huw Morys. Extremely radical during the first phase of the French Revolution, he had by 1797 " toned down " and is found in that year supporting his quondam adversary Ned Môn in hot debate against Owain Myfyr and a good minority of the " Caradogion "—" and the violent patriots," says he, " call me an aristocrat."

To the man in the street in Welsh-speaking Wales today, the name, at least, of John Jones of Glan-y-gors (1767-1821) is beyond doubt more familiar than that of any other of the Gwyneddigion—was he not the creator of " Dic Siôn Dafydd," that representative in literature of the Welshman who has forsworn his language ? and the writer of revolutionary political pamphlets which alarmed, nay, horrified good men in Wales in his day ? John Jones, born at Glan-y-gors (Cerrig-y-drudion), came up to Town at a date which is not known, and for reasons attested only by legend. He found work in a haberdasher's shop ; but in the winter of 1789-90 returned home presumably to settle affairs on the death of his father and his uncle, and again in the summer of 1790, when his friend David Samwel notes that he " saw him off "—the " seeing-off," from the " Blue Boar " in Holborn, took " three or four hours " ! Perhaps John Jones benefited financially from these family deaths, for early in 1793 he took over the " Canterbury Arms " inn, in the Borough. Later, he removed to the " King's Head " on Ludgate Hill, the house which is always remembered along with his name ; and there he died in 1821, greatly respected—the first Welsh Baptist minister in London (Evan Evans) officiated at his funeral and afterwards delivered an encomium upon him.

The facts mentioned in the last sentence are in odd contrast with the generally accepted view that " Jac Glan-y-gors " was one of the wildest of " Bohemians "—even Twm o'r Nant, writing to Owain Myfyr as late as 1799, judged that " John Glan-y-Gors and Edward Charles were quite bad enough to satisfy London." But Twm had his serious side, and it is possible that the odium in which John Jones's political views were held in Wales had frightened him. Or again, it may be that there were in the bard's life two periods—an irresponsible phase, and a more " settled " existence as a responsible householder. To be sure, we are not for a moment to suppose that John Jones (or indeed any of the Gwyneddigion) at any time made a fetish of abstinence or of solemnity of demeanour. Not so would he have merited Leathart's description, " one of the wittiest and best comic and satirical song-writers ; . . . . . it was at the Gwyneddigion his effusions generally appeared, sung by himself, with no small portion of humour "—Leathart takes care to add that John Jones was " a highly competent judge " of poetry and " likewise in other respects a well-informed man." He was elected to the Society in 1790, and was Vice-President in 1801 and again in 1813, but ",could never be persuaded to sit as *Llywydd*."

Edward Charles (1757-1828) of Clocaenog, styled by himself for some reason " Siamas Wynedd," but by his fellow-Gwyneddigion " Sierlyn Fardd," became a member in 1790, but held no office higher than that of Secretary (1796)—one wonders whether this fact reflects the Society's considered opinion of him, for extremely few of its secretaries stopped at that point. Perhaps it would not be unfair to describe him as a Glan-y-Gors who never made good. He was in Town at least as early as 1789, as a draper's assistant. In later years, he fell into adversity ; the Cymreigyddion are found doing a little for him in 1821, and the Gwyneddigion in 1823 ; he died, says Leathart " very badly off." Yet he was a man of very considerable ability. His MSS. (letters, and copies of poems) in the British Museum and the Cardiff City Library are valuable, and incidentally contain information about London-Welsh life which cannot be got elsewhere. For fifteen months (he says) in 1803 and 1804 he was employed by Owain Myfyr, from 7 a.m. to 8 p.m. daily, to transcribe old poetry—"Myfyr" was no doubt a hard taskmaster. Edward Charles's particular friends were John Jones and Siôn Ceiriog, though he opposed John Jones's political opinions and indeed had a journalistic controversy (1796) with him. Methodism he hated like poison, attacking it not only in the pages of M. J. Rhys's *Cylchgrawn Cyn-mraeg* (1793-4) but also in a pamphlet, *Epistolau Cymraeg at y Cymry* (1797), which was so violent that his disgusted fellow-Gwyneddig Thomas Roberts replied to it (under the pseudonym "Arvonius") in 1806, and that Twm o'r Nant too attacked it, in verse. Nevertheless, Edward Charles's pamphlet (like all his writings, indeed) is written in most racy Welsh.

Thomas Roberts (1767-1841), just mentioned, is a more substantial figure. The details of his life have been painstakingly elucidated in an unpublished essay by Mr. Robert Owen of Croesor, who has most kindly permitted the use of his researches in these pages. Born at Llwyn'rhudol Uchaf in Abererch (near Pwllheli) in August 1767, to a lawyer who was himself the son of a lawyer, Thomas Roberts was well educated—where, is not known. He left home, according to his own (later) reckoning, in 1780 or 1781 ; but here again we do not know where he went. Indeed, we lose sight of him completely till he emerges again, a married man, in 1791. By that time he had become a Quaker, for the advent of his eldest child Hannah, born in October 1791, is recorded in S. Botolph's parish, Aldgate, and he and his wife were members of the "Devonshire House Meeting" of the Society of Friends. Mrs. Roberts's name was Mary, and she is said to have hailed from Warwickshire ; she died in 1829. They had five daughters and a son, Maurice, who showed much promise as a writer of Welsh, but he and four of his sisters pre-deceased their parents. Mary Roberts was wealthy, and her husband (who may up to that time have followed the Law) became a "goldsmith" upon marriage. They lived successively in Aldgate, Clerkenwell, and Poultry ; on his wife's death, Thomas Roberts returned to Aldgate, moving thence to Bond Street, where he died on May 24th, 1841 (again the date comes from a Friends' Register) ; he was buried with his wife in Bunhill Fields. It seems probable that he was the " Thomas Roberts " who took part in the inauguration of the Stock Exchange building in 1801. But towards the end of his days he sustained heavy losses (caused, so the story goes, by the loss at sea of a shipload of bullion) ; and latterly he lived on a pension from the Goldsmiths' Company. There had clearly been no aspersions cast upon his personal integrity, for otherwise he would have been disowned by the Society of Friends.

The career thus outlined—the English marriage—the Quaker associations—may at first sight seem not wholly appropriate to a member of the blithe company of the Gwyneddigion. But in the first place, the Friends could be as lively as any other folk (we have read, in the preceding chapter, of that quaint character Silvanus Bevan) ; we know that they could be boon companions—and it was Thomas Roberts who on one occasion stubbornly withstood a proposal that smoking should be forbidden at Cymreigyddion meetings. Next, despite his English marriage (indeed, obviously with his wife's concurrence), Thomas Roberts was an ardent Welshman. His children were brought up in Welsh, his son in particular showed every sign of becoming a Welsh writer ; the family paid frequent visits to Wales, making long sojourns with Thomas Roberts's nephew who lived at Llwyn-du, Llanllyfni. The goldsmith was in constant correspondence with men of letters in Wales, and was a collector of folk-verse, and particularly of *penillion telyn*— he had more than a hundred of these. And while he wrote much in English (in the *Cambro-Briton* and the *North Wales Gazette*), his best-known work *Cŵyn yn Erbyn Gorthrymder* (1798), is in Welsh, and he wrote in the *Geirgrawn*, the *Greal*, *Seren Gomer* and other Welsh periodicals, and published several translations in Welsh, notably and characteristically, in 1839, *Y Ffordd i Gaffael Cyfoeth*, by Benjamin Franklin. " Characteristically," for despite what was said, a few lines back, about Thomas Roberts's lighter side, the Quaker was still there : the earnestness which joined in the " self-improving " debates of the Cymreigyddion Society ; the canniness which could not away with improvidence ; the dissent in religion. His pseudonymous reply to Edward Charles was inspired partly by disgust with Edward Charles himself, and partly by a sturdy Quaker dislike of the Establishment—certainly not by any love of Methodism, for what his argument comes to is this : that great as might be the faults of Methodism, the Established Church was much worse !

Although we know a good deal about other members of the Gwyneddigion Society, there is no further room to dilate upon them. Nearly every notable Welsh man of letters at the time was either a resident or an honorary member : among the latter we may specify Twm o'r Nant (Thomas Edwards) and "Bardd Nantglyn" (Robert Davies)—Davies indeed was a resident member (and Secretary, 1802-3) during his brief sojourn in London. In this way, the Society continued and extended the function of the old Cymmrodorion, in providing a gathering-ground for well-wishers of Welsh literature, in London and in Wales.

The Rules ("*Gosodaethau*," this time) of the Society were amended on October 6th, 1777. Every member had to be Welsh-speaking ; he had also (as it is prudently put) to "avow" a fondness for singing, or at least for *hearing* poetry sung to the harp—but members were begged "not to sing the *same* penillion too often." At the very first, innkeepers were excluded, but it is obvious from the history of John Jones that this rule must have been abrogated. Visitors could be introduced, but their sponsors had to tell the Secretary, pay 1/3d. for their entertainment, and guarantee their good behaviour. The Rules were revised in 1784-5 and again in 1799. Officials (from 1785 on) wore silver badges, made by Hugh Samwel (a cousin of David's, and third President, 1773), which cost the Society £23 6s. 9d. : a harp for the President, a wren for the Vice-President (a newly-created office, 1785), a key for the Treasurer, a quill for the Secretary, druids' heads for members of Council. There was no statutory "Bard" till 1800 ; his badge (if any) is not known to us.

Members were ceremoniously initiated (after proposal in the preceding month, and a ballot at which five negative votes excluded) in Welsh, according to a form devised in 1785 by Pughe. They were asked by the President whether they desired to become "Friends" of "Y Gymdeithas Wyneddig," whose members assembled in amity for mutual delight, and further to uphold the honour of their country and to cherish its history and poetry and language." After avowing this, they were ordered to lay the right hand upon a symbolic harp, and to declare their loyalty to the Society and its rules. They were then admitted, and had afterwards to greet each member singly. Then came the Initiation song, " *Cydunwn, Wynedd-igion,*" written by old Rhys Jones of Blaenau and sung to the air " Toriad y Dydd."

The subscription in 1771 was 12/- a year. According to the 1777 Rules, there was a payment of 3/- (whether once for all or annually is not clear) " to the Chest," and another of a shilling per meeting (*that* seems to be the 1771 annual 12/-) " for the entertainment "—if you left before 10 p.m., you paid 6d. Leathart gives us a rather confused account of the fluctuations of the subscription ; by 1823 it had become 10/6d. per annum. To go back to the 1777 Rules : there was a fine for coming in drunk, another for " discourteous and unkindly language," and yet another for talking so loudly that your voice could be heard above the sound of the harp. Small wonder that the Minutes of November 4th, 1783, record : " a bothersome evening—but Abraham [the collector of fines] was pleased, having to take his collecting-box around so often." A New Year's Gift (*calennig*) of 5/- to the cook is mentioned in 1778. The 1784-5 revision of the Rules seems to have raised the 3/- payment to the Chest to 5/-.

Meetings were held on the first Monday in the month— later on in the history of the Society (1826) there were no meetings between June and October. There was an " Annual Dinner." On this point, the Gwyneddigion differed from the Cymmrodorion. The Society seems in 1771 to have fallen in with the Cymmrodorion practice of attending the " Antient British " Festival. But, to be frank, the Gwyneddigion Society seems at no time to have been over-enthusiastic about the " Antient Britons." In 1772, it broke away (as a Society— individual members did attend the Festival), and held a ball on S. David's Day, at the " George and Vulture." The ball was discontinued in 1777, and the " Annual Dinner," hitherto held " in the course of the summer " at such rustic resorts as Highbury Barn or Copenhagen House, was removed to March 1st, and held at the " George "—not without opposition. The habit of dining in summer was *also* kept up—the dinner wandered around the suburbs ; Denmark Hill in Camberwell is mentioned, and the " Horns " in Kennington ; we observe that in 1778 (at Highbury Barn) the more agile of the Gwyneddigion " showed their valour in putting the stone, pole-jumping, leaping, racing, and football," *before* dinner, one supposes. The " Annual " Dinner remained at the " George " for a long time ; the toasts in 1785 were *King and Church, Prince and Principality* and *Long Life to the Welsh Language.* But in 1790, only " a few members " dined at the " George " ; the rest, " in accordance with a resolution to that effect " (taken in 1787, " for the benefit of the Welsh School," and repeated in 1789), " joined the Antient Britons at their table." By 1814, the Gwyneddigion as a Society had " omitted to celebrate S. David's Day," though most of them went to the Antient British Dinner. The " Summer " Dinner had by that time become the " Annual " Dinner, but was held on the second Monday in December. When the change was made is not known, but it was before 1825, for in that year we hear of " curious and diverting mistakes "—the adjectives can rarely have been used in so exact a sense, however unintended— caused by the tickets being printed in Welsh ; English visitors " perambulated the whole district of Cornhill, on a disagreeable evening in December," because they could not understand their tickets. Tickets, thenceforth, were printed in English. In 1823, members drank not only the three ancient toasts, but four others : " The Memory of Owain Myfyr," " The Welsh School," " The Cymmrodorion "—this was the Second Cymmrodorion—and finally, " Sir Watkin Williams Wynn, in gratitude for the venison on which we have feasted this day."

There has been some misunderstanding about the regular place of meeting of the Gwyneddigion. The very frequent mention of the " Bull " has led many to suppose that the Society always met there. But in truth, there are three quite distinct " uses " of this famous (or notorious) old tavern. First (as for instance in the lampoons of Dr. John Jones and Iolo Morganwg), there is the " parlour," or *public* room, of the " Bull " ; here you would normally meet Owain Myfyr, " between 8 and 10 or 12," amid his rout of " fiddlers " and so on. Next, there was the room upstairs containing the famous " round table," where the *Council* of the Gwyneddigion met for many years on Monday nights, just because the " Bull " was Owain Myfyr's " house of call " ; Dr. John Jones confesses that " the transactions in the club-room, on the first floor, were more meritorious " than the gatherings downstairs—here, too, met the " *Caradogion*," of whom more will be said later. Thirdly, the " Bull " *did* become at one time the regular meeting-place of the Gwyneddigion Society itself.

The Society, in fact, wandered about a good deal, and it is not always easy to follow its movements in detail. It began with the " Goose and Gridiron " in S. Paul's Churchyard. Then (very soon) it moved to the " George and Vulture," George Yard, Lombard Street ; the house still stands, and is now said to be the oldest surviving " chop-house " in London ; it has old associations with famous English men of letters, and readers of Dickens in particular will remember its name. There the Society remained till 1798, when " on the motion of Owain Myfyr " it moved to the " Coopers' Arms " in Silver Street, whose Welsh landlord Robert Hughes (a Gwyneddig since 1792) undertook to re-name it " The Cambrian Arms." But in 1801 there was a fresh move, to the " Butler's Head " in White-Rose-Court, Coleman Street. It was not till 1802 that the Society set up at the " Bull's Head " (" the Bull ") in Walbrook ; there can be no doubt that the decision was Owain Myfyr's. The Welsh landlord, Evan Roberts, a Gwyneddig, who had been so well known to the members, had been dead (says David Samwel) for some years before that time ; but they still called the house " Y Crindy " as they did in his lifetime, for Evan had been either wizened or stingy, and was therefore nicknamed by Siôn Ceiriog " *y Crin* "—it should be explained (if it has not already become clear) that all the Gwyneddigion had such nicknames, but further that these are *not* " bardic names," queer as those often are. Let us hear David Samwel further :

> In Walbrook stands a famous inn
> Near ancient Watling-street,
> Well stored with brandy, beer, and gin,
> Where Cambrians nightly meet.
>
> If on the left you leave the bar
> Where the Welsh landlord sits,
> You'll find a room where a wordy war
> Is waged by Cambrian wits

The lines were written in (or very soon after) 1791, ten years or more before the Gwyneddigion officially camped in the house

—" Cambrians *nightly* met " there, but that was in a private capacity.

And there the Gwyneddigion Society assembled for thirteen years. When Iolo Morganwg described it as " a very creditable bawdy house," he may have been a trifle censorious ; but in truth it does not appear that Gwyneddigion who regarded themselves as " respectable " felt altogether comfortable there. Says Quaker Thomas Roberts of Llwyn'rhudol, writing in 1806 to John Roberts (Siôn Lleyn ") of Llanarmon : " I haven't been near the Gwyneddigion for a long time ; . . . . . the Society is being ruined by the badger-like obstinacy (" *tyrcheidd-dra* ") of Owain Myfyr, who won't budge from the *Crindy*, while others won't go there because it is too low-down for them." The old " badger " died in 1814, and the Society moved to the " New York Coffee-house " ; but 1817 saw it at the " Woolpack," S. Peter's Alley, Cornhill, kept by a Welsh landlord named Parry, where it remained till 1831. Its home in 1831 (naturally, the last mentioned in Leathart's book) was the " Owain Glyndwr," 163, Aldersgate Street.

The meetings of the Gwyneddigion were from the first unashamedly merry. The *Cyfeillion* were never bored by " communications " on whales or ancient coins, as a prelude to their evening's enjoyment. They were less " high-brow " than Lewis Morris would have *liked* the Cymmrodorion to be. But it is fair to add that they were in one rather important sense *more* " high-brow " than a modern Welsh " literary society " tends to be. For the Gwyneddigion, one and all, had a keen (however uncritical) interest in *literature*, a considerable (however undisciplined) knowledge of it ; our modern societies have (perhaps) more *general* interests, but are less well-informed on Welsh literary matters. An *englyn* or a *cywydd* would arouse lively discussion among them. And they were more musical than the Cymmrodorion had been ; the harp, and singing to the harp, occupied much of the time of the meetings. And with all this went merriment and leg-pulling and nonsense in general.

For, let us remember, the Gwyneddigion (though there were certainly among them some who were very well-to-do), were socially more homogeneous than the old Cymmrodorion had been. They had no aristocrats among them, and they were pretty clearly anti-clerical ; there would be no one at their meetings who would " cramp their style." Their minute-book, especially when Siôn Ceiriog was Secretary, abounds in such summings-up as " digon o grwth a thelyn "— " mwyniant a diddanwch "—" canu a chellwair." A harpist attended every meeting in the early days—the principal *penillion*-singer was " Siôn Collen," Jonathan Parry of Llangollen. But by 1793, harpists (so we are told) were becoming increasingly difficult to get, and about 1800 the harp was confined to alternate meetings. There might indeed be other instruments—John Vaughan of Conway, for instance, the artist, could play the fiddle and the flute, and Siôn Ceiriog, that versatile man, would sing to his accompaniment. *Smoking* was prodigious—in 1802 there was a smoking-match between William Owen Pughe and a John Davies of Wood Street. The duellists puffed into each other's faces—says the learned lexicographer : " Mr. John Davies, a great smoker, whom I fairly smoked out of the chair ; I beat him hollow." Leathart, writing in the distant year 1830, notes that by his time the habit of " smoking in Societies had become unfashionable," so that " meetings are less sociable than they were fifty years ago—indeed, altogether clubs have degenerated."

It was before the Gwyneddigion, though it cannot have been a " regular " meeting of the Society, on October 15th, 1791, in " the great room " of the " Seven Stars " near London Bridge (where Siôn Ceiriog, as we remember, used to haze the sea-captains), that Edward Charles " produced " Twm o'r Nant's famous interlude *Tri Chryfion Byd ;* the three characters were impersonated by Glan-y-Gors, Daniel Davies of Tooley Street, and his brother Peter Davies : three actors from the very heart of the interlude-country, one of them the very incarnation of that countryside's ethos, with exactly the " right " audience. Yet, let us confess it, a respectable London-Welsh draper, of say, 1851, could he have been wafted in a dream to that show at the " Seven Stars," would have been fully as bewildered as if it had been Shakespeare's " Globe " hard by, in 1600.

Poetry, of varying merit, was regularly offered to the Gwyneddigion, without fear of that unflattering reception which, according to Lewis Morris, the old Cymmrodorion gave it. We are, naturally, not surprised that Glan-y-gors's pungent satires were received with acclamation. But Edward Charles (the first official "Bard"—1800—of the Society), Siôn Ceiriog, Bardd Nantglyn, Daniel Ddu o Geredigion (at a later date) and many others contributed *awdlau* and *cywyddau*. Daniel Davies (who acted in *Tri Chryfion Byd*) was a notable *englynwr* : Bardd Alaw was always ready to fit a tune to new words, or words to a new tune. And when the Gwyneddigion Eisteddfodau began, the poems sent in were discussed at length (sometimes, it must be admitted, with more heat than light) by the fraternity. Indeed "debates" were at the beginning (though the practice declined at a comparatively early date) regarded as a regular part of the proceedings. Perhaps the most famous of their debates was the "Madog" debate of 1791, in which the "Caradogion" Society was also involved. Credulous Pughe and hot-headed David Samwel fervently believed in the story of Prince Madog's voyage and in the existence of red-skinned Cymry across the Atlantic ; money was collected to send Iolo Morganwg and the missionary John Evans of Waunfawr out West to them—fortunately (or unfortunately ?) Iolo stayed at home ; but the cooler Ned Môn and (out of mischief, one suspects) Siôn Ceiriog were sceptical ; Owain Myfyr, it need hardly be said, sided with Pughe. An argument (at the "Bull") waxed so hot that David Samwel celebrated it in the famous squib *Padouca Hunt*. As this squib *must* be read, we break the "no references" rule laid down for this book, to inform the reader that it can be read, together with its interesting footnotes, either in the 1926-7 *Cymmrodorion Transactions* or in the *National Library of Wales Journal* for 1942. The issue was again raised in the Society some twenty-five years later ; the reader will know that it was finally settled by Thomas Stephens in 1858, to the immense wrath of the credulous. To go on : the practice of set debate "fell into disuse" among the Gwyneddigion, and lovers of such debates felt themselves compelled in 1794 to establish a new Society, the "Cymreigyddion," for that purpose.

Like the Cymmrodorion, the Gwyneddigion dispensed charity—for example, to John Humffreys Parry's "helpless family," and to Edward Charles. They saw to Robin Ddu's tombstone at Heneglwys, set up a memorial to Twm o'r Nant at Whitchurch (Denbigh), and intended to set up a gigantic

cairn in memory of Owain Myfyr on a hilltop in Denbighshire—
fortunately the scheme fell through. The Society also interested
itself in church matters, very odd " churchmen " though many
of its members were—and though, indeed, there were strong
Dissenters among them. We have on a previous page spoken
of their protest against the appointment of an English-speaking
vicar at Caernarvon in 1817. And, again like the Cymmrodorion, they talked of a " Welsh church " in London—as
early as 1794, it would seem that Gwallter Mechain was thought
of as a chaplain. In or about 1819, Gwyneddigion and
Cymreigyddion together are found printing a " prospectus "
inviting subscriptions (in Wales as well as in London) for a
Welsh church ; it was to be in Lambeth, but the idea, so
Leathart says, " was coldly received by the ecclesiastical
powers," and nothing came of it—Leathart's remark, in
passing, that there were in 1819 " 60,000 " Welshpeople in
London takes some believing. We have, however, tantalising
references which indicate that some provision of services in
Welsh *had* been in existence, round about 1800 ; the clergyman
concerned is known to us only as " *Jones feddw* " (fortunately
for him, the surname amounts to almost complete anonymity),
and Thomas Roberts of Llwyn'rhudol tells us that Edward
Charles was his " clerk " ; nothing more is known of this
somewhat inauspicious arrangement. To round off this scrappy
tale of " miscellaneous " Gwyneddigion activities, we may note
that the Society from 1827 hobnobbed at intervals with Breton,
Gaelic and Erse societies ; and that in 1830 it joined the Cymreigyddion in a vain attempt to prevent the abolition of the
Court of Great Sessions in Wales.

But it is safe to say that the Gwyneddigion Society is to-day
remembered primarily for its great services to Welsh literature.
Yet in the early years of the Society, there is no hint of any
aspirations of this kind—all the stress is laid on good-fellowship
and an *affection* for things Welsh. The conscious adoption of
the literary projects which the leaders of the old Cymmrodorion
had cherished was to come later. The sequence of the Society's
minutes is significant. It was on August 6th, 1787, that the
Society formally accepted the Presidential Chair of the Cymmrodorion—this may perhaps be construed as the overt act of
dissolution of the older Society. And it was on October 1st
that it resolved " to publish the work of Dafydd ap Gwilym,

under the auspices and in the name of the [Gwyneddigion] Society." Owain Myfyr thus showed a tact with which he is not commonly credited. The Society which he and his friends had founded, as far back as 1770, was not to be regarded as a *rival* of the Morrisian Cymmrodorion ; not even on Richard Morris's death, though we have ample evidence that Owen Jones had long been collecting and copying MSS. of the Dafydd ap Gwilym poems, did he launch forth—it is of course possible too that he had not as yet acquired the wealth which enabled him in the end to realise his desires. In other words, the Gwynedd-igion Society in 1787 became the literary executrix of the Cymmrodorion. We have now, as it were, a Richard Morris who had plenty of money—and a Richard Morris who had energetic collaborators at call, and (to do the rank and file of the Gwyneddigion justice) the backing of a well-disposed and intelligent Society. Thus, after a remarkably short interval, *Barddoniaeth Dafydd ap Gwilym* (1789) was actually published, under the editorship (however nominal) of Owain Myfyr, who wrote the Welsh preface, and of William Owen Pughe, the real editor, who wrote an English introduction ; and with the collaboration of Iolo Morganwg (he " collaborated " not only with his two friends but with Dafydd ap Gwilym himself !), and the help of David Samwel, Siôn Ceiriog, the brothers Ned Môn and Owen Môn, Meredith Jones, and " Bardd y Brenin." This famous edition, with all its very grave defects, had to suffice students of Welsh throughout the nineteenth century—it was reprinted in 1873. Sir Ifor Williams published (1914) a critical edition of a selection of the poems, and Professor Thomas Parry's complete edition is now awaited.

The second *magnum opus* of the Gwyneddigion Society, undertaken in 1798, was the *Myvyrian Archaiology of Wales* in three volumes (I and II, 1801 ; III, 1807), under the editorship of Owain Myfyr (who probably did little more than paying for it), Iolo Morganwg and Pughe—with a shadowy committee which included Fenton, Gwallter Mechain, and John Lloyd of Caerwys. The first volume, containing the pre-1282 poetry, is still in use (in the form of an excerpt from the 1870 reprint of the whole work) ; it has only in part been replaced by a better text of some of the " Poets of the Princes " and by a series of scholarly modern editions of the poetry of the " Ancient Books." In fact, only from the " *Myvyrian*," either in the original form or in the 1870 reprint, have students of pre-1282 Welsh poetry, throughout the nineteenth century, been able to acquire a comprehensive (however imperfect) view of its achievements. A projected fourth volume, to contain a considerable collection of the post-1282 *cywydd* poets—Hugh Maurice, for one, had collected much material for it—had to be abandoned. The second and third volumes, of prose, were less satisfactory—they were be-devilled by Iolo Morganwg's fabrications. The three volumes were priced at a guinea each, and no doubt sold rather badly—Dr. John Jones's " eight or ten copies." is of course nonsense. It may be added in passing that the adage *Cerid doeth yr encilion*, " the wise man loves the things of old," which in its imperative form *Cared doeth*, etc. (" let the wise man love ") was adopted as the motto of the Second and Third Cymmrodorion Societies, appears on the half-title of Vol. II of the " *Myvyrian*." The only other *official* publications of the Gwyneddigion Society were the " Chair " poems of its Eisteddfodau, and its periodical *Y Greal*.

The example of Richard Morris, who had given kindly though critical help to the sponsors of *Yr Eurgrawn* in 1770, was followed by the Gwyneddigion, who supplied a good deal of the purely literary matter contained in Morgan John Rhys's short-lived *Cylchgrawn Cyn-mraeg* (1793-4), and even more of the contents of David Davies's *Geirgrawn* (1796)—indeed, the wordy warfare between Edward Charles and John Jones of Glan-y-gors concerning Glan-y-gors's political views was fought out on its pages. So also, the *Cambrian Register* (1796, 1799, 1818) and J. H. Parry's *Cambro-Briton* (1819-22) printed contributions by the leading Gwyneddigion. But *Y Greal* (nine numbers, 1805-7) is a different matter. It was *officially* published, jointly, by the Gwyneddigion and the Cymreigyddion, through a Committee on which the former Society was represented by Pughe (editor) and Humphrey Parry (*ca.* 1772-1809, of Clynnog Fawr ; he kept a grammar-school in Hackney), and the latter by Thomas Jones (Bardd Cloff) and Glan-y-gors—all four were members of *both* Societies. We have already seen that Pughe's insistence (backed by Owain Myfyr) on his spelling caused trouble between the Societies ; the Cymreigyddion quite rightly held that the common man would not abide Pughe's whims, and Glan-y-gors further complained that the contents of the periodical were too " antique." The Welsh public evidently agreed with him, and sets of *Y Greal* are today much-esteemed rarities.

Another opportunity of supporting the press in Wales was seized by the Gwyneddigion when in 1814 Joseph Harris ("Gomer"; 1773-1825), Baptist Minister at Swansea, began to publish *Seren Gomer*, the first Welsh newspaper, changed later into a monthly. They gave it their active support, both before and after Harris's death, and his successors in the editor-ship were honorary members of the Gwyneddigion. As a result, *Seren Gomer* gave much space to the activities of all the London-Welsh Societies, and is indeed our chief printed source for their history in the years following the publication of Leathart's book.

We have from time to time caught glimpses of the political and religious opinions of the leading Gwyneddigion. Both sets of opinions have a common origin—the London-Welshman's *nostalgia*. These men had left Wales, yet they loved it. On the one hand, they deemed that the pattern of Welsh life which had flourished in their young days, and which they now viewed from a distance which lent enchantment to it, had been ruined by a "kill-joy" Methodism—which in any case their free-and-easy life in Town would have made repugnant to them. And on the other hand, most of them had been forced to leave their native land because they could not live in it—because of economic distress, or at least of lack of opportunity for advancement in life. They felt a sense of social injustice ; what was more (to do them credit), they felt that the home-keeping Welshmen who had not (as they had) escaped from this bondage should be encouraged to strive for betterment. And here again, the ferment of political Radicalism in London had worked within them—London was full of "left-wing" Associations, and London Welshmen were found in their ranks. Pughe, for example, bewailed the arrest of Horne Tooke and his friends in 1794 ; when they were released, many Welshmen were at the "celebration" dinner at the "Crown and Anchor," and Iolo Morganwg was asked to produce a song for the occasion.

Two of the Gwyneddigion in particular strove (in vain) to awaken the home-keeping Welshman to the need for political and social reform. John Jones of Glan-y-gors published in 1795 *Seren tan gwmmwl*, and in 1797 *Toriad y Dydd* ; and Thomas Roberts of Llwyn'rhudol, in 1798, *Cŵyn yn erbyn Gorthrymder.*

These little pamphlets may seem paradoxically " out of character." One would have expected the satirical inn-keeper's two pamphlets to be " homespun " in appeal and illustration, and the more sophisticated and wealthy Quaker's to be more concerned with abstract principles. On the contrary, John Jones just paraphrases Tom Paine, and deals in generalities, while Thomas Roberts attacks what he considers the specific evils of Wales itself—Methodism, Church Establishment, Tithe, swindling apothecaries and pettifogging lawyers (himself a lawyer's son, and quite possibly a former lawyer himself !), and above all the English administration of the Law in Welsh Wales. The three pamphlets were " born out of time," and their only effect was to give the Gwyneddigion a bad name in a conservative Wales which the 1797 French landing at Fishguard not unnaturally frightened out of any dallyings with " revolution " and whose Methodists promptly dubbed Glan-y-gors an " atheist."

For the Gwyneddigion, like the Cymmrodorion, were anti-Methodist. There were, indeed, Dissenters among them, but these (like M. J. Rhys and David Davies in Wales whose periodicals they had encouraged) were " left-wing," and had a rooted dislike of Methodist " enthusiasm." Nor did the Welsh Methodists take their strictures lying down. Iolo Morganwg, writing to Pughe from North Wales in 1799, picturesquely tells him that " North Wales is now as Methodist-ical as South Wales, and South Wales as Hell "—Iolo was a Unitarian. Owen Myfyr himself was reputed by the Methodists and other Tories to have egged on M. J. Rhys and David Davies for political purposes. Later, we are told that " some gentlemen and clergymen of Wales " regarded the *Myvyrian Archaiology* itself as a mere device for " publishing democratic stuff under the fictitious title of the works of the Ancient Bards " ! To return to Iolo : he tells Pughe that " Huw Maurice, Glan-y-gors, and Sierlyn [Edward Charles] are now considered 10,000 times worse than Tom Paine—and all this," he adds, " on the word of Ginshop Jones " at the Methodist Association at Bala.

Poor " Ginshop Jones "—Edward Jones, to put it more politely—was soon to deliver himself into the hands of the enemy ; and indeed not in him could the Gwyneddigion have seen Methodism at its best. He was a Llansannan man, who had at one time been a trooper in the Life Guards but had afterwards set up as an inn-keeper, and later as a "rum and brandy merchant." An early convert to Methodism, he attached himself to Whitefield's Tabernacle ; then began "exhorting" among the London-Welsh (without abandoning his spirituous trade), and was one of the two founders of what is today the Jewin C. M. Church. In 1785, he had built his flock a meeting-house in Wilderness Row (off Clerkenwell Road), of which he was the unofficial pastor (but unordained—the Methodists did not ordain ministers till 1811). In or about 1800, he was injudicious enough to incur an action for breach of promise of marriage—he married a wealthy widow of 63 (about his own age), having previously engaged himself to a Miss Gwen Prydderch, a young Denbighshire lady of 28, daughter of a former sheriff of Carmarthenshire. The case was tried before the Lord Chief Justice, Lord Kenyon (appropriately enough another Denbighshire man !), in January, 1801; Edward Jones had to pay £50 damages. The opportunity for Gwyneddigion vengeance was too good to be missed. The blow did not indeed ostensibly come from the Gwyneddigion, but from the Cymreigyddion—the right hand took care not to know what the left hand did. Glan-y-gors composed a ribald ballad, " *Gwenno Bach*," in which poor Edward Jones is made to cite some of the less edifying amatory exploits of Old Testament notabilities ; this was received with shouts of joy at a Cymreigyddion meeting—the collected volume of Glan-y-gors's verse omits all but one of its eight stanzas ! And in March, the Cymreigyddion published 1,000 copies of a 24-page booklet containing a full account of the trial, and including the unhappy Jones's love-letters (read out in court), with Glan-y-gors's ballad as an appendix.

A modern Welsh Calvinistic Methodist will waste no sympathy on this worthy Stiggins. For his tyranny was soon to come near wrecking Welsh Methodism in London. Holding as he did the trust-deeds of the chapel, he turned his protesting congregation out of it ; Methodist leaders of unimpeachable Toryism (men who loathed the Gwyneddigion) had to come up from Wales time after time to try to bring him to reason ; not till 1806 was he forced to surrender the chapel and (in the words of a Methodist writer) " to retire, snarling." And though London-Welsh Methodism was for some time to come to continue anti-Radical, changes of temperament (on both sides) brought peace between it and the Gwyneddigion (and Cymreig-yddion) ; Hugh Hughes ("the Welsh Artist") and Thomas Edwards ("Caerfallwch," the lexicographer), members of the Gwyneddigion Society, were indeed expelled from Jewin in 1829 for their Radicalism, but in 1833 the Methodist poet Robert Owen ("Eryron Gwyllt Walia") who was, in long years to come, to become an ordained minister, was the official "Bard" of the Gwyneddigion Society. James Hughes, the minister of Jewin who took the drastic action of 1829, had no quarrel with literature, and was indeed one of the active supporters of the Second Cymmrodorion ; and London-Welsh ministers, of the Methodist as of other denominations, have figured quite prominently among the later Cymmrodorion.

The political views of the early Gwyneddigion tinged, at first, what may well be regarded as the Society's second main contribution to the life of Wales—the rehabilitation of the Eisteddfod. Had not Owain Myfyr declared in 1789 that "Liberty in Church and State is the aim of this Society" ?—and with his rather "single-track" mind, it seemed to him perfectly right that the newly-restored Eisteddfod should be a form of propaganda for political Radicalism. His opportunity came in 1789, when Thomas Jones of Clocaenog, an exciseman then stationed at Corwen, resolved to promote, in the May of that year, an *eisteddfod*, that is, a gathering of bards, of the type (held usually in taverns) which during the eighteenth century had replaced the then defunct mediaeval and Tudor "professional" eisteddfodau whose function had been the regulation of admission into the closed corporation of officially-recognised bards and musicians. Wishing to "do the thing well," Thomas Jones wrote up to the Gwyneddigion for advice—we note, once more, how a London-Welsh Society had come to be regarded *in Wales* as an "authority" on Welsh literary matters—and Pughe, as Secretary, sent him a lengthy reply, which included an offer of a "chair" and medals, and made the important suggestion that the chief prize should be given, not, as in the "tavern" eisteddfodau, for *englynion*, but for a "heroic" poem. When the Corwen eisteddfod came to be held, the adjudicators of the "chair" competition disagreed, and the compositions were all sent up to London for the verdict of the Gwyneddigion Society—in October, the Society (i.e., quite certainly Owain Myfyr himself) awarded the Chair to Gwallter

Mechain, though all men now agree that Twm o'r Nant should have had it. It was in this indirect way that the Gwyneddigion came to take a hand in eisteddfodau in Wales.

The Society now took a further step—of promoting eisteddfodau in its *own* name, under its own entire control, and at its own expense—i.e., at Owain Myfyr's. From September, 1789 (at Bala), for a series of subsequent years, it did so, and thus set the pattern for what was eventually to become the National Eisteddfod of Wales. And although this particular run of eisteddfodau were all held in North Wales, it is fair to Owain Myfyr to record that even as early as 1789 he looked forward to extending the reorganised eisteddfod to South Wales as well. However, here we have the *pattern* with which we are so familiar : a *single* " authorised " eisteddfod annually, with notice given, a year in advance, of place and of programme; the association of the Chair with the *awdl* ; the submission of competitive efforts pseudonymously to a panel of adjudicators (however much in fact Owain Myfyr may have " rigged " the adjudication) ; the *central* controlling authority. The subjects set for competition, as has been hinted, were mainly of Owain Myfyr's choice : in 1790 (at S. Asaph) the main subject was " Liberty "— the Chair was awarded to David Thomas (1760 ? —1822), a most important figure in the bardic tradition of North Wales, and the master of a whole school of disciples ; the medal for the essay in prose went to Gwallter Mechain. But this political bias was not to continue—the outbreak of war naturally made a difference. And in fact, these Gwyneddigion eisteddfodau are important mainly as *patterns*. At the time, they were not over-successful. At Bala, in 1789, it proved impossible to get the assembled bards (there were not many of them) to settle down, as Pughe had hoped, to technical discussions on the Art of Poetry—they could not shake off the free-and-easy eighteenth century conception of the " tavern " eisteddfod ; and the " tempestuous weather " kept them indoors *in* the taverns. The hopeful idea of selling copies of the new *Dafydd ap Gwilym* proved a complete fiasco, much to Owain Myfyr's wrath. With the public, the only thing that " went down " well was an interlude, " presented " by Twm o'r Nant in person. The 1793 eisteddfod at Bala was an even more complete failure—good Thomas Jones the exciseman judged that it had been " folly to hold it there, among the [Methodist] saints." The new Eisteddfod needed some considerable time to get over its growing-pains.

It may have been noted that nothing has been said of "Gorsedd y Beirdd." In truth, that institution was known neither to the mediaeval "professional" eisteddfodau nor to the tavern-eisteddfodau nor to the Gwyneddigion Eisteddfodau. For Iolo Morganwg had not yet invented it. The growth of the idea in his fertile brain could be traced, step by step, if space allowed. But it was on June 21st, 1792, and on Primrose Hill, that Iolo set up "the Throne of the Bards of the Isle of Britain," aided and abetted by Pughe, David Samwel, Bardd Cloff, and Bardd y Brenin, whom he solemnly initiated, to their great pride. One wonders why Owain Myfyr (who surely deserved Gorsedd honours !) was absent—was he perchance sceptical ? And further, why has Leathart not a word to say about this historic event ? At any rate, the Gorsedd was not grafted on to the Eisteddfod till 1819.

The Gwyneddigion Society was not uninterruptedly prosperous throughout its long career. In 1800-1, says Leathart, it was "visibly on the decline, through a bad attendance of members " ; in 1801, the leaders, "disgusted with such unbecoming apathy, had almost resolved to abandon the Society " ; Leathart further comments on the "discouragement of penillion-singing "—his own hobby—"to make room for speeches or matters of less importance " ; were these, one wonders, political speeches ? It is indeed hard not to feel that the vivacity—the brio—which had signalised the initial years of the Gwyneddigion, was ebbing by 1800. However, "it was decided to keep on." But by 1827, again, Leathart has to report that "little business had been transacted in the last three or four years," and to speak of "the disgrace of still existing, yet doing nothing." In 1830, he notes that members in the old days of the Society (which, by the way, he knew only from Pughe's reminiscences) "were better acquainted with each other ; they are now more numerous and more dispersed ; the meetings are consequently less social than they were, forty or fifty years ago." Leathart as Secretary did his best, but is it unkind to hint that he was not quite the man to start a revival ?—efficient, but staid and formal, as he seems from his book to have been. Then again, one cannot help noticing the increase of "social consideration" apparent in the last two pages of Leathart's membership-list. Have we here a repetition of the old tale of 1770 ? Did the Cymreigyddion sap the ground from beneath the Gwyneddigion, as the Gwyneddigion had formerly (and equally unintentionally) undermined the Cymmrodorion—and for somewhat similar reasons ? Mr. Robert Owen holds that the two societies had become to all practical purposes amalgamated, in the middle 1830's. Certainly, in 1837 a writer in *Seren Gomer* alleges that the Gwyneddigion Society as such was " dying of dissension " ; though it seems not to have formally expired before 1843— the very year in which the Second Cymmrodorion Society too, as we shall see in the next chapter, came to an end.

It is hard not to believe that one very important reason for the decline of the Gwyneddigion was the *multiplication* of London-Welsh Societies—societies which in the very nature of things drew upon the same personnel (amplified though that was as time went on), and " splintered " its interests and energies. Professor G. J. Williams has pointed out how very busy a keen London-Welshman must have been, in the heyday of these societies : Monday night, once a month, at the Gwyneddigion ; *every* Thursday at the Cymreigyddion ; *every* Saturday at the Caradogion—and if you were on the Council or Committee of one or the other, you had more meetings ; all this on top of the nightly " dropping-in " into the " Bull " or some other house of call !

The first-established of these Societies (about 1790—in the turmoil caused by the French Revolution) was the Caradogion Society, which had English-speaking as well as Welsh members. Most of the Gwyneddigion belonged to it ; Leathart tells us that " it was, in fact, an off-shoot of [the Gwyneddigion], a branch of it." It was a debating-society ; and its debates were naturally held in *English*. It met every Saturday night at the " Bull," in that upper room in which the *Council* of the Gwyneddigion met, and around that mahogany table of which we have already heard. Indeed, this table, called by David Samwel " Arthur's Board," at first suggested " The Arthurian Society " as a name for the new Society, but the half-mythical Arthur was replaced by the not-so-very-much less mythical Caratâcus, whose portrait, " addressing the Roman emperor," was hung on the wall of the room. The " debates " can hardly have been other than political, though on one occasion, in 1791, unhappy English members of the Society became involved, with the Gwyneddigion leaders, in the heated " Welsh-Indian " controversy, with results celebrated in verse by David Samwel ; according to him, men fled in terror from the fray :

> So seeking out the various holes,
> Alleys, and lanes, of London,
> Routed Caradogs ran in shoals,
> Like damnèd spirits undone.

One of the drawbacks of debating in English in London, in time of war, is that the police may overhear you or hear of you.   On one occasion, the constables entered, and impounded the Caradogion Society's books and papers, but " nothing more was heard of the matter."   Some of the Society must have taken fright, for in 1797, in a discussion of the (1795) " Treason and Sedition Acts," a prudent two-thirds of the members (including the bellicose David Samwel) supported the Acts— Owain Myfyr, one observes, spoke and voted with the minority. We hear nothing of the Caradogion after 1798.

Very much more important was the Cymreigyddion Society, frequently mentioned already.   According to Leathart, it was founded in 1795 ; but Edward Charles speaks of a meeting on November 19th, 1794.   It was founded by twelve men, most if not all of them members of the Gwyneddigion ; the best known are John Jones of Glan-y-gors and Thomas Roberts of Llwyn'rhudol—by 1831, Thomas Roberts was the sole surviving founder. Its Rules, it seems probable, were settled in 1797, printed in 1798, and revised in 1810 and 1827 ; they are known to us only from a reprint of the 1827 Rules.   The declared aims of the Society were " to increase good-fellowship, and to maintain the Welsh language pure and undefiled, to the best of their ability, by holding debate on substantial and moral topics, and promoting the development of mental powers ; always avoiding, however, such topics as promote theological or political argument."   We have, as has been said, only the 1827 version of the Rules, and the wording does rather suggest the solemn earnestness of Welshmen (including London-Welshmen) of that period—we may readily agree with Professor G. J. Williams in wondering whether in 1794 the scope of debate would have been limited to non-political or even to non-theological subjects ; indeed, we shall have to note evidence to the contrary.   But, especially in view of Leathart's statement that debating had "fallen into disuse" among the parent Gwyneddigion, we can feel little doubt that debating was the *differentia* of the Cymreigyddion.

There was no subscription—only an entrance-fee of half-a-crown ; but there were fines for absence, fines for being late, a three-halfpenny levy per head, at each meeting, for tobacco, and a fine of a shilling for "smoking without paying" ; it is to be presumed that each man paid for his drink when he called for it. Meetings were on every Thursday night, apparently at seven o'clock. The tale of the wanderings of the Cymreigyddion is complicated, and can be only hazardously elicited from references in their minutes down to 1826, and afterwards from *Seren Gomer*. In 1794, Edward Charles locates them at the "Seven Stars" in the Borough. Then we find them at the "Cambrian Arms" in Silver Street (which also for a short time housed the Gwyneddigion) ; the "Horns" at Kennington is also mentioned—possibly occasional suburban junketings, similar to those of the Gwyneddigion, were held there. In 1811, they were at the "Queen's Arms" by S. Paul's (the last home of the old Cymmrodorion), where they spent £25 on "improving" their room. In 1815, they moved to the "Golden Fleece" in Queen Street, Cheapside, which they left in October, 1818, for Glan-y-gors's "King's Head," but afterwards returned to it. Afterwards came the "Red Lion" in Basing Lane ; the "Southwark Bridge" in Queen Street, Cheapside (landlord, R. Evans) ; the "Salutation" in Newgate Street ; the "Three Tuns" in Coleman Street (1828-30) ; the "Crown" in Bow Lane (1830-1) ; the "Owen Glyndwr" in Aldersgate Street (1831-9—it will be remembered that the Gwyneddigion also met there in those years) ; "Old Parr's" in the same street (1840) ; and finally the "Green Dragon" in Fore Street, where the Society ran its course out.

Their register and minute-book, untidy and badly blotted, strengthens the impression left on us by their very modest entrance fee, that the Cymreigyddion were a more "democratic" body—the Welsh adjective *gwerinol* fits better—than the Gwyneddigion. And it will not be out of place to observe here, in passing, that when Welsh literary Societies began to spring up all over Wales itself, in the first quarter of the nine-teenth century, they almost invariably called themselves

" *Cymreigyddion* "—in all probability in conscious imitation ;
the use of " Cym(m)rodorion " is much later, and mostly
confined to the larger towns. Yet, Gwyneddigion must have
formed a large part of the Cymreigyddion Society, very well-
known Gwyneddigion too, like Glan-y-gors, Thomas Roberts,
Thomas Morris ("Morcyn" to his fellow-Gwyneddigion ;
a Wrexham man and a great wit), Daniel and Peter Davies of
Corwen, Hugh Maurice, Humphrey Parry of Clynnog, William
Jones (" Wil Môn," one of Ned Môn's two brothers), Edward
Charles, Iolo Morganwg. Pughe was a " visitor " at a meeting
in 1827. Members were elected after a week's notice ; the
" Initiation Song " celebrated Madog's voyage to America—
this Society had no doubts upon that matter !

While, as we have seen, the specific object of the Cymreigyddion Society was the holding of *debates*, we have taken leave
to doubt whether the rather portentous wording of its Rules,
in the 1827 form in which we know them, really reflects
the spirit of the founders in 1794. We may indeed think it
conceivable that Thomas Roberts should talk of " substantial
and moral topics " and of " developing the moral powers,"
but it seems odd language for John Jones of Glan-y-gors ; and
neither of these Radical pamphleteers seems at all likely to have
insisted, in 1794, on eschewing political or religious controversy. Professor G. J. Williams indeed goes so far as to
tack the adjectives " Bohemian " and " irresponsible " on to
the Cymreigyddion. And for that matter, it is obvious from
their records that " cheerfulness would keep breaking in."
Indeed, " *crashing* in " would better fit Edward Charles's
account of a meeting in 1794, when one David Evan " came in
drunk, and staggered around the room drinking people's beer,
setting the empty pots down before them and bidding them call
for more, wasting much tobacco and working havoc among the
[churchwarden] pipes, making horrible grimaces," etc., for
which he was duly " arraigned before the President, John
Jones of Glan-y-gors." And we have noted that it was the
Cymreigyddion, not the more " serious " Gwyneddigion, who
took in hand the condign punishment of " Ginshop Jones "—
this booklet, by the way was their only *separate* " publication."
There was certainly singing, and in 1810, the Society decided
to keep a harpist ; a minute records " good singing to the harp—
five of the best singers in London." Charitable aid was freely

given—as much as £20 in nine months during 1818. We note with amusement that Richard Robert Jones, far better known as " Dic Aberdaron," became a member, but that very soon afterwards money was collected to send him back to Wales.

Yet there *were* debates ; the subjects are noted in the minutes. In April, 1802, for instance, there was a furious argument, " for four nights running " (four weeks ?) on the question " are the people called Quakers nearer the Apostolic Church than are the other religious folk of today ? " Glan-y-gors (according to his own account of the debate) " tore the Quakers to tatters, asserting that scripture forbids women to speak at Church meetings, and that Quakers are snakes in the grass, etc. Thereupon Thomas Roberts clean lost his temper, and in an angry speech, quivering with rage, asserted that Glan-y-gors was a weapon of the Devil's to destroy all religion— and that he had succeeded only too well." This hardly seems like " avoiding theological . . . . . argument." Indeed, the 1827 wording of the Rules may have been the result of an attack upon the Cymreigyddion, in that very year, by clerical writers in *Y Gwyliedydd*, who accused them of " dicing " (the context rather suggests that dice were in fact used as a form of " black-ball " at elections of members), of chauvinism, and of irreligion. The members must have taken serious note of these charges, for in 1828 there is a long letter in *Seren Gomer* setting forth the aims of the Society as the use of Welsh, the practice of charity, and the holding of debates " on philosophical subjects, but not on theology or politics."

In 1829, we hear for the first time of *lectures*, on astronomy, navigation, etc. ; later, on money, mining, geography, temperance, acoustics, hydrostatics, and what not. Among the lecturers we notice the names of Hugh Hughes of Conway (" the Welsh Artist ") and of Griffith Davies, F.R.S., the mathematician and actuary. The ban on politics proved short-lived, for in 1832 we have a lecture on " Nonconformity in Wales "— an uneasy note added to the report explains that the Society was not responsible for the lecturer's opinions. In the same year (that of the Reform Bill), the Welsh voter is exhorted to use his vote to demand improvements for Wales ; and Caerfallwch, lecturing on the National Debt, made a fiery attack upon the Royal Family. Not unnaturally, clerical and conservative writers in *Y Gwyliedydd* resumed their attacks upon the Society as a "political club"; and Griffith Davies, a sober-sided Methodist who held to his Connexion's traditional "non-interference" in politics, quitted the Society. It is as certain as can be that Thomas Roberts of Llwyn'rhudol was behind this Radical trend, which became stronger in the following years. Yet the Society's programme continued to give large place to the Welsh language and its literature ; eisteddfodau, too, were frequently held—in chapels now, not in taverns.

The Cymreigyddion, indeed, were clearly becoming more seriously-minded—more "respectable," if you will. An attempt, in 1840, to prohibit *smoking* at meetings, as a "degrading" habit, was defeated by only one vote—Thomas Roberts withstood it, pleading that the object of the Society was the maintenance of the Welsh language and *of the Welsh way of life*—which included smoking ! Thomas Roberts, that pillar of our ancient liberties (smoking included) died in 1841. It becomes fairly clear that the considerable increase of Welsh Nonconformity in London was modifying the whole tone of London-Welsh life. Men were still keen enough on their language, interested enough in its literature and song, sedulous at eisteddfodau (though they now held these in chapels) ; *here* lies the element of continuity in London-Welsh life, from the days of Richard Morris and of Owain Myfyr to our own. But there were new interests. There was politics. And there was the church or chapel, making increasing (and natural) demands upon the time and energies of a loyal member.

To us today, who have learnt once more to appreciate the Wales (and the "London-Wales") of the eighteenth century, these London-Welshmen of the 1820-50 period may seem uninteresting when compared with their forbears—with Owain Myfyr in his bar-parlour at the "Bull," with leg-pulling Siôn Ceiriog, with mischievous Ned Môn, with sparkling Glan-y-gors, in the days when there were cakes and ale, and ginger was hot in the mouth. But in truth, we have in these last few pages been beholding a very important development in the life of the Welsh people. Two powerful forces had seemed in the latter half of the eighteenth century to be bent on a head-on collision : the old Welsh literary and musical tradition, and the new Welsh Methodist movement, which had by 1800 permeated the older Dissent too in Wales. Hearken to Howel Harris (and for that matter to Griffith Jones of Llanddowror before him), and you will snap your fiddle across your knee, call damnation upon ballad and interlude, regard the four-and-twenty metres as godless waste of time, look upon dancing and cards as inventions of the devil. Hearken to others, and you will deem religion a kill-joy, and drunkenness a sure proof of poetic genius. Was either side to have it all its own way ? The one would have flung our whole cultural tradition away ; the other would have left us with an undisciplined and irresponsible populace, blind to larger issues, incapable of political thought and indeed of sustained thought in general.

A compromise was reached—compromises, to be sure, are not completely satisfactory. Though the older literary culture was still for some time to be primarily supported by some of the clergy of a Church which in that particular epoch seemed to be rather in a backwater of our national life (the next chapter will have much to say of these), changes were coming : the Methodist—even the Methodist preacher—was imperceptibly being encouraged to follow a submerged instinct, to move on from stringing pious elegies to shaping verse of higher excellence on older patterns and on themes not so obviously " religious." We were moving towards a day in which prominent Nonconformist ministers and laymen were to be conspicuous figures in our literature and even in our antiquarian studies—it was a Baptist minister who was in 1864 to reprint Rhys Jones's *Gorchestion Beirdd Cymru* and in 1872 to reprint the Gwyneddigion *Dafydd ap Gwilym* ; it was an Independent layman who in 1870 reprinted the *Myvyrian Archaiology* ; it was a Methodist printer who ventured in 1872 to reissue (Latin and all) the *Specimens of Antient Welsh Poetry* of that violent anti-Methodist Evan Evans. Not in the wildest flights of their fancy could the Morrises or Owain Myfyr have conceived that such things could be possible. And after all, these serious be-lectured London-Welshmen who had qualms about smoking may claim our interest and respect as participants in the painful (and indeed the confused) working-out of this compromise which was to ensure the survival, in however modified a form, of that older Welsh tradition which was so near to the heart of the Morrises of Anglesey in 1751.

Yet, the Cymreigyddion Society was evidently flagging. Perhaps the last hope of reviving the ancient *brio* came with the advent in 1843 of " Talhaiarn " (John Jones, 1810-69), the whimsical architect-poet (manager for Paxton) who would have been so perfectly at home amid the conviviality and " ragging " of the older Gwyneddigion and of the earliest Cymreigyddion. Born at the " Harp " in Llanfair Talhaearn (where Ieuan Fardd had been curate in 1761-5), he had hitherto contented himself mostly by translating English verse into Welsh ; and it was in London and among the Cymreigyddion that (as he puts it), he " began seriously to write poetry "—to do him justice, he promptly adds " did I say *seriously ?* but hang me if anyone knows when I *am* serious ; I'm sure *I* don't ! " In fact, he never bothered much with the " strict " metres ; we know him primarily as a song-writer and a hitter-off of amusing or satirical verse. Still, there he was, and it is through his reminiscences that we catch our last glimpse of the London Cymreigyddion Society. One of his chief friends there, " when we tippled together in the *Green Dragon*," was " Twrog " (O. W. Thomas), who once informed Talhaiarn that " poetry springs from indigestion ; for no happy man ever took to writing poetry." Another was " Gwrgant " (William Jones, 1803-86), a London-Welsh solicitor from Montgomeryshire, a dabbler in literature who perhaps interests us more as having been a member not only of the Cymreigyddion but also of the Second and Third Cymmrodorion ; his name will recur in the ensuing chapters.

Talhaiarn has a not very good quasi-dramatic sketch, in English, *The last Dying Speech and Confession* of that " garrulous, querulous old dame " the Cymreigyddion Society. The old lady, now " in her sixtieth year " (1794-1854), complains of her neglect by her " children "—" Tal, Twrog, Gwrgant," and the rest. Once upon a time, " all the Welshmen in London were in love with me ; . . . I was petted by that wonderfully witty poet Glan-y-gors, and by the learned Doctor W. Owen Pughe, and by Owain Myfyr, John Humffreys Parry, Bardd Môn, Llwyn'rhudol, and a host of others." Her nurse tartly reminds her that all her " children " were forever " tippling, smoking, and gabbling like a lot of geese." But the dying woman rambles on : where were " my chief officer, Meredydd " and others ? " Meredydd " was William Meredith of Barmouth, who had been at one time secretary of the Welsh Charity-School in Gray's-Inn Road ; let us note what the old lady has to say about him : " he used to be kind to me, but he ruled my children with a rod of iron ; he would insist upon their being sober, sedate, and moral ; but the poor bairns got a distaste for me under his adamantine rule." *There*, one feels, is the explanation of the end. "Tal" (who had been President in 1849) did turn up to comfort the poor old dame, but in a few moments " her spirit had flown with a murmur . . . to join the ghosts of Cymmrodorion and Gwyneddigion Societies." This was printed in 1855. When in 1858 a correspondent asked for information about the society, his letter brought no reply.

There were even then, and there had been from time to time, other London-Welsh Societies, mostly serving sectional or regional interests. The Ofyddion, a literary society founded by Pughe in 1794 (and of course called by him " *Ovyzion* ") were to meet on the first Friday in the month, " at Peele's Coffee-house," but their days were brief. The Canorion Society, again, was founded (says Leathart) in 1820 : " it was a convivial Welsh meeting at the *Freemasons' Tavern*, upon the first Saturday in the month, when the members supped, and afterwards proceeded with *penillion* and other singing ; it lasted four or five years." The " Freemasons' Tavern " in Great Queen Street was, as every Cymmrodor will know, to become the *locus originis* of some of the most important Welsh cultural and educational movements in the nineteenth century ; within its walls, for instance, the Second and Third Cymmrodorion Societies were born. The Treasurer and Secretary of the Canorion, throughout its short life, was James Davies of Llandaff, lieutenant in the Hon. Artillery Company ; he was Vice-Treasurer of the Second Cymmrodorion at the time of his death in 1828. We may further name the Gomerian Society of 1822 of Welshmen from Mid and South Wales ; and the Saint David's Society of 1831. But a little more should be said of Undeb Cymry, 1823, for *penillion*-singing. Leathart informs us in 1825 that it had two " Lodges," the first at the " Coach and Horses " in Little-Compton Street, Soho ; the second at the " Lock and Key," West Smithfield (landlord, John Edwards—the house, by the way, was a great resort of Welsh drovers) ; *penillion*-singing could also be had at Morgan Jones's, Basing Lane ; at the " Southwark Bridge " off Cheapside, of which we have already heard ; at the " Bell " in Doctors'-commons (kept by John Jones) ; at Cadwaladr Jones's " Vine " off Tooley Street, Hugh Morris's " Ship " off the Strand, and " David Jones's,

Pickle-herring-stairs, Southwark "—" and," he adds, " at Gwyneddigion meetings." Nothing more would be needed than a mere mention of the Ymofynwyr Cymreigyddawl, of 1829, were it not for the interesting fact that it was a revolt against the Cymreigyddion—a protest of the more puritannically-minded against that Society's meeting in taverns and admitting " Deists and Atheists " into its membership.

When the Cymreigyddion Society expired, London Welshmen were left, for the first time since 1751, without a dominant and *general* Society (as distinguished from sectional societies) to bring them together. From 1751, there had always been one, and from 1770 two or at times three or more such societies. Clearly, however much we may discount Leathart's " 60,000 Welshpeople " (even if we reduce it to 12,000 Welsh *men*) in London, the Societies can have accounted for no more than a microscopic fraction of them, But it was a fraction composed of (or at least including) men who *mattered*, so to speak, in the preservation and enhancement of the Welsh tradition, not only in London but also in Wales. There was, as has often been said already, no comparable body in Wales itself which could have assumed leadership, in the eighteenth century and the early nineteenth, or whose leadership would have been accepted if it had been assumed. And though there will now be a gap of some twenty years before the Third Cymmrodorion Society comes on the scene, it is significant that even then Wales—though vastly transformed, though possessing by that time religious, political, educational, and literary figures of great distinction—did not yet feel that it could dispense with the co-ordinating and guiding hand of patriotic Welshmen in London.

V.—THE SECOND CYMMRODORION SOCIETY

THE re-establishment of the Cymmrodorion Society was directly due to the rise and growth of the Cambrian Societies and to the Eisteddfodau held under their patronage, and it is as part of this activity in Wales that the achievements and failures of the Second Cymmrodorion Society must be assessed.

The formation of the Cambrian Societies and the founding of the Eisteddfod in its modern form can be traced to the activities of a group of Welsh clergymen in the second decade of the nineteenth century. They cannot be called great poets or great scholars, but they were zealous, sincere Welshmen who endeavoured to promote the Welsh language among all classes in Wales, and especially among the nobility, who since Tudor times had gradually turned their backs on the native tongue. These clerical literati sought through Societies and Eisteddfodau to win back their allegiance, and hoped that the Welsh language, which had once been the language of princes and poets, would once again be spoken and cherished by the descendants of those princes.

The most famous member of this clerical group was the Rev. Walter Davies (1761-1849) of Manafon in Montgomery, who was known by the bardic name of Gwallter Mechain, being a native of Llanfechain in that county. He was a prolific writer, and his works show knowledge of poetry, antiquities and philology ; evidence of his wide and varied interests and of his large circle of correspondents may be found in the Crosswood MSS. deposited in the National Library at Aberystwyth. Walter Davies won the Gwyneddigion Medal at their first Eisteddfod in 1789, and during the subsequent years won so many medals that the Society (of which he was elected a corresponding member as early as 1790) deemed it necessary to ask him to refrain from competing. He was held in great esteem by his contemporaries—a more critical age today regards his work as mediocre—and he exercised considerable influence on the literary ideas of his fellow-clergymen.

Two of these clergymen—the Rev. W. J. Rees (1772-1855) of Cascob in Radnorshire, and the Rev. John Jenkins (1770-1829) of Kerry in Montgomeryshire,—worked out the details of the Cambrian Societies. Jenkins (usually referred to as Ifor Ceri), was a keen Eisteddfodwr, and a patron of the poets, but confessed himself "a complete ignoramus" on literary matters, and continually turned to Walter Davies for advice. Rees, who also was on intimate terms with Davies for over fifty years, was of a more literary turn of mind ; he contributed regularly to the periodicals of his day and played a prominent part in the establishment of the Welsh MSS. Society. Among his publications are the *Lives of the Cambro-British Saints* and the *Liber Landavensis*—a work begun by his nephew, Professor Rice Rees of S. David's College, Lampeter. These two friends worked in close collaboration over a period of years, as may be seen from their letters (preserved in the Crosswood MSS. already mentioned, and in the Tonn MSS. at Cardiff Central Library), and when Jenkins died, Rees remarked sorrowfully— "I feel as if I had lost my right hand." Rees was present at the formation of all four Cambrian Societies in Wales, and spent six weeks in London helping to resuscitate the Cymmrodorion Society, and the officials of all these Societies received from him constant guidance, counsel and encouragement. The credit, however, for originally suggesting the formation of the Cambrian Societies goes to the Rev. David Rowland (1783-1820), curate of Carmarthen, who plays but a fleeting part in this story, as he died shortly after the first Eisteddfod held under the auspices of the Cambrian Societies.

The Rev. Thomas Richards of Darowen, who succeeded to the curacy at Llanymawddwy vacated by Thomas Charles of Bala when the latter became a Methodist, corresponded with Walter Davies on antiquarian topics. Of Richards's five sons, who were all incumbents in Montgomeryshire, two were intimately connected with this circle. The elder of the two, David Richards (1783-1826 ; Dewi Silin), took a leading part in the formation of the Eisteddfodau in North Wales and was Secretary of the Wrexham Eisteddfod in 1820. He does not appear to have been a very efficient secretary—W. J. Rees in one letter complains that "Mr. Richards is so indolent that nothing material can be trusted to be done by him," and in a subsequent letter, states that the delay of the report of the

Eisteddfod was due solely " to the incompatible and impracticable indolence of the Secretary, which his worthy brother of Berriew has endeavoured to the utmost to remedy." This brother was Thomas Richards (1787-1856), who had been licensed by the Bishop of St. Asaph to the free school of Berriw, Montgomery (an old institution established in 1655). He had among his pupils the Rev. Evan Evans (Ieuan Glan Geirionydd) and the Rev. John Blackwell (Alun), who spoke highly of his work as a schoolmaster. Thomas Richards was also closely identified with the Welsh magazines which appeared at this time.

Another clergyman-schoolmaster who associated himself with the movement was the Rev. Eliezer Williams (1754-1820), the eldest son of the Rev. Peter Williams, the Biblical annotator. He was appointed to the living of Lampeter in 1805, and opened a Grammar School, which at once became a formidable rival to the more famous Grammar School at Ystrad Meurig. It is said that in those early days more clergymen were educated in Lampeter School than in any other school in Wales, not even excepting Ystrad Meurig itself, and the prosperous condition of the school helped materially to decide in favour of Lampeter as the home of S. David's College. Eliezer Williams was a student of literature and antiquities, and wrote extensively on those topics. His works were published by his son, who states that the great eighteenth century scholar, Evan Evans (Ieuan Fardd) helped and influenced his father in the study of the Welsh language—" The Rev. Evan Evans was in the habit of frequently visiting Gelly, the residence of my grandfather, and with him our young student formed an intimate acquaintance. In investigating the structures of his native tongue, and in learning to feel and estimate its beauties, he was materially assisted by Mr. Evans' extensive and familiar knowledge of Welsh literature, as well as by his taste and eloquence of mind."

A rare and notable figure among the women of her day was Angharad Llwyd (1780-1866), another member of this circle. She inherited her literary talents from her father, the Rev. John Lloyd of Caerwys, who accompanied Pennant on his tours through Wales. Angharad Llwyd was a zealous transcriber of MSS., and a competitor in the Eisteddfodau; her essay on the history of Anglesey was awarded the silver medal at the Beaumaris Eisteddfod in 1832, and was published.

Archdeacon Thomas Beynon (1744-1833), the oldest member of the circle, generously encouraged the publication of Welsh books, and was largely instrumental in having the Welsh language included in the curriculum of the S. David's College, Lampeter, towards which foundation he made a substantial monetary contribution. Some of our modern poets would have welcomed the Archdeacon's championship of blank verse and would have applauded his demand for abolishing the twenty-four metres, although they would hardly agree with his reasons for making the suggestion—" there isn't a good metre among them " was his verdict—and they would surely disagree with his sweeping denunciation of the *Cynghanedd* as " the invention of the barbarous and dark ages " !

This circle was responsible for the establishment of that valuable publication *Y Gwyliedydd* which appeared in 1822. John Jenkins, who was the chief promoter of the project, gives the following reasons for the need of such a publication— " There are at present four magazines published in Welsh by the four sects of Baptists, Methodists, Independents and Wesleyans. It struck me that a publication of Church principles, a more respectable appearance, containing a little of Natural History, Antiquities, etc., with Theology, might have the patronage of the Clergy."

This project and their other literary activities did not receive support from all the clergy, rather indeed they met with considerable opposition from a certain section, who feared dire consequences from a revival of the Welsh language. Letters to this effect appeared in the *Gentleman's Magazine*, the *Salopian Journal* and the *Carmarthen Journal* : they were answered in a very spirited fashion by Walter Davies, and more mildly, but no less effectively, by W. J. Rees, and the private correspondence of this circle abounds in references to the subject. " It is difficult to think too meanly of the dignitaries and wealthy non-residents throughout the Welsh diocese on account of their lethargic apathy," is an opinion frequently expressed in their letters.

This reference to apathetic dignitaries was certainly not applicable to Dr. Thomas Burgess (1756-1837), Bishop of S. David's, who approved and encouraged the activities of this group of literati. He insisted that applicants for incumbencies in his diocese should have a knowledge of the native language, and he emphasised the Celtic aspect of the Church ; two of his publications are concerned with the antiquity of the British Church, and its independence of the Church of Rome. Bishop Burgess also raised the educational standard of the clergy in his diocese ; he licensed new Grammar Schools for their education and was the leading spirit of the movement to establish Lampeter College.

In the correspondence of this circle we find numerous references to meetings called " clerical Eisteddfodau." John Jenkins kept open house during the first week of every year when poets, harpists and singers were welcomed and feted ; and on account of his hospitality he was affectionately referred to as " Ifor Hael o Geri," on an analogy with that more famous Ifor, the " patron " of Dafydd ap Gwilym. The time was spent in singing Welsh songs to the harp, and in composing and reciting poetry. It was at one of these gatherings (in 1818), that David Rowlands, then newly returned from the mission field in Newfoundland, suggested that a poet should be sought to " teach prosody to the clergy." " By that means " he said, " bardism may be revived in South Wales, and a new era formed." He repeated his suggestion in a letter to Jenkins later in the year, and also mentioned the matter to the Bishop of S. David's, who subsequently suggested the formation of Cambrian Societies and the revival of the Eisteddfodau. John Jenkins, in a letter to W. J. Rees, stresses the important part played by Bishop Burgess—" When you speak of the origin of the Cambrian Societies " he said " you ought carefully to avoid taking the credit of it from the Bishop. The subject must be handled with great delicacy indeed. The first suggestion was certainly that of Rowland at Kerry in January, 1818, which he shortly afterwards communicated to the Bishop. No notice was taken of it at the time, but when the Bishop came to Kerry in the following August, he was most intent on a plan of that nature, and in travelling towards the Hay reduced it into form and fixed on the name of the Cambrian Society."

Thus it was Bishop Burgess who inaugurated the Cambrian Societies by improving, as W. J. Rees affirms, " on the original idea, and suggesting the revival of the ancient Welsh Eisteddfodau, and the forming of a Society, whose activities would not only embrace Mr. Rowland's objects, but also other objects, connected with Welsh literature and antiquities." A contemporary writer attributes the Bishop's zeal to his desire to improve the position of the Church. " But it is to the exertions of an Englishman that the present enthusiasm is principally owing. A few years since, the Bishop of S.David perceiving that sectarian preachers from their intimate knowledge of the Welsh language possessed important advantages over the regular clergy, proposed to revive the Bardic congresses, and distributed prizes as an incentive to the study of Welsh." The condition of the Church is described by a writer in the *Cambro-Briton* who comments on the marked decline in Church membership owing to the Anglicising tendencies of the clergy. He speaks of the " evils which arise from neglecting the Welsh in the Church . . . the clergy give part of their services in English . . . and the monoglot Welshmen turn from the English Church and betake themselves to the Chapel."

Although the " foundation of the Cambrian Societies was laid on principles immediately concerned with the origin of the Episcopal Church," according to an Eisteddfod programme preserved in the Crosswood MSS., this did not exclude Non-conformists ; the rules of the Cambrian Societies proclaimed that " All Dissenters from our Church who are natives of the Principality and are distinguished as authors of creditable works of literature and religion may be Honorary members." But the great majority of Nonconformists, intensely and exclusively concerned with religious questions, regarded poetry and song as frivolous vanities to be avoided at all costs, and the clergy of this period emerge as the sole guardians and promoters of Welsh culture. There were two notable exceptions, however, from among the Nonconformists—the Rev. John Hughes (1776-1843), author of *Horae Britannicae* (1817), one of the ministers sent by the Methodist Conference to introduce (Wesleyan) Methodism into North Wales, and Joseph Harris (1773-1825), already mentioned in the preceding chapter.

Joseph Harris as editor of that valuable monthly periodical *Seren Gomer* writes to W. J. Rees—" As you are so closely connected with all the Eisteddfodau we should be particularly grateful to you for sending, or causing to be sent to us an account of all the proceedings . . . And indeed to be plain with you we hardly consider it fair that the first Welsh publication of this kind (i.e. *Seren Gomer*) be so far disregarded by the

Eisteddfodwyr as to be compelled to copy from English publications the account of their proceedings. It may be urged that the Editor is a Dissenter, true, but he is not so in *Seren Gomer*, there he is nothing but a Welshman."

The account of the Carmarthen Eisteddfod of 1819 which he received and published in *Seren Gomer* shows the widely different views held by Dissenters and Churchmen at this time. The editor, writing for a Nonconformist public, testifies that the Eisteddfod had been held in a seemly and highly commendable way ; and that the presence of the harp was not a sign of licentiousness as was generally supposed. Hitherto, the editor adds, his acquaintance with that instrument had been slight, as he had always associated it with the taverns (where he had heard the strains as he passed—and, as he hastens to add, it would not have been seemly to tarry and listen) but the Eisteddfod at Carmarthen had proved to him that the harp, in spite of its disreputable past, could be used to a good purpose. In this way the broadminded editor of *Seren Gomer* paved the way for the Nonconformists to take part in the Eisteddfodau.

The first meeting of the Cambrian Societies was held on the 28th of October, 1818, when the Cambrian Society of Dyfed was formed, and its promoters met again the following day at the Palace, Abergwili, to discuss their plans for the establishment of three other Cambrian Societies—in the provinces of Gwynedd, Gwent and Powys, and to make arrangements for holding Eisteddfodau quadrennially in each province. The first Eisteddfod, under the auspices of the Dyfed Society, was to be at Carmarthen in the following year, and the subjects for the poetical compositions aroused controversy at the Abergwili meeting. Walter Davies was not present, and John Jenkins writes to him—" Your absence was much regretted by everyone, and particularly by the Bishop, as the assistance you could have given would be most essential. . . . No one present, except E. o Lanbedr (who was too shy to offer his sentiments, though he trembled at the idea of any innovation) was acquainted in any tolerable degree with the Construction and Rules of Welsh Poetry." The innovations which the reticent Eliezer Williams feared were the abolition of some of the metrical forms and of the *cynghanedd*. Jenkins himself was opposed to any change, not because he had any knowledge of the traditional structure of Welsh poetry, but because " it would certainly alarm the Bards and make them believe that the Society intended under cover to barbarize and not preserve the National language.'' He turns for advice to Walter Davies as the acknowledged authority in the whole field of Welsh literature, and urges him to send his views to the Bishop.

Jenkins was hardly justified in saying that no one at the meeting had any knowledge of Welsh poetry, as Iolo Morganwg, the inventor of the Gorsedd of the Bards of Britain, was present. '' Old Iolo '' as he was affectionately called, was on intimate terms with the clerical literati, and one suggestion put forward was that he should reside for part of every year at Carmarthen to superintend the Dyfed Society's publications, and to teach the rules of poetry to young students. Another suggestion which shows Iolo's influence was that meetings should be held annually in the four provinces, and that all the surplus money from these Eisteddfodau should be accumulated until the fifth year when a '' grand Gorsedd '' would be held in London, and the money spent on publishing the winning poems and other works. Neither of these suggestions materialised, but at Carmarthen a '' Gorsedd of the Bards of Britain '' was held for the first time in connection with an Eisteddfod, and the Gorsedd, which in all probability, according to Professor G. J. Williams, would not otherwise have survived Iolo himself (who died in 1826), became an integral part of the Eisteddfod.

The Carmarthen Eisteddfod—the first of the great modern Eisteddfodau—proved a great success, and the clerical literati proceeded with their plans for forming Cambrian Societies in the other provinces. Bishop Burgess wrote to the leading gentry urging them to form committees, but the organising work fell to W. J. Rees. He visited the provinces, and addressed meetings ; he wrote speeches for the elected Presidents on the objects of the Cambrian Societies, and sent drafts of resolutions to the Secretary of each Province with detailed instructions how to proceed, even enclosing copies of advertisements for the newspapers.

One of these advertisements appeared in the *North Wales Gazette*, calling a meeting '' of the friends of Cambrian literature in Caernarvon,'' on the 16th of September, 1819, and at this meeting the Cambrian Society of Gwynedd was formed. In the previous July, Rees had suggested that steps should be taken to interest the " Gentlemen at the Jesus College meeting " at Dolgellau in the formation of a Society in Powys, and then sent to the Secretary a copy of resolutions containing even the names of the President, Vice-President and Committee, and the most appropriate time of meeting, viz. during the Wrexham races. There only remained for those present to adopt the resolutions ; this was done at a meeting held at the " Eagles Inn," Wrexham, on the 6th of October, 1819, and the Cymmro-dorion Society of Powys came into being. The designation of the Society was the only one of Rees' recommendations to be refused ; Sir Watkin Williams Wynn, who was elected President, insisted that the Welsh word " Cymmrodorion " should be used rather than " Cambrian," which he regarded as a Latin term. The clerical literati opposed his suggestion, saying that there should be uniformity in the names of the Societies which were designed to work in union ; this dis-agreement was an augury of the disunity that was to follow.

Dissension delayed the establishment of the Gwent Society, and the Central Society in London was formed before this last link in the chain was completed. Sir Charles Morgan and Colonel Wood were contesting a Parliamentary seat, and the dispute between their rival factions delayed—until December, 1821—the establishment of the Gwent Society, when once more W. J. Rees played an active part, sending two drafts of resolutions, for the formation of the Society and the Committee respectively, to the Gwent Secretary, and preparing a lengthy speech on the Society's objects.

From the beginning the clerical literati had felt the need of a central organisation to direct the four Cambrian Societies and the Welsh Olympics, as the Eisteddfodau were called, and they instinctively turned their eyes to London. The officials of the provincial Societies, who were almost all members of Parliament, would find the capital their most convenient meeting-place ; for almost a century Welshmen at home had derived encouragement and inspiration in cultural matters from the Welsh Societies in London. Here also—in the Welsh School—were to be deposited the collection of Welsh printed books, which the provincial Societies hoped to acquire, and the MSS. which were to be transcribed by a "Literary Agent." The quinquennial Gorsedd, already mentioned, was to be in

London, and the Abergwili meeting stressed the need for a Metropolitan Central Committee.

So inevitably London was to be the centre, and even before the Abergwili meeting plans had been made to form a Society in London. There is a letter extant written by John Jones of Glan-y-Gors in support of the project, and its contents seem surprising to us who have always regarded Glan-y-Gors as the avowed enemy of squire and cleric. Here is an extract from the letter :

" Several of your friends, upon hearing of the proposed Society for the encouragement of Welsh literature, and of your interesting yourself therein, beg leave to suggest through me, that much good would result from such an institution, if carried into effect with becoming energy. In the first place it is observed that the clergy ought to take a prominent part therein, in order to give it a character of dignity suitable to the object, that is the four Welsh bishops ought to sanction it with their names and influence."

It is evident that the nature of the Society was known, but the project of reviving the Cymmrodorion Society is not mentioned, and again at a meeting held in June, 1819, at Lord Dynevor's town house to consider the formation of a Society, no reference was made to the Cymmrodorion.

Glan-y-Gors's letter quoted above was written to Richard Edmunds, who may be regarded as the resuscitator of the second Cymmrodorion Society. Edmunds, described as a barrister in the Exchequer Office of Pleas, and a native of Montgomeryshire, was a friend and correspondent of Walter Davies and was the first London Welshman to be consulted as to the possibility of reviving the Cymmrodorion Society. He had been a member of the First Cymmrodorion Society, though not of the Gwyneddigion Society, and was one of the pillars of the Welsh School over a long period ; when retiring from the post of Treasurer to the School in 1818, he states that he had been connected with the school for fifty years, and after his death he is referred to as " the zealous and steady friend of the Welsh School."

He cannot have been a very active Cymmrodor, for we find him writing to an old member, Rowland Jones (1740 ?-1829), for information about the history and dissolution of the Society. Unfortunately, the latter's memory was failing, but he directs

Edmunds to Meredith Jones, another old Cymmrodor, who would be able to give him all the information he desired. Meredith Jones "dines punctually at 3 o'clock every day at the King's Head Tavern" and Edmunds was to go there to meet him ; unfortunately no record of that conversation in Glan-y-Gors's famous tavern has been preserved, but it must have encouraged Edmunds in his plans to revive the Society, for at the end of 1819, at a meeting of the Powys Society, it was resolved "that the re-establishment of the Cymmrodorion Society in London instituted in the year 1751, has the cordial approbation of this meeting."

W. J. Rees once again actively participated in the arrangements. In the beginning of the month of May, 1820, he set out for London to re-establish the old Cymmrodorion Society as a Central Society to direct and govern the Provincial Societies. Among his correspondence has been preserved a piece of paper bearing the instructions given to him by John Jenkins :—

"Memoranda of the Rev. John Jenkins. Mr. Rees will get Silver Chair Prize Medals. Mr. Rees will do what he can to urge the necessity of a Central Society in London on the friends of the Cambrian and Cymmrodorion whom he may meet. Mr. Rees will call on Mr. Parry (Bardd Alaw), No. 26, Lower Throgmorton Street, Bedford Square, to present John Jenkins's compliments to him and give him all the information he can respecting the Eisteddfod Music Meetings. Mr. Rees (if he can afford time) will also call on Mr. Edward Jones (Bardd y Brenin), His Majesty's Head (sic) Officer of the Robes, Lord Steward's Court Yard, St. James's Palace and present John Jenkins's compliments to him. He will learn from Mr. Jones whether he will attend as Judge of the Musical Performances at the Eisteddfod."

Armed with this memorandum, W. J. Rees arrived in London. In the meantime, Walter Davies had notified Sir Watkin Williams Wynn of Rees's visit—"He has told him how desirable it would be that steps should be taken towards the revival of the old Cymmrodorion Society and has spoken of you as well qualified to give information on the subject, and ready to give your assistance by his direction in forming and arranging a primary meeting." So wrote John Jenkins in a letter to W. J. Rees on May 19th, 1820, and in the same letter he emphasises the desirability of collaborating with the Welsh

School, thus carrying on the tradition of the old Cymmrodorion Society. "It should be as much as possible in union with the Society of Ancient Britons and extend the means of usefulness of that excellent Institution and make the Library the Repository of its researches. This perhaps would be serving both."

In another letter written three days later, he encloses correspondence to be shown to Sir Watkin Williams Wynn, from the Secretaries of the Gwynedd and Powys Societies, advocating the union of all the Societies. W. J. Rees returned the proposals and resolutions from London, and suggested certain alterations, which John Jenkins adopted without consulting any of his friends. " The Alterations . . . were so evidently judicious, the time being short (the morning being also so rainy that I could not go to Manafon), that I did not hesitate to adopt them. I shall see Mr. Walter Davies on Monday, and I have no doubt that he will approve of every item." Two days later he speaks of his proposed visit to Thomas Richards of Berriew, accompanied by Walter Davies and David Rowland, to discuss the letters of W. J. Rees and John Parry (Bardd Alaw).

Rees's visit to London was prolonged for six weeks, but his mission was successful and the Cymmrodorion Society was revived. John Jenkins pays a tribute to his efforts to establish the Society on a firm basis—" Your correspondence is particularly interesting to me at present. You have been indefatigable, and as usual have done everything that could be done, and if the Society does not go on after the great trouble you have taken, it is vain on our part to take any further steps." The secretary of the new Society writes to W. J. Rees a few months later to " express the gratitude of the members for your patriotic zeal. They will never forget how they are indebted to you for whatever benefit may result from the establishment of the Institution."

The first meeting of the second Cymmrodorion Society was convened by public advertisement and held at the " Freemasons' Tavern " on the 24th June, 1820. Owing to its twofold character, the Society was to be known as the " Cymmrodorion Society or the Metropolitan Cambrian Institution." The resolutions adopted at the meeting were as follows :—

1.   That the Welsh language and literature are eminently worthy of cultivation, therefore it is highly desirable that a

Literary Institution connected with this object be established in London.

2. That accordingly, the Cymmrodorion Society instituted in 1751 be revived and that the present meeting do form themselves into such a Society under the designation of Cymmrodorion or Metropolitan Cambrian Institution.

3. That this Institution be in connection with the Societies already formed in the Provinces of Dyfed, Powys, Gwent and Gwynedd, having the same object in view, and that it can be considered a point of union between such Societies.

4. That for the furtherance of this object it shall be the paramount aim of this institution to preserve and illustrate the ancient remains of Welsh Literature and to promote its cultivation in the present day by every means in their power.''

The first step was to find members, and for this purpose advertisements were inserted in the newspapers. The following is the notice that appeared on the cover of *Seren Gomer* in September, 1820 :

CYMRU.
SEFYDLIAID CYMROAIDD Y BRIFDDINAS

Er cefnogaeth i
Leënaeth Gymreig
Ei Fawrhydi, y Noddwr
Syr W. W. Wynn, Barwnig, Llywydd.

Deisyfir yn barchus ar y cyfryw Bendefigion a Boneddigion ag a ddichon fod a thuedd ynddynt i ymgeleddu gwrthych y Gymdeithas wladgarol hon, i ddanfon eu HENWAU A'U TANYS-GRIFIADAU i Mr. Thomas Jones y Trysorydd, 90, Long Acre, neu i Gyhoeddwr y Greal Hon.

Tanysgrifiad—Un gini ac uchod yn y flwyddyn . . . . . ''

All gentlemen of title who had any connection with Wales were chosen members, and eminent persons, other than Welshmen, were elected—foremost among these we may mention Sir Walter Scott. The result of this indiscriminate choosing of members was that the Society had a long list of Vice-Presidents, which led to a correspondent in one paper observing

" that every individual who can boast of a long pedigree or of a few hundred acres of bog or marshland appears in the list of Vice-Presidents." Soon after this a new regulation was adopted ; a candidate for membership had to be nominated by three subscribers ; this was " to ensure the respectability of the Institution." A printed (1824) List of Members has 108 names, including those of T. L. Peacock and Sharon Turner. There are also six " Lady Subscribers " and 32 " Honorary Members "—among these are Bardd Nantglyn, Iolo Morgannwg, John Jones (" Tegid "), and Robert Southey.

The first President of the Society was Sir Watkin Williams Wynn (1772-1840), the son of the second Chief President of the old Cymmrodorion Society, and like his father a strong supporter of the Welsh School. He was a Member of Parliament for Denbighshire and Lord Lieutenant of that county. He raised a regiment to cross to France in the Napoleonic War ; but although he arrived when the battle of Waterloo was over, the reception given to him on his return by London Welshmen was so enthusiastic that the Prince Regent observed that Sir Watkin was the Prince in Wales. His clemency as a landlord also claimed for him this title ; and he is described as " the most liberal patron of agricultural improvement in Wales."

Another notable President of the Society was Edward Clive Herbert, second Earl of Powis and grandson of the famous Clive of India. He is best remembered as one of the most strenuous opponents of the plan to unite the sees of Bangor and S. Asaph.

The chief members of the Gwyneddigion became the first officials of the new Society ; Walter Davies suggested William Owen Pughe, then President of the Gwyneddigion, as the Secretary of the Society, but the post went to John Humffreys Parry (1787-1825). Parry was called to the Bar in 1811, and for a time practised successfully ; but having inherited property on the death of his father, he devoted his time to literary pursuits. He died a comparatively young man, as a result of a drunken brawl in a tavern. He was the editor of the first volume of the *Cymmrodorion Transactions* (published 1822) and in 1820-1822 he edited three volumes of the *Cambro-Briton*, a publication dealing with the history and antiquities of Wales. In 1824, he published a biography of eminent Welshmen which he called the *Cambrian Plutarch* and as " Ordovex " he was a regular contributor to the newspapers. A writer in the *Literary Chronicle* states that Parry was engaged on a new edition of Dr. Johnson's dictionary at the time of his death.

After holding office for one year, Humffreys Parry was followed by James Evans who was Secretary until 1824, when he resigned the office. Nothing is known of him and his name does not appear in the list of members of the Gwyneddigion Society.

The Secretary from 1824 to 1828 was Griffith Jones, a native of Dolgelley, Merioneth. A writer in *Old Wales* informs us that he was an attorney, and that his office was at 7, Birchin Lane. The *Cambrian Remembrancer* contains a short paragraph about him—" The Cymmrodorion Society in the days of its chief glory never had a better Secretary than Griffith Jones, a devoted Welshman, a distinguished speaker, and a man whose heart prompted him at all times to befriend his countrymen. He died in 1832." W. J. Rees in his correspondence also refers to him as a fluent speaker ; and as the representative of the Cymmrodorion Society his name appears in the accounts of the provincial Eisteddfodau. The close connection between the three London Societies is clearly illustrated in Griffith Jones. He was elected a member of the Cymreigyddion Society in the month of February, 1818, was Vice-President from April till July of that year, Secretary in 1820, 1822 and 1823 and President of the Society in 1821. He was elected a member of the Gwyneddigion Society in 1821, was Secretary during 1822 and 1823, President in 1824 and at the end of that year was presented by the Gwyneddigion with a silver medal for his services as Secretary, as well as in recognition of his work as President. He was also Treasurer of the Gwyneddigion in the years 1827 and 1828. Lastly, he was the Sub-Librarian of the Cymmrodorion during the years 1822 and 1824, and Secretary for the next four years. Griffith Jones corresponded with W. J. Rees and Walter Davies, and in his first letter to the latter he introduces himself as a lover of the language and refers to their common friend " Dafydd Ionawr " (David Richards).

The first Treasurer of the Society was Thomas Jones, " Bardd Cloff " (1768-1828). He removed to London at an early age, entered a coach-building business, and eventually became a partner in it. Bardd Cloff composed an " Ode on the Re-establishment of the Cymmrodorion," and on his death in 1830, the Society offered a Silver Medal for an elegy on their late treasurer and bard.

It will be seen that music was an important factor in the London Society and in the provincial Eisteddfodau, and the " Registrar of Music " for these functions was John Parry (1776-1851) " Bardd Alaw " (a title conferred on him in the Gorsedd of 1821). He was a prolific composer and his publications formed altogether forty thick folio volumes. Parry was Honorary Treasurer of the Royal Society of Musicians and Secretary to the Melodists Club.

Henry Davies (1804-1890) moved from his native town of Bridgend to London at an early age and played an active part in the Cymmrodorion Society during the years 1827-1829. He was Librarian for two consecutive years. His ambition was to be " a Librarian to some noble Londoner, and get a literary occupation." and he was given a testimonial for this purpose by W. J. Rees. According to the latter, he possessed con-siderable literary talents, and at one time was considered for the post of editor of the *Cambrian Quarterly*. He left London about 1830, to take charge of the Montpelier Pump-Room at Cheltenham, and in 1833 he established the *Cheltenham Looker-on*, a social notebook of fashionable doings, " conducted with considerable literary ability " for over fifty-six years. He is described as " a prominent figure in the political, municipal and commercial life of Cheltenham for sixty years." He fulfilled his ambition of being a Librarian, by establishing a Library adjoining the Pump-Room. Henry Davies lived to be a member of the third Cymmrodorion Society.

Another Librarian to the Society was Richard Evans of Llanbrynmair, Montgomeryshire (1793-1832), who is described as the " Conservator of the Ancient Welsh Manuscripts of the Royal Cambrian Society." He was also connected with the two other London Societies. He was a benefactor of London Welshmen. " In the neighbourhood of his warehouse he gathered together quite a colony of his compatriots, comprising about twenty families, to whom he gave medicine and surgical advice, and once a week delivered a lecture in Welsh for their instruction in manufactures, mechanics, and kindred topics." He had formed a plan for founding a Society to co-operate with the Cymreigyddion for the purpose of translating some of the simplest and most approved elementary English books on several branches of science into Welsh, and proposed to sell them at a price that would render them available to Welshmen of the humblest class. It is not known what became of his proposal.

Arthur James Johnes (1809-1871) of Garthmyl, Montgomery, was chosen Librarian of the Society in 1830. In his youth he had come under the influence of Walter Davies and John Jenkins, who had encouraged him to learn Welsh. He strongly supported the demand for Welsh-speaking bishops, and was Secretary of the Commission sent to London to protest against the union of the sees of Bangor and S. Asaph ; he published an account of the case in 1841. Johnes was a County Court Judge, and one of the first directors and promoters of a railway between Oswestry and Newtown, and Shrewsbury and Welshpool. He published an English translation of the works of Dafydd ap Gwilym in 1834 and won the Cymmrodorion Prize for an essay on the *Causes of Dissent* in Wales. He was also a member of the Cymreigyddion Society.

The Librarian of the Second Society at its dissolution forms a link between the Second and Third Societies, for he was present at the establishment of the Third Society in 1873, and was elected a Vice-President. He was William Jones, " Gwrgant " (1802-1886), a native of Llanfihangel, Montgomery, and a lawyer of Furnival's Inn. Gwrgant, already mentioned in the preceding chapter, was a prominent Eisteddfodwr, and adjudicator.

By 1836 the Society had a Chaplain—The Rev. Arthur Butler Clough (1797-1870). He was a correspondent of the clerical literati, and befriended Rice Rees and John Blackwell at Oxford, giving considerable financial assistance to the latter. Clough contemplated establishing a branch of the Cymmrodorion Society at Oxford, and other large towns.

Another office established in the last decade of the Society's existence was that of a Welsh Correspondent—which was held by the Rev. John Jones, " Tegid " (1792-1852). Tegid took a leading part in the controversy on the orthography of the Welsh Bible, and was the greatest opponent of Chancellor Bruce Knight, to whom Sir John Morris-Jones gives the credit for "saving the Welsh Bible from the vandalism of Pughe's followers." Tegid undoubtedly was the greatest of these "vandals." In 1829 he published "*A Defence of the Reformed System of Orthography*" and "*A Reply to the Rev. W. B. Knight's Remarks on Welsh Orthography.*"

These then were the leaders of the new Society, this Janus which was to attempt to carry on the tradition of the old Cymmrodorion, but also was to act as a Central Committee to direct the provincial Societies and to ensure that one grand Eisteddfod would be held every year in rotation in the provinces, i.e., it was to do the work of the modern Eisteddfod Council.

This plan of a "national" Eisteddfod had an auspicious beginning. The nobility took a great delight and interest in this novelty, and the Dyfed Eisteddfod at Carmarthen in 1819, and the Wrexham Eisteddfod held by the Powys Society in the following year were very successful, and the question of disposing of the surplus funds of both functions soon arose. The Powys Society proposed that the surplus money received from the provincial Eisteddfodau should be at the disposal of a Committee from the four provinces to co-operate with the London Institution, and that the money should be used for *particular purposes*, i.e., the holding of Eisteddfodau in rotation in the provinces. A similar resolution by the Dyfed Society advocated that the union should be founded on the "common objects" of the Societies, viz., organising Eisteddfodau and fostering literature. The London Cymmrodorion however felt that the money should be entrusted to them for their own general objects, and not used exclusively for organising quad-rennial Eisteddfodau. W. J. Rees was naturally opposed to this, and expressed his regret that "the Funds of the Metropolitan Society are not in a more flourishing state," suggesting that the Society desired to appropriate the money to alleviate its own financial difficulties. This refusal to act as a Central Committee was responsible for the failure to ensure the permanence of an annual Eisteddfod.

The inevitable result of this disagreement was that the surplus fund of each province was retained in that province for four years, and the "National Eisteddfod" did not materialise for half a century. Even the "provincial" Eisteddfodau soon lost their significance ; in 1824 the Welshpool Committee decided that their £200 surplus money should be kept "to assist the next Eisteddfod at Welshpool, and if one does not take place within eight years, then the Committee is to determine on its final disposal," disregarding the fact that the fund belonged to the province, and not to a local committee.

The Gwynedd Society does not seem to have been very active. An Eisteddfod was held at Caernarvon under its auspices in 1821 and the Secretary, Joseph Goddard, complains of lack of enthusiasm. The Gwynedd poets were not favourably disposed to the Eisteddfodau and the nobility refused to patronise them, so that no great enthusiasm, either for or against a union, could be expected from that province. It was owing to the inability of the Gwynedd Society to hold an Eisteddfod in 1825 that the rotation of the provincial Eisteddfodau was broken.

But the most important point of disagreement between the London and the provincial Societies was the question of orthography. The leading London Cymmrodorion were greatly influenced by William Owen Pughe, and accepted his eccentric innovations. In 1822 there appeared a statement in the *Cambro-Briton* and in the Cymmrodorion Society's *Transactions* (both publications were edited by J. Humffreys Parry) that the London Society recommended the substitution of the letter " v " for " f " and of the letter " f " for " ff " in Welsh orthography, giving as a reason that " the alteration was sanctioned, as well by the practice of all other tongues, as by the ancient mode of writing the Welsh language itself." The editor declares that " this Resolution previously recommended by the Council, was adopted and acceded to, as far as we could discern, without one dissentient voice." W. J. Rees, however, emphatically denied this, and said that Humffreys Parry had deliberately misreported the minutes. This is Rees' testimony —" I was in London where the alteration from ' f ' to ' v ' was proposed by Mr. Humffreys Parry, but no one seconded the motion, and I considered it as lost, but it was mentioned in the proceedings as carried, and has accordingly been since acted upon."

The Dyfed Society refused to accept these innovations and offered a prize medal at the Carmarthen Eisteddfod in 1825 for an essay on the subject. A memorandum of John Jenkins explains the sentiments of the Dyfed Society :—" At the next Eisteddfod at Caerfyrddin it will be attempted to fix the

Orthography of the Welsh language which is to be brought back as nearly as possible to the standard of the Welsh Bible produced by Richard Morris in 1746."

The Gwent Society agreed with these sentiments, and was also embittered by an attack made by Humffreys Parry on John Hughes, the aforementioned Methodist minister who was one of the Gwent Society's most prominent members. At the Brecon Eisteddfod in 1822 Hughes won a medal for an essay on *The Present State of the Welsh Language* and Humffreys Parry attacked the orthographical opinions expressed in it. The Gwent Society resented this reflection on its powers of literary criticism, and the London Society fell into disfavour. Rees deplores the lack of wisdom shown by Humffreys Parry. "As the essay was published with the authority of the Society, respect and prudence should have dictated to him to be very cautious in what he advanced in such circumstances, but poor man, he has no tact."

Rees was keenly aware of the difficulties of co-operation, and opposed any superficial union. When the Powys Society advocated the publication of the successful essays of the provincial Eisteddfodau in the Cymmrodorion *Transactions* he expressed his disapproval, and spoke disparagingly of the leaders of the Cymmrodorion, viz., Humffreys Parry, William Owen Pughe and Griffith Jones . . . " They are not three I should be inclined to vest with authority with respect to what should and what should not be printed in the *Transactions* . . . The two first, who would of course influence the third, have a particular bias, and anything which would not accord with their opinions would, of course, not be adopted, or if inserted would be accompanied with somewhat harsh observations." Indeed, he seems to have held no very high opinion of the literary capabilities of any members of the Council in London—" Were there among the leading members of the Cymmrodorion Council half a dozen persons of enlarged minds, extensive information and principles, and I mention it without intending to throw any reflection on those who take the trouble to guide its concerns, such a proceeding might do very well, but as the Council is at present constituted, I doubt its success."

Another reason for the failure to unite was the opposing views held on the function of the Eisteddfodau. The clerical literati rightly regarded them as a means of fostering Welsh culture, but John Parry, "Bardd Alaw," the Registrar of Music to the London Cymmrodorion, made them merely grand musical entertainments. An important factor in deciding the nature of these Eisteddfodau was the interest evinced in them by the nobility ; the wealthy residents of Wales had held aloof from the life of the nation, and the promoters of the Cambrian Societies had hoped to regain their allegiance through the Eisteddfodau, and one of the essential requirements at these meetings was the harp, regarded as a novelty by the gentry. The organiser of the first Cambrian Eisteddfod in 1819 stressed the importance of having a harpist "otherwise Ladies of Distinction who intend coming from a distance will be miserably disappointed." The harpists received handsome remuneration —Thomas Blayney at Carmarthen Eisteddfod received thirty guineas towards his expenses, and a gratuity, and Henry Humphries received fifteen guineas and a gratuity—this was to encourage the custom of harp playing—"taking into consideration that the future success of the Society in exciting Emulation in this branch mainly depends upon the Manner it treats those who are successful at the first meeting." But the clerical literati soon realised that a series of musical entertainments, with literature as a very secondary consideration, would not achieve the destined object. Instead of the gentry becoming Welsh through the Eisteddfodau, the Eisteddfodau themselves became Anglicised, and the Welsh language and literature were still ignored.

"A recital of the Awdl at the Eisteddfod," said W. J. Rees in a letter to Walter Davies "would probably be thought tedious to the Anglicised part of the audience, which I expect was by far the majority." He also quotes a letter from the Rev. Thomas Price, "Carnhuanawc" (1787-1848), stating that the meeting of the Cymreigyddion at Brecon on St. David's Day was well attended, but that the success of the meeting was "due purely to the patriotism of the common people ; the gentry kept aloof as usual, but they received the intelligence of an Eisteddfod with much cordiality."

The optimism of the Welshpool Committee of 1824 in suggesting that a Prize should be given for an epitaph of six englynion—"to be inserted on the Tomb of Dic Shon Dafydd, an imaginary personage supposed to be the general representative of anti-Cambrian feeling, who departed this life during the Eisteddfod at Carmarthen (1823) after a lingering consumption of four years " was hardly justified, for by this time the clerical promoters themselves had realised the futility of the Eisteddfodau. John Jenkins pointed out that " our great people as they have in a measure lost their nationality can only be brought together by Musical Entertainments of a superior style, but these, by frequency will be considered too expensive and the novelty will wear off "; he proposed a triennial Eisteddfod as a solution to the problem and consulted Walter Davies to find out whether such a procedure was sanctioned by tradition.

His plan did not mature ; no Eisteddfod was held in 1825 ; the following year the Gwent Society held one at Brecon, but in 1827 when the Gwynedd Society again decided not to hold a meeting, Rees approved rather than regretted their decision. " No Eisteddfod will be held at Caernarvon this year " he wrote " in consequence of the gentry not coming forward to support it. I am not sorry for the circumstance, as music is made too prominent a part of the proceedings." Jenkins did not attend the 1829 Eisteddfod as he considered that these meetings had lost sight of their primary object and were dwindling into " an Anglo-Italian farce."

The clergy held John Parry, " Bardd Alaw," responsible for this Anglicisation. They considered his " Anglo-Italian music extremely ill-judged, besides taking all the profits," and Angharad Llwyd regretted that "our bards should be made catspaws of the musicians " ; and although they still supported the Eisteddfodau, the correspondence of the members of the clerical circle shows that they had lost faith in the project as a means of reviving the Welsh language, and despaired of persuading the London Society to act as a Central Committee. Thus one of the primary objects of the second Cymmrodorion was abandoned and the work of establishing a National Eisteddfod was left to the Third Cymmrodorion Society to undertake fifty years later.

The Cymmrodorion themselves did not attach any great importance to this object, for in their first volume of *Transactions* published in 1822, no reference is made to it, but the Society's aim is said to be " the fostering of literature by awarding medals and by collecting and publishing rare books and MSS." In these editorial remarks it is made evident that they based their aims on the first Society although their objects were not as comprehensive ; they were not proposing to emulate the first Society in " contributing towards the instruction of the ignorant and the relief of distressed countrymen." This was a reference to the Welsh School and to charitable gifts to poor Welshmen : lack of data makes it difficult for us to arrive at any definite conclusions on these two points.

The Second Cymmrodorion still used the Welsh School as their Library ; the Society's President and several of the leading members were prominent supporters of the School and once, at least, the Society organised a concert in aid of the School (which incidentally, benefited the School no more than did Pennant's *British Zoology*) but we have seen no reference to substantial contributions to the School, as were made by the first Society. Neither have we come across any references to constant charitable work such as undertaken by the First Cymmrodorion by means of their " Poor Box " and the quarterly levy for sending " decay'd distressed Welshmen " by the waggon to their former homes in Wales. But there is evidence that the second Society did dispense charity ; according to a report in the *Cambrian Quarterly* one Richard Owen of Anglesey sent an appeal for a pair of spectacles ; his appeal was accompanied by a Welsh poem declaiming his poverty and old age. A pair of spectacles was bought for him—" a handsome pair of silver ones "—and engraved on them the words " Cymmrodorion Caerludd i'r Bardd Richard Owain." It seems quite possible that this may have been the " Richard Owen, schoolmaster at Holyhead " born in 1751, a nephew of the Morrises—son of their sister Ellen.

Lack of data also makes it difficult to determine on the nature of the Society's meetings. Weekly meetings held in the beginning soon gave place to monthly ones, but only a few references occur to them. A series to discuss " Poetry " was arranged for the winter, and Samuel Roberts, Llanbrynmair, writes of a visit to another meeting with Richard Evans, when an address was given on " Shipbuilding," and the democratic " S.R.," then a young man, was much impressed by the splendour of the gathering. Judging from Henry Davies's letters to W. J. Rees, the Society was declining by 1827 ;— " the meetings," he said, " are mere push-pin play, for scarcely any of our members attend and I can plainly see, unless something is done to establish the thing on a bona fide literary basis it will soon crumble to nothing." He voiced the same complaint as the clerical literati against "Bardd Alaw,"—"Mr. Parry is the only regular member, and he, as you know, studies little save the musical celebrity of the Institution." The following year he again complained of the little spirit existing among the members of our Cymmrodorion."

The Society had now confined itself to bi-monthly meetings, when papers on any subject connected with Wales were to be given and Henry Davies appealed to Rees for essays to be read. John Jenkins commiserated with Rees over the frustration of his plans, "but," he added "you have done what you could and what you ought to do, to excite a good taste among your countrymen, but the obstacles proceeding from apathy and a fanatic spirit are insurmountable"—undoubtedly another reference to John Parry. By the following year, the meetings were better attended and Henry Davies and Richard Evans were hopeful of "placing the Society on a more literary footing." Unfortunately the Secretary misplaced the contributions sent in for the premiums—elegies on the death of Bardd Cloff and essays on the hospitality of the Ancient Britons—and this led to an unpleasant controversy at the ensuing meetings, but the matter was finally settled and the Secretary, according to Henry Davies, "promised to behave better in the future."

Eighteen Hundred and Thirty proved a more successful year then the three preceeding ones. Meetings were now reported to be "respectably attended" and "of an unusually interesting character." Fortnightly meetings were again started and literary and historical subjects were discussed.

These few references, gleaned from letters and periodicals, give only a glimpse at the activity of the Society, but they show that the same struggle was taking place in London as in the provincial Eisteddfodau and in this literature versus music contest, music undoubtedly won. John Parry seems to have been a strong character and he concentrated his efforts on the anniversary meetings of the Society. He himself says in one of his letters that "matters as usual are at a standstill here, but I must start them up by the anniversary meeting."

It must also not be forgotten that there were the two other Societies, the Gwyneddigion and the Cymreigyddion, still in existence, and literary topics were discussed regularly at their meetings, so that John Parry's apologia might be that he was providing fare differing from theirs. It is rather ironical that the Gwyneddigion Society, which was formed in 1771 because the " Cymmrodorion did not foster the harp and penillion singing," should have been surpassed in its enthusiasm for music by the Second Cymmrodorion Society.

It must also be kept in mind that the Second Cymmrodorion Society catered for all classes of Welshmen and as the clerical promoters had found, it was infinitely easier to interest the wealthier classes—who formed a large part of the Cymmrodorion at this time—in music, than in literature and in the revival of the Welsh language.

The anniversary meetings of the Society (held not on June 24th, but on the 22nd of May—as this was the birthday of the heir of Wynnstay) undoubtedly attracted the nobility ; the average attendance was 600—800 guests. These meetings combined business and conviviality—in the morning the financial report of the Council was adopted and premiums for the next year were chosen ; a musical concert, or an " Eisteddfod," as it was called, was held in the afternoon and followed by a dinner in the evening. The President's chair of the First Cymmrodorion Society, a "handsome piece of mahogany, excellently carved"—now the property of the Gwyneddigion, was sometimes borrowed for these occasions.

The afternoon " Eisteddfod " commenced with a presidential address in English on the Society's objects, followed by a Welsh address on the same subject by one of the members of the Council. During the interval in the concert which followed, medals were presented to winners in the literary competitions, and the reading of the successful poems and essays was proposed, but was never carried out with any great success.

As early as 1823, Humffreys Parry complained to Rees of the undue emphasis laid upon music—" But our Registrar of Music is as usual on the alert and as far as ' harp and song ' go, our ensuing Eisteddfod will not be without its wonted attractions . . . . But I see no reason why our Eisteddfod should be converted, as it was last year, into a mere concert. For so far from introducing any literary recitation, the prize competitions written expressly for the occasion were not allowed to be read." He remarked dryly that the title of the Society should be abridged to the " Cymmrodorion Society for the encouragement of music."

At the beginning at least, Welsh airs and songs had a prominent place and penillion singing was encouraged. A report of one meeting states that—" The bards (about twenty in number) were ranged behind the instrumental performer and each in succession took up the strains and sang on an extempore stanza in the Welsh language and at the close of the air all joined in the chorus." The harpist was one William Pritchard, " whose style of playing has procured for him the distinction of being harper to the Society." John Parry regarded these meetings as an opportunity for London Welshmen to hear their native music, and a contemporary describes them as " the reign of song, hilarity and good fellowship." There was a verse to be sung at these meetings to the air of " Ar hyd y nos "—

> Cadw cov am hen arverion
> Ydyw gwledd y Cymmrodorion
> Man mae Telyn, man mae canu
> A phob mwynder er dyddanu
> Ydym val ar vryniau Cymru.

The words were written by William Owen Pughe and were rendered into English by Humffreys Parry in this form :—

> Ancient customs still to treasure
> Cymmrodorion is our pleasure
> Rapture in each heart exciting
> As on Cambria's hills delighting.

These nostalgic songs and the strains of the harp gave the exiled Welshmen great pleasure and made the Cymmrodorion anniversary meetings the most popular in London, but those of the members who had hoped for encouragement for literature, were grievously disappointed. Henry Davies, while the Society was still in its infancy, wrote to W. J. Rees that he now expected " a mere musical display at the meetings. Poor literature goes quite to the bad as usual . . . . I think the Literateurs of the Principality will be sorry to see the objects originally proposed by the Society so entirely lost of." One year, John Parry decided that no annual meeting should take place, owing to the difficulty of obtaining suitable artistes. Rees opposed this decision, as he considered that the very continuance of the Society depended on the annual meeting, and if no subjects were chosen for competition for the next year, there would be no real Eisteddfod. He again deplored John Parry's excessive zeal for music. " I consider that though music is important on such an occasion it is no compliment to the Cymmrodorion to conclude that they are governed by it," and sent a strong appeal to Parry to support the Society's real objects.

But Parry remained obdurate, and his " Eisteddfodau," like the Provincial ones, grew more foreign to Welsh life and culture. He secured the services of the most famous vocalists and instrumentalists of the day, regardless of cost, and Welsh songs had to take second place to such items as " Signor Pozzi executing some difficult variations on the French horn." One year Parry arranged " A grand Concert " to procure funds for the Welsh School. Richard Roberts the blind harpist from Caernarvon was brought to London to perform at the meeting and celebrated English artistes were engaged. But the concert was a financial failure and the Cymmrodorion were faced with a deficit of £100. Another concert, arranged for Parry's own benefit, " in recognition of his services to music," proved successful, but Angharad Llwyd, in her forthright way denounced him—" that money which Mr. Parry pocketed ought to have been divided between Mr. Humffreys Parry's widow and printing the Mabinogion."

And so the London Eisteddfodau became Anglicised concerts, and Literature " ranked but secondary in the Bill of Fare," to quote Henry Davies. But efforts were made to promote literature, by the publication of books and by the awarding of medals to successful candidates in competition of prose or poetry. Over thirty medals were thus given during the Society's existence and medals were also given for distinguished services in the field of literature or art, a practice which is continued by the present Society. Three recipients of these medals were William Owen Pughe, John Parry and Angharad Llwyd.

The Society's medal was designed by Flaxman ; on the obverse side was depicted a poet, holding in his right hand the " Coelbren y Beirdd " and reclining on a harp. In the background was Stonehenge with Druidicial altars. The medal bore the new motto of the Society—" Cared Doeth yr Encilion " in bardic characters ; this had replaced the motto "Undeb, a Brawdgarwch" favoured by the old Cymmrodorion Society.

The first medal to be awarded was won by Thomas Jones, "Bardd Cloff," for a Welsh ode on the re-establishment of the Cymmrodorion Society. Elegies on prominent Welshmen formed favourite subjects ; odes in memory of Bardd Cloff and William Owen Pughe serve as examples. The Society also chose subjects of historical and national interest such as Owain Glyndŵr and Caswallon and an equally prominent place was given to the connection of Wales with England ; thus the birth of Edward II at Caernarvon Castle was the subject of an englyn in 1822 and the accession of the Tudor family to the English throne the subject of a Cywydd in the same year. There are also a few references to English poetical compositions.

The essays were for the most part in English, and dealt with the ancient history of Wales. Antiquity was a favourite subject of the Second Cymmrodorion Society, as of the First, and the traditions, customs and coinage of the Ancient Britons formed the subject of many essays. Premiums were also awarded for accounts of castles and monasteries in Wales and other essays dealt with the vernacular language and literature ; these show traces of the influence of William Owen Pughe's orthographical innovations and accept his conclusions without demur. The discussions on the strict metres and free verse which took place in 1780 in the First Cymmrodorion Society were also reflected in the following competition by the Metropolitan Institution—"Whether the twenty-four metres have been of benefit to the language or otherwise." This essay was to be in Welsh or English and there is a record of one other Welsh essay—Caledfryn's on the "Advantages and Disadvantages of Cultivating the Welsh language as a Living Tongue."

Medals were also offered annually as prizes to students in Grammar Schools for Welsh essays on a given subject and were intended to encourage the study of the Welsh language, thus counteracting the discouragement given to it in the Grammar Schools, as, to quote a writer of that period, " the Welsh language in these schools (we speak most particularly of North Wales) has been for many years, not only not encouraged, but absolutely discountenanced by severe penalties." Just as the Cambrian Societies were formed to promote the study of the language among the clergy, so these medals were awarded " to encourage native genius and for stimulating young men who are destined for the Church to make themselves masters of the language, in which they are to read divine word to their flock."

The first of these medals was won by David James (1805-1871) then a pupil at Cardigan Grammar School. Dewi o Ddyfed, as he was later named, was to be a keen Eisteddfodwr and a prominent member of the Association of Welsh Clergymen in West Riding. The medal awarded to him bears the following inscription :

" Cymru Vu, Cymru Vydd.
Cymmrodorion Llundain.
Arobryn i
David James
O Athrova Aberteivi
Am ei Draethawd sev, Gwladgarach
Rhagfyr 22 1821."

The Welsh language naturally found a place among the subjects of these essays—David James won another medal in 1823 on " The Cultivation of the Welsh Language." It is difficult to estimate the consequences of this bestowal. It undoubtedly created an interest in Wales among the pupils of the schools and this may have had far-reaching results, even though they were not always those contemplated by the Society. The medal was won twice by " S.R." who may have been encouraged to literary efforts in his student days by this early patronage, but who was by no means to become an upholder of the Church. The winning of these two medals by " S.R." may indeed have had far-reaching results—it may be that the present Society owes its very existence to this bestowal, as will be shown in the next chapter.

Richard Morris had dreamt of a library of all printed Welsh books in the Welsh School ; the clerical literati also favoured the project and the Second Cymmrodorion appealed for assistance to procure Welsh Books and MSS., which together with the books and MSS. deposited in the Welsh School by the First Cymmrodorion " may prove the foundation of a valuable national library." A valuable library of books was thus formed, which were available to any member of the Society and the most important addition to their collection of MSS. was the Myvyrian MSS.—the books and MSS. belonging to the late Owen Myfyr, comprising a hundred volumes—forty-seven volumes of ancient Welsh poetry and fifty-three volumes of prose, the latter being a varied collection of historical, geographical and miscellaneous treatises in Welsh. This collection was purchased by the Society from the widow of Owain Myfyr for the sum of £50, by means of a subscription fund inaugurated by Sir Watkin-Williams Wynn and Bishop Burgess. A catalogue of its contents was made by William Owen Pughe and published in the first volume of the Society's *Transactions*. When Edward Jones, " Bardd y Brenin," died, his collection of MSS. was offered for sale, but the Society, owing to lack of funds, was unable to buy it. Having acquired the Myvyrian Collection the Society decided to publish an additional volume of the *Myvyrian Archeology*, under the editorship of Pughe and Walter Davies, but the work never appeared. Suggestions were also made for the publication of cheap periodicals, containing extracts from ancient Welsh literature, but these did not materialise, again through apathy and lack of funds. When the provincial Societies wanted to publish their winning essays in the Cymmrodorion *Transactions* John Parry puts the matter bluntly—" we must have a little assistance in the cash way, say the odd £25—we are miserably poor, but something must be done at our next general meeting to get us out of hot water." An appeal was sent to the provincial Societies, but the majority of the members were apathetic and the Powys Secretary, Thomas Richards of Berriew, gives the following reason for not placing the appeal before the Society—" I have been dissuaded from calling a meeting, because the Anglo-Saxons would certainly outvote us." The other provincial Societies proved equally unwilling and the carefully prepared scheme of the Cambrian Societies was never carried out.

Yet the clerical literati endeavoured to stimulate the Cymmrodorion. In 1829 John Jenkins was in London, and at the anniversary meeting of the Society stressed the importance of publishing literary productions of merit, " which would be more beneficial . . . than any mere amusement of an hour however splendid." He reminded them that the Society "was a continuation of the Cymmrodorion Society of 1751 and that their appropriation of the funds of the Cymmrodorion Society for an annual Eisteddfod was an infringement of the Constitutions of the Cymmrodorion." This appeal was made on the day of the "Grand Concert" for the benefit of the Welsh Charity School and the literati were justly annoyed with the Cymmrodorion—"we are decidedly opposed to such sacrifices, for while the valuable Myvyrian Manuscripts are sealed from the literary world, the Society in whose custody they lie, are from time to time expending considerable sums in retaining eminent vocal and instrumental professionals."

Up to 1827 the publications of the Society had been *Reports* of the annual Eisteddfodau and two volumes of *Transactions*. The Editor of the first volume was Humffreys Parry ; he was succeeded by David Lewis, a successful competitor at the Eisteddfodau and a member of the Cymreigyddion Society. Part IV of the second volume did not appear until 1843—the year of the dissolution of the Society—and the Editor was W. J. Rees, who remained faithful to the Society to the end. The *Transactions* contain some of the successful poems and essays of the London Eisteddfodau and articles on the history and language of Wales. William Owen Pughe wrote articles for the first volume ; and John Parry and Humffreys Parry also contributed, while W. J. Rees supplied some material. Catalogues of MSS. also found a place in these volumes ; the Myvyrian Catalogue by Pughe has already been mentioned ; descriptions are also given of the MSS. of Edward Llhuyd and Sir Watkin Williams Wynn. Aneurin Owen and Angharad Llwyd both made catalogues of MSS. in the various private libraries in North Wales and their work was published in these volumes.

In 1831 the Cymmrodorion medal was awarded to A. J. Johnes for an essay on *The Causes of Dissent in Wales*. The work was recommended for publication by the adjudicator, William Owen Pughe, and was published by the Society in the same year. Though the author confused the Methodists and the Dissenters of the 18th century, this essay contains much valuable information on the condition of the Welsh Church.

In the same year the Rev. Robert Williams (1811-81) won a silver medal for biographical sketches of eminent Welshmen, born after the Reformation. The Society decided to translate the essay into Welsh and to publish it ; the work appeared in 1833. The name of the translator is not mentioned, but Tegid in a note written in one copy stated that it was translated by "Iago Trichrug," i.e. Rev. James Hughes, minister of Jewin Chapel, London and author of a commentary on the Bible. An English version of the biographical dictionary was published by the author in 1836 and an enlarged edition appeared in 1852.

In 1833 the Cymmrodorion Council had appointed Tegid and Walter Davies to undertake the editorship of the works of Lewis Glyn Cothi, one of the great 15th century poets. The work had not appeared by 1836 and John Parry, who had by now become the Society's secretary, writes to the Secretary of the Denbigh Eisteddfod (which had been a very successful one) asking for a grant towards the work; " so that," he said, " the entire work of the merry old chap can be committed to the press forthwith." Fortunately the anniversary Cymmrodorion Eisteddfod of that year yielded a profit of £100 and the money was devoted to the publication. Charles Watkin Williams Wynn, a keen Cymmrodor, approved of this as a step in the right direction—" these (i.e. publications of ancient literature and historical research) are the legitimate objects of such a Society as the Cymmrodorion, and not musical Concerts and Prizes offered to multiply the quantity of indifferent poetry. If the Cymmrodorion apply themselves to the encouragement of Poetry and Music in preference to the other objects I should be glad that another Society exclusively literary, historical and antiquarian should be formed." He evidently felt that the Cymmrodorion did not fulfil their legitimate objects, for he became one of those responsible for forming the Welsh MSS. Society.

Acting on the recommendation of W. J. Rees, the Society decided to invite kindred institutions to communicate with it on antiquarian topics. In this way, correspondence was started with the Society of Antiquaries in France, who sent to the London Cymmrodorion a copy of their *Mémoires*. It was then resolved to transmit a copy of John Hughes's *Horae Britannicae* to the French Society, at the earnest request of the author, who wished to draw the attention of the Celtic Institute of Paris, incorporated with the Society of Antiquaries, to the need for translating the Bible into the Breton language. This work was later undertaken by Thomas Price (Canhuanawc) who acknowledges his indebtedness to John Hughes for the suggestion. W. J. Rees was chosen to take the copy of *Horae Britannicae* personally to France. He gives an interesting account of his adventure to John Jenkins ; the visit took seventeen days, of which eight were spent in travelling and when he arrived in Paris he found that he had omitted to procure the address of the Secretary of the Society of Antiquaries and he was most considerably handicapped by his lack of knowledge of the language. However, being the bearer of a letter to a friend of an acquaintance from Glamorgan, he visited this Parisian, a M. Fauriel, who, fortunately, was able to converse in English. Being informed by M. Fauriel that the Society would not meet during his sojourn of eight days in Paris, Rees entrusted to him the book for the Antiquarian Society and gave him also a sketch of the plans, objects and proceedings of the London and Provincial Societies and suggestions as to subjects for essays relating to Celtic matters, which would be of interest to both Societies. A notice of the formation of the Dyfed Society had already appeared in the *Révue Encyclopédique* for 1819 ; after Rees's visit, an account of the re-establishment of the Cymmrodorion Society appeared in the *Mémoires* of the French Society. Subsequently volumes of *Transactions* and *Mémoires* were exchanged by the Societies.

One of the objects of the Cymmrodorion was to establish a Welsh Church in London and a reference to the project appears as early as 1821. The next reference is ten years later when it was announced in the *Cambrian Quarterly* that the Bishop of London proposed to arrange evening services in the Welsh language and that the Cymmrodorion Society had invited the Rev. John Price of S. John's College, Cambridge, to conduct them. It is not known what happened to this proposal, but the matter was again in abeyance for ten years— until 1841, when a meeting was held under the chairmanship of the Earl of Powis. He was then President of the Cymmrodorion, and the Society's Vice-Presidents were also present ; and the day of the meeting was the 22nd of May, the Society's anniversary, which suggests that it was at a Cymmrodorion meeting that the matter was brought forward. We may at least claim that the Society's anniversary was taken as an opportunity for meeting and according to the testimony of the Earl of Powis the movement owed its origin to the suggestion made by the First Cymmrodorion. The outcome of the meeting was the establishment of a Welsh Church in Ely Place in 1843.

The last reference to a meeting of the Second Cymmrodorion appears in *Seren Gomer* in 1837. Gwrgant, speaking at the inauguration of the Third Society (in 1873) stated that the work of the Second Cymmrodorion was suspended in 1837, but that meetings were again held in the following year. He gave the date of the final dissolution as 1843 and mentioned the members who were present at that last meeting ; they were the Marquis of Bute, Charles Watkin Williams Wynn, Rice Trevor, D. Lewis, H. Hughes, Gwrgant himself, and the Secretary, John Parry, " Bardd Alaw," who was authorised to convey the books and papers of the Society to the British Museum. The MSS. were taken but the books in the library were kept at the Welsh School and the story of their removal belongs to the next chapter. John Parry, like the Secretary of the first Society, omitted to take care of the minute books and no trace of them has been found.

Gwrgant offers no reason for the dissolution of the Society, but one reason was the lack of wise leadership among London Welshmen—one man of the calibre of Richard Morris would have been invaluable to the Society, for the furtherance of its objects and for acting as a magnet to rally the London Welshmen to the cause of Wales. John Parry proved too strong for the other members and expended its resources entirely on music. Mention has already been made of Charles Watkin Williams Wynn's observation on the shortcomings of the Cymmrodorion ; this is endorsed by the Editor of the *Archaelogia Cambrensis* when he gives the following reason for the establishment of the *Cambrian Archaelogical Association* (in 1846)— " Had the Cymmrodorion maintained its pristine energy and known how to anticipate the wants and wishes of the Antiquarians of Wales, the *Archaelogia Cambrensis* might never have existed."

The Gwyneddigion Society had probably disappeared even before the dissolution of the Second Cymmrodorion—a writer in 1837 states that the Gwyneddigion had ceased to meet owing to dissension and apathy. There is a reference in *Seren Gomer* in 1840 to an Eisteddfod held under the auspices of the Cymreigyddion and the Gwyneddigion and it may be that the two Societies had been combined. The Cymreigyddion Secretary, writing in 1844, says that "the other London Societies of a similar nature are dead to all intents and purposes and have left no issue except good deeds."

The Cymreigyddion Society itself disappeared about 1855, and with its passing, the history of the old London Societies comes to an end. Apathy and indifference are the reasons given for their disappearance, but the real cause was the change that had come over Welsh life in London. The old leaders, lovers of poetry and song and harp, were replaced by serious, sober-minded men—earnest reformers who were concerned only with the educational and social problems confronting Wales. The old convivial spirit disappeared and the various places of worship superseded the taverns as the centres of Welsh Social life in London ; indeed even the Cymreigyddion Society at one time during the last years of its existence had turned its back on the taverns and frequented a more respectable meeting-place ; the innovation however met with little success and the Society soon returned to the old haunts. It is also significant that the Cymreigyddion during the last years of its existence appointed a Committee with the object of forming a Society for promoting secular knowledge in Wales, but the Society did not materialise. One of the members of this Committee (although he was not a member of the Cymreigyddion) was Hugh Owen, a native of Anglesey (later Sir Hugh Owen) who was to become a pioneer of education in Wales and who had already written a *Letter to the Welsh People*, advocating the acceptance of the Government Grant for education in Wales. This pamphlet was written in 1843, the year of the dissolution of the Second Cymmrodorion Society, and this year may be taken as the dividing line between the old period and the new. From this time London Welshmen were to be intimately concerned with the social problems of their native land and although their activities were not to be centralised into a strong Society for another thirty years— until the formation of the Third Society—a London Society established in the sixties prepared the way for the Third

Cymmrodorion. In 1852 the Rev. John Williams (Ab Ithel) severed his connection with the Cambrian Archaelogical Association (which he himself had formed in 1846) and founded the Cambrian Institution, and a branch was started in London in 1855. The Chairman was Gwrgant, already mentioned, the Secretary the Rev. Robert Jones of Rotherhithe, who was to become the Editor of the Third Cymmrodorion Society, lastly, the Treasurer was Hugh Owen, who was to be one of the two founders of the Third Cymmrodorion Society. This London Branch of the Cambrian Institution differed greatly from the previous London Societies ; more emphasis was laid upon the moral aspect of its work. Robert Jones stressed the importance of preventing the meetings from degenerating into mere convivial gatherings. Gwrgant, too, appeared as a renagade from the ranks of the old Cymmrodorion, when he emphasised rather the educational value of the Cambrian Institution—" in as much as it would call the rising generation . . . away from places of dangerous amusement or demoralising habits, to devote their leisure hours to the study of science, literature, music and the fine arts."

Little is known of the activities of this Society, but it had pointed the way to the establishment of a London Society on a basis not precisely identical with those on which its predecessors had been established.

VI.—THE THIRD CYMMRODORION SOCIETY

THIRTY years were to elapse before the Cymmrodorion Society was re-established, and during that time, the need for a national Society to promote literature was keenly felt. Moreover, as the Eisteddfodau had become universally popular, and hundreds were being held throughout Wales, there was a growing desire for one annual National Eisteddfod, and an " Eisteddfod Council " was formed for this purpose during the 'sixties, but after a brief existence, it was dissolved because of the financial failure of the Ruthin Eisteddfod of 1868.

Education had also become a subject of paramount importance in Wales, and this interim period had witnessed considerable educational activity. Hugh Owen, in spite of the indignation aroused by the notorious 1847 Report, succeeded in his advocacy of the acceptance of State grants for day schools, and numerous schools were established by agents of the British Society in North and South Wales. The efficiency of these schools was greatly increased by the training of teachers at the Training College founded at Bangor in 1862 ; the National Society already possessed its own Training Colleges—the Carmarthen College had been established in 1848, and in 1849 a training school at Caernarvon had been converted into a College for North Wales.

It was during this period that the first University College was established. Several Schemes had been put forward, but it was among London Welshmen that the successful scheme was inaugurated ; a committee was formed (which met at the Freemason's Tavern, the home of the Second Cymmrodorion Society), to collect funds for the establishment of a College. This College, which was opened at Aberystwyth in 1872, had to rely on voluntary subscriptions for eighteen years, and depended literally on the " pennies of the poor," which were collected largely by Hugh Owen, who with his famous black bag became a familiar figure in all the remote villages of Wales.

But there was a vital link missing from the educational system—intermediate schools to fill the gap between the primary schools and the Aberystwyth College.

With all these problems awaiting solution, it was natural that Welshmen should seek some central organisation to direct their energies, and as a result the formation of three Societies was proposed almost concurrently. At the Portmadoc Eisteddfod of 1872, the project of an Antiquarian Society was mooted ; the leading spirit in the venture was J. R. Elias (1819-1881), a nephew of John Elias, and usually known as " Y Thesbiad." He was a keen Eisteddfodwr, and a student of literature and antiquarian topics ; he and Dr. Evans ("Tudur"), of Llannerch-y-medd, were appointed secretaries of the proposed Society, and a statement was published, signed by the Rev. D. Silvan Evans, The Rev. Thomas Jones (" Llallawg "), F.S.A. of Nethertong, The Rev. John Peter (" Ioan Pedr ") of Bala, and the Rev. Richard Parry (" Gwalchmai "), referring to the mass of antiquarian knowledge uncollected in Wales, and enumerating the benefits that would accrue from disseminating this knowledge among the Welsh people. As a result of the publication of this statement, three hundred applications for membership were received by the Secretaries, and at the Mold Eisteddfod in 1873, J. R. Elias formally proposed the establishment of a Welsh Antiquarian Society, and the publication of an Antiquarian Journal. No resolution was passed, however, the meeting being terminated on the understanding that other motions of a similar nature would be proposed and considered on the following day.

On that day, the formation of a Society of all recognised Welsh literati and musicians was suggested by the poet Ceiriog. This Society was to be designated " The Order of the Round Table " (Urdd y Ford Gron), and was to safeguard the prestige of the Eisteddfod by forbidding its members to take part in small literary gatherings. Its principal aim was to reform the management of the Eisteddfod, but the form of procedure was vague—" the Society for years would exist unostentatiously, but could in course of time merit the respect of the country as far as to enable it to diminish the disorder and confusion of the Eisteddfodau and utilise the great power which the national gathering possessed." The Order was to follow the example of the Second Cymmrodorion Society in providing prizes at the Eisteddfodau and all the adjudications were to be published.

In the course of the discussion which followed, a third suggestion was put forward, namely, the revival of the Cymmrodorion Society by London Welshmen. In that year, a Musical Prize Fund Committee had been formed in London for the purpose of collecting money towards the expenses of the South Wales Choral Union on its visit to London to compete for the £1,000 prize trophy, offered by the Directors of the Crystal Palace. When the Union had secured the trophy, the Committee met to decide on the disposal of the surplus money, and it was felt that the Committee should remain in existence for the benefit of Wales. One of its members, John Griffith, popularly known as " Gohebydd," proposed that " the Musical Prize Fund Committee should be the nucleus of a Society for the encouragement of literature and fine arts in Wales." This resolution was seconded by Hugh Owen, and was approved by those present, among whom were Sir J. H. Puleston (as Chairman), Stephen Evans, Brinley Richards, R. G. Williams, Q.C., the Rev. Robert Jones of Rotherhithe, G. Osborne Morgan, M.P., and Sir Thomas D. Lloyd, M.P. Gohebydd and Hugh Owen had repeated consultations as to the form and character of their proposed Society and the suggestion of reviving the Cymmrodorion Society was made by Gohebydd. This is the testimony of Hugh Owen—" to Gohebydd alone belongs the credit of proposing that the Society which we felt to be needed, should take the form of a revived Cymmrodorion Society." Gohebydd was a nephew of Samuel Roberts of Llanbrynmair, and he was probably led to take an interest in the history of the old Cymmrodorion by the fact that he had in his possession the letter sent by Griffith Jones, as Secretary of the Second Cymmrodorion in 1826, to Samuel Roberts, congratulating him on being awarded the Society's Medal for students in Grammar Schools. Furthermore, two articles published by Gohebydd prove that he had carefully studied the *Constitutions* of the First Society, and the *Transactions* of the Second Society, doubtless from the copies preserved in the British Museum.

Thus at the Mold Eisteddfod, Gohebydd announced the resolution of the Musical Prize Fund Committee and the plans made for the reviving the Cymmrodorion Society ; he also suggested that the promoters of the two other Societies, the

Antiquarian and the Eisteddfodic Societies, should merge their proposals with that of the London Welshmen, in order to have London as a centre, and to ensure a really powerful and influential Society. This suggestion was seconded by Hugh Owen, and was accepted by the meeting, whereupon a sub-committee was appointed to form proposals to be discussed the following day— the committee consisting of Gohebydd, Ceiriog, Tudur, Gweirydd ap Rhys, Alfardd (J. J. Hughes), with Ioan Arfon (J. O. Griffith) as Chairman. The report of the committee, expressing approval of the work of the London Welshmen and proposing that corresponding members should be chosen to enrol members in Wales, was adopted on the following day. Two corresponding members for North Wales were chosen, viz., Ceiriog and William Hughes ("Tegerin") of Llannerch-y-medd, and in September, printed notices appeared requesting all the Welsh literati and musicians intending to become members of the Cymmrodorion Society to communicate with these two.

Meanwhile four Welshmen met from time to time in London to make arrangements for the formal revival of the Society ; they were Hugh Owen, Gohebydd, Stephen Evans and Brinley Richards, and the rules of the new Society were drafted by Hugh Owen, and sent to Ceiriog for approval. Thus, Gohebydd claims the honour of being the resuscitator of the Cymmrodorion Society, while the foundations were laid by Hugh Owen. Robert Jones of Rotherhithe, who is usually associated with the establishment of the Third Society, took no active part in the formation, but became a leading figure in the activities of the Society, while Gohebydd's name appears only rarely in the minutes of the Council ; his frequent absence from London as the *Baner* correspondent probably accounts for this.

Thirty people were invited to the first meeting of the Society, which was held in London on the 10th of November, 1873, but only fifteen were present. They were—Hugh Owen, who was elected Chairman of the meeting, Sir J. H. Puleston and J. Roland Phillips, who were chosen Treasurer and Secretary respectively ; Gohebydd, Gwrgant, Stephen Evans, Robert Jones of Rotherhithe, Brinley Richards, the Rev. Evan Jones, William Davies (" Mynorydd "), Morgan Lloyd, Q.C., R.G. Williams, Q.C., B. T. Williams, Q.C., Ellis Jones and Erasmus

Jones. T. Marchant Williams attended on the invitation of Hugh Owen to take notes.

These fifteen men constituted themselves the Council of the Cymmrodorion Society and proceeded to draw up its Rules. The anniversary of the Society was to be held on November 9th—that day being the birthday of the Prince of Wales—and Sir Watkin Williams Wynn was chosen President of the Society ; a long line of distinguished Presidents has followed him ; Sir Harold Idris Bell is now the President. Addresses were delivered on the proposed character of the new Society ; the Chairman emphasised the need of a Society of a more permanent character and having a wider scope than the Eisteddfod ; Brinley Richards suggested that it should supplement the work of the Eisteddfod by publishing the successful poems and essays, and that it should develop the Eisteddfod as an educational institution ; Gohebydd stressed the importance of using the Society for the encouragement of literature, science and arts in Wales. Robert Jones of Rotherhithe and Gwrgant connected the new Society with the previous Cymmrodorion Societies, the former by speaking of the Morris brothers and the work accomplished by them, and the latter by referring to the dissolution of the Second Society.

It will be convenient here to anticipate and to refer to the subsequent meetings of the Society. They were of two kinds—the London meetings and the Cymmrodorion Section meetings of the National Eisteddfod. The latter, which will be described more fully on a later page, dealt with topics of immediate interest to Wales, and advantage was taken of these gatherings to secure co-operation for the Society's ideals. As will be seen, many a movement owes its origin to these Section meetings, and they were also the means of obtaining various reforms. The London meetings took the form of periodical gatherings for the reading of papers on literary, scientific or artistic subjects, all bearing on Wales. The Society was singularly felicitous in obtaining men of note to lecture ; and the addresses given were printed in the publications of the Society and will be dealt with in that connection.

Of the fifteen men present at the historic meeting on the 10th November, 1873, the most notable figure is Sir Hugh Owen (1804-1881), not only because he was a pioneer in Welsh education and the promoter of the new Society, but also because he induced others to join the Society and to work for Wales. During a long career as Chief Clerk of the Poor Law Commission he devoted all his leisure to social and educational reforms and gathered around him collaborators who were to carry on the work after his death. As already mentioned, he advocated State-aided day schools, and introduced the British Schools into Wales ; he was also chiefly instrumental in founding the Training College at Bangor in 1858. The University College of Wales at Aberystwyth (1872) owes its origin to him, and on the formation of that institution he resigned his post at the Poor Law Board to devote himself to its welfare. Through his influence and that of Lord Aberdare, the Departmental Committee for Intermediate and Higher Education was set up, and in his evidence before the Commission he submitted a complete scheme for intermediate education in Wales. He also perceived the need of reforming the Eisteddfod ; he formed a Social Science Section, and was a member of the Eisteddfod Council, already mentioned. Numerous philanthropic institutions were promoted by him, such as the Cambrian Association for the Education of the Deaf and Dumb, and the London Welsh Charitable Aid Society. Although Hugh Owen himself would have no interest in a purely literary Society in which social reform did not play a part, yet he came into contact with the Cymreigyddion Society, his name appears on the Committee set up by that Society to promote secular knowledge in Wales, referred to in the previous chapter, and he was on intimate terms with two prominent Cymreigyddion, Caerfallwch and Griffith Davies, the actuary, who were both members of Jewin Chapel when Owen went to London in 1825.

John Griffith (Gohebydd) (1821-1877), a native of Barmouth Merionethshire, came to London on the recommendation of Samuel Roberts of Llanbrynmair to assist Hugh Owen in the establishment of British Schools ; this was the beginning of a life-long friendship. When Owen was able to dispense with his services, Griffith remained in London, and for the last twenty years of his life was the London correspondent of the *Baner*, and became known as Gohebydd. Through his accounts of the proceedings of Parliament, he made monoglot Welshmen conversant with contemporary history and also helped to create strong Liberal feeling in Wales. Many a great movement in

Wales owes its success to the interest taken in it by Gohebydd, in advocating meetings, and in faithfully reporting the proceedings. To many, indeed, he *was* the *Baner*. A thorough-going Independent, he did great work as a political agitator ; he was the prime mover in convening the great meeting at Aberystwyth held to express sympathy with the evicted Cardiganshire tenants. Gohebydd believed with Hugh Owen that the Eisteddfod should be, primarily, an educational institution ; and that, with certain improvements, it could be of paramount importance in the moral and intellectual advancement of the people. In all the progressive movements of his time Gohebydd took a leading part, and his presence at every Eisteddfod and all political and religious meetings earned for him the sobriquet "Pobman." Robert Jones of Rotherhithe (1810-1879) was the first Editor of the *Cymmrodor*, and one of the most active members of the Society during the first years of its existence. He was born at Llawr y Cwm, a farm situated three miles outside Llanfyllin in Montgomeryshire, and was educated at Oswestry Grammar School and Jesus College, Oxford. After holding curacies at Connah's Quay and Barmouth he was appointed incumbent of All Saints' Church, Rotherhithe, where he remained for thirty-seven years. He was a staunch supporter of the Eisteddfod and of all Welsh movements, and was a keen supporter of the University College at Aberystwyth, being convinced that its establishment would prove an inestimable benefit to the Church of England in Wales, by educating candidates for Holy Orders from the ranks of the people. He considered that the bishops, by indifference towards the Welsh language, had alienated the people, and articles on behalf of the language were written by him and published in the *Times*. His knowledge of Welsh literature was remarkable ; it was said that if all the Welsh books in the British Museum were to be destroyed they could be reproduced from the remarkable memory of Robert Jones. In his earlier days he was a frequent contributor to the *Shrewsbury Chronicle* and throughout his life published articles in the Welsh magazines ; the *Montgomeryshire Collections*, in particular, contain many of his publications. Robert Jones brought out the *Cymmrodor* at his own expense, as will be seen later. His other publications consist of a Welsh Hymn-Book, published when he was a curate at Barmouth, a reprint in 1864 of *Flores Poetarum Britannicorum*, the work of Dr. John Davies of Mallwyd, and an edition of the *Poetical Works of Goronwy Owen* (1876), containing notes on the poems and a biography of the poet. In 1887, he edited *Salesbury's English-Welsh Dictionary* for the Cymmrodorion Society. The following notice appeared in the minutes of the Council on the death of Robert Jones—" One of the earliest promoters of the Society, and one who, by his large experience, unremitting attention, wide knowledge of Welsh literature, and especially by his labours as the Editor of the publications of the Society, did so much towards securing it on a firm basis, and furthering the objects for which it was re-established. The Council desire to record also its profound sense of the true patriotism and self-sacrificing devotion with which Mr. Jones, amid many other important avocations, and under many trying difficulties, undertook this work."

Sir Hugh Owen acted as Chairman of this first meeting and of a few subsequent meetings, but the future Chairman of the Council, who was to hold that post for many years, was also present. Stephen Evans (1818-1905), was chosen Chairman of the Society on the 14th January, and held that office without a break for over thirty years until his death in 1905. He was a native of Llannon, Cardiganshire, and at an early age went to London, where he established a prosperous business as a warehouseman ; towards the end of his life, however, he was to suffer reverses of fortune. Stephen Evans was another Welshman who came under the influence of Sir Hugh Owen, and he regarded the latter as his leader in all matters relating to Wales. An intimate common friend of Stephen Evans and Hugh Owen depicts their differing temperaments in the following words— " Sir Hugh was of an astute laborious Northern type, the calm unruffled temper, working by conciliatory methods, but never giving way when persuaded it was right. Stephen Evans, of the more fiery and impetuous type of the South, loud-voiced . . . bluff in manner and hasty sometimes . . . a little imperious perhaps, but always deferring in the long run to the calmer judgment of his revered leader."

Yet another of the original fifteen members had come into contact with Sir Hugh Owen in his youth, and was led to co-operate with him in later life in the cause of Higher Education in Wales. When Sir John H. Puleston (1830-1908) left his native village of Llanfair Dyffryn Clwyd and came to London to study medicine, he became a member of Jewin Welsh chapel, and thus became acquainted with Hugh Owen and Stephen Evans. After a few years' sojourn in London, he emigrated to the States, and remained there until 1870, when he returned to England, and opened a bank in London. In the following year he was elected Conservative M.P. for Devonport, and continued to represent that constituency until 1892, when he unsuccessfully contested the seat for Caernarvon Boroughs against David Lloyd George. He became a member of the Established Church and inaugurated an annual St. David's Day service at St. Paul's Cathedral. His connection with Welsh national movements was mainly non-political, and in London, charitable work among the poor engaged much of his sympathy. At the first meeting of the Cymmrodorion Society he was chosen Treasurer, an office which he held for three years.

The Secretary chosen at the first meeting was John Roland Phillips (1844-1887), a native of Cilgerran, Pembrokeshire. At an early age he was a successful competitor at local Eisteddfodau, and as a youth, when articled to a Cardigan solicitor, was the author of a prize essay on *The History of Cardigan*, At the Cardiganshire Eisteddfod of 1886, his *History of Cilgerran* was awarded the first prize and published in the following year. In London he was called to the Bar and was eventually appointed first Stipendiary Magistrate for West Ham. His literary activities did not cease after his departure from Cardiganshire ; for many years he edited the legal columns of one of the public journals, and his leisure was devoted to acquiring a knowledge of the Welsh MSS. in the Record Office and in the British Museum. As a result of his studies he compiled a history of the *Civil War in Wales and the Marches* which was published in 1874. He also contemplated the publication of a History of Wales during the Tudor period and an account of the Castles and Abbeys in South Wales. His last publication was *A Short History of the County of Glamorgan* (1879).

From a literary standpoint he seemed well qualified for the post of Secretary, but his career in that office was of short duration and unsatisfactory. His failure may have been due to lack of interest in the work of the Society ; he omitted to pay the debts of the Society and on one occasion was unable to furnish the report for the annual meeting. His post was honorary, and when on the 24th of February, 1875, after holding office for little more than a year, the Secretary appealed for pecuniary remuneration, the Society decided to appoint a new Secretary at a salary of £20 a year, and to retain the services of J. Roland Phillips as Honorary Secretary, promising to pay him an honorarium of £25 a year, when the Society should have an annual income of £120. The new Secretary acted as recorder of the minutes of the Council, and numerous complaints are entered in the minutes regarding the delinquent Honorary Secretary. Continued criticism of his work led to the resignation of Roland Phillips on the 3rd of May, 1876, and the Secretary took over the work.

Two officials of the Second Cymmrodorion Society were to witness the revival of the Society in 1873—viz., Henry Davies of Cheltenham (1804-1890) and William Jones, " Gwrgant " (1803-1886). The former was to take no active part in the proceedings of the Third Society, but Gwrgant was present at the first meeting, and became a member of the Council and eventually a Vice-President of the Society. Gwrgant was a member of the one Welsh Church in London at the time, at Ely Place (later removed to St. Benet's, Blackfriars), and in 1867, as a Warden of the Church, he had been chosen by the congregation to oppose the appointment of the incumbent chosen by the Selection Committee and to propose the Rev. Evan Jones, curate of Oakwood in the diocese of Llandaff, in his place. The Rev. Evan Jones was appointed and held the incumbency until 1898. His name appears among those present at the first meeting and he was a faithful, but not a very active member of the Council for many years ; he died in 1903.

Gwrgant appeared in the first Council meeting as the only surviving member of the Council of the Second Society, but there was also present one who had been connected with the old Cambrian Eisteddfodau. Brinley Richards (1819-1875) was born in the year in which the Cambrian Eisteddfodau were inaugurated at Carmarthen (his father being the organist of St. Peter's Church, where David Rowland, the promoter of those Eisteddfodau, was then curate), and in 1834 he won a prize at the Cardiff Eisteddfod, and was presented with the prize by John Parry (Bardd Alaw), the Registrar of Music of the Second Cymmrodorion Society. In the same year he entered the Royal Academy and gained there a King's Scholarship, being the first Welshman to win that honour. Later he was made a Professor, then a Director and official examiner of the

Academy. Brinley Richards published a great quantity of music, especially Welsh music, and with the aid of Lady Llanover he encouraged harp-playing and singing with the harp in Wales. The Eisteddfod received his ready support, and he was a member of the " Eisteddfod Council."

Three Queen's Counsel present at the meeting were R. G. Williams, B. T. Williams and Morgan Lloyd. B. T. Williams was at one time leader of the South Wales Circuit and Recorder of Carmarthen. He was M.P. for Carmarthen from 1878 to 1881, and in that year was appointed Judge of the Glamorgan County Courts. In 1876 he was co-editor with D. Silvan Evans of Thomas Stephens's *Literature of the Cymry*, prefacing it with a memoir of Stephens. He was also for some time editor of the *Law Magazine and Commercial Compendium*. He championed the cause of Higher Education as early as 1852 and he published a pamphlet upon the desirability of founding in Wales a University similar to the University of Glasgow, and was chosen one of the two Honorary Secretaries of Aberystwyth College in 1885.

Morgan Lloyd (1822-1893) was the other Honorary Secretary of the College at the time. He was educated at Edinburgh University and was called to the Bar at the Middle Temple in 1847. Morgan Lloyd sat as a Liberal for Beaumaris from 1874—1885 ; in that year, however, he unsuccessfully contested Anglesey as a Unionist. His career at the Bar, on the other hand, was eminently successful. He practised on the North Wales and Chester Circuit, where his knowledge of Welsh proved an invaluable asset. He was greatly in demand, as to be represented by him was to win a case, indeed it has often been said that juries, being mostly monoglot Welshmen and therefore at a loss to understand the proceedings, invariably got out of their dilemma by siding with Morgan Lloyd's client. He was the author of two publications on law—" *The Law and Practice in Law Courts* " and " *The Supreme Courts of Judicature* " (1873 and 1875). Morgan Lloyd was considered by his contemporaries to be one of the three Welshmen who rendered the greatest service to the University College at Aberystwyth on its formation.

Two prominent business men in London, Ellis Jones and Erasmus Jones, and a sculptor-musician, complete the list of the fifteen original members. William Davies (" Mynorydd," 1828-1901), a native of Merthyr Tydfil, was intended for a musical career, but forsook the study of music for sculpture.

He worked with Noble, the chief London sculptor of his time, in completing a statue of Queen Victoria and one of Sir Robert Peel ; for thirty years he was an exhibitor at the Royal Academy. Mynorydd was the father of Dr. Mary Davies, the well-known singer. Ellis Jones was a native of South Caernarvonshire and went to London in connection with one of the largest firms of Manchester warehousemen. He is described as a generous subscriber to Welsh Charities and to the funds of Welsh Wesleyan Methodism.

Although his name is not recorded in the minutes of the first meeting, Sir Thomas Marchant Williams (1845-1914), according to his own testimony, was present, having come at the request of Hugh Owen to make a report of the proceedings. A few years previously, as a student at the Training College at Bangor, Marchant Williams had come under the influence of the Rev. John Phillips, the Principal of the College, and had become acquainted with Hugh Owen during Owen's periodical visits to the College. As one of the first Welsh " pupil-teachers," he had worked at Aberdare under Dan Isaac Davies, the educationist ; he was also one of the first students of Aberystwyth College. Marchant Williams removed to London as an Inspector of Schools when the Cymmrodorion Society was in its infancy. In London he took up law, was called to the Bar, and afterwards became Stipendiary Magistrate of Merthyr Tydfil. He was the author of a satirical work on the Welsh Members of Parliament of his day, and as the Editor of *The Nationalist*, a non-political magazine for the encouragement of nationalism in Wales, he was a caustic commentator on contemporary events in Wales. Marchant Williams was a member of the Council of the Cymmrodorion Society for over forty years.

This concludes the list of those present at the first meeting of the Society ; the following pages contain the names of the officials and prominent members up to the present day, with more detailed reference to those members who were prominent in the Society, but who were not so well-known in other spheres of Welsh life.

Stephen Evans was succeeded as Chairman in 1905 by Sir John Rhys (1840-1915), Principal of Jesus College, Oxford, and first Jesus Professor of Celtic. Rhys will be remembered as a folk-lorist and as a pioneer in twentieth century Celtic linguistic research, as through his efforts the study of Welsh philology became scientific, and was saved from the pernicious influence of Pughe and his coterie. He was a member of the Cymmrodorion Society from an early date, and was Chairman of the Council for ten years. *The Welsh People*, a result of searching inquiries for the Royal Commission on Land in Wales (1895), was written by Sir John Rhys in collaboration with Sir David Brynmor Jones, K.C. (1852-1921), who also acted as Chairman of the Council for one year (1919-1920). Brynmor Jones, like his more famous brother, Principal Viriamu Jones of Cardiff, evinced a strong interest in all matters relating to Wales, paying especial attention to Welsh laws and history, and contributing articles on these subjects to the *Cymmrodor* and the *Transactions*.

Another Chairman of the Council, Dr. Henry Owen of Poyston (1844-1919) requires more comment. Dr. Owen practised law for more than forty years, and in the course of doing philanthropic work in London was brought into contact with Sir John Williams, afterwards the benefactor of the National Library, on whose suggestion he joined the Cymmrodorion Society. Vincent Evans as the Secretary of the Society induced him to read a paper to the Cymmrodorion which led him to compose his first literary work—*Gerald the Welshman* (published in 1889). Practically the whole of his literary work was done for, or in connection with, the Cymmrodorion Society. He was engaged during his lifetime on a series of works connected with his native county, Pembrokeshire. He edited the work of the Elizabethan historian George Owen of Henllys, which was published in four volumes entitled *Pembrokeshire*, and perceiving lack of published data for investigating the history of Wales, he produced three volumes of *A Calendar of Public Records Relating to Pembrokeshire*. Further references will be made to his work in connection with the Cymmrodorion Record Series. Dr. Owen was Chairman of the Society from 1916 to 1919, and also Treasurer during this time (1906-1918).

The Rev. Dr. Griffith Hartwell Jones (1854-1944) was elected Chairman of the Council in 1921, and for some time combined the offices of Chairman and Treasurer. He was a great-grandson of that David Jones of Trefriw who has appeared in our Chapter III, and he was at one time Professor of Latin at University College, Cardiff ; he became a member of the Cymmrodorion Council in 1892, when he was appointed

Rector of Nutfield in Surrey. In addition to being an active Cymmrodor, Dr. Hartwell Jones was Chairman of the National Eisteddfod Association, and a member for over thirty years of the Royal Commission on Ancient Monuments in Wales. His substantial work, *Celtic Britain and the Pilgrim Movement* was published by the Society in 1912. The present Chairman of the Council, following Hartwell Jones, is Sir Wynn Powell Wheldon.

Two others who held the post of Treasurer to the Society were H. Loyd Roberts, a barrister of the Middle Temple, who filled the office for a quarter of a century (1881-1906), and John Hinds (1862-1928), an M.P. for Carmarthen, and at one time President of the Baptist Union in Wales. Hartwell Jones was followed as Treasurer (1934-1950) by Mr. T. D. Slingsby-Jenkins ; the present Treasurer is Mr. T. Arnold Lewis.

On the death of Robert Jones of Rotherhithe in 1881, the editorship of publications was undertaken by Thomas Powel, who held the office until 1886, when he resigned owing to ill-health. Powel was a native of Llanwrtyd, Breconshire, and was educated at Llandovery College and Jesus College, Oxford. After serving as Headmaster of Bootle College, he was appointed lecturer in Celtic at the newly opened Cardiff College, and later became the first Professor of that subject in Wales. In this capacity, he gave distinguished service to Wales for thirty-four years. Powel was responsible for securing, for the Cardiff College, the Salesbury Library, and on his suggestion the Welsh manuscripts from the collection of Sir Thomas Phillips, Bart., were bought for the Cardiff Free Library. Reference will be made to his work as Editor of the *Cymmrodor*, and to his articles advocating a place for the vernacular language in education.

Another Editor of the Society's publications was Egerton Grenville Bagot Phillimore (1856-1933), a native of Shiplake-on-Thames. His mother was a descendant of the Salesburys of the Vale of Clwyd, and this may account for the fact that Phillimore learnt Welsh and interested himself in the historical and topographical antiquities of Wales. He studied its lore, early history and place names, and his chief scholarly work was to compile the notes appended to George Owen's *Pembrokeshire*. Phillimore edited *The Gossiping Guide to Wales* and was for some time editor of the *Archaeologia Cambrensis*. In 1897 he was awarded the Cymmrodorion Medal for distinguished service to Wales.

Among the educationists who from time to time were members of the Council of the Society may be mentioned Dr. Thomas Nicholas (1820-1879), a nonconformist minister who resigned his post as professor at Carmarthen College and removed to London to devote himself to literary pursuits and to the cause of education in Wales. He was responsible for stimulating the University movement, originated in the fifties, by writing a series of letters in the *Cambrian Daily Leader* in 1863, which brought him to the notice of Hugh Owen, with the result that a Provisional Committee for establishing a University College in Wales was formed and Dr. Nicholas was appointed the Secretary of the Committee, a post which he held until 1867, when the Aberystwyth building was purchased.

Henry Austin Bruce (1815-1895), first Lord Aberdare and a Vice-President of the Cymmrodorion Society, played a prominent part in the educational movement. He is remembered as the Chairman of the Departmental Committee of Education formed in 1880 to investigate into the condition of Intermediate and Higher Education in Wales, and which led to the establishment of the University College and Intermediate Schools. The "Grand Old Man of Welsh Education," as he was called, presided over the most of the meetings held to found the University, and on its foundation became the first Chancellor.

From the Council of the Society came the first Registrars of the University Colleges of Cardiff and Bangor. Ivor James was in London earning his livelihood partly as a journalist for the *Western Mail*, and was on the Council of the Society, when chosen the first Registrar of the University College of Cardiff. In 1895, on the formation of the University of Wales he became its first Registrar. William Cadwaladr Davies, the first Registrar of the Bangor College, was a member of the Cymmrodorion when in London as Assistant Secretary to the University College of Aberystwyth, under the immediate direction of Hugh Owen, who had aroused his interest in Welsh matters. He married Dr. Mary Davies, whose father, "Mynorydd," has been mentioned as one of the original members of the Cymmrodorion Council. Dr. Mary Davies was also to be chosen a member of the Council later.

Another educationist and member of the Council who had come under the influence of Hugh Owen was Sir Lewis Morris (1833-1907), a great-grandson of the famous Lewis Morris. He was a poet who enjoyed considerable vogue during his lifetime, and hoped vainly for the Poet-Laureateship on the death of his friend Tennyson. In politics he was an advanced Liberal and unsuccessfully sought a Parliamentary seat. Lewis Morris, induced by Hugh Owen, became one of the Joint Honorary Secretaries of the University College at Aberystwyth in 1878, and was later made a Vice-President of that College ; he was also Chairman of the Executive Committee of the National Eisteddfod Association from its formation. The Cymmrodorion Society elected him a member of the Council in 1877 and Vice-President in 1892.

Foremost among the Cymmrodorion who performed signal service to the University of Wales must be mentioned Sir Isambard Owen (1856-1927). Although educated wholly in England, he was an untiring worker in the struggle for a Welsh University, and was largely responsible for bringing the movement for an independent University to a successful issue. On the formation of the University he became its first Senior Deputy Chancellor. He has been described as " a man who had been especially prepared by Destiny for the role of University-builder," owing to his brilliant gift of administration and unbounded energy. Isambard Owen was introduced to the Cymmrodorion Society almost on its revival, by Joseph Edwards the sculptor, and was elected a member of the Council as early as 1897. He also acted as editor of the Society's publications for a brief period.

Another famous member of the Council, Sir John Williams (1840-1926) will always be remembered for his valuable work in connection with the National Library of Wales, and the University College at Aberystwyth. During the whole of his successful medical career in London, his leisure time was devoted to one ideal—that of founding a National Library of Wales, and with this end in view he collected a fine library of valuable books and MSS. ; this collection, now known as the Llanstephan MSS., together with the Shirburn and Peniarth MSS. which he procured, he presented to the National Library.

In addition to London Welshmen who took a prominent part in the educational and other progressive movements at the end of the last century, the Council also included scholars who had removed to London to devote themselves to literary pursuits. One of these was Howell W. Lloyd, M.A. (1816-1893), a convert to the Roman Catholic faith, who fought vigorously for Higher Education for Roman Catholics. His chief study was the language and archaeology of Wales, and he was a member of the Powys-land Club and other associations. Another such member was the Rev. John Davies, M.A., a former Rector of Walsoken, Norfolk, who had resigned his living to devote himself to the study of literature, especially to the study of Sanskrit. Yet another litterateur and member of the Council was Colonel George Grant Francis (1814-1882), historian and archaeologist. He was the founder of the Royal Institution of South Wales, took part in the establishment of the Cambrian Archaeological Society, and contributed to its transactions.

Membership of the Council was not confined to Welshmen. Alfred Nutt (1856-1910), the publisher, was elected a member because of his work for Celtic folk-lore and antiquities. A more interesting figure, and one who took an active part in the deliberations of the Society, was Prince Louis Lucien Buonaparte (1813-1891), the fourth son of Lucien Buonaparte the brother of Napoleon. Lucien Buonaparte had been taken a prisoner by a British ship in the first decade of the last century and was sent on parole to Ludlow, and the son, Prince Louis, took up his abode in England and devoted himself to philological researches. He was a member of most European academies, and the Cymmrodorion Society in particular found in him a keen supporter. He was elected honorary member of the Society in 1880, and became a frequent attendant at the meetings ; he presented to the Society for publication (1880) his copy of *Athravaeth Gristnogavl*, the work of Griffith Roberts of Milan. Prince Louis was President of the Welsh Dialect Society, and, accompanied by Robert Jones of Rotherhithe, who taught him to speak Welsh, he made a tour through Wales to discover where the purest dialect was spoken.

Well-known barristers appear on the list of Council members. The following two will suffice as examples—J. W. Bowen, a leading barrister of the South Wales Circuit, and W. Llewelyn Williams, K.C., M.P. (1867-1922), historian and novelist, and almost the only one of the members of the

Young Wales Movement to remain an enthusiastic Welsh Nationalist. Two prominent sculptors also served on the Council. James Milo Griffith (1843-1897), was an exhibitor at the Royal Academy for many years and his chief work is the statue of Hugh Owen in Caernarvon. The other sculptor, Joseph Edwards (1814-1882) was an early member of the Council, and, as has been already mentioned, introduced Isambard Owen to the Society. Joseph Edwards bequeathed to the Society his library and collection of engravings, and was the designer of the Cymmrodorion Medal.

Famous ministers in charge of Welsh churches in London were elected to the Council. Two of these were the Rev. John Evans of Eglwysbach (1840-1897), regarded as the most eloquent preacher among the Wesleyans in Wales, and the Rev. Rowland Williams, Hwfa Môn (1823-1895) of wide repute as an Archdruid, and one of the chief bardic adjudicators of the Eisteddfod in his day.

We shall conclude our list of prominent members by referring to the Secretaries of the Society. Mention has already been made of Roland Phillips's unsuccessful career as Secretary ; he was succeeded by Charles William Jones who was chosen on the 24th February, 1875, at a salary of £20 per annum. Charles William Jones was the brother of Robert Jones of Rotherhithe and like his brother, was educated at Oswestry Grammar School. He seems to have been intended for a scholastic career, but at the time of the revival of the Cymmrodorion Society was a clerk in the Poor Law Department, which was then reorganized as the Local Government Board, and Charles Jones became a prominent official of the Board. Following the tradition of the officers of the two previous Cymmrodorion Societies, this Secretary of the Cymmrodorion was a supporter of the Welsh Charity School—by this time a school for girls (but not yet a High School), and situated at Ashford, Middlesex, having been removed from Gray's-Inn-road in 1850. In the year 1883, Charles Jones was the Secretary of the House Committee of the Welsh School, and the Committee paid a tribute to his services— " to whose efforts the successful position of the Welsh Girls School as regards the number of students is largely due." Unlike his more famous brother, references to him in the journals and periodicals of the time are scarce, but at the Merthyr Tydfil Eisteddfod of 1881 his address was singled out for mention—"Of incidental speeches other than those delivered in the course of adjudications, . . . the most noticeable was that of Charles W. Jones . . . upon the permanence of the language . . . demanding attention to it." A contemporary writes of him thus—"Charles Jones never appeared to me as a personage of importance, and as far as I knew or ever heard, had never done anything to distinguish himself . . . essentially a quiet and friendly companion." A member of the Council gave the following testimony to his work—"He discharged the secretarial duties with scrupulous care and devotion, coupled with the strictest formality. The Society is largely indebted to this very quiet, very affable and very polite man." He held the office of Secretary until the 27th of October, 1887, when he was compelled to resign through ill-health. His death occurred in 1895.

In the absence of the Secretary due to the illness which caused his resignation, John Owens of the India Office acted as Secretary. A special meeting of the Council was convened on the first of November, 1887, to elect a permanent Secretary. A prominent member, W. E. Davies, was offered the post, but he refused the office, and two other candidates were named, John Owens and Evan Vincent Evans. As a result of the voting each gained the same number of votes (eight), and the Chairman of the Council (Stephen Evans) was called upon to give the casting vote, which he did in favour of Vincent Evans. The Secretary was to receive a salary of twenty-five guineas, and a commission of five per cent on all subscriptions of membership collected after the first hundred pounds and ten per cent profit on the sale of back publications.

It is of interest to note that the three named for the Secretaryship were all to survive for almost forty years, and since this appointment had far-reaching consequences on the history of the Society, it is instructive to compare the three men. John Owens of the India Office was a native of Llandwrog, Caernarvonshire. After spending eighteen years in the India Office in London, he became Secretary to Edward Davies of Llandinam, and was until 1902 connected with the management of the Llandinam fortunes, when he removed to Chester as a stockbroker, and became a power in the civic life of Chester. "John Owens of Chester," as he was usually called, was a pillar of the Calvinistic Methodists, and held the office of

Moderator of their North Wales Association. In London he was the Secretary of the Welsh Calvinistic Church in Nassau Street (later removed to Charing Cross Road), and in Llandinam was connected with the Forward Movement in South Wales. He was also responsible for inaugurating the C.M. Infirm and Aged Ministers' Fund and for the formation of the C.M. Central Fund.

William Edward Davies (1851-1927), was better known in Welsh circles in 1887 than John Owen or Vincent Evans, and had exerted considerable influence in Welsh matters for some time before this, so that it is not surprising to learn that he was offered the secretaryship by the unanimous wish of the Council. By means of letters and original articles to the *Wrexham Advertiser*, the *Western Mail*, and other journals he had expressed his opinion on such pressing problems as the Welsh Education Bill and Aberystwyth College. Before his departure for London in 1878, he had been the Secretary of the Caernarvon Eisteddfod in the previous year, and a few months before he received the offer from the Cymmrodorion Council, he had been the Secretary of the London National Eisteddfod. He was one of the founders of the National Eisteddfod Association, and although Vincent Evans acted as Secretary, and Marchant Williams as Honorary Secretary, it was W. E. Davies who drew up the rules, drafted the articles, and wrote the annual reports. He had also become well-known as the author of the biography of Hugh Owen, published in 1885 by the National Eisteddfod Association. Indeed he was one of the most prominent London Welshmen until 1891, when he left London to become the General Manager and Secretary of the Anglesey Limestone Company. Previous to this he had been an accountant in London, and after five years in Anglesey he returned to the Metropolis to follow the same profession, and eventually became a partner in the firm with which he was connected. On his return he resided outside London, a circumstance which forced him to be less active in Welsh affairs, and in this way he lost touch with London Welsh life ; however, he remained a member of the Cymmrodorion Council until his death.

As has already been mentioned, Vincent Evans was comparatively unknown in London in 1887. He had come to London fifteen years earlier, and was gaining recognition as a correspondent for the newspapers, and had been chosen the Secretary of the National Eisteddfod Association, and of the Cymmro-dorion Section of the Eisteddfod. The casting vote given by Stephen Evans was to make him a well-known figure in Wales as well as among London Welshmen, and for almost half-a-century he was to direct the affairs of the Cymmrodorion Society. Evan Vincent Evans (1852-1934) was a native of Nantcaw, Merionethshire, which explains the pseudonym which he later adopted for writing to the newspapers—"Nancaw Hen." As his family moved to Trawsfynydd a few years later, he received his education at the National School in Trawsfynydd, and his first situation was as a pupil teacher in that school. In 1867 he was apprenticed to the owner of the village store, one Jarrett Jarrett, who had three brothers in London, and this may have influenced his young assistant to follow them ; he was also doubtless attracted there by the success of another Trawsfynydd boy—Morgan Lloyd. It seems that he finally decided on the move to London with the view to enlarging his experience in journalism ; his connection with the Press had begun at an early age, and he was the local correspondent of the *Baner*.

He arrived in London on the eve of S. David's Day, 1872. In Trawsfynydd he had been known as Evan Evans ; on his arrival in London he provided himself with the additional name, Vincent, the name of his grandfather, Evan Vincent, who hailed from an agricultural family near Dolgelley. He did not devote himself entirely to journalistic pursuits, but took up another career in which he proved very successful. After a brief period in a solicitor's office, he was appointed by a firm of chartered accountants to special work in connection with the Chancery Lane Safe Deposit and Offices Company, and in time became Managing Director. However, he maintained a close connection with the Press ; soon after his arrival in London he became a member of the Parliamentary Press Gallery, and it is also of interest to note that on the death of "Gohebydd," Vincent Evans took his place in contributing a weekly London letter to the *Baner*.

It was as a Press representative that he first came into contact with the Cymmrodorion Society. On the 13th of December, 1883, he was invited as a representative of the *South Wales Daily News* and other newspapers to be present at a meeting of the Council, and the Society soon perceived his worth. In 1884 he became the Secretary of the Cymmrodorion Section of the National Eisteddfod, having been previously appointed Secretary of the National Eisteddfod Association. According to the minute-book, he was not yet a member of the Society ; he joined it on the 2nd of October, 1886, and he became a member of the Council in the same year. He was therefore only gradually becoming a well-known figure when he was appointed Secretary of the Society in the following year. In 1889, when the temporary arrangements made at the cessation of Thomas Powel's editorship came to an end, he was appointed Editor of the Society's publications. He retained both offices for almost half a century—until his death in 1934.

The 1887 report of the Society contains the following notice—" The Council have elected Mr. E. Vincent Evans whose qualifications for the post are already well-known to a large number of the members . . . and believe that the interests of the Society are safe in his hands." This trust was amply justified. Under his direction, the Society enlarged its sphere of work, and deepened its influence on the national life. Urgent problems in the social life of Wales were dealt with at the Society's meetings, and Vincent Evans possessed the great quality of attracting eminent persons to support these reforms and express their views in the meetings. The Society acted as a centre where all who laboured for the good of Wales might meet, and in this way, under his wise leadership, the Society became the most powerful organisation for the advancement of Welsh culture. He made it the supreme Welsh literary Society, and the same might be said of him as of Owain Myfyr, that, although not a man of letters, yet he gathered them around him, and these scholars contributed articles of lasting value to the Society's publications. Vincent Evans also gave many writers an opportunity, which they would not otherwise have had, of publishing their work. The *Transactions*, the *Cymmrodor*, and the *Cymmrodorion Record Series* are his monument. He was followed as Secretary by J. L. C. Cecil-Williams (now Sir John Cecil-Williams) and as Editor of Publications by Llewelyn Wyn Griffith.

One of the first achievements of the Third Cymmrodorion Society was to attain the object which had been the cause of the formation of the Second Cymmrodorion Society, namely, the establishment of an annual National Eisteddfod. With the decay of the Cambrian Societies had come disorder and confusion as to the time and place of holding the Eisteddfodau, which by now had secured the allegiance of the Nonconformists, and had become universally popular. Any body of men could claim the privilege of holding a " National Eisteddfod," provided that a Gorsedd was held in connection with it.

Two classes of Welshmen endeavoured to reform matters. They were the poets and the social reformers ; the former were actuated by a desire to uphold the prestige of the Eisteddfod, while the latter had discovered its possibilities as an educational institution. The result of their efforts was the Eisteddfod Council, already mentioned, which had a brief and stormy existence, owing to denominational bickerings, and which was dissolved when its members, faced by the financial failure of the Ruthin Eisteddfod of 1868, had to pay large sums to liquidate the debt. Various other proposals for a Central Board or permanent organisation were made again, and the next important step was Ceiriog's proposal, and the suggestion by London Welshmen that the Cymmrodorion would undertake the work of regulating the Eisteddfodau.

The reform of the Eisteddfod was thus made one of the objects of the newly-established Cymmrodorion Society. At its first meeting the Council expressed concern as to the fate of the successful poems and essays in the Eisteddfodau, and proposed that the Society should supplement the work of the Eisteddfod. As the three promoters of the Society, Gohebydd, Hugh Owen, and Robert Jones, had been members of the Eisteddfod Council, it was natural that they should suggest to the Society the formation of a new organisation on the same lines as the Eisteddfod Council. In the month of March, 1880, Hugh Owen, at the request of the Cymmrodorion Council, read a paper to the Society on " Eisteddfod Reform," which resulted in the unanimous adoption of the following resolution—" that the proposal submitted by Mr. Hugh Owen be referred to the Council of the Honourable Society of Cymmrodorion with a view to taking such steps as they may deem necessary for the formation of a permanent organisation to assist in the conduct of the National Eisteddfod." The Council agreed to the resolution and requested Hugh Owen to submit his proposal at a Cymmrodorion meeting to be held in connection with the Eisteddfod in Caernarvon in the month of August. At this meeting, a paper was also read by Mrs. Anna Walter Thomas of Bethesda, who advocated a Royal Charter for the Eisteddfod ; but Hugh Owen's proposal for forming an organisation to be known as the National Eisteddfod Association, was preferred. A motion was brought forward in favour of authorising the Cymmrodorion to carry his suggestion into effect, but opposition was shown to the motion by those who objected to the centralisation of Welsh affairs in London, and a compromise was effected by establishing a Provisional Committee of literati to work in conjunction with the Cymmrodorion ; a joint meeting was subsequently held in Shrewsbury when the work of the Association was defined.

The history of the National Eisteddfod Association has been described in the *Transactions* of the Cymmrodorion Society for 1933-1935, and from a perusal of this article it will be seen that the most important achievement of the Association was to ensure the holding of one annual National Eisteddfod in North and South Wales alternately. Publication has played an important part in its work ; successful poems and essays, and the reports of the Association have been published. Special prizes for literary work requiring detailed research, have been given by the Association, and a Trust Fund was formed (in 1924) to give financial aid, when necessary, to local Committees.

The close connection between the National Eisteddfod and the Gorsedd was the work of the Association. Believing in the antiquity of the Gorsedd, the Association proclaimed that its members " will uphold the Gorsedd, with its mystic rites and high claims of veneration." Since it was then universally believed that the Gorsedd had been connected with the Eisteddfod from olden times, it was described as " the governing Eisteddfodic power, and that in the Gorsedd alone vested supreme authority." In the account of the Association referred to above it is described how members of the Gorsedd came to be automatically elected members of the Association.

The members of the Association, on its formation, regarded the Eisteddfod primarily as an educational institution. In this, they were influenced by the ideal cherished by the old Eisteddfod Council. In 1861, the Eisteddfod was considered as " a powerful engine for public good " ; the same sentiment was expressed at the first meeting of the Council of the Cymmrodorion Society " the Eisteddfod should afford a wholesome recreation to the people," and the Association described the Eisteddfod as " the upholder of public virtue as well as the promoter of literature and the arts." The Association was to guard the Eisteddfod against corrupting influences. " It will be their endeavour to assist in excluding from the Eisteddfod proceedings whatever may be deemed low, vulgar, or in bad taste, as this high court of the nation ought to be characterised in all aspects by propriety, decorum and even dignity." Objections to this conception were expressed by W. E. Davies at the Liverpool Eisteddfod in 1884, and many years later in the *Nationalist*. He was of the opinion that the Eisteddfod was not primarily an educational institution—"the only instructional work is that connected with the offering of prizes and the delivery of adjudications." It is of interest to note that he suggested the establishment of a " Pabell Lên " to be attached to the Eisteddfod, where the adjudications might be consulted during Eisteddfod week. He also objected to attaching undue importance to Gorsedd degrees—" they do not denote achievement, but [are] certificates of the possibility of the Eisteddfod."

Thus under the auspices of the Third Society, and at the instigation of its leaders, the work of the Second Cymmrodorion Society was accomplished. The Third Society, in the matter of Eisteddfod reforms, as with other problems, did not attempt the impossible task of undertaking the burden of the work, but rather acted as a stimulus to achieve the necessary reforms, and allocated the work to other bodies. The National Eisteddfod Association was in 1937 transformed into a " Council of the National Eisteddfod."

From the beginning the Cymmrodorion Council realised the possibilities of the Eisteddfod meetings for the furtherance of the Society's objects. During the first years of the Society's existence, a sum of five guineas was granted annually to the Secretary to enable him to visit the Eisteddfod to gain new members and to give publicity to the objects of the Society. In this way the newly-established Cymmrodorion Society became known throughout Wales, and there was a substantial increase in the number of members from Wales, e.g. forty new members were enrolled at the Wrexham Eisteddfod in 1876.

We have seen that the National Eisteddfod Association was based on the Eisteddfod Council ; another activity connected with the Eisteddfod and inaugurated by the Society had its origin in an organisation formed at the same time as the Eisteddfod Council. At the Aberdare Eisteddfod held in 1861, Hugh Owen had proposed the formation of a Social Science Section, to be held in connection with the Eisteddfod, for the discussion of practical questions relating to Wales. This Section, which first met at the Caernarvon Eisteddfod in the following year, existed for some years, and afforded an opportunity for the reformers to bring their plans to the notice of the people of Wales. It was at a meeting of the Social Science Section in 1863 that Dr. Nicholas, at Hugh Owen's request, read a paper which led to the first University movement and the establishment of the Aberystwyth College in 1872. Since the Cymmrodorion included social and educational reforms among their avowed objects, it was felt that meetings similar to those of the Social Science Section would prove beneficial for propagating knowledge of these intended reforms. Hugh Owen, who had suggested the establishment of the Section in 1861, was again responsible for proposing at a meeting of the Council that meetings to be known as the meetings of the " Cymmrodorion Section of the National Eisteddfod " should be held annually during the Eisteddfod week, and an extensive and varied list of subjects for discussion was drafted. Health, food, houses, occupations, earnings, thrift, morals, education, and other questions of public interest were the topics chosen for discussion.

The first attempt at establishing a Cymmrodorion Section was a comparative failure owing to the meagre attendance at the Section meetings inaugurated at the Birkenhead Eisteddfod of 1878 ; and the attempt was abandoned. However, two years later, at the Caernarvon Eisteddfod (where, it will be remembered, the Social Science Section was first successful, eighteen years previously) the meetings, held tentatively, proved so successful that it was decided to institute the Cymmrodorion Section as an integral part of the Eisteddfod proceedings ; it has remained so to this day. The example set by the Cymmrodorion has been widely followed ; all kinds of movements and Societies now take the opportunity of meeting during the Eisteddfod week.

It has already been pointed out that Vincent Evans was the Secretary of the Cymmrodorion Section before being elected Secretary of the Society, and he held the office for half a century (1884-1934). It is difficult to over-estimate his work in this connection ; the success which has attended these meetings may be attributed to him, for he chose the subjects for discussion, which were always topical, and requiring immediate attention, and he also secured speakers who were authorities on these subjects. The reforms advocated by the Cymmrodorion would probably never have been realised were it not for these Section meetings, originated by Hugh Owen, and organised so successfully by Vincent Evans.

As already mentioned, it was at a Cymmrodorion Section meeting of the Caernarvon Eisteddfod that Hugh Owen read his paper on " Eisteddfod Reform " and that the National Eisteddfod Association was formed ; reference has also been made to the paper on the same subject given by W. E. Davies at the Liverpool Eisteddfod of 1884. Other Section meetings from time to time were devoted to papers on the Eisteddfod, where its connections with Art, the Drama and the Colleges were discussed.

Education has played an important part in the proceedings of the Section ; for the first twenty years, one meeting, at least, of the Section was devoted to some aspect of Welsh education. These meetings gave the leaders of the educational movement an opportunity of acquainting the public with their ideals, and with their plans for the reform of the Welsh educational system, and as will be seen, some of these meetings changed the form and character of certain elements of the educational system and even led to legislation on the part of the Government. Mention will also be made of the profitable discussions held at these meetings in connection with the formation of a National Library and Museum.

Some Societies owe their origin to these Section meetings and will be dealt with later ; among them we may mention the Society for the Utilisation of the Welsh language, and the National Council for the Preservation of Rural Wales.

At the Caernarvon Eisteddfod in 1880 the hope was expressed that the Cymmrodorion Society would not confine its Section meetings to educational and social problems, but that discussions on philology and archaeology would be included. However, at the beginning, the latter were not given a prominent place, except when they became questions of national importance, such as the debate on Welsh Orthography in 1893, when the revised orthography was proposed. Literature, history, and archaeology were left to the London meetings, while problems of more immediate importance and dealing directly with the future of the whole of the nation were discussed in the Section meetings. However, as the social and educational problems were solved, the Society paid more attention to literary and antiquarian topics in the meetings in Wales. At first, papers in Welsh were the exception rather than the rule in these Section meetings, except when they dealt directly with the language itself, such as the papers on orthography at the 1893 Eisteddfod, but in recent years, the Section meetings have been conducted in Welsh.

Since one of the objects of the Society was to bring into closer contact those who wished to advance the welfare of Wales, it was natural that education, the topic which created most interest in Wales at the time, should have a prominent place in the early meetings, and the Society performed a signal service to Wales in holding meetings and discussions, which led to a better realisation of the difficulties, and which sometimes had a definite practical outcome. As already mentioned, the Section meetings at the Eisteddfodau, in particular, were of paramount importance, as they provided an opportunity for all the promoters of education in Wales itself, of all parties and creeds, to meet on common ground. The unsectarian character of the Society proved an invaluable asset in this connection and the announcement "that the Society would not advocate any institution, or become the organ of any tenets, whether religious or political, which shall savour of party" was essential to the furtherance of a scheme requiring national support. From the establishment of the *Cymmrodor*, accounts of meetings, and articles dealing with educational problems, were published in that journal, since, to quote the editor, "the time is fast approaching when a definite policy must be framed on the matter and it is one to which the Cymmrodorion cannot remain indifferent."

Education was first discussed by the Society on the 20th February, 1877 when a paper (later published as a pamphlet) was read by Marchant Williams, then an Inspector of Schools under the London School Board, on " The Educational Wants of Wales." The paper contained an outline of the provision for education in Wales, and also suggestions for reforms ; it is worthy of note that an assessment of the Grammar Schools by examinations was advocated ; a degree-conferring University was not included in the scheme.

The Cymmrodorion Society was well represented on the Departmental Committee of 1880. Mention has already been made of Lord Aberdare as its Chairman; John Rhys and Lewis Morris were both members; B. T. Williams submitted valuable information, while Hugh Owen supplemented his evidence with a complete scheme for secondary education in Wales—a scheme which in its main form was embodied in the Intermediate Education Act of 1889.

The first of the Section meetings, at Caernarvon, dealt with education, and heard an address by Hugh Owen on intermediate education in Ireland, and secondary education in Wales. Considerable time was devoted to the same subject at the Section meetings at Cardiff in 1883, but no definite progress was made. However, at a London meeting during the following winter, the Cymmrodorion discussed a measure for Intermediate Education which had been awaited since the establishment of the Departmental Committee. The continued delay led to the Society urging on the Government the need of the immediate introduction of such a measure, and continual efforts were made to bring about practical legislation in this respect. On the 14th March, 1884 a memorial was presented by the Cymmrodorion Council to the Right Hon. A. J. Mundella, Vice-President of the Committee of the Council on Education, at the Education Offices at Whitehall. Although composed only of members of the Society, the deputation was of a most representative character. Every county in North Wales was represented by one of its members of Parliament, and in some cases the Lord Lieutenant and Chairmen of the Quarter Sessions were present also. The members of the deputation were, to quote the words of Lewis Morris, " of every variety of political creed, and held almost every conceivable variety of theological opinions."

The following resolution was submitted in the memorial :
"The Honourable Society of Cymmrodorion begs respectfully to urge on Her Majesty's Government the

. pressing need for the immediate introduction of their long promised measure re Intermediate Education. The Society would especially invite the attention of the Government to the fact that the success of the Colleges which they have so generously aided in establishing in Wales depends absolutely upon the existence of an adequate number of efficient intermediate schools in active work, such as a Government measure alone can provide."

The varying political opinions of the members of the Council led to the adoption of another resolution : "That the above resolutions are not intended in any way to commit the Society, or any member of it, to any approval or disapproval of any supposed detail of the forthcoming Government measure, but simply to urge the necessity of the provision of an adequate number of Intermediate Schools in Wales and Monmouth, and that this resolution be made an instruction to all who take part in the deputation and speak in the name of the Society or Council."

In replying to the memorial the Vice-President of the Council expressed his intention of introducing the proposed Bill in Parliament at the first possible opportunity.

But no measure for an Intermediate Education Act for Wales was then brought before Parliament, and in 1887 the Society decided that the Section Meetings of the London Eisteddfod of that year should be devoted solely to educational purposes. Thus the Cymmrodorion meetings held at the Central Technical Institute, Prince's Gate, became an Educational Conference to discuss the Future Development of the Welsh Educational System. The meetings were well attended by the authorities of the colleges and schools in Wales, and by the promoters of education. Papers were read by Principal Viriamu Jones of Cardiff, Principal Reichel of Bangor, Beriah Gwynfe Evans (as the Secretary of the Society for the Utilisation of the Welsh language) and William Edwards, Her Majesty's Inspector of Schools for Merthyr Tydfil. Contributions to the subject of Education of Girls in Wales were made by Miss E. P. Hughes, Newnham College, Cambridge, and Miss Dilys Davies.

During subsequent discussions the Warden of Llandovery, the Rev. John Owen (later Bishop of S. David's) suggested that a Conference on elementary, intermediate and higher education in Wales should be held, and that the Cymmrodorion Society should convene it. This suggestion was subsequently brought forward as a proposal by Owen Owen, Headmaster of Oswestry Grammar School (later the first Chief Inspector of the Central Welsh Board), and seconded by the original promoter of the plan. This resolution, which was carried unanimously was as follows : "That in the opinion of this meeting a Conference of representatives of the Colleges, intermediate schools, and elementary schools of Wales should be summoned at a convenient place at an early period, and that the Society of Cymmrodorion be requested to take the initiative in convening it." Dr. Isambard Owen consented to the proposal on behalf of the Society. The conference was summoned by the Cymmrodorion Society to meet at Shrewsbury on the 5th and 6th January, 1888, and in due course the conference was held under the presidency of Professor Rhys. The following were invited to the Conference : the Principals, Professors and Permanent Lecturers of the University, Theological and Normal Colleges of Wales and Monmouthshire; the Headmaster (or Mistress) of every endowed school, and of the leading unendowed schools in Wales, Monmouthshire and the Oswestry district, and the Headmistress of the Welsh School at Ashford ; two representatives to be named by each of the Associations of Elementary Teachers in Wales, Monmouthshire and the Oswestry district ; Her Majesty's Inspectors and the Sub-Inspectors of Schools for Wales and Monmouthshire; two representatives of each of the following Societies : the North Wales Scholarship Association, the Society for Utilising the Welsh Language and the Association for promoting the Education of Girls ; the surviving members of the Departmental Committee upon Intermediate and Higher Education in Wales, viz. Lord Aberdare, Lord Emlyn, Henry Richard, Professor Rhys and Lewis Morris.

The subject of the Conference was defined as "The Future Developments of the Welsh Educational System, considered from an academical point of view." The first resolution passed at the Conference was as follows : "That in the opinion of this Conference, an important step towards the development of the Welsh Educational System must be establishment of numerous and efficient Intermediate Schools."

Another resolution was that those existing intermediate schools which had already proved efficient, should be considered in the new scheme. These two proposals (together with the other resolutions adopted by the Conference) were laid before the Welsh Peers and Members of Parliament and were accepted by them. As a result, in the following year (1889) a Bill for Intermediate Education in Wales was introduced, passed through both houses and received the Royal Assent on August 12th, 1889. In this way, Wales secured a national system of intermediate education some ten years before England, and much of the success was due to the impetus given to the movement by the Cymmrodorion Society.

Higher and elementary education became possible for women by the establishment of the University College at Aberystwyth and by the passing of the 1870 Act respectively, but the provision for intermediate education was still totally inadequate. Private Schools offered a very limited source of education for a small minority, while out of the thirty publicly endowed Grammar Schools in Wales in 1880, only three were for girls, viz. the two endowed after the reconstitution of the Howell Trust, at Llandaff and Denbigh, and the one endowed out of the funds of the Daniel Williams Trust at Dolgelly. The Welsh School at Ashford had only a very small percentage of Welsh girls at this time, and was of no consequence as an educational force in Wales. The Departmental Committee commented on the urgent need for improvement in the education of girls, but public opinion was not in its favour ; the medical profession, for example, regarded with disfavour the prospect of equal education for boys and girls.

The Cymmrodorion Society, however, warmly supported the cause ; various Section Meetings from 1882 to 1888 were devoted to discussions on the subjects, and thus the sympathy of the public was gradually gained. As the Intermediate Education Bill, proposed in 1886, contained no reference to the education of girls, an Association was formed to remedy this deficiency. It was known as the Association for promoting the Higher Education of Girls, and came into being at the Section Meetings of the Caernarvon Eisteddfod in 1886, a resolution of approval of the project being passed unanimously on the motion of Isambard Owen, seconded by T. E. Ellis, M.P. To create a desire for better education for girls, the Association published pamphlets which consisted of the papers read at the previous Section Meetings. At a meeting of the Cymmrodorion

Section of the London Eisteddfod (1877) the following resolution was passed—"That this Meeting of the Cymmrodorion Section of the National Eisteddfod is strongly of the opinion that in any provision for intermediate education in Wales, the interests of girls should be considered equally with those of boys." This same resolution was adopted by the Shrewsbury Conference with the result that the education of girls was placed on the same status as that of boys in the 1889 Intermediate Act.

The Third Cymmrodorion Society, unlike the two former Societies, had no official connection with the British Charity School, especially after its reorganisation in 1882 as a school providing intermediate education. Since the removal of the School to Ashford in 1857, the number of Welsh pupils had been gradually decreasing, a fact which led the Cymmrodorion Council in 1877 to form a Committee to inquire into the condition of the school, and to suggest reforms. However, the subsequent reforms did not meet with the approval of some of the Cymmrodorion. W. E. Davies and Marchant Williams, for example, by means of newspaper articles, criticised the Governors of the Ashford School for utilising the funds of the Charity Institution to provide education for middle-class girls ; on the other hand, prominent Cymmrodorion, such as Brinley Richards and J. H. Puleston, still acted on the Committee of the School. But there was no official connection between the two Institutions, and in 1883, the Cymmrodorion made an unsuccessful request for the return of their books which had been in the possession of the Charity School since the dissolution of the Second Society.

Technical education also received attention from the Cymmrodorion Society at its Section Meetings. Before 1889 the Society discussed the question of introducing technical subjects into the curriculum of the Intermediate Schools and the Shrewsbury Conference passed a resolution that a scheme of intermediate education should include technical and commercial subjects. It is known that some of the Schools proposed to provide instruction in varied subjects such as architecture, slate-work, lithographic and mosaic work, and the intermediate schools were "not intended to be as completely academic as they became," but even after the passing of the 1889 Act, when academic subjects had become almost the sole subjects taught in the schools, the Society continued to discuss technical instruction. Technical Institutes and Colleges in the mining areas were advocated at the Cymmrodorion Section of the Cardiff National Eisteddfod in 1899 while at the Liverpool Eisteddfod in the following year, a department of commerce was suggested, and the development and extension of the agricultural departments were urged.

A suggestion made at a Cymmrodorion Section meeting of the Denbigh Eisteddfod of 1882 led to the formation of a National Educational Council, and so to the establishment of the Bangor University College. Thomas Gee drew attention to the fact that nothing had been done in North Wales, and very little in South Wales, to carry into effect the most important and valuable recommendation of the Departmental Committee ; and upon his motion, it was unanimously resolved to form a National Educational Council, to further the educational interests of Wales in the direction indicated in the report of the Departmental Committee. As a result, a meeting was held in London in the autumn, convened by Marchant Williams, and under the presidency of Lord Aberdare, when the question of a University College for North Wales was discussed ; this led to the Chester Conference and so to the establishment of the Bangor College.

The movement for a University for Wales coincided with the struggles for the Intermediate Education Act, a fact which considerably impeded the progress of the University Scheme, for the attention of the educationists was concentrated on the passing of the Intermediate Education Bill. Also there was considerable difference of opinion as to the character of the proposed University, whether it should be a teaching University or an examining University ; and the educationists had to face indifference on the part of the general public, for it seemed immaterial to the majority whether Wales had a University or only University Colleges.

Through their Section Meetings, the Cymmrodorion endeavoured to draw attention to the question and the character of the proposed University was extensively discussed. At the Education Conference of the London Eisteddfod of 1877, the Cymmrodorion arranged a discussion on the subject. Principal Thomas Charles Edwards was in the Chair, and Principal

Viriamu Jones, who was in the forefront of the movement to secure a University, opened the discussion on "The Future Development of the Welsh Education System." He advocated a closer connection between the Elementary Teachers and the Colleges, by placing the University Colleges in the same position as Training Colleges, as regards the reception of grants for the training of elementary teachers. The University should be a teaching and a degree-conferring body. He pointed out that without University organisation it was impossible to have a well-arranged educational system in Wales. Principal Reichel also contributed a paper on the same subject and at a meeting of the Section the following resolution was unanimously accepted: "That in the opinion of the Cymmrodorion Section of the National Eisteddfod, the University Colleges of Wales ought to be placed in the same position as training colleges as regards the reception of Grants for the training of elementary teachers." The Shrewsbury Conference of 1888 adopted the following resolutions with regard to the University : "that in the opinion of this Conference the University Colleges should be utilised in the training of elementary teachers ; that in the opinion of this Conference it is expedient that the provision for intermediate and collegiate education in Wales and Monmouthshire should be completed by a University organisation ; and that the inspection of state-aided intermediate schools should be committed to the Welsh University, with due provision for the representation of such schools upon its executive body." The last resolution was never to be realised, but the other resolutions were soon to be achieved, for the Shrewsbury Conference had stimulated the authorities of the University Colleges to take some practical steps towards securing a University. Two invitations to a joint conference were issued to the other University Colleges by the authorities of the Bangor College in 1888 and 1891 respectively. At the latter conference the Welsh University Conference came into being, and the result was the formation of the University Charter which received the Royal Assent in 1893.

The Education Act of 1870 had made no provision for the Welsh language, and the Departmental Committee of 1880, while commenting on the prevalence of the language, regarded it as a serious impediment to the progress of education, and was unable to offer a solution of the problem, dismissing the subject with the remark "that there is every appearance that the Welsh language will be cherished by the majority of Welsh people." The two languages were considered incompatible in the schools, but no systematic effort had been made to cope with the difficulties of this situation until the matter was taken up by the Cymmrodorion Society. In this matter the Society was actuated chiefly by educational motives, rather than by a desire to preserve and perpetuate the language. The Society's chief care was to provide education for the children of Wales, and since in Welsh-speaking districts elementary education was interpreted as knowledge of English, it was the deficiency in knowledge of English which led the Society primarily to investigate the matter. Two problems confronted the Cymmrodorion—the necessity for Welsh children to be acquainted with the English tongue for their own material advancement, and the existence of the Welsh language, "which had proved its claim to vitality by refusing to be exterminated," in spite of overwhelming difficulties. For this reason it was resolved "that, granting the existence of the language in Wales, it would be more compatible with practical wisdom to utilise than to affect to ignore it." They were not primarily concerned with its duration, which they felt "might safely be left to a higher power," their concern was the intellectual life of Wales which was inextricably bound up with the language, and for this reason the Society advocated a rational use of the language in education.

In its endeavours to include the Welsh language in the curriculum of the Schools, the Society was influenced by another consideration, namely the fact that the disparagement and indignity inflicted on the language in schools inevitably resulted in a lack of self-confidence and a loss of self-respect in the children. An additional reason for its efforts was the realisation that the great majority of those educated in the elementary schools in the Welsh-speaking districts would not require a thorough knowledge of the English language, while at the same time, a knowledge of the grammar of the language, and the ability to write it correctly, would prove beneficial.

The matter was first brought forward by a member of the Cymmrodorion Council, the Rev. D. J. Davies, Rector of North Benfleet, Essex, in a paper read before the Society in 1882. His chief concern was the fact that children in the Welsh-speaking districts, after several years of elementary education, left school with their knowledge of English confined to mechanical phrases and isolated words. As a remedy for this defect, he suggested that the prevailing system of encouraging the English language by discouraging the native tongue, should be discontinued, and that the one language should be taught by means of the other. He believed that "there would be no necessity to teach the children to write Welsh, as the object was not to teach Welsh, but English," and considered that what Wales needed most was an efficient method of teaching English. A resolution was passed at the meeting in favour of the suggestion and copies of the paper were circulated, accompanied by a short article by Thomas Powel, then editor of the *Cymmrodor*. A not very successful endeavour was made to solicit replies and criticism of the circular. In the same year the editor of the *Cymmrodor* included an article in that publication on the work which was being done in Ireland by the Society for the Preservation of the Irish language (which had been established in 1877), gave a list of the concessions granted by the Government of Ireland at the instigation of that Society, and advocated a similar scheme for Wales.

Two years later the matter was again taken up by the Society. Professor Powel read a paper on "The Advisability of the Teaching of Welsh in Elementary Schools," endorsing the suggestions made by D. J. Davies and proposing to introduce the language as a "specific subject" in elementary schools. The meeting, which was attended by members from Wales, as well as from London, expressed agreement with his views, and the Council of the Society at its next meeting appointed a Sub-Committee, consisting of W. E. Davies, Isambard Owen, John Owens, Professor Rhys Davids and Marchant Williams, to make enquiries as to the extent to which the Welsh language was used to teach English, and as to the advisability of introducing Welsh as a specific subject. The sub-committee submitted seven questions to the Inspectors of Schools, to certain Chairmen of the School Boards and to a few Head-masters ; and from the answers received it was seen that the general opinion was that there should be no formal regulation on the subject. The Society printed the "Preliminary Report upon the use of the Welsh Language to Elementary Schools in Welsh-speaking Districts, by a Sub-Committee of the Council" in time for discussion at the Liverpool Section Meeting in the same year, when a further paper was read on the subject by Professor Powel, who pointed out that the use of the Welsh language in education would be advantageous for the advancement of learning and not a stumbling-block as was generally believed. A resolution was passed at the meeting expressing unanimous approval of the work done by the Society, and desiring the inquiry to be continued.

Accordingly the Council of the Society, at its first meeting in the following October, re-appointed the Committee ; and at the end of the year it was resolved to ascertain from the headmasters and headmistresses of the elementary schools in Wales whether they approved of Professor Powel's proposal. For this purpose, the following questionnaire was drawn up : "Do you consider that advantage would result from the introduction of the Welsh language as a 'specific subject' into the course of elementary education in Wales? The reply may be given by a simple affirmative or negative or reason may be stated." A copy of this question paper with a short circular letter explaining the reasons for the Society's action, with the preliminary report of the Committee and a stamped addressed envelope for reply, was forwarded by the Society, in the months of February and March, 1885, to the headmaster or headmistress of every public elementary school (not being an infant school) throughout Wales and Monmouth. There was also included an illustrated syllabus drawn up by Marchant Williams, showing how a graduated course of instruction in Welsh might be made. Fourteen hundred copies of this inquiry were sent out. Less than half that number of replies were received, but, by a small majority, the prevailing opinion was that the Welsh language should be included as a specific subject. It may be mentioned that a great proportion of the negative replies received came from the English-speaking districts, on the ground that the Welsh language had no commercial value ; many headmasters from the Welsh-speaking districts also disapproved of the suggestion, giving as a reason that the scheme would be strongly opposed by parents, whose main purpose in sending their children to school was to enable them to learn the English language, and who laboured under the impression that the exclusion of Welsh from the school curriculum would inevitably lead to a knowledge of English. It should also be remembered that knowledge of the Welsh language was often a deciding factor in forming the views of the headmasters ; to quote one of the correspondents—"the answers to this question will, to a very great extent, reflect the ability of the teacher to teach the Welsh language."

After the important Cymmrodorion meeting at the Liverpool Eisteddfod, Dan Isaac Davies (1839-1887), became the most zealous and devoted supporter of the bilingual movement. In an enthusiastic speech at Aberdare in the month of January, 1885, at a joint meeting of a deputation from the National Eisteddfod Association and the Aberdare National Eisteddfod Committee, he pressed forward the claims of bilingualism, with the result that the Chairman and Secretary of the Cymmrodorion induced him to read a paper at a Cymmrodorion meeting in London. At this meeting, held on April 16th, 1885, Dan Isaac Davies read a paper on "bilingual Wales" of which a summary was published in various newspapers.

It was this paper which led to the formation of the "Society for the Utilisation of the Welsh language." A Cardiganshire Justice of Peace, Henry Tobit Evans, on reading a summary of the article in the *South Wales Daily News*, suggested the formation of such a Society. This suggestion was published by Dan Isaac Davies in his series of nine articles in *Baner ac Amserau Cymru*, June-August, 1885, which later appperaed as a pamphlet entitled, *1785, 1885, 1985, neu Tair Milion o Gymry Dwy-ieithiog mewn Can Mlynedd*. During the months preceding the Eisteddfod at Aberdare he enlisted support for his project.

The Cymmrodorion Society had been so impressed with the reply (accompanied by a draft of a systematised scheme of graduated translation from Welsh into English, and vice-versa) received form Beriah Gwynfe Evans, then an unknown village schoolmaster in Carmarthenshire, that they invited him to give a further exposition of his views at the Cymmrodorion Section of the National Eisteddfod at Aberdare.

The crowded attendance at these meetimgs testified to the interest aroused by Dan Isaac Davies. After the Cymmrodorion Report on the inquiries had been presented, the results of inquiries by the Society into the methods of education adopted by bilingual countries on the Continent were given, letters of information being read from the Belgian, French, Austrian and German Embassies. A further contribution to the subject was made by Beriah G. Evans and followed by a discussion.

As a result the following resolution, proposed by Archdeacon Griffiths and seconded by William Abraham ("Mabon") was unanimously carried : "that it is desirable that a Society should be formed for the purpose of promoting the utilisation of the Welsh language as an instrument of education in Wales and Monmouthshire." On the following day, another meeting was called for the formal establishment of the Society, and it was resolved that the Society should, if possible, be in connection with the Society of Cymmrodorion, and that the Council of the latter should be asked to nominate one-fourth of its executive body. At a public meeting held at Cardiff in the same year, the following resolution was unanimously adopted : "that the best thanks of this meeting be tendered to the Honourable Society of the Cymmrodorion for their thorough inquiry into the question of the advisability of the introduction of the Welsh language into the course of elementary education in Wales, and their excellent report on the result of the inquiry." The Council of the Cymmrodorion Society at its meeting on October 8th granted permission to the new Society to append to its name the words "in association with the Honourable Society of Cymmrodorion."

The Society was for some time called "The Society for Utilising the Welsh Language for the Purpose of Securing a Better and More Intelligent Knowledge of English " ; this designation would seem to imply that the Society was wholly English in aims and sympathy. But Sir John Edward Lloyd, who was present at the first Aberdare meeting and who witnessed the establishment of the Society, held (1931) that the English title of the Society was rather a blind, disguising its real nature ; and that the protestations of unconcern as to the fate of the native language were merely made to persuade the educational authorities to accede to the plan. He added that Principal Thomas Charles Edwards, playing on the words *dwy-ieithiog* and *dau-wynebog*, used to refer to it as "the two-faced Society," as it was known among its members by the Welsh name *Cymdeithas yr Iaith Gymraeg.*

A glance at the work accomplished by that Society confirms this suggestion. The chief object of the Society was to endeavour to prevail upon the Government to introduce the native language into the curriculum of the schools. Soon after the formation of the Society, the opportunity arose—through the appointment of a Committee to inquire into Elementary Education. The matter was brought before this Royal Committee by the Society, and the unanimous approval of the Committee was elicited with the result that permission was given to use the native language as a substitute for English, as a means of instruction, in the Welsh districts. Welsh also became a recognised "specific subject." The Society forthwith pressed upon the public to adopt the recommendation of the Committee. Bilingual reading and writing books might be used in the schools; and the History and Geography of Wales might be taught to some extent. The Society provided for the preparation and publication of adequate text-books for this new scheme.

In 1899, those who had been prominent in the establishment of the Society met to form a new Society—*Cymdeithas yr Iaith Gymraeg* (adopting the Welsh title of the original Society), which accorded a no less important place to the native language in education, but recommended the "Direct Method" in the teaching of English as of Welsh. This Society was merged into the New Wales Movement (Undeb Cymru Fydd) in 1942.

In preparing a series of bilingual books, the Society found itself confronted by a serious difficulty, owing to the various modes of spelling employed by different Welsh writers, and it was decided to appeal to Welsh philologists to devise a standard system of orthography. A standard system had already been adopted by the "Dafydd ap Gwilym" Society at Oxford, and in 1889, at the meetings of the Cymmrodorion Section of the National Eisteddfod at Brecon, papers (in Welsh) were read by John Morris-Jones and J. E. Lloyd on the reforms needed in Welsh spelling. These reforms were adopted by the Society for the Utilisation of the Welsh language and were published in 1893. On this book was based the University of Wales handbook on orthography which appeared in 1928.

The formation of a National Library had always been an aim of the Cymmrodorion Society from the days when Richard Morris collected books to be deposited in the Welsh School, and a National Museum had been a Cymmrodorion project from the same time, when William Morris sent fossils and shells to London to " Almari'r Cymmrodorion." But the proposal for a National Library in Wales itself originated at the Llangollen Eisteddfod of 1858, although no steps were taken at the time to put the suggestion into effect. It was the educational movement in Wales which gave the necessary impetus to the project, since a library and museum were considered essential to each of the Colleges. At the Mold Eisteddfod of 1873, the promoters of the Cymmrodorion Society also proposed the formation of a National Library ; Stephen Evans suggested that a National Library should be formed, as the complement of the newly-established College at Aberystwyth. Although the numerous educational problems connected with higher and intermediate education proved a hindrance to the realisation of the proposal, the authorities of the Aberystwyth College proceeded to form a collection of valuable books and MSS. which eventually was to be a deciding factor in determining the site of the National Library.

In 1876, Professor Rudler of the University College of Aberystwyth, read a paper before the Society on " A National History Museum for Wales," in which he suggested that the Museum should be affiliated to some large educational establishment. The University College at Aberystwyth alone fulfilled this requirement at the time. The matter was raised in Parliament from time to time, but it was not until 1895 that the subject was discussed in Wales, when Brynmor Jones, at the request of the Secretary of the Cymmrodorion Society, addressed the Pontypridd Eisteddfod Section Meeting on the subject of a National Museum. He suggested that the Museum and Library should be one institution, i.e. a Museum which should be a repository for works of art, literature and science, and he stressed that the Museum should be truly national, containing primarily, objects relating to Wales.

In the month of July, 1903, a Parliamentary Conference was convened, of Members of Parliament, representatives of the three University Colleges and representative of the County Councils as the new educational authorities. The Principals of the Colleges proposed that the grant offered by the Government should be used for the establishment of institutions attached to each of the three Colleges ; in this they were supported by the educational authorities. But since the Members of Parliament, who were in the majority at the meeting, favoured a central institution, their motion was adopted. However, as a compromise between the two divergent views, it was proposed that a generous share of the Museum grant should be devoted to the circulation of loan collections throughout Wales.

The Cymmrodorion Section of the Llanelly Eisteddfod in the following month, devoted wholly to discussions on a National Museum, criticised the work of the Conference. The proposal of a Central Museum was fully approved, but the loan system was considered impracticable. It was pointed out that lending exhibits from the Museum, if done on a large scale, would be laborious and well-nigh impossible, and the scheme of a lending library of rare books and valuable MSS. was also condemned : it was felt that copies of books and rare manuscripts should be confined to one locality. Strong disapproval was again expressed of the proposal of the educational authorities to establish three Libraries and Museums, attached to the three Colleges. The addresses given before the discussions were delivered by Brynmor Jones, J. Herbert Lewis, and Principal T. F. Roberts, and since it was evident from the discussion that there was considerable difference of opinion with regard to the nature of the institution, a resolution was passed unanimously requesting the Parliamentary Committee, before finally committing itself to any particular scheme for a National Museum or Museums for Wales, to convene a thoroughly representative meeting of Welsh authorities to discuss the matter further. As a result of the re-discussion it was decided to appeal to the Treasury for a grant for two Institutions, a National Library and a National Museum, and the scheme of a lending Museum and Library was withdrawn.

Isambard Owen, a member of the Council of the Society, was chosen by the Parliamentary Committee to draw up a scheme for the establishment of the two Institutions; before drafting the plan, he visited various Museums, including the national Museums at Dublin and Edinburgh. At the next Cymmrodorion Section meetings, held at Rhyl in 1904, he gave an address on a National Library; papers were also read by John Williams and Marchant Williams. In the following year, at the Mountain Ash Eisteddfod, John Williams again spoke on the Welsh National Museum. The Cymmrodorion thus stimulated the movement, and clarified the situation by repeated discussions, and when the National Library and Museum were eventually established, Vincent Evans was appointed to the

Court of Governors of both institutions. The nucleus of a "national library" formed by the First Cymmrodorion Society remained in the Welsh School until the 1939-1945 war, when the books were brought to the National Library at Aberystwyth (the MSS., as the reader will remember, had long since gone to the British Museum) and Richard Morris would have been pleased to know that his dream had been realised, and that his collection had found a final resting-place in a National Library

The Cymmrodorion Society promoted and effected the formation of various societies which were felt to be needed from time to time. The same procedure was invariably followed— the Cymmrodorion stimulated interest in the cause by holding a discussion at the Section meeting, when the desirability of forming a Society was expressed; they then convened a Committee, and in some cases a Conference, at which the proposed Society came into being. This ended the official connection between the two Societies, and allowed the Cymmrodorion Society to proceed unhampered to inaugurate further reforms.

Two such organisations have already been dealt with, namely the Society for the Utilisation of the Welsh Language and the National Eisteddfod Association. Another such society was the National Musical Association inaugurated in 1888. Music had not occupied such a prominent place in the proceedings of the Third Society as had been accorded to it by the Second Cymmrodorion, but it had been a favourite topic for discussions and lectures, and it was felt that an organisation was needed for the development of music in Wales, especially instrumental music. At a Section meeting during the Wrexham Eisteddfod in 1866, this question was discussed, and the Cymmrodorion were asked to convene a Conference. This conference met at Shrewsbury, and the National Musical Association was formed. The first meeting was held during the Brecon Eisteddfod in the following year, but no great success attended the meeting, and the Association lapsed. However, this was the fore-runner of the National Council of Music to be established later. A Folk Song Society formed by the Cymmrodorion Society at the 1906 Section meeting, on the other hand, has been very successful, and has done invaluable work in preserving the folk-songs which still remained extant in Wales.

The Society also gave its blessing to the formation of the Welsh Bibliographical Society at the Swansea Eisteddfod of 1907, and it was with the view of assisting the newly-formed Society and of putting into practice the recommendations made at that meeting, that the Cymmrodorion undertook to print and publish a *Bibliography of Welsh Ballads* compiled for the Society by J. H. Davies.

The formation of the Council for the Preservation of Rural Wales is a fairly recent occurrence. From its establishment the Cymmrodorion Society had encouraged the development of the fine arts among the people of Wales, and with this end in view had included in its journal descriptions of works of architecture in Wales. At the Section Meetings during the Mold Eisteddfod in 1923 the protection of the beauty of the Welsh countryside was discussed, and a development plan considered. No steps were taken in the matter until four years later when the preservation of rural Wales was the topic of discussion at the Holyhead Eisteddfod Section meeting. The usual procedure was followed; the Cymmrodorion were requested to consider what steps should be taken, and were given full power to act. A Sub-Committee elected by the Society for this purpose convened a Conference at Shrewsbury to which were invited representatives of public bodies and Associations connected with Wales, and at this meeting the Council for the Preservation of Rural Wales was formed, all the expenses being undertaken by the Cymmrodorion Society.

" Gohebydd " suggested the awarding of a Cymmrodorion medal for the encouragement of the native language in the schools of Wales as had been done by the Second Society; it was later proposed that the medal should be used to stimulate native talent, and offered as a prize of merit to persons connected with Wales by birth or residence. However, after prolonged discussions, it was finally decided to confer the medal " as a recognition by the Cymmrodorion Society, of distinguished services rendered to Wales in connection with Literature, Science and Art." Thus it was not given as an incentive but as a reward for a lifetime devotion to Wales, and has been described as " a sort of literary canonisation." The medal, designed by Joseph Edwards, bears the inscription—" Cymru, a phob peth mawr, doeth a sanctaidd." The imposing list of recipients proves that this medal has been well bestowed.

It was awarded in the first instance, in 1882, to the Rev. William Rees, (Gwilym Hiraethog), in recognition of his services to Wales as a publicist and preacher, lecturer and social reformer, author, essayist and poet for more than half a century, and it is interesting to note that " Hiraethog " had won the medal of the Second Cymmrodorion Society fifty years earlier, (in 1828) at the Royal Denbigh Eisteddfod for an essay on " Cantre Gwaelod." The medal has subsequently been awarded to the Rev. D. Silvan Evans, Sir John Rhys, Sir John Williams, Sir John Edward Lloyd, Dr. Henry Owen, Sir Isambard Owen, Sir Owen Morgan Edwards, Sir John Morris-Jones, Rev. Dr. G. Hartwell Jones, Sir Henry Jones, Edward Owen, H.R.H. The Duke of Windsor (at that time Prince of Wales), Sir Evan Vincent Evans, Sir John Herbert Lewis, Sir William Goscombe John, Dr. Mary Davies, Ben Davies, Sir John Ballinger, Ernest Rhys, Rev. Howell Elvet Lewis, Dr. Thomas Gwynn Jones, Sir Ifor Williams, Sir Daniel Lleufer Thomas, Dr. John Lloyd Williams, Dr. Thomas Jones, Sir Harold Idris Bell, Dr. William John Gruffydd, Prof. T. H. Parry-Williams, and Mr. Saunders Lewis.

During the 1939-45 war, the Society interested itself in matters of immediate moment to Wales, such as the formation of the Cymmrodorion Welsh War Relief Committee. It prepared a memorandum on Wales and the Armed Forces, and pressed for the establishment of a Welsh Division. Since the end of the war the Society has concerned itself with the protection of the land of Wales in face of the demands of the Services. Thus the Third Cymmrodorion Society has met the needs of the day.

But from its inception, its distinctive work has been the promoting and publishing of literary and historical studies, and some of the most valuable contributions to Welsh scholarship have appeared in the Society's publications. The history of its publications goes back to 1875 when Robert Jones outlined a scheme which was adopted by the Council in the following year. He proposed that the Society's Journal, which was to be known as Y Cymmrodor, should be a half-yearly periodical; the first section was to contain the report of the Society's work, a summary of the lectures given at the meetings, and notices of Eisteddfodfau and of current matters bearing upon the literature, history and antiquities of Wales: the second section was to be devoted to the printing of valuable Welsh MSS.; while the third section was to consist of reprints of rare and interesting works, chiefly in English, relating to the history and literature of Wales. This scheme, however, was doomed to failure. The half-yearly system of publication was discontinued in 1884, as it was found impossible to adhere rigidly to this rule, owing to lack, or over-abundance, as the case might be, of material submitted, and it was resolved that the time of publication should depend on the matter at the disposal of the Society. Difficulties also arose in publishing, in the ordinary issues of *Y Cymmrodor*, the papers read during that particular year, and in 1893 Vincent Evans proposed that the papers read during each lecture session should be printed apart in an annual volume, to be known as the *Transactions of the Honourable Society of Cymmrodorion*. These two journals appeared annually up to the war, when the difficulty of obtaining paper inevitable delayed publication. The *Transactions*, therefore, correspond to the second section proposed by Robert Jones, and *Y Cymmrodor* to the first section. The third section, namely reprints of rare works and publications of MSS. developed into the " Cymmrodorion Record Series."

The original proposal made by Robert Jones suggested an Editor for each section, and a Chief Editor to superintend the work of the three sections. Silvan Evans was proposed as Chief Editor, the two brothers, Charles Jones and Robert Jones were to be responsible for the first section, while the second and third were allotted to Roland Phillips and Cadwaladr Davies respectively. This plan was not adopted, and the first volume of the *Cymmrodor* finally appeared under the sole editorship of Robert Jones, who took upon himself the whole expense of printing, on the condition that the Society paid fourteen shillings per number per subscriber, so long as its members were limited to a hundred and fifty; this sum was to be reduced as the Society's membership increased. The magazine was to be the property of the editor, and at the end of each year, he was allowed to dispose of back numbers of *Y Cymmrodor* to non-members of the Society. It was also decided that the Society, in the event of the editor's death, was to have the right of continuing the publication on the payment of a certain sum. This plan was adopted in 1878.

When the death of Robert Jones occurred after the publication of two volumes, the editorship was offered to John Rhys, who declined the offer, and the following notice was inserted in *The Athenaeum* and later in Welsh newspapers: "Wanted, a gentleman, connected with the Principality, and acquainted with its literature, to edit the annual publication of a Society established for the purpose of promoting literature, science, and art in Wales. Only a moderate honorarium can be offered at present." As a result of the advertisement, Thomas Powel was chosen to be Editor, at a salary of fifty pounds per annum. Powel, with the active assistance of Isambard Owen, edited the next five volumes, but after six years of office he resigned, and the Society, acting on the recommendation of John Rhys, chose Egerton G. B. Phillimore, who had already contributed transcripts from MSS. to the *Cymmrodor*. Phillimore, also assisted by Isambard Owen, supervised the work up to Volume XI, and on his resignation was succeeded by an Editorial Committee. However, most of the work devolved on the Secretary of the Society, and so Vincent Evans was for nearly fifty years responsible for the publication of the *Cymmrodor*, the *Transactions* and the *Cymmrodorion Record Series*.

The articles in the *Cymmrodor* and *Transactions* cover a wide range of subjects, and deal with every aspect of Welsh Life; archaelogy, music, folk-lore and science, to name only a few, have found a place in these pages. There has been a remarkable diversity of topics discussed in these publications, but one subject has been scrupulously eschewed. The Society, to emphasise its thoroughly undenominational character, has avoided theology, a subject which in the past has aroused considerable controversy in Wales, and has published one or two articles only on the subject—and even these dealt with the theology of the *ancient* British Church. The history of Wales has been the predominant feature, and valuable documents from the Public Record Office, throwing light on various periods in Welsh History, have been used in many of the contributions. Indeed the wealth of material in the Record Office accounts for the great number of historical articles, and is one reason why history soon superseded pure literature; the latter, during the brief editorship of Robert Jones, had occupied the foremost place. In the field of history, every period has been represented, from Hartwell Jones's *Celtic*

Britain and the Pilgrim Movement up to our own day. The laws of Wales have found a prominent place in the publications, which is not surprising when we recall the many eminent members of the legal profession who have been connected with the Society. In recent years, literature has again been much to the fore in the lectures of the Society, and there has been a notable increase in the number of lectures given in the Welsh language, so that the charge made in the past that the Society was prone to neglect the native language has no longer any foundation.

The " Cymmrodorion Record Series " was inaugurated by Henry Owen, John Williams and Vincent Evans, and was a work which the Society had in view since its revival in 1873. The matter was discussed at the Brecon Eisteddfod Section meeting in 1889, when it was decided that for the publication of Welsh Historical Records and MSS. a Cymmrodorion Record Series Fund should be established. In this way the results of original research in Welsh History, Antiquities, and Literature were published, and valuable books printed which appealed only to a limited circle of students. Among the works thus published are the works of Gildas; the *Black Book of S. David's;* the *Ruthin Court Rolls* containing manorial documents; the *First Extent of Bromfield and Yale* (1315), the oldest surviving extent dealing with Wales ; the *Register of the Council of the Marches in Wales* (1569-1591) ; George Owen's *Pembrokeshire* (1603); and a *Catalogue of MSS. relating to Wales in the British Museum.*

EPILOGUE

IT MAY fairly be claimed that the Third Cymmrodorion Society has already done a good day's work. The preceding chapter has sketched two rather different phases of its activities—two phases which we may associate respectively with the names of Hugh Owen and Vincent Evans. For although Hugh Owen died before the Third Society became a power in the life of modern Wales, yet we have seen that his conception of the Society as an originator or stimulant of movements for the good of Wales was not allowed to die with him. It can never be wholly right to attribute great changes in the life of a nation to a single individual; yet it is Hugh Owen's name which most readily occurs to us when we survey the cultural institutions of Wales today—its Eisteddfod, its schools, its colleges, its University and Library and Museum. On the other hand, the serried ranks of Cymmrodorion publications on our shelves, their sumptuous type and paper, their luxuriance of illustration, evoke the massive and imperious figure of Vincent Evans, a man who neither counted pence nor weighed trouble when the fruits of Welsh scholarship were to be offered to the public in his ancient Society's name. There can hardly be a scholar or man of letters in Wales today who has not been indebted to the Honourable Society for publishing some of his work— not a few of them can testify that it has been their very first patron.

But Vincent Evans (perhaps unlike Hugh Owen in this respect) also cherished a still older Cymmrodorion tradition. The Society of 1751 was a London society, a society in which London Welshmen could come together and enjoy the company of their compatriots. The "succession-societies," too, were above all sociable—when Robin Ddu o Fôn was forced by ill-health to leave London and spend his last days at Caernarvon, he tells us that what irked him most was the loss of that colourful social life which he had enjoyed among Cymmrodorion and Gwyneddigion during his twenty years' sojourn in Town. And despite the changes of intervening years—the multiplication of London-Welsh societies of all sorts, religious, professional, "county," and what not—the Honourable Society, in its late

Secretary's mind, was still to be the predominant meeting-ground of Welshmen in Town. It would no doubt be blasphemy to suggest that Vincent Evans ranked a Cymmrodorion Dinner (or similar function) above a National Library or a well-produced Calendar of Records; but a greatly-daring leg-puller might at times have been tempted to twit him with such a charge. Like Richard Morris, and like Owain Myfyr, he was a gregarious man.

With his death in 1934, and more still with the war in 1939, came a changed world. No one could take his place in its entirety. The direction of the National Eisteddfod passed to a newly-constituted Council; the Secretaryship of the Honourable Society was separated from the Editorship of its publications; and those responsible for these sundered activities have found their energies taxed to the utmost. They have all stood up to the work manfully: the Eisteddfod (now mistress of its own house) is more flourishing than ever—the membership of the Honourable Society now exceeds 2,000—the *Cymmrodor* and the *Transactions*, though (as with all societies) there has been a lag in publication, have abated not a whit of the high standard of their contents.

The two-hundredth birthday of the Society, not unnaturally, finds its Council and officers in a reminiscent mood, reflected not only in the present volume of *Y Cymmrodor* but also in its immediate predecessor, the great collection of *Additional Morris Letters*, running to nearly a thousand pages, whose publication was a fitting expression of piety towards our founders of old, But an anniversary which could not also look forward would be a dismal thing; and the Society has no intention of quitting the field. Publication has become terribly costly; no longer can we afford the Vincentian splendours, and our Honorary Editor has to " make do " with crammed pages of thinner paper, rarely relieved by illustration. To be sure, we are no longer without coadjutors: Eisteddfod and University (through its Board of Celtic Studies and its Press Board), Library and Museum, Bibliographical Society and church historical societies, new and vigorous county historical societies—not to mention that doughty centenarian, *Archaeologia Cambrensis*—are bearing an increasing share of the burden. Yet even so there is plenty of work for *Y Cymmrodor*. The *lengthy* historical essay—the contribution which on the one hand cannot be made within brief compass, or on the other is not bulky enough to need a volume—still looks to our Editor for its opportunity, and has so far not looked in vain.

Our Council has certainly not lacked courage. In what now seems a very remote age, it conceived the project of publishing a new Dictionary of Welsh Biography, in a Welsh and in an English edition. As has been the custom of the Third Society, the scheme was introduced to the public at a meeting held during the National Eisteddfod of 1938, at Cardiff; the late Sir John Edward Lloyd, who had been chosen to edit the Dictionary, then explained the project. All was going well enough when war came, and set the clock back. With peace came an enormous rise in printing and publishing costs, and what had once seemed a reasonably adequate sum, voted by the Society or collected from well-wishers, practically ceased to count. Further, death removed the distinguished Editor when the planning had only just been resumed. But those who were responsible for the enterprise did not flinch. Sir John's assistant-editor was commissioned to succeed him, and had his hands enormously strengthened by associating with him the National Librarian—not only that, but the Council of the National Library, graciously acknowledging its debt to the Society which had done so much towards founding the Library itself, put the whole resources of the Library, whether in searching for information or in secretarial help or in technical advice, at the disposal of the two editors. On the financial side, the problem was energetically tackled by appealing to the County (and County Borough) Councils of Wales to grant a small percentage of the money which had come to them from the Commissioners of the ancient Church endowments—and the appeal met with a gratifying response. The " copy " of the whole Dictionary has now been assembled, and even the type-setting of the Welsh edition has reached a point far down the alphabet; publication is now well within sight.

In other ways too, the Society is showing great activity. A London society it still is, as it has always been. But a large proportion of its members, and even one-fourth of its Council, is now composed of residents in Wales. Indeed, the Society itself has of late become more " extra-mural." The days of Vincent Evans's majestic annual descents upon Wales are over, and the Society's officials have in recent years frequently left its gracious home in Bedford-square to mingle with their fellow-Welshmen at home. Meetings in Wales have become a regular feature, not only in the larger towns but in the smaller market-towns. Indeed, the Society's motto *Cared doeth yr encilion*, which those who adopted it seem to have construed as " Let the wise cherish antiquity," may now be said to be applicable in the literal sense of *encilion*—" the out-of-the-way " —for remote villages and hamlets have welcomed meetings of the Honourable Society. It is safe to say that never has Wales been made more aware of the Society's existence. But to return for a moment to London: no question affecting the interests of Wales in late years has evaded the Society's notice, and prompt action has been taken when that seemed to be called for. There will, it is very sure, be further problems, in these anxious times, but they too will be faced.

The Cymmrodorion Society, phoenix-like, has twice arisen from its own ashes. Today there is no question of " ashes," for the Third Society has already far surpassed the span of either of its predecessors (indeed, of both put together), and is still in full vigour. The writers of this book may confidently end their task with the salutation *esto perpetua*.

_____

CONSTITUTIONS

OF THE HONOURABLE SOCIETY OF

CYMMRODORION
IN LONDON (1755).

THE INTRODUCTION

SHEWING THE USEFULNESS AND NECESSITY OF AN ASSOCIATION OF *ANCIENT BRITONS* IN LONDON.

THERE is implanted in the Nature of Mankind, a strong Attachment to that Country which gave them Birth, and a laudable Curiosity to acquaint themselves with the genuine History and Antiquities of those People from whom they are immediately descended.

But to arrive at any great degree of certainty in these Researches, is an arduous task, and requires certain previous and necessary Qualifications.—No one can be ignorant, that in order to explain the ancient Monuments, Customs, and Manners of any People, a competent Knowledge of their Language is absolutely necessary : And as the *British* or *Welsh*, is the Language of the original Inhabitants of *Great Britain ;* without a Critical Knowledge of it, it will be found extremely difficult, if not impracticable, to investigate the most ancient *British* Antiquities with any degree of Success. This Observation, sufficiently evident in itself, is likewise supported by the Authority of a Person very eminent in this as well as other Parts of Learning, the late Bishop *Nicholson*, who, in his *English Historical Library*, recommends the Study of the *British* Language, as a necessary Acquisition to compleat an *English* Antiquary : Having advertised his Reader that there are many curious Manuscripts, of a very great Age, still remaining in *Wales ;* he farther adds, " But it will be to no purpose for a Man to seek out these venerable Remains, unless he be able to understand the Meaning of what he meets with ; and therefore it is requisite that our Antiquary, if he be not a Native of *Wales*, should furnish himself with a competent Skill in the *British*, or *Welsh* Language."

The World in general, as well as our Island of *Britain* in particular, is greatly indebted to the *Greeks* and *Romans* for transmitting down to us those few, though imperfect, Fragments of ancient History. But when we reflect upon the Disadvantages they lay under in this respect, as being entire Strangers to the several Languages of those People they affected to call *Barbarous ;* the high Opinion we may have entertained of the Accuracy and Credit of their Accounts, will be considerably abated.

Nor is this asserted without good Authority ; for *Humphrey Llwyd*, who had the Reputation of being one of the best Antiquaries of this Kingdom, in a Book of his, intitled *Commentarioli Britannicae Descriptionis Fragmentum*, plainly shews how imperfect all the Accounts of this Island are, which we have from the *Roman* Writers, and how dark, for want of Skill in the old *British* Language.

We have had indeed, in almost every Age since, a great number of learned and ingenious Persons, Natives of *Britain*, who have laudably laid out their Time and Pains in these Researches ; but however well qualified they might otherwise have been for a Work of this Nature, yet for want of this Requisite, namely, an intimate acquaintance with the *British*, or *Welsh*, Tongue ; they have been so far from contributing anything considerable towards illustrating our *British* Antiquities, that they have frequenlty committed the most gross and palpable Mistakes.

The diligent and ingenious *Camden*, with a few others, ought here to be excepted : He it was, of *English* Writers, who first took the right Method of studying Antiquities. " *Plato*, in his *Cratylus, says he*, directs us to trace the Original of Names to the *Barbarous Tongues*, as being the most antient ; and accordingly, in all my Etymologies and Conjectures, I have constant recourse to the *British*, or (as it is now called) the *Welsh* Tongue, which was spoken by the first and most ancient Inhabitants of this Country." He saw the Impossibility of coming at any degree of certainty in these Researches, without being first acquainted with the *British* Language. This was indeed a laborious Task ; but as he found it to be necessary to the Execution of his Plan, he cheerfully underwent it, and it seems acquired some Knowledge of that ancient and venerable Language. By these Helps, joined to an uncommon degree of Diligence and Penetration, he reflected more light upon the History and Antiquities of this Island than ever had been done before.

But notwithstanding the many useful Discoveries this accurate and industrious Antiquary, and others after him, have made in this Field of Knowledge, the Subject is far from being exhausted. There is still Employment enough for the curious Inquirer into Antiquity, and abundant Treasure, if he will be at the Pains to search for it. But to prosecute it with Success, a right Method must be pursued ; a competent Knowledge of the *British* Language must be attained : Without this necessary and previous Preparation, the Attempt will be vain, the Labour will be fruitless.

It is indeed readily granted that the Knowledge of Languages, where they serve not to convey the Knowledge of Things, is a mean and trifling Accomplishment : But this Objection, so commonly urged by the Ignorant and Unlearned, against the Study of the *British* Language, is without Foundation : For, notwithstanding the Losses it must have sustained by the Devastations of War, the Injuries of Time, and other Casualties, it can still boast of many curious and valuable Manuscripts in Poetry, History, Mythology, &c.

The learned and ingenious Dr. *Wotton*, whose critical Knowledge of this kind cannot be called in question, in a Dedication of a Work of his to the Society of ANCIENT BRITONS, gives this remarkable Attestation to what has been advanced : " You (says he) have the Usages and Constitutions of your Ancestors still extant in your Mother-Tongue. It argued a true Love for your Country to preserve such a Record so long entire. *France* has no Monuments left of its primitive Language before *Julius Caesar's* Time ; the *French* must apply themselves to you, if they would know what Tongue the old *Gauls* conversed in. *Spain* has little or nothing of their original Tongue to boast of : The poor Remains of the old *Cantabric* Language, are by no means comparable to your antient Stores.'' Nor are these relative Uses of the *British* Language its only Recommendation ; it has perhaps as much intrinsic merit as any living Language whatsoever. In the Strength of its Expressions, it is inferior to none ; in the Harmony of its Numbers, which admirably fits it for Poetry, it is superior to most ; nor is it an inconsiderable Proof of its Copiousness and Independency, that, without the Assistance of any foreign Words, it fully expresses all the Conceptions of the Mind : And, which is a remarkable Excellency peculiar to it, not commonly taken notice of, it is easily formed into Compounds, which not only serve for Signs of Things, but are likewise expressive of their principal Modes and essential Properties.

And whereas most other Languages have been changed and corrupted, so as in length of Time to become in a great Measure unintelligible ; we have undoubted Proofs that the *British* has continued very near the same, at least for twelve hundred Years past ; the Compositions of the famous Poet *Taliesin*, the two *Merddins*, *Aneurin Wawdrydd*, and Prince *Llywarch hen*, who all flourished in the fifth Century, being, at this Day, perfectly intelligible in this Language.

These intrinsic Excellencies of the *British* Language, among other Things, give us a high Idea of the natural and acquired Abilities of the *Antient Britons ;* and are presumptive Proofs that they were a polite and learned People : For, if we consider how great an Effort of the human Mind it is to form a Language, how rude and imperfect the first Models of it generally are, and by what slow Graduations it advances towards Perfection : it must be confessed to have been the Work of great Art and Genius to carry the *British* Language to such a Degree of Beauty and Exactness. But, as it frequently happens, that no Excellency can always be secure from Detraction and ill Treatment, it has been the Fate of this truly ancient and noble Language to be despised ; and that for no other visible Reason, but because it is not understood ; and even amongst those whose Mother-Tongue it is, whether from an Affectation of Novelty, or an Indolence of Temper, or from whatever other Cause it proceeds, few take the Pains to attain a critical Knowledge of it, and to study its Beauties.

To cultivate therefore a Language so excellent in itself, so fruitful in many venerable and undoubted Monuments of Antiquity, so highly useful and indeed necessary, to the Restoration and Improvement, not only of the History of *Great Britain* and *Ireland*, but likewise of several Countries upon the Continent ; and to make it more thoroughly and generally understood ; Grammars and Dictionaries of it have been written by several Persons of great Ingenuity and Learning. But as the Field is large, and a Work of this kind is not without length of Time and much Difficulty brought to any degree of Perfection ; it is reasonable to suppose, that what the utmost Efforts of a few have not been able to accomplish, will be more successfully effected by the united Labours of many.

To this End, a considerable Number of Persons, Natives of the Principality of *Wales*, now residing in and about *London*, inspired with the Love of their common Country, and consulting the Honour of the *British* Name, propose to establish a general Monthly Society, distinguished by the Name and Title of *Cymmrodorion*.[1]

But though the Cultivation of the *British* Language, and a Search into Antiquities, be the principal End of our meeting together ; it is not, however, by any Means intended to make these Inquiries and Speculations the sole Object of our Attention. We likewise propose to render this Society as useful in general as the Nature of the Thing will admit of ; to facilitate which laudable Design, and to make its Influences as extensive as they appear to us to be beneficial ; it is our Desire not only to establish a general Acquaintance amongst our Countrymen, but also a friendly Intercourse and Correspondence with all candid Inquirers into Truth ; to whom we shall gratefully acknowledge ourselves indebted for their kind Assistance towards the Propagation and Improvement of any other Branch of Learning and useful Knowledge.

And as we glory in being the Offspring of the *Ancient Britons*, it will be our endeavour to approve ourselves worthy of that honourable Appelation, by imitating those social and generous Virtues for which our Ancestors were so justly renowned. More particularly we shall be attentive to the true Interest of our Native Country, and endeavour to promote its Welfare and Prosperity. And that we may not be wanting in the noblest and most Christian Virtue, we shall contribute our Endeavours towards the Instruction of the ignorant and the Relief of the distressed Part of our Countrymen.

With regard to ourselves, as Members of this Society, it will be our constant Care strictly to observe a just Order and Decorum at our several Meetings ; to conduct ourselves unblameably and inoffensively, to discourage all Vice and Immorality, to promote every private and public Virtue, to testify our firm Attachment to his Majesty King GEORGE, and his mild and auspicious Government, to cultivate a good Understanding amongst ourselves, and to extend our Charity and Benevolence towards all Mankind.

---

[1] Or *Aborigines*.

CONSTITUTIONS

OF THE SOCIETY OF

CYMMRODORION IN LONDON

I.

THE Society shall consist of Twenty-four Managers, *viz.* Two Presidents (one of whom distinguished by the Title of Chief), Four Vice-Presidents, Sixteen Council, a Treasurer, and Secretary ; and an unlimited Number of Members : All born or bred in the *Principality of Wales*, or whose Ancestors were of that Country, or who are allied to the Country by Marriage, or are possessed of landed Estates therein ; and who can speak the antient *British* Language, or are desirous of becoming acquainted therewith ; and who profess themselves hearty Well-wishers and Promoters of the Honour and Welfare of the Principality and its Inhabitants, and shall be of the Age of one and Twenty Years or upwards

II.

There shall be a General Meeting of the Society on the first *Wednesday* of every Month, at some convenient House near the Center of the City.[1] The Hours from Eight to Eleven in the Evening, from *April* to *September*, and from Seven to Ten from *October* to *March*, both Months inclusive. The Officers shall take their Seats, and the Chairman shall call the Society to Order, at half an Hour after the appointed Time of Meeting : and the Form of sitting shall be as represented in the Following Figure. [*omitted*].

When the Chief President is in the Chair, the other President shall sit on his right Hand. When both Presidents are absent, the first Vice-President shall take the Chair, and so on by the others.   And the Vice-Presidents Chairs shall be filled in their Absence by the Senior Members of the Council, in the order they stand on the Book. When the Treasurer or the Secretary are absent, the Chairman shall depute proper Persons to officiate for the Night in their Stead.

III.

Every Person desirous of entering into the Society, must first get himself proposed by one of the Members at a General Meeting, who shall deliver the Chairman a Paper Writing, containing his Name, Calling or Occupation, Place of Abode, and place of Birth, signed by the Proposer : And at the same Time shall deposit Half a Guinea for him in the Treasurer's Hands for the general Use of the Society.   The Chairman shall read the said Paper in the Hearing of all the Members, that the Character of the Candidate may be enquired into, if thought necessary, against the next Monthly Meeting, when he shall be

[1] The present House is the Half-Moon Tavern in *Cheapside*.

231

balloted for : But if his Proposer be absent, the Ballot shall be postponed till such Time as he is present. If Five Negatives[2] appear on the Ballot he shall be rejected ; if there does not appear Five Negatives, he shall be admitted a Brother, according to the Society's standing Form of Initiation. Provided always, that the Half a Guinea Deposit-Money shall be returned to the Proposer in Case the Person shall be rejected.

IV.
CYFRINACH.

V.

The Officers and Council shall be elected yearly by Majority of the Members present, at a full Meeting, between the hours of Eight and Nine in the Month of *January* ; whereof previous Notice shall be given in one of the public Papers, and also in circular Letters to all the Members in Town. Agreed unanimously that the following Gentlemen be the first named Officers, to continue as such till *January* 1753, *viz.*

Chief President.

WILLIAM VAUGHAN of *Cors y Gedol* and *Nannau* in *Merionethshire* Esq. ; *Custos Rotulorum* of the County, and Member of the Honourable House of Commons.

President.

Mr. RICHARD MORRIS, of the *Navy Office.*

Vice Presidents.

Mr. DAVID THOMAS.
Mr. DAVID JONES.
Mr. ANDREW JONES.
Mr. ROBERT EVANS.

Treasurer.

Mr. DAVID HUMPHREYS.

Secretary.

Mr. DANIEL VENABLES.

VI.

The Council is to be composed of Gentlemen of Learning and Knowledge in the *British* and other Languages ; vers'd in the History, Poetry, Genealogies and Antiquities of the *Antient Britons*, and acquainted with the present State of *Wales*, with respect to Learning, Trade, Manufacturers, Fisheries, Mine-works, Husbandry, &c., of whom Eight new Members at least to be chosen annually. They are to meet occasionally upon the President's Summons, to assist him in conducting the Affairs of the Society : To direct the Disposal of their Money to proper Uses, as in Acts of Charity, Purchase of Books and other Necessaries, or (when it rises to a considerable Sum) put it out to interest in the public Funds, in the Names of the President, Treasurer and Secretary, till such Time as it may be wanted. Audit the Treasurer's Accounts Yearly. Enquire into the Character and Qualification of Candidates for Members, whether they be Persons of good Fame and Reputation, and qualified as required

[2] The Negative was Three till the Members became One hundred in Number.

by the first Article of the Constitutions. Consult with the Secretary, and give their Opinion on ancient Manuscripts and Letters from Correspondents what Part thereof may be proper to be published among the Society's Memoirs. And they are to have always in view the Encouragement of Industry among the Inhabitants of *Wales*, by promoting Schemes for improving their Trade and Manufactures, by Premiums or otherwise : As the only Means of enriching and better peopling the Country ; which is continually drained of its most able Hands for want of Employment.

VII.

The Master of the *British Charity School* at *Clerkenwell*, for the Time being, shall be admitted a Member without any Expence at Entrance or otherwise. He is to officiate as perpetual Clerk to the Society, to enter the Minutes of their Proceedings, call over the Members Names every Night, and collect the Reckoning : Direct the circular Letters, and send them by his Boys to the Member's Houses : put Advertisements into the News Papers, one Monthly in *Welsh* for the general Meeting : Give Notice to the Members to attend the Funerals of deceased Brethren : And occasionally any other Business of the like Nature. His necessary Expences on those Accounts shall be defrayed out of the common Stock ; and the Society shall make him a Compliment at Christmas yearly, adequate to the Nature of his Services.

VIII.

A Messenger shall be appointed to attend the Inside of the Room Door, to call for and receive every Thing wanted from the Waiter, and deliver the same at the Table. And also to take Care of the Fire and Candle, and see that every Thing in the Room is in proper Order for the Conveniency of the Members. And after the Society breaks up, shall see that their Moveables be taken Care of against the next Meeting. He shall be allowed one Shilling a Night for his trouble, and a further Gratuity at Christmas yearly at the Discretion of the Members.

IX.

A Door-Keeper shall be also appointed to attend the Outside of the Door, who is to receive the Commands of the Society from the Messenger, and must take particular Care that none but Brethren enter the Room, during the fixt Hours of Sitting on any Pretence whatsoever ; and shall have the same Allowance with the Messenger for his Trouble and Attendance.

X.

The Chief President is empowered to constitute three subordinate Houses, under his Hand and Seal of the Society, by the Names of the *Westminster*, *Southwark* and *Eastern Societies ;* each of which to be conducted by a President, Treasurer and Secretary, and governed by the same Constitutions. Those Gentlemen shall always act in Conjunction with the principal Society in every Thing respecting the main Scope of the Original Institution, and shall pay a Visit to the Chief President once a Year ; and the Societies shall likewise respectively visit one another.

XI.

When the Officers, or their Representatives, are all seated their proper places, the Chairman shall drink *Yr* EGLWYS *a'r* BRENHIN, which shall be pledged by all the Members. Then they shall proceed on Business to ballot for Candidates proposed at last Meeting, and take Cognizance of such as may be then proposed for the next Meeting : Receive Reports of the Council, and determine upon all Motions relating to the Concerns of the Society. When the current Business is over they shall drink *Jechyd* TYWYSOG CYMRU, *a Llwyddiant i Dywysogaeth* CYMRU : Then to mixt Conversation. When the Hours of sitting are expired, the Clerk shall call over the Members, and the Treasurer shall adjust the Reckoning, allowing therein one Shilling to the Drawer, and also the Messenger and Door Keeper's Allowances ; which being discharged, they shall conclude the Night with drinking *Jechyd y* PENLLYWYDD, *a Llwyddiant i'r* GYMDEITHAS : And the Chairman shall adjourn the Meeting to that Day Month, according to the prescribed Form in the *Antient British* Language. Not any Liquors called for before the Hour of Meeting, or drank out of the Meeting Room, nor any Eatables to be charged to the general Reckoning, each Member being to defray the whole of such Expence out of his own Pocket. If any Member shall have Occasion to depart the Society before the Hour of breaking up, he shall signify the same to the Chair, and lay down Thirteen Pence at least for his Reckoning.

XII.

The Discourse of the Society shall be as much as possible in the *Antient British* Language, which they are specially bound to cultivate. And all Motions regarding the immediate Concerns of the Society are to be directed to the Chair, the Person speaking standing up uncovered, and only one Person to speak at a Time : And if the Matter should render it necessary, a Committee of the Vice Presidents and Council shall be appointed to take the same into Consideration, who shall withdraw into another Room, and Report their Opinion thereof to the Society.

XIII.

The Chairman is to be treated with the greatest Respect, and his Orders obeyed by all the Members. He shall see that due Harmony and Decorum be kept up in the Conversation ; and if any Member shall be guilty of Drunkenness, profane Cursing or Swearing, using any obscene or irreligious Expressions in his Discourse ; or shall create any unnecessary Disputes, cavilling or wrangling, to the Disturbance of the Company ; (particularly Religious and Party Disputes, the Bane of Civil Society) the Chairman shall call the Offender to Order, and admonish him to better Behaviour. If notwithstanding such Admonition he still persists in being troublesome, he shall be immediately turn'd out of the Room as a common Disturber ; and if the Majority think proper shall be utterly expelled the Society. And if any Member shall be guilty of any atrocious Crime without Doors against the Public ; or shall commit any unworthy Action to the Dishonour of the Society, or Prejudice of any of its Members ; upon Complaint thereof he shall be heard in his Place, then ordered by the Chairman to withdraw, and Sentence shall be pronounced in the Case, according to the Opinion of the Majority, to a Reprimand from the Chair, Fine to the Poor's Box, or Expulsion. If he shall be absent at the

Time of the Complaint, the Clerk shall give him Notice to attend the next Meeting, to make his Defence. If he disregards the Notice, he shall be proceeded against as if Personally present ; and if he refuses to pay the Fine imposed on him, he shall be expelled the Society.

XIV.

The following Particulars shall be purchased for the Use of the Society, out of the Money received on Admission of Members ; *viz.*

1. A great Chair properly ornamented for the President, with the Society's Arms over it.
2. A proper Table to stand before it.
3. White Wands with Mottos for all the Officers.
4. Desks for the Chairman, Treasurer and Secretary, with Inkstands and Stationary.
5. A balloting Box and Counters.
6. A large Seal of Arms.
7. A Copper Plate of Blank Notices in *Welsh* for the Monthly Meetings.
8. A well-bound Book in Folio, to enter therein the Constitutions of the Society, Register of the Members Names, Catalogue of the Society's Moveables, expressing their Value, and whether given or purchased ; and a Cash Account for a Check on the Treasurer.
9. A Book for a Monthly Call List, and Minutes of the Society's Proceedings, whereof so much as deemed necessary shall be transcribed once a Year into the great Book, to be preserved on record.
10. A Charity Box, with two Locks and different Keys for the President and Treasurer.
11. A Cabinet for the Society's Books and Rarities, with Locks and Nine Keys for the Eight principal Officers and the School-Master.
12. A *Morthwyl mawr* for the Chairman to command Silence.

XV.

Each Member shall put a Sum not less than six Pence every Quarter into the Charity Box ; and any overplus Money in Reckonings shall also be put into it, if the Company present approve of it. And it shall be recommended to every Brother at his Admission to remember the Poor's Box. Which Box shall be kept in Custody of the Landlord, and shall be opened every Month, and the Money told in the Presence of the Society. When any of the Country, from unavoidable Losses, Sickness, large Families, or Want of Employment, shall be reduced to Distress in *London*, and come properly recommended to the Society, as real Objects of Charity ; the Managers may give them casual Subsistence, discretionally in Time of Need, to be reimbursed out of the Poor's Box ; and if from Home, a Sum to enable them to travel thither. The Clerk shall keep an Account of all the Charities in a Book, and a Report thereof shall be made to the Society in the Month of *December* Yearly. Persons inclined to promote so useful a Charity, are requested to send their Contributions for that Purpose to the Society at their general Monthly Meeting.

XVI.

The Society's Museum and Library shall be at the *School-house* on *Clerkenwell Green*, till a more commodious Place can be fixt on : and the Schoolmaster is to frame and continue in Order a proper Catalogue of all the Books and Curiosities contained therein, and take particular Care that no Part of them are damaged, or taken away by any Person whatever. The Librarian, with the Approbation of the Managers, shall purchase at the Society's Expence one Copy (if to be had) of every Book that hath ever been printed in the antient *British* Language ; and of every one that shall be printed hereafter : also as many antient *British* Manuscripts as can be procured at a reasonable Price : Likewise such Books in any other Language, treating of the History and Antiquities of *Britain*, as shall be judged useful and necessary towards carrying on the Designs of the Society : Each Book to be lettered on the Cover *Eiddo'r Cymmrodorion yn Llundain*. All Donations to the Society of Books, Manuscripts, Medals, Fossils, Ores, Shells, or any other curious Productions of Art or Nature, shall be entered on Record with the Donors Names in the Book of Constitutions : And honourable mention shall be made of the Donors in the Society's *Memoirs :* and the Society's Thanks under their Seal shall be transmitted by the Secretary to every such generous Encourager of our Institution.

XVII.

The Library, Collection of Curiosities, Great Chair, Table and other Moveables, are to be deemed the joint Property of the Society for ever. But if by any unforeseen Accident the Society should in future Time be dissolved, the Whole shall devolve to the Trustees of the *British Charity School* on *Clerkenwell Green*, to be preserved by them at the School-House entire : And if that Foundation should cease, then the same to go to the Use of *Jesus College Oxon* for ever.

XVIII.

The Secretary shall be the Librarian, and Keeper of the *Cymmrodorion Museum*. He shall make Extracts from the Letters of Correspondents, and regularly digest them into a Book ; which, with any new Discoveries or Improvements that the Society shall make on the Subject of History, Poetry, Antiquities, &c., after having been approved of in Council, shall be published under the Title of *Memoirs of the Society of* CYMMRODORION *in* LONDON ; from such a Time to such a Time. The Society also propose to print all the scarce and valuable *antient British Manuscripts* with Notes Critical and Explanatory : To which End, the Possessors thereof are desired to communicate the same, that they may be preserved from being lost to the World. The Copies of all such Books shall be vested in the Society, and the Profits arising from the Sale of them shall be appropriated for other Publications in the *British* Language, such as the Society shall deem useful and necessary for promoting Knowledge and Virtue among their Countrymen. And a Printer and Bookseller to the Society shall be appointed, for the better carrying on the said Publications.

XIX.

Corresponding Members shall be elected of the Curious and Learned in the Country : And the Society do heartily invite their Brethren of the *Welsh* Colony in *Pensylvania* to correspond with them ; being very desirous of perpetuating the antient *British* Language in that Province : To which End they will give them all the Assistance in their Power, by supplying them with Books on the same Terms with their Countrymen in *Old Wales*. They are also desirous of Correspondence with all Historians and Antiquaries, of what Nation soever, who may have Occasion to treat concerning the former State of this Island : Such of whom as the Society shall approve of shall be elected Honorary Members ; and the Society will assist them all they can in their laudable Pursuits of tracing the true History and Antiquities of *Britain*, and in rectifying the numerous Errors which abound in most books written on those Subjects, through the Author's Want of Knowledge of the Original Language of the Country. The Secretary shall write to the Corresponding and Honorary Members elect, to acquaint them therewith, which Letters shall be subscribed by the Chief President, or in his Absence by the President, and the Seal of the Society affixt thereto. Correspondents are desired to address their Letters to Mr. *Richard Morris, at the Navy Office, London*. The Originals of which, after they have been considered by the Secretary, shall be carefully preserved for the Inspection of the Curious among the Archives of the Society.

XX.

The Society shall make Rules and Orders for the better regulating and conducting the Annual Feast of the Antient *Britons* on St. David's Day, in order to retrieve the Credit and Dignity of that honourable and charitable Institution, which was heretofore conducted with solemn Splendor and Magnificence by the Nobility and Gentry, to the Honour of the *Principality of Wales*, and the great Benefit of the poor Children supported by this Charity : But of late entirely neglected by the Great, and but little regarded by any, for want of proper Regulations. Not any other Feast, Annual or otherwise, shall be held by the Society ; but they shall use their best Endeavours for supporting the *British Charity School* on *Clerkenwell Green*, by their own Subscriptions thereto, procuring Charity Sermons for their Benefit, and recommending the same to all their Friends and Acquaintance : And shall also consider of the most proper Methods to render that Establishment as useful as possible to the Public.

XXI.

And as the Protestants of all Nations in *Europe* (the *Antient Britons* excepted) have their particular Churches in *London*, for the Worship of God in their own Language, the Society have under Consideration the Building, purchasing, or hiring a Place of Worship here, and supporting an able Minister to perform Divine Service, and Sermons therein Weekly, according to the established Doctrine of the *Church of England*, in the *Antient British Language* : A Foundation greatly wanted and wished for by a numerous Body of People of truly religious Disposition, and firmly attached to his Majesty and his Government in Church and State. They have the greater Reason to hope for Success in this good Work, when they reflect on the noble and truly Christian Spirit which now universally prevails through the whole Nation, in the extraordinary Encouragement of public Charities in general, such as has not been known in any former Age : And which more immediately regards themselves, the late Publication of Thirty thousand *Welsh Bibles*, besides Five thousand more Testaments and Common Prayer Books, distributed, by the worthy *Society for promoting Christian Knowledge*, among the poor Inhabitants of *Wales*, for less than half their Value. The Society therefore doubt not, but that the same gracious Providence which so plentifully supplied their Countrymen with the precious Word of God in their own native Language (in which only they can understand it) will also provide them a House for his Worship in this Capital, where they have not hitherto enjoyed that Blessing. Persons inclined to promote this noble Design, are desired to specify in Writing the Sums they are willing to contribute to Mr. *Morris* at the *Navy Office, Crutched Friers ;* Mr. *Humphreys* in *St. Martins le Grand ;* the Reverend Mr. *Evans* in *Cowley Street, Westminster*, or to the Society at their Monthly Meetings. And when a sufficient Sum shall be promised, the Society will give Notice in the public Papers for the Money to be paid into a Banker's Hands, and will take the necessary Measures to accomplish the Work with all Speed, under the Care and Inspection of a Committee to be chosen for that Purpose.

XXII.

The Treasurer shall keep a fair and regular Account of his Receipts and Payments, which shall be audited by the President and Council in the Month of *December* yearly ; and an Abstract thereof, distinguished under proper Heads, reported to the Society, at their General Meeting in *January*. He must produce Vouchers for all his Payments, that will admit thereof, together with the President's written Directions for disbursing the Money.

XXIII.

The Members shall attend at the Funeral of every deceased Brother, if within the Bills of Mortality, in Procession, preceded by the Officers with their Wands, and the *British Charity Boys* shall walk before the Corps, singing Psalms, to the Grave.

XXIV.

The Constitutions, with the Introduction thereunto, and general Heads for Correspondence, shall be printed at the public Expence, in *British* and *English* (the Form of Initiation excepted) for the Use of the Members in Town and Country, and one Copy thereof delivered to each Member gratis. *Provided always*, That the Society shall be at Liberty to make additional Laws, if found necessary, for their better Government, so as the same be regularly proposed at a General Meeting, and Notice thereof given to all the Members in Town, who shall determine the Matter by Majority of Voices at their next Meeting : The Chairman to have Two Votes in this and all other Matters relating to the Society. In like Manner, they may alter or amend any of these Articles, the first only excepted, which is hereby declared to be the fundamental Qualification of the Members, never to be deviated from upon any Pretence whatsoever.

CANIAD *Y CYMMRODORION*

Ar ôl dewis Brawd o'r Gymdeithas.

——————

I.

CYD unwn, *Gymmrodorion*,
A'n gilydd yn un galon,
I ganu clod i'n Gwlad a'n Iaith ;
Dewisol waith Cymdeithion.

II.

Wrth ddewis Brodyr ffyddlon,
I fysg y *Cymmrodorion*,
Caned pawb ar flaenau 'i draed,
O 'wyllys gwaed ei galon.

III.

Cymraeg fydd ein penillion,
Hen famiaith, heb wehilion ;
Na chaffer neb, yn hyn o waith,
Yn sisial Iaith y *Saeson*.

IV.

Dowch yfwch, *Gymmrodorion*,
At Iechyd $\begin{cases} \text{ein brawd} \\ \text{brodyr} \end{cases}$ rhadlon
A ddaeth i'n mysg, mewn dysg a dawn,
Yn llawen iawn $\begin{cases} \text{ei galon.} \\ \text{eu calon.} \end{cases}$

V.

Nyni yw'r Hen Drigolion ;
Cynyddwn ein hamcanion :
Am garu'n gilydd haeddwn glod :
Bid hynod *Gymmrodorion*.

VI.

Ein Llongau pan ollyngon'
Yn rhydd i'r Moroedd mawrion ;
Y Daran fawr a deifl ei bollt,
I Laenio'n holl Elynion.

239

VII.

A gwnawn i'r *Ffrancod* duon,
Fyn'd ar eu gliniau noethion :
Gwae nhwy 'rioed y dydd a fu
Ffyrnigo *Cymru* a *Saeson*.

VIII.

Bydd yno'r *Spaeniaid* beilchion,
Yn crynu 'u hesgyrn crinion :
Ni rown mor cleddyf yn ei wain,
Nes curo rhain yn 'sgyrion.

IX.

Dowch llenwch bawb yn llawnion,
Ag yfed pawb yn gyfion :
Na adawn ddiferyn ar ein hol,
Drag'wyddol ddoniol ddynion.

Nodwch : Ni chenir y 6, 7, a'r 8 bennill, ond pan fyddom mewn rhyfel a'r *Ffrancod* a'r *Yspaeniaid*.

GENERAL HEADS

Of Subjects to be occasionally considered and treated of (among others) in the Correspondence of the Society of *Cymmrodorion*.

ANTIQUITIES

1. Of the ancient Names of the Isle of *Britain*.
2. Of the *British* Book of *Triades*, and its Authority.
3. Of the Book of ancient *British* Proverbs, and their Authority in History.
4. Of the ancient *British* Genealogies, and their Authority from written and oral Tradition ; and of the Use of that Science.
5. Of old Inscriptions in *Wales*, *British* and *Roman*, and ancient Coins.
6. Of the historical and poetical *British* Manuscripts mention'd in Mr. *Lhuyd's Archaeologia Britannica*, and several not seen by Mr. *Lhuyd*, &c., with an Account in whose Hands they are.
7. Of the *British* Character or Letter ; and of the *Saxon*.
8. Of Monsieur *Pezron's* Book (the Antiquities of Nations), its Excellencies and Defects.
9. Of the Uncertainty of ancient History, *Greek* and *Roman*, when they treat of the Affairs of *Britain*.
10. Of *Gildas*, *Nennius*, *Asserius Menevensis*, *Giraldus Cambrensis*, *Galfridus Monemuthensis*, *Ponticus Virunnius* ; and other ancient Writers among the *Britains*, who wrote our History in the *Latin* Tongue.
11. Of *Tyssilio*, the true Author of the *British History*, translated out of *British* into *Latin* by *Galfrid* Bishop of *St. Asaph*, called in Derision *Geoffrey of Monmouth*, and of the Translation and several Editions of it : Also of the Original Manuscript Copies, and in whose Hands they are.
12. Of *Camden*, *Milton*, *Lloyd* Bp of *St. Asaph*, and their Opposition to *Tyssilio's British History*.
13. Of their great Character to *Bede* the *Saxon* Historian ; and a Comparison between *Bede* and *Tyssilio*.
14. Some Extracts out of *Howel Dda's* Laws (or the ancient Laws of the *Britains*), particularly their Method of exposing Vice.
15. Of the ancient Tenure of Lands in *Wales*.
16. Of the true Orthography of ancient Names of Men and Places, the best Proof of them from the Poets ; and of mistaken Translations of Names, as *Merlin* for *Merddin*, &c., which have occsion'd the wild Guesses of Etymologists.

17. Of the Names of Mountains, Lakes, Rivers, Promontories, Towns and Countries in *Britain ;* being the most ancient Names, especially among unconquered Nations : These will help to explain *Antoninus's Itinerary*, i.e., The ancient *Roman* Stations in *Britain*.

18. Of ancient Churches, Bridges, and other noted Buildings : by whom built or erected.

19. Of the Carn, Cromlech, Meini gwyr, Bedd y Wrach, Coeten Arthur, Rocking Stones, Barrows, Barclodiad y Widdon, Maen Tarw, Maen Arthur, Cader Arthur, Gorsedd, Eisteddfa, Din, Dinas, Castell, Caer, and other ancient Fabrics or Erections of Stones found in *Wales*.

Poetry, *and the Welsh Language.*

1. Of the most ancient *British* poetical Writers ; Proof of the Genuineness of their Works : and of the Antiquity of Poetry among the *Britains*.

2. Of the *Druids* and *Bards*, in *Gaul* and *Britain*.

3. Of the most ancient Kind of heroic Verse used by the *Britains*, now called *Englyn Milwr*, and of the lyric Verse *Triban*, being of the same Original.

4. Of the present Twenty four Measures in the *British* Poetry, and about what Time they were instituted ; and of the Affinity between them and the Twenty four Measures in the ancient *British* Music.

5. Of the Congresses of the *Bards*.

6. Of the Secrets of the Poets.

7. Of the Decline of *Welsh* Poetry upon the Death of Queen *Elizabeth ;* not one Poem having been well wrote since, till the present Age : with a Guess at the Reason of it.

8. Of a Comparison between Dr. *Davies*, and Mr. *Edward Llwyd*, as Dictionary and Grammar-writers, and how each of them excell'd in his Way ; with their Characters.

9. Of the Character of *Humphrey Llwyd* the Antiquary.

10. Of *Robert Vaughan* of *Hengwrt*, the Antiquary ; and of his valuable Collection of *British* Manuscripts in Poetry, History, Genealogy, &c.

11. Of the valuable *British* Manuscripts in *Llanvorda*, *Llannerch*, and *Mostyn* Libraries ; also in Possession of his Grace the *Duke of Ancaster*, *Earl of Macclesfield*, *Sir Thomas Sebright*, Baronet, or in whatever other Hands they may be.

12. Some old *British* Penills set to the ancient Music, with a Prose Translation into English, or a Verse Translation if can be procured.

13. Of the Similitude between the *British* Tongue and the *Eastern* Languages.

14. Of the Softness of the *British* Tongue, as well as Roughness ; and of Verses in this Language composed of Vowels only.

15. Of Dr. *Swift's* Complaint, that the English is too full of Monosyllables, and of *Erasmus's* Observation on the same Head.

16. Of the excellent Song Writer *Hugh Morris*.

17. An Enumeration of some of the most noted modern *Welsh* Poets, *David* ap *Gwilym*, *Lewis Glyn Cothi*, and *Iolo Goch*, &c., with their Characters ; and some of their Works occasionally printed with Notes and Translations.

18. Some *Welsh* Poems of the present Age to be published with Notes.

19. The great Affinity between the *Welsh* and *Irish* Languages, and between the Customs of the two Nations ; and that there is some strange Language mixt with the *Irish*, and what it is.

20. That the *Irish* are a Colony from the first Inhabitants of *Britain ;* proved from the Names of Mountains, Lakes and Cytiau Gwyddelod in *Wales*.

21. Of the *Welsh* Words *Porthmon, Hwsmon, Allmon,* &c., had from the *Teutons*.

22. Of the Translation and different Impressions of the *Welsh* Bible.

23. Of *Welsh* Grammars and Dictionaries, printed and manuscript.

24. Of *Welsh* printed Books in general.

The present Customs and Manners of the Welsh.

1. Of the Similitude between the *Welsh* Customs and the *Graecian ;* and of the *British* Chariots of War mentioned by *Caesar*.

2. Of Surnames in *Wales*, of what Standing ; and of the ancient Method of Pedigrees, like the *Eastern* Nations.

3. Of their deriving themselves from the Fifteen Tribes of *North Wales;* and why the Writers of Genealogies in later Times thought it sufficient to derive any Family from those Tribes.

4. Of their particular Method and Custom of Singing with the *Harp ;* and an Account of the *Crwth,* a *Welsh* Musical Instrument.

5. Of the Ferocity of the *English* formerly to Strangers ; and of Mr. *Lambard's* Observation that seems to point out the Cause why the *Welsh* and *English* were not sooner incorporated.

6. Of the hot Passions of the *Welsh ;* and whether there be any Foundation in Nature for that common Expression, *His Welsh Blood is up.*

7. Of some *Druidical* Remains of Customs, &c., among the *Welsh*.

8. Of the *Welsh Awen*, and their Fondness to Poetry and Antiquities.

9. Of their long Lives, and the most common Diseases in *Wales*.

10. Of the present State of Religion in *Wales*, and of the Circulating *Welsh* Charity Schools.

Natural Philosophy.

1. Of Plants found in some Parts of *Wales*, not hitherto described by any Botanists who travelled those Parts, or of those that are rare.

2. Of Fossils found in *Wales*, either not hitherto known, or not described by any Writer, or very scarce.

3. Of Fish upon the Coast of *Wales*, or in Lakes or Rivers.
4. Of Birds, Beasts, and Insects in *Wales*.
5. Of Medicinal Waters.

Manufactures.

1. Of burning Tang for Kelp, and the present Practice.
2. Of burning Lime, and the present Practice in different Parts of *Wales* ; and of the different kinds of Limestone : some for White-washing, some for Manure, some for common Mortar, some for Bridges or Works under Water.
3. Of burning Fern for the Use of Refiners, Soap-makers, &c., and the present Method in *Wales*.
4. Of Millstone and Slate Quarries.
5. Of the Lapis Asbestos, and Salamanders Wool.
6. Of Marble.
7. Of Manurement of Ground with Marl, Sand, and Lime and Method of Manuring.
8. Of the Lead, Sliver, and Copper Mines.
9. Of the Collieries.
10. Of the Woollen Manufactures.
11. Of the Fishery on the Coast of *Wales*.
12. Of Improvements in Husbandry, Trade, and Navigation.
13. Of charking Wood and Turf.

Queries of the Invisible World *whether it be true or false what is reported of*.

1. Apparitions and Dreams.
2. Haunted Houses, and Treasures discovered by that Means.
3. Knockers in Mines, a kind of beneficent Spirits.
4. Appearances in the Day-time of Funerals, followed soon after by real Funerals ; the same with Pslam-singing heard in the Night.
5. Corps Candles.

Caniad i'r Hybarch GYMDEITHAS O GYMMRODORION yn LLUNDAIN; ac i'r Hen odidwag Iaith GYMRAEG : ar y Pedwar Mesur ar Hugain

Englyn Unodl union.

1. MAWL i'r Ion ! aml yw ei Rad,—ac amryw
I *Gymru* fu'n wastad :
Oes Genau, na chais Ganiad,
A garo Lwydd Gwŷr ei Wlad ?

Prost Cadwynodl.

2. Di yw ein Twr, Duw, a'n Tad,
Mawr yw'th Waith ym Môr a Thud,
A oes modd, O Iesu mâd,
I neb na fawl na bo'n fud ?

Prost Cyfnewidiog.

3. Cawsom Fâr Llachar a Llid,
Am ein Bai yma'n y Byd ;
Torres y Rhwym, troes y Rhod,
Llwydd a gawn, a llawn wellhâd.

Unodl grwcca.

4. Rhoe Nefoedd yr Hynafiaid
Dan y Gosp, a Dyna gaid ;
Llofr a blin oll a fu'r Blaid—flynyddoedd
Is trinoedd Estroniaid.

Unodl gyrch.

5. Doe *Rufeinwyr*, Dorf, unwaith,
I doliaw'n Hedd, dileu'n Hiaith,
Hyd na roes Duw Ion, o'i Rad,
O'r Daliad wared eilwaith.

Cywydd Deuair hirion-

6. Aml fu alaeth mil filoedd,
Na bu'n well, ein Bai ni oedd,

Cywydd Deuair fyrion ac

7. Treiswŷr trawsion
I'n Iaith wenn hon

Awdl Gywydd ynghyd.

8. Dygn Adwyth digwyn ydoedd
Tros Oesoedd Tra y *Saeson*,

Cywydd llosgyrnog.

9. Taer flin oeddynt hir flynyddoedd,
Llu a'n torrai oll o'n Tiroedd
I filoedd o Ofalon,

a

Thoddaid ynghyd.

10. Yno, o'i Rad, ein Ner Ion—a'n piau
A droe Galonnau Drwg Elynion.

Gwawdodyn byr.

11. Ion Trugarog ! onid rhagorol
Y goryw'r Iesu geirwir rasol ?
Troi Esgarant traws a gwrol—a wnaeth
Yn Nawdd a phennaeth iawn ddiffyniol.

12. Coeliaf, dymunaf, da y mwyniant,
Fawr Rin *Taliesin*, fraint dilysiant,
Brython, Iaith wiwlon a etholant
Bythoedd, cu ydoedd, hwy a'i cadwant,
Oesoedd, rai Miloedd, hir y molant—Ner :
Moler ;—I'n Gwiwner rhown Ogoniant.

13. A dd'wedai Eddewidion—a wiriwyd
O warant wir ffyddlon,
Od âi'n Tiroedd dan y Taerion,
Ar fyr dwyre wir *Frodorion*,
Caem i'r Henfri *Cymru* hoenfron,
Lloegr yn dethol Llugyrn doethion,
Llawn Dawn Dewrweilch *Llundain* dirion—Impiau
Dewr weddau *Derwyddon*.

14. Llwydd i chwi, Eurweilch, Llaw Dduw i'ch arwedd,
Dilyth Eginau da Lwythau *Gwynedd*,
I Yrddweis *Deheu* urddas a Dyhedd,
Rhad a erfyniwn i'r hydrwiw Fonedd,
Bro'ch Tadau a Bri'ch Tudwedd—a harddoch
Y mae, wŷr, ynoch Emmau o Rinwedd,

15. Iawn i ninnau
Er ein Rhadau   } roi Anrhydedd

Datgan Gwyrthiau
Duw, Wr gorau   } Ei Drugaredd.

16. Yn ein Heniaith
Gwnawn Gymhenwaith,   } gynnil union,
Gan wiw lanwaith

Gwnawn Ganiadau
A phlethiadau   } Moliant wiwdon.
Mal ein Tadau

17. Mwyn ein gweled mewn un Galon,
Hoenfrwd Eurweilch, *Hen Frodorion*,
Heb rai diddysg, hoyw Brydyddion,
Cu mor unfryd, *Cymru* wenfron.

18. Amlhawn Ddawn, Ddynion, i'n mad Henwlad hon,
E ddaw i Feirddion ddeufwy urddas
Awen gymmen gu, hydr Mydr o'i medru,
Da ini garu Doniau gwiwras.

19. Bardd a fyddaf, ebrwydd ufuddol,
I'r *Gymdeithas*, wŷr gwiw, a'm dethol,
O fri i'n Heniaith, wiw frenhinol,
Iawn, Iaith geinmyg, yw ini'th ganmol.

20. Fy Iaith gywraint fyth a garaf,
A'i theg Eiriau, Iaith gywiraf,
Iaith araith eirioes, wrol, fanol foes,
Er f' Einioes, a'r fwynaf,

21. Neud, Esgud, un a'i dysgo,
Nid Cywraint ond a'i caro,
Nid Mydrwr ond a'i medro,
Nid Cynnil ond a'i cano,
Nid Pencerdd ond a'i pyngcio,
Nid Gwallus ond a gollo
Nattur ei Iaith, nid da'r wedd,
Nid Rhinwedd ond ar honno.

22. Medriaith Mydrau,
Wiraith Eiriau,   } wyrth eres.
Araith orau,

Wiwdon wawdiau
Gyson Geisiau,   } lan wiwles.
Wiwlon olau,

23. Gwymp odiaethol Gamp y Doethion,
A'r hynawsion wŷr hen oesol :
Gwau naturiol i Gantorion
O Hil *Brython*, hylwybr ethol.

24. O'ch arfeddydd wych wir fuddiol
Er nef, fythol wŷr, na fethoch :
Mi rof ennyd amrwy fanol,
Ddiwyd rasol, weddi drosoch ;
Mewn Serch Brawdol, diwahanol,
Hoyw-wŷr doniol, hir y d'unoch,
Cymru'n hollol o Ddysg weddol
Lin olynol, a lawn lenwoch.

1. Am a'i prydawdd, o dawr pwy,
Sef a'i prydes *Goronwy*
Neud nid llyth na llesg Faccwy.

2. Ys oedd mygr Iaith gyssefin,
Prydais malpai mydr *Merddin*,
Se nym lle, nym llawdd Gwerin.

Tri Englyn
Milwr, yn ôl
yr hen ddull.
3. Neu, nym doddyw Gnif erfawr,
Gnif llei no lludded Echdawr,
Am dyffo clod, Gnif nym dawr.

[GORONWY OWEN]

AN

ALPHABETICAL LIST

OF THE

SOCIETY OF CYMMRODORION

With each Member's Place of Abode, and Place of Birth, from its first Institution to the 7th of May, 1755.

Those marked★ are of the Council.

NAMES	PLACES OF ABODE	COUNTIES WHERE BORN
	A.	
Aaron Ashton,	Southampton Buildings,	*Caermarthen.*
	B	
Edward Baxter,	Dev. Street, Qu. Square,	*Montgomery.*
William Bowling, *dead*	Chancery Lane,	*Pembroke.*
	C.	
William Carter,	Garlick Hithe,	*Caermarthen.*
	D	
★John Davies,	(1) Love Lane, East Cheap,	*Caermarthen.*
John Davies,	(2) Lincoln's Inn,	*Radnor.*
John Davies,	(3) Newgate Street,	*Merioneth.*
Thomas Davies,	(1) Navy Office,	*Anglesey.*
Thomas Davies,	(2) Bloomsbury,	*Merioneth.*
Hugh Davies,	Devereux Court,	*Anglesey.*
★Francis Davies,	Arundel Street,	*Pembroke.*
Maurice Davies,	Dalston,	*Merioneth.*
Moses Davies,	Qu. St. Go. Square,	*Montgomery.*
David Davies,	Islington,	*Caermarthen.*
	E.	
David Evans,	Fenchurch Street,	*Caermarthen.*
★Revd. John Evans	Cowley Street, Westmr.,	*Ditto.*
Robert Evans,	Spittle Fields,	*Montgomery.*
Thomas Evans,	Middle Temple,	*Anglesey.*
	F.	
★Revd. Henry Foulkes,	Rood Lane,	*Montgomery.*
	G.	
Sir Richard Glyn,	Lombard Street,	*Welsh Descent.*
John Griffiths,	Abchurch Lane,	*Montgomery.*
Emanuel Gunnis,	Cavendish Street,	*Caernarvon.*

H.

John Herbert, Esq.,	Serj. Inn, Fleet Street,	*Montgomery.*
Charles Hickman,	Bell Yard, Temple Bar,	*Ditto.*
★William Holland,	Lincoln's Inn,	*Denbigh.*
★Francis Howel,	Strand,	*Glamorgan.*
George Hudson,	Smithfield,	*Montgomery.*
Edward Hughes,	Threadneedle Street,	*Salop.*
Richard Hughes,	Parliament Street,	*Caernarvon.*
Robert Hughes,	York Street, Co. Garden,	*Ditto.*
Thomas Hughes, *dead.*	Clerkenwell Green,	*Cardigan.*
William Hughes,	High Holborn,	*Anglesey.*
★Revd. Cornelius Humphreys,	Tower,	*Caermarthen.*
David Humphreys, *Treasurer.*	St. Martin's le Grand,	*Montgomery.*
Capt. Hugh Humphreys, *dead.*	Gulston Square,	*Caernarvon.*

J.

★Thomas Jenkins,	Black Fryers,	*Glamorgan.*
Abel Johnson,	Victualling Office,	*Welsh Parent.*
Rev. Row. Johnson,	Gold. Sq., Crutch. Fryers,	*Merioneth.*
★Andrew Jones,	Breadstreet Hill,	*Denbigh.*
★David Jones,	Borough, Southwark,	*Cardigan.*
Edward Jones,	1, Castle St., White Chapel,	*Radnor.*
Edward Jones,	2, Paternoster Row,	*Salop.*
Henry Jones,	Barebinder Lane,	*Montgomery.*
Hugh Jones,	Bishopgate Street,	*Caernarvon.*
John Jones, Esq.,	(1) Chiswick,	*Montgomery.*
John Jones,	(2) White Chapel,	*Merioneth.*
John Jones,	(3) Newgate Street,	*Caernarvon.*
Maurice Jones,	Carolina,	*Denbigh.*
Michael Jones,	Old Fish Street,	*Glamorgan.*
Robert Jones, *dead.*	Field Lane,	*Denbigh.*
William Jones,	(1) Chancery Lane,	*Caermarthen.*
William Jones,	(2) Seething Lane,	*Caernarvon.*

L.

Howel Lewis,	Jermyn Street,	*Anglesey.*
John Lewis,	Bread Street,	*Montgomery.*
★Watkin Lewis,	Inner Temple,	*Cardigan.*
Henry Lloyd,	Hollywell Street,	*Montgomery.*

M.

★William Mathews,	Silver St., by Wood St.,	*Caermarthen.*
John Mathews,	Grays Inn,	*Montgomery.*
Charles Meredith,	St. Dunstan's, Fleet St.	*Brecon.*
Thomas Merrick,	Billingsgate,	*Glamorgan.*
Charles Morgan,	Temple,	*Caermarthen.*
David Morgan,	Maiden Lane, Co. Garden,	*Ditto.*
David Morris,	Coleman Street,	*Montgomery.*

Lewis Morris, Esq.,	Gallt Fadog, Cardiganshire,	*Anglesey.*
Richard Morris, *Pres.*	Navy Office,	*Ditto.*
Robert Morris, *V. Pr.*	Dowgate Hill,	*Denbigh.*

O.

Jeremiah Oliver,	Jermyn Street,	*Radnor.*
Hugh Owen,	Doctors Commons,	*Denbigh.*
Richard Owen,	Holborn Bridge,	*Montgomery.*

P.

John Parry,	Rhiwabon, Denb. Shire,	*Caernarvon.*
William Parry, *Secretary.*	Mint Office, Tower,	*Anglesey.*
John Paterson, Esq.,	Barbers Hall,	*Welsh Descent.*
William Paynter,	Navy Office,	*Denbigh.*
Robert Peters,	Dean Street, Soho,	*Caernarvon.*
Henry Price,	Threadneedle Street,	*Brecon.*
Rice Price,	Bow-lane,	*Radnor.*
William Prichard,	Cross St., Carnaby Mark.,	*Anglesey.*
John Prince,	Arundel Street,	*Welsh Descent.*
Evan Pugh,	White Chapel,	*Montgomery.*
Philip Pugh	Wood Street,	*Brecon.*

R.

Hopkin Rees,	Cursitor Street,	*Glamorgan.*
David Reynolds,	Golden Lane,	*Montgomery.*
*David Rice,	Ivy Lane,	*Caermarthen.*
Morgan Rice,	Thames Street,	*Glamorgan.*
Roder. Richardes, Esq.	Navy Office,	*Cardigan.*
Frederick Roberts,	Highgate,	*Denbigh.*
Henry Roberts, *dead.*	College Hill,	*Caernarvon.*
John Roberts,	Great Trinity Lane,	*Denbigh.*
Robert Roberts,	Black Fryers,	*Flint.*
Evan Rogers,	Saffron Hill,	*Cardigan.*
James Rowles,	St. James's Street,	*Monmouth.*

T

*David Thomas,	(1) Moorfields,	*Flint.*
David Thomas, Esq.	(2) Chancery Lane,	*Glamorgan.*
*John Thomas,	(1) Fenchurch Street,	*Caernarvon.*
Revd. John Thomas,	(2) St. Saviour's, Southwark,	*Merioneth.*
John Thomas,	(3) Strand,	*Glamorgan.*
Noah Thomas, M.D.	Leicester Square,	*Ditto.*
Richard Thomas,	(1) Moorfields,	*Flint.*
Richard Thomas,	(2) Lowman's Pond,	*Brecon.*
V. President.		
James Tomley,	Minories,	*Montgomery.*
Richard Tomley,	Borough, Southwark,	*Ditto.*

V.

William Vaughan, Esq.,	Haymarket,	*Merioneth.*
Ch. President.		
Daniel Venables, *dead.*	Princess Street,	*Flint.*

W.

Walter Watkin,	Cannon Street,	Brecon.
Edward Williams,	Finsbury,	Glamorgan.
Evan Williams,	Brooke Street, Gro. Square,	Caernarvon.
Francis Williams,	Charles Street, Westminster,	Montgomery.
*Henry Williams	Fleetditch,	Glamorgan.
Hugh Williams,	Cheapside,	Flint.

V. President.

John Williams,	At Sea,	Caermarthen.
Thomas Williams,	Clare Street,	Brecon.
Walter Williams,	Symmonds Inn,	Caermarthen.

V. President.

Abstract of Counties, &c.

Anglesey	9	Flint	5	Radnor	4
Brecon	6	Glamorgan	11	Salop	2
Cardigan	5	Merioneth	7	Welsh Descent	4
Caermarthen	14	Monmouth	1		
Caernarvon	12	Montgomery	21	Total	112
Denbigh	9	Pembroke	2		

CORRESPONDING MEMBERS

Revd. Thomas Ellis, B.D., *Flint*, Senior Fellow of *Jesus College, Oxon.*, Minister of *Holyhead, Anglesey.*

Rev. Evan Jenkin Evans, *Cardigan*, Curate of *Manafon, Montgomery.*

Rev. Peter Evans, *Denbigh*, Rector of *Harlington, Hants.*

Owen Holland, of *Plas Isaf* in *Conway, Caernarvonshire*, Esq.

Revd. Hugh Jones, Rector of *Bodffari, Denbighshire.*

Revd. Richard Jones, Curate of *Bewmares, Anglesey.*

William Morris, Comptroller of the Customs, and Collector of the Salt Duty, *Holyhead, Anglesey.*

Revd. Gronow Owen, *Anglesey*, Curate of *Walton, Lancashire.*

Revd. Lewis Owen, *Merioneth*, Curate of *Llanallgo, Llaneugrad* and *Penrhos Lligwy, Anglesey.*

Thomas Pennant, of *Downing Flintshire*, Esq., F.A.S.

Revd. Thomas Richards, Curate of *Coychurch, Glamorganshire.*

Revd. William Wynne, M.A., Rector of *Llangynhafod, Denbighshire*, and *Manafon, Montgomeryshire.*

HONORARY MEMBERS

John Bevis, M.D., Fellow of the Royal Academy of Sciences at *Berlin, Red-Lion Street Clerkenwell.*

John Warburton, Esq., F.R.S., *Somerset Herald, Heraldry Office.*

LIST OF MEMBERS, 1759

(As printed in *GOLUD YR OES*, *1863*)

Enwau	Trigfan, A Galwedigaeth (* Aelodau o'r Cyngor)	Genedigol Wlad

A.

Aaron Ashton,	Southampton buildings, Peruke maker	*Caerfyrddin.*

B.

Thomas Baker,	Arundel Street, Mason,	*Mynwy.*
Edward Baxter,	Dev. Street, Queen's Square, Linendraper,	*Trefaldwyn.*
Syr Charles Bond, Bart.,	Ensign in the Army.	*Caernarfon.*
Essex Bowen, Esq.,	at sea, Lieut., in the Navy.	*Penfro.*
Ynyr Burges,	East India House, Gent.	*Lloegr, mam Gymreig.*

C.

William Carter,	Garlick Hythe, Carpenter.	*Caerfyrddin.*
Thomas Cross, Esq.,	Wine Office Court, Attorney	*Lloegr, mam Gymreig.*

D.

David Davies,	(1), Islington, Schoolmaster.	*Caerfyrddin.*
David Davies,	(2), White Hart Court, Drury Lane, Haberdasher.	*Trefaldwyn.*
David Davies,	(3), Bush Lane, Merchant.	*Aberteifi.*
Francis Davies,	Deveraux Court, Gent.	*Mon.*
John Davies,	(1), Coffeeman.	*Maesyfed.*
John Davies,	(2), Newgate Street, Watchmaker.	*Meirionydd.*
Moses Davies,	Queen Street, Go. Square, Bricklayer	*Trefaldwyn.*
Thomas Davies, Esq.,	(1), Navy Office, Accountant.	*Mon.*
Thomas Davies,	(2), Bloomsbury, Japanner.	*Meirionydd.*
Edmund Day,	Fulham, Schoolmaster.	*Lloegr, gwraig Gymreig.*

E.

*Thomas Edward,	St. Giles, Soapmaker.	*Trefaldwyn.*
David Evans,	Fenchurch Street, Chinaman.	*Caerfyrddin.*
Rev. John Evans,	Cowley Street, Chaplain to White Hall.	*Caerfyrddin.*
Thomas Evans, Esq.,	(1), Inner Temple, Attorney.	*Mon.*
Thomas Evans,	(2), Long Acre, Goldbeater.	*Aberteifi.*
*William Evans,	Hogston, Excise Officer.	*Maesyfed.*

F.

Rev. Henry Foulkes,	*Islywydd*, St. Thomas Apostle, Lect. of St. Mary Aldermen.	*Trefaldwyn*.

G.

Rt. Hn. Sir R. Glyn, Kt., M.P. (Lord Mayor of London), Mansion House, Banker.		*Lloegr, hil Cymry.*
John Griffiths,	(1), Abchurch Lane, Merchant	*Trefaldwyn.*
Rev. John Griffiths,	(2), Chiswick.	*Caerfyddin.*
John Griffiths,	(3), Honey Lane Market, Poulterer.	*Lloegr, tad Gymreig.*
John Griffiths,	(4), Little Newport Street, Gent.	*Morganwg.*
Maurice Griffith,	Newgate Street, Tobacconist.	*Maesyfed.*
*Emanuel Gunnis,	Cavendish Street, Carpenter and Joiner.	*Caernarfon.*
Morgan Gwynn,	New Inn, Attorney.	*Caerfyrddin.*

H.

Thomas Harris,	York Buildings, Tailor.	*Brecheiniog.*
William Harris,	Ordnance Office, Draughtsman.	*Morganwg.*
John Herbert, Esq.,	Montgomery, Attorney.	*Trefaldwyn.*
Charles Hickman,	Bellyard, Temple Bar, Cuttler.	*Trefaldwyn.*
William Holland,	Lincoln's Inn, Attorney.	*Dinbych.*
*Francis Howel,	Strand, Mathematical Intru. maker.	*Morganwg.*
John Howel,	Cecil Street, Surgeon.	*Caerfyrddin.*
Valantine Howel,	Ryder Street, Farrier.	*Penfro.*
George Hadson,	Dock Head, Brewer.	*Trefaldwyn.*
David Hughes,	Leicester Street, Tailor.	*Caerfyrddin.*
Edward Hughes,	Threadneedle Street, Chocolate maker.	*Mwythig.*
Elis Hughes,	At sea, Surgeon in the Navy.	*Meirionydd.*
Richard Hughes,	Parliament Street, Slater to His Majesty.	*Caernarfon.*
*Robert Hughes,	York Street, Perfumer.	*Caernarfon.*
William Hughes,	*Islywydd*, High Holborn, Watchmaker.	*Mon.*
Rev. Corn. Humphreys,	Tower, Rector of St. Mary, Somerset.	*Caerfyrddin.*
David Humphreys,	*Trysorwr*, St. Martin's le Grand, Hosier.	*Trefaldwyn.*

J.

John James,	Old Bond Street, Hatter and Hosier.	*Penfro.*
William James,	Norris Street, Grocer.	*Aberteifi.*
James Jenkins,	Leather Lane, Cabinet-maker.	*Maesyfed.*
Thomas Jenkins,	Prerogative Office, Gent.	*Morganwg.*
Abel Johnson,	Victualling Office, Gent.	*Lloegr, tad Gymreig.*
Andrew Jones,	Wales, Merchant.	*Dinbych.*
Cooper Jones,	Southampton Buildings, Apothecary.	*Dinbych.*
David Jones,	(1), Borough, Southwark, Linen-draper.	*Aberteifi.*
David Jones,	(2), Bank of England, Gent.	*Morganwg.*
Edward Jones,	(1), Brewer.	*Maesyfed.*
Edward Jones,	(2), Paternoster Row, Bees-man.	*Mwythig.*

Griffith Jones,	Bishopgate Street, Brewer.	Caernarfon.
Henry Jones,	Birchen Lane, Attorney.	Trefaldwyn.
Hugh Jones,	Bishopsgate Street, Brewer	Caernarfon.
John Jones, goch, Esq.,	(1), Chiswick.	Trefaldwyn.
John Jones,,	(2) White Chapel Bars, Distiller.	Meirionydd.
John Jones,	(3), Newgate Street, Apothecary.	Caernarfon.
John Jones,	(4), Ruper Street, Brewer.	Aberteifi.
John Jones,	(5), Friday Street, Mercer.	Dinbych.
Maurice Jones,	South Carolina, Merchant.	Dinbych.
★Michael Jones,	Old Fish Street, Apothecary.	Morganwg.
Thomas Jones,	East Smithfield, Customhouse Officer.	Caernarfon.
★Wheldon Jones,	Shad Thames, Glover.	Mon.
William Jones,	(1), Chancery Lane, Surgeon.	Caerfyrddin.
William Jones,	(2), Seething Lane, Customhouse Officer.	Caernarfon.
William Jones,	(3), Cheapside, Glover.	Lloegr, tad Gymreig.

K.

William Keay,	Fleet Street, Surgeon.	Flint.

L.

Howel Lewis,	Islywydd, Jermyn Street, Surgeon.	Mon.
John Lewis,	Leadenhall Market, Druggist.	Trefaldwyn.
Thomas Lewis,	Tufton Street, Carpenter.	Caerfyrddin.
Watkin Lewis,	Inner Temple, Attorney.	Aberteifi.
Henry Lloyd,	Holywell Street, St. Clements, Woollen-draper.	Trefaldwyn.
Richard Lloyd,	Smithfield Bars, Grocer.	Meirionydd.
William Lloyd,	(1), Cornhill, Woollen-draper.	Meirionydd.
William Lloyd,	(2), White Chapel Bars, Vintner.	Dinbych.

M.

Rev. Abraham Maddock,	Grange Inn.	Lloegr, hil Cymry.
Roger Mascal,	Newgate Street, Druggist.	Brecheiniog.
John Matthews,	Gray's Inn, Attorney.	Morganwg.
★William Mathews,	St. Dunstan, Fleet Street, Watchmaker.	Morganwg.
Charles Meredith,	St. Dunstan, Fleet Street, Hatter and Hosier.	Morganwg.
Thomas Merrick,	Billingsgate, Vintner.	Morganwg.
Edmund Miles,	Ordnance Office, Gent.	Morganwg.
Charles Morgan,	Gough Square, Fleet Street, Attorney.	Morganwg.
David Morgan,	Marden Lane, Covent Garden, Cord-wainer.	Caerfyrddin.
John Morgan,	Leather Lane, Tailor.	Caerfyrddin.
David Morris,	Colman Street, Apothecary.	Trefaldwyn.
Hugh Morris,	Downing Street, Peruke-maker	Dinbych.
Lewis Morris, of Penybryn, Esq., Bardd. Cardiganshire.		Mon.

Richard Morris, Esq.	*Llywydd*, Navy Office, Accountant.	*Mon.*
Robert Morris,	Barbadoes, Merchant.	*Dinbych.*
John Mostyn, of Segrwyd, Esq., Wrexham.		*Dinbych.*

O.

Jeremiah Oliver,	Jermyn Street, Tailor.	*Maesyfed.*
Rev. Goronwy Owen,	*Bardd*, Williamsburgh, Virginia.	*Mon.*
Rev. Henry Owen, D.D.,	Essex, Vicar of Terling.	*Meirionydd.*
Hugh Owen,	*Islywydd*, Printing House Yard, Blackfriars, Gent.	*Dinbych.*
Richard Owen,	Holborn Bridge, Haberdasher.	*Trefaldwyn.*
William Owen,	At sea, Lieut. in the Navy.	*Lloegr, rhieni Cymreig.*

P.

John Parry,	(1), Market Street, St. James, *Musician.*	*Caernarfon.*
John Parry,	(2), Bridge Row, Vintner.	*Dinbych.*
William Parry, Esq.,	*Cofiadur*, Mint and Navy Office, Dep. Comp. of the Mint.	*Mon.*
John Paterson, Esq.,	Barber's Hall, Attorney, Flanders.	*Hil Cymry o du ei Fam.*
William Paynter,	Navy Office, Gent.	*Dinbych.*
*Thomas Peake,	Lincoln's Inn, Attorney.	*Dinbych.*
Vaughan Phillips, Esq.,	Customhouse, King's waiter.	*Caerfyrddin.*
William Phillips,	Charles Street, Westminster, Brewer.	*Maesyfed.*
Henry Price,	Threadneedle Street, Apothecary.	*Brecheiniog.*
James Price,	Oxford Road, Brewer.	*Lloegr, Tad Cymreig.*
*Rice Price,	St. Lawrence Jury, Warehouseman.	*Brecheiniog.*
Richard Price, of Rhiwlas, Esq., M.P., Somerset Co. House.		*Meirionydd.*
William Price,	Southampton Buildings, Coffeeman.	*Brecheiniog.*
William Prichard,	Cross Street, Corn Market, Lieut. of Marines.	*Mon.*
John Price,	Arundel Street, Carpenter.	*Mynwy.*
Edward Pugh,	Holborn, Linen-draper.	*Trefaldwyn.*
Ellis Pugh,	Spring Gardens, Toyman.	*Meirionydd.*
Evan Pugh,	Bishopsgate Street, Soapmaker.	*Trefaldwyn.*
Humphrey Pugh,	Spitalfields, Scarlet dyer.	*Trefaldwyn.*
John Pugh,	Fulwood Rents, Tailor.	*Brecheinog.*
Phillip Pugh, Esq.,	Wales, Apothecary.	*Brecheinoig.*

R.

*William Rea,	Peartree Street, Coal merchant.	*Trefaldwyn.*
Hopkin Rees,	Censitor Street, Attorney.	*Morganwg.*
David Rice,	Ivy Lane, Apothecary.	*Caerfyrddin.*
Morgan Rice,	Thames Street, Brandy merchant.	*Morganwg.*
Roderick Richards,	o Penclais, Esq., Navy Office.	*Aberteifi.*

Thomas Richards,	Holywell Street, Woollen-draper.	*Maesyfed.*
Edward Roberts,	Long Lane, Smithfield, Leather-cutter.	*Mwythig.*
Frederick Roberts,	Putney, Schoolmaster.	*Dinbych.*
John Roberts,	(1), Great Trinity Lane, Distiller.	*Dinbych.*
John Roberts,	(2), Holborn, Oilman.	*Dinbych.*
Robert Roberts,	Shoemaker Row, Blackfriars, Tailor.	*Flint.*
William Roberts,	(1), Chancery Lane, Attorney.	*Lloegr, rhieni Cymreig.*
William Roberts,	(2), Abchurch Lane, Printer.	*Caernarfon.*
Evan Rogers,	Saffron Hill, Carpenter.	*Aberteifi.*
James Rowles,	St. James's Street, Coffeeman.	*Mynwy.*

T.

John Taylor,	Skinner Street, Brewer.	*Morganwg.*
*David Thomas,	(1), Ropemakers' Alley, Moorfields, Stocking-presser.	*Flint.*
David Thomas, Esq.,	(2), Censitor Street, Solicitor in Chancery.	*Morganwg.*
Edward Thomas,	St. Paul's Church-yard, Mercer.	*Meirionydd.*
John Thomas, Esq.,	(1), Brenton Street, Ensign in the Army.	*Caernarfon.*
John Thomas, Esq.,	(2), Temple Bar, Banker.	*Morganwg.*
Noah Thomas, M.D.,	Leicester Square.	*Morganwg.*
*Richard Thomas,	(1), Ropemaker's Alley, Moorfields, Stocking-presser.	*Flint.*
Richard Thomas,	(2), Lawmans pound, Soapmaker.	*Brecheiniog.*
William Thomas,	Lambeth Hill, Dep. Marshal Admiralty.	*Morganwg.*
James Tomley,	Minories, Stationer.	*Trefaldwyn.*

V.

| Wm. Vaughan, Esq., M.P., | *Penllywydd*, of Nannau and Gorsygedol, Spring Gardens. | *Meirionydd.* |

W.

Walter Watkins,	Exchange Alley, Breeches maker.	*Brecheiniog.*
John Wilding,	Pope's Head Alley, Insurance broker.	*Trefaldwyn.*
Edward Williams,	Finsbury, Stable keeper.	*Morganwg.*
Evan Williams,	Hol. St., Shoreditch, Excise Officer.	*Caerfyrddin.*
Francis Williams,	Cha. St., Westminster, Coal-merchant.	*Trefaldwyn.*
Henry Williams,	At sea, Purser in the Navy.	*Morganwg.*
*Hugh Williams,	(1), Cheapside, Hosier.	*Flint.*
Rev. Hugh Williams,	(2), Anglesea, Rector of Aberffraw.	*Caernarfon.*
John Williams,	At Sea, Purser in the Navy.	*Caerfyrddin.*
Robert Williams,	Strand, Hatter.	*Mynwy.*
Thomas Williams,	Hermitage Bridge, Chair and Cabinet maker.	*Brecheiniog.*
Walter Williams, Esq.	Symmonds Inn, Attorney.	*Caerfyrddin.*

Y.

| William Yates, | *Ysgrifenydd*, Clerkenwell Green, School-master. | *Lloegr, gwraig Gymreig.* |

AELODAU GOHEBOL.

A.

Rev. Stephen Aldridge,	Clerkenwell, Rector of St. John.	*Lloegr.*

B.

John Beard, Esq.,	St. Martin Lane.	*Lloegr.*
John Bevis, M.D.,	Clerkenwell Close.	*Lloegr.*
John Bradford,	*Bardd*, Bettws.	*Morganwg.*

D.

Griffith Davies, Esq.,	Harwich, Collector of Customs.	*Aberteifi.*

E.

Capt. Edward Edwards,	Boston, New England, Mariner.	*Mon.*
John Ellis, Esq., F.R.S.,	Lawrence Lane, Merchant.	*Iwerddon.*
Thomas Ellis, B.D.,	Holyhead, Minister of Holyhead.	*Flint.*
Rev. Evan Evans,	Llanllechid, Caernarfon.	*Aberteifi.*
Michael Evans,	Llanerchymedd, Saddler.	*Mon.*
Rev. Peter Evans,	Hants., Rector of Haslington.	*Dinbych.*

F.

Rev. David Foulkes,	Sussex.	*Meirionydd.*

H.

Joseph Harries, Esq.,	Mint Tower, King's Assay Master.	*Brecheiniog.*
Owen Holland, Esq.,	Conway.	*Caernarfon.*
Hugh Hughes,	*Bardd*, Llwydiarth Esgob, Anglesey.	*Mon.*

J.

Rev. Rowland Johnson, D.D.,	Hertfordshire, Rector of Hampstead.	*Meirionydd.*
William Johnson, Esq.,	Broad Street, Soho.	*Lloegr, tad Cymreig.*
David Jones,	*Bardd*, Trefriw.	*Caernarfon.*
Rev. Hugh Jones,	Rector of Bodfari.	*Dinbych.*
Rev. John Jones,	Holborn Court.	*Morganwg.*
Rev. Richard Jones,	Beaumaris.	*Mon.*
Thomas Jones, Esq.,	Exchange Office.	

L.

Rev. Pierce Lloyd,	Ingat Stene, Essex.	

M.

William Morris,	Holyhead, Com. Customs, &c.	*Mon.*

O.

John Owen,	*Bardd, a Thelynor*, at sea, Cl. of His Majesty's Ship " Edgar."	*Mon.*
Rev. Lewis Owen,	Anglesey, Rector of Llanallgo.	*Meirionydd.*

Paul Panton, Esq.,	Plas Gwyn, Anglesea, Barrister-at-Law.	*Flint.*
Rev. Thomas Pardoe, D.D.	Oxford, Principal of Jesus College.	*Caerfyrddin.*
Thomas Pennant, Esq., F.A.S.,	Downing.	*Flint.*
Rev. Ellis Price,	Holyhead.	

Rev. Thomas Richards,	(1), Coychurch, Glamorgan.	
Rev. Thomas Richards,	(2), Montgomery, Rector of Llanfyllin.	*Aberteifi.*

Thomas Salmon,	May's Buildings, Historian.	*Lloegr.*
George Scullard, Esq., F.A.S.,	Chancery Lane, Barrister-at-Law.	*Lloegr.*

Morgan Thomas,	Bristol, Merchant.	*Caerfyrddin.*

John Warburton, Esq., F.A.S.,	Heraldry Office, Somerset Herald.	*Lloegr.*
Evan Williams,	*Bardd a Thelynor*, Brook St., Grosvenor Square, Musician.	*Caernarfon.*
George Williams,	Dover, Surgeon.	*Caernarfon.*
Brown Willis, Esq., LL.D., F.A.S.,	Wheddon Hall, Staffordshire.	*Lloegr.*
Rev. William Wynne, M.A.	*Bardd*, Denbighshire, Rector of Llangynhafal.	*Meirionydd.*

YR AELODAU A FUONT FEIRW ER DECHREUAD Y GYMDEITHAS, RHWNG 1751 a 1759.

William Bowling,	Attorney.	*Penfro.*
Maurice Davies,	Schoolmaster.	*Meirionydd.*
Robert Evans,	Scarlet dyer.	*Trefaldwyn.*
William Evans,	Tailor.	*Aberteifi.*
Thomas Hughes,	Schoolmaster.	*Aberteifi.*
Capt. Hugh Humphreys,	Mariner.	*Caernarfon.*
Robert Jones,	Brewer.	*Dinbych.*
Robert Peters,	Merchant.	*Caernarfon.*
David Reynolds,	Tobacconist.	*Trefaldwyn.*
Henry Roberts,	Sugar boiler.	*Caernarfon.*
Rev. John Thomas		*Meirionydd.*
Gwynn Vaughan, Esq.,	Compt. of Customs.	*Penfro.*
Daniel Venables,	Book-keeper.	*Flint.*

LIST OF MEMBERS, 1762

COFRESTR CYMDEITHAS Y CYMMRODORION.

Y rhai a Nodir â Seren,* ydynt y CYNGHOR am y Flwyddyn gydrychiol.

ENWAU.		GENEDIGWLAD.	TRIGFAN.	GALWEDIGAETH.
			A.	
Aaron Ashton,		*Caerfyrddin*,	Southampton Buildings,	Gwalltweydd.
			B.	
Thomas Baker,		*Mynwy*,	Arundel Street,	Saer Maen.
Daniel Ball,		*Penfro*,	Garlick-hythe,	Porthmon Gwin.
Edward Baxter,		*Trefaldwyn*,	Devonshire St., Qu. Square,	Lliain-werthwr.
Sir Charles Bond, of Gorddinog, Bart.,		*Caernarfon*,	In the Army,	Rhaglaw.
Essex Bowen, Esq.,		*Penfro*,	In the Navy,	Rhaglaw.
Ynyr Burges, Esq.,		*Lloegr*,	East India House,	Bonheddig, *Cymraes ei Fam.*
			C.	
William Carter,		*Caerfyrddin*,	Garlick-hythe,	Saer Coed.
John Chettoe,		*Dinbych*,	Warwick Street,	Bonheddig.
James Christian,		*Manaw*,	Grigsby's Coffee House,	Coffiydd.
Cadwalader Coker, Esq.,		*Lloegr*,	Old Street,	Darllawydd, *Hil Cymry.*
*Thomas Crosse, Esq.,		*Lloegr*,	Wine Office Court,	Cyfreithiwr, *Cymraes ei Fam.*
			D.	
David Davies,	(1)	*Caerfyrddin*,	Islington,	Ysgolydd.
David Davies,	(2)	*Trefaldwyn*,	White-hart Court, Drury Lane,	Gwerthwr mân bethau.
David Davies,	(3)	*Aberteifi*,	Bush Lane,	Masnachwr.
Francis Davies,		*Penfro*,	Carey Street,	Poticari.
Hugh Davies,		*Mon*,	Beaumares,	Uchelwr.
John Davies	(1)	*Maesyfed*,		Bonheddig.
John Davies,	(2)	*Meirionydd*,	Newgate Street,	Awrflychydd.
Moses Davies,		*Trefaldwyn*,	Queen Street, Golden Square,	Saer Priddfaen.

259

Thomas Davies, Esq., *Islywydd* (1)	*Mon,*	Navy Office,	Cyfriydd.
Thomas Davies, (2)	*Meirionydd,*	Bloomsbury,	Cabolydd.
Edmund Day	*Lloegr,*	Fulham,	Ysgolydd, *Cymraes ei Wraig.*

E.

Edward Edwards,	*Trefaldwyn,*	Old Change,	Lliwydd Sidan.
*Thomas Edwards,	*Trefaldwyn,*	Broad St. Giles's,	Sebonydd.
Charles Evans,	*Mwythig,*	Rotherhithe,	Gwerthwr Cyfreidiau Llong.
David Evans, (1)	*Caerfyrddin,*	Fenchurch Street,	Gwerthwr Tfini.
David Evans, (2)	*Trefaldwyn,*	Horsleydown,	Cadpen Llong.
Rev. John Evans,	*Caerfyrddin,*	Cowley Street,	Caplan y Brenin.
Morris Evans,	*Meirionydd,*	Cheapside,	Gwerthwr Sidanau, &c.
Thomas Evans, Esq., *Islywydd* (1)	*Mon,*	Inner Temple,	Cyfreithiwr.
Thomas Evans, (2)	*Aberteifi,*	Long Acre,	Aurddeilydd.
William Evans,	*Maesyfed.*	Antigua,	Masnachwr.

F.

Rev. Henry Foulkes,	*Trefaldwyn,*	St. Thomas Apostle,	Eglwyswr.

G.

Sir Richard Glyn, Knt. and Bart., M.P.,	*Lloegr,*	Birchin Lane,	Bancwr a Seneddwr *Hil Cymry.*
John Griffiths, (1)	*Trefaldwyn,*	Abchurch Lane,	Masnachwr.
Rev. John (2) Griffiths,	*Caerfyrddin,*	Chiswick,	Eglwyswr.
John Griffiths, (3)	*Lloegr,*	Honeylane Market,	Adarwerthwr, *Cymro ei Dad.*
John Griffith (4)	*Morganwg,*	Little Newport Street,	Bonheddig.
John Griffith, (5)	*Trefaldwyn,*	Carter Lane,	Crydd.
Maurice Griffith,	*Maesyfed,*	Newgate Street,	Tybacydd.
William Griffith,	*Trefaldwyn,*	Spittal-fields,	Lliwydd Ysgarlad.
*Emanuel Gunnis,	*Caernarfon,*	Cavendish Street,	Saer Coed.
Morgan Gwynn,	*Caerfyrddin,*	New Inn,	Cyfreithiwr.

H.

Hon. Thomas Harley, Esq., M.P.,	*Lloegr,*	Aldersgate Street,	Marsiandwr a Seneddwr, *Cymraes ei Fam.*
William Harris,	*Morganwg,*	Ordnance Office,	Darluniwr.
John Herbert, Esq.,	*Trefaldwyn,*	Montgomery,	Cyfreithiwr.
Charles Hickman,	*Trefaldwyn,*	Bell-yard, Temple Bar,	Cyllellwr.
William Holland,	*Dinbych,*	Amsterdam,	Maelier.
John Howel,	*Caerfyrddin,*	Cecil Street,	Meddyg.
Valentine Howel,	*Penfro,*	Ryder Street,	March-Feddyg.

Name	County	Address	Occupation
George Hudson,	*Trefaldwyn,*	Dockhead,	Darllawydd.
David Hughes,	*Caerfyrddin,*	Leicester Street,	Dilladwr.
Edward Hughes,	*Mwythig,*	London Wall,	Cocolatydd.
Ellis Hughes,	*Meirionydd,*	In the Navy,	Meddyg.
Hugh Hughes, Esq.,	*Mon,*	Wales,	Bonheddig.
Richard Hughes,	*Caernarfon,*	Fishmarket, Westminster,	Cerrigdowr y Brenin.
★Robert Hughes,	*Caernarfon,*	York Street,	Peraroglydd.
William Hughes,	*Mon,*	High Holborn,	Awrflychydd.
Rev. Cornelius Humphreys,	*Caerfyrddin,*	Tower,	Person St. Mary, Somerset.
David Humphreys, *Trysorwr,*	*Trefaldwyn,*	St. Martins le Grand,	Hosaneuwr.

J.

Name	County	Address	Occupation
John James,	*Penfro,*	Old Bond Street,	Hetiwr ac Hosanydd.
William James,	*Aberteifi,*	Norris Street,	Siopwr.
James Jenkin	*Maesyfed,*	Leather Lane,	Saer Cist.
★Thomas Jenkins,	*Morganwg,*	Prerogative Office,	Bonheddig.
Edward Johnson, Esq.,	*Maesyfed,*	Petty-france,	Bonheddig.
Andrew Jones,	*Dinbych,*	Wales,	Masnachwr.
Cooper Jones,	*Dinbych,*	Southampton Buildings,	Poticari.
David Jones, (1)	*Aberteifi,*	Borough Southwark,	Lliain-werthwr.
David Jones, (2)	*Morganwg,*	Bank of England,	Bonheddig.
Edward Jones, (1)	*Maesyfed,*		Darllawydd.
Edward Jones, (2)	*Mwythig,*	Paternoster Row,	Bacynydd.
Evan Jones,	*Fflint,*	In the Navy,	Meddyg.
Griffith Jones,	*Caernarfon,*	Bishopsgate Street,	Darllawydd.
Henry Jones,	*Trefaldwyn,*	Lombard Street,	Cyfreithiwr.
Hugh Jones, (1)	*Caernarfon,*	Bishopsgate Street,	Darllawydd.
Hugh Jones, (2) *Bardd,*	*Dinbych,*	Llangwm,	Cyhoeddwr Cerddlyfrau.
John Jones (1) Goch, Esq.,	*Trefaldwyn,*	Chiswick,	Bonheddig.
John Jones, (2)	*Meirionydd,*	White Chapel Bars,	Diferwr.
John Jones, (3)	*Aberteifi,*	Rupert Street,	Darllawydd.
John Jones, (4)	*Dinbych,*	Friday Street,	Gwerthwr Sidanau.
Maurice Jones,	*Dinbych,*	South Carolina,	Masnachwr.
Michael Jones,	*Morganwg,*	Old Fish Street,	Poticari.
★Richard Jones,	*Aberteifi,*	Strand,	Siopwr.
Robert Jones, Esq.,	*Dinbych,*	Dover Street,	Bonheddig.
Thomas Jones, (1)	*Caernarfon,*	East Smithfield,	Swyddog y Dollfa.
★Thomas Jones, (2) Esq.,	*Aberteifi,*	Cowley Street,	Bonheddig.

Thomas Jones, (3)	*Trefaldwyn,*	Broad St. Giles's,	Sebonydd.
Thomas Jones, (4)	*Caernarfon,*	Staples Inn,	Cyfreithiwr.
Valentine Jones, Esq.,	*Aberteifi,*	In the Army,	Cadpen.
★Wheldon Jones,	*Mon,*	Shad Thames,	Gwneuthurwr Hwyliau.
William Jones (1)	*Caerfyrddin,*	Chancery Lane,	Ffiol-waedwr.
William Jones, (2)	*Caernarfon,*	Tower Street,	Swyddog y Dollfa.
William Jones, (3)	*Lloegr,*	Cheapside,	Menig-werthwr, *Cymro ei Dad.*

K.

John Keay,	*Fflint,*	Chester,	Meddyg.

L.

John Lewes,	*Aberteifi,*	Customhouse, London.	Bonheddig.
Thomas Lewis,	*Caerfyrddin,*	North Street, Redlion Square,	Saer Coed a Mesurwr.
★Watkin Lewis, Esq.,	*Aberteifi,*	Inner Temple,	Cyfreithiwr.
Ambrose Lloyd,	*Dinbych,*	Holborn,	Bonheddig.
Richard Lloyd,	*Meirionydd,*	Clothfair,	Siopwr.
William Lloyd, (1)	*Meirionydd,*	Cornhill,	Brethyn-werthwr.
William Lloyd, (2)	*Dinbych,*	White Chapel Bars,	Gwinydd.

M.

Rev. Abraham Maddock,	*Lloegr.*	Bedfordshire,	Eglwyswr, *Hil Cymry.*
Roger Mascal,	*Brecheiniog,*		Cyfferiwr.
John Mathews,	*Morganwg,*	Gray's Inn,	Cyfreithiwr.
★William Mathews,	*Morganwg,*	St. Dunstan's, Fleet Street,	Orfanegydd.
Charles Meredith,	*Morganwg,*	Ditto.	Hettydd ac Hosanydd.
Thomas Merrick,	*Morganwg,*	Billingsgate,	Gwinydd.
Edward Miles,	*Morganwg,*	Ordnance Office,	Bonheddig.
Charles Morgan,	*Morganwg,*	Gough Square, Fleet Street,	Cyfreithiwr.
John Morgan,	*Caerfyrddin,*	Leather Lane,	Dilladwr.
David Morris,	*Trefaldwyn,*	Coleman Street,	Poticari.
Hugh Morris,	*Dinbych,*	Downing Street,	Gosodwalltwr.
Lewis Morris of Penbryn, Esq., *Bardd,*	*Mon,*	Cardiganshire,	Ustus Heddwch.
Richard Morris, Esq., *Llsywydd,*	*Mon,*	Navy Office,	Cyfriydd.
Robert Morris,	*Dinbych,*	Barbadoes,	Masnachwr.
John Mostyn of Segrwyd, Esq.,	*Dinbych,*	Wrexham,	Bonheddig.

O.

Jeremiah Oliver,	*Maesyfed*,	Jermyn Street,	Dilladwr.
Rev. Gronow Owen, *Bardd*,	*Mon*,	Williamsburgh, Virginia,	Athraw'r Coleg.
*Rev. Henry Owen, M.D.,	*Meirionydd*,	Hart Street, Crutched-fryars,	Person, St. Olaves.
Hugh Owen,	*Dinbych*,	Chancery Lane,	Bonheddig.
Richard Owen,	*Trefaldwyn*,		Gwerthwr mân bethau.
Robert Owen, Esq.,	*Mon*,	In the Army,	Cadpen.
William Owen,	*Lloegr*,	In the Navy,	Rhaglaw, *Rhieni Cymreig*.

P.

John Parry, (1)	*Caernarfon*,	Market Street, St. James's,	Telynior.
John Parry (2)	*Dinbych*,	Budge Row,	Gwinydd.
William Parry, Esq., *Cofiadur*,	*Mon*,	Mint and Navy Offices,	Cyfarchwyliwr y Mint, &c.
John Paterson, Esq.,	*F flanders*,	Barbers Hall,	Cyfreithiwr a Seneddwr, *Cymraes ei Wraig*.
William Paynter,	*Dinbych*,	Navy Office,	Bonheddig.
Thomas Peake,	*Dinbych*,	Lincoln's Inn,	Cyfreithiwr.
Vaughan Phillips, Esq.,	*Caerfyrddin*,	Custom House, London,	Disgwylydd y Brenin.
William Phillips,	*Maesyfed*,	Charles Street, Westminster.	Darllawydd.
Rev. William Powell,	*Aberteifi*,	Nant Eos,	Eglwyswr ac Ustus Heddwch.
James Price,	*Lloegr*,	Oxford Road,	Darllawydd, *Cymro ei Dad*.
Jonathan Price,	*Aberteifi*,	Salters Hall,	Cyfreithiwr.
Rice Price, (1)	*Maesyfed*,	Bow Lane,	Siopwr.
Rice Price, (2)	*Brecheiniog*,	Wales,	Ystorwr.
Richard Price of Rhiwlas, Esq., M.P.	*Meirionydd*,	Somerset Coffee House,	Seneddwr.
William Price,	*Brecheiniog*,	Southampton Buildings,	Coffiydd.
William Prichard,	*Mon*,	In the Army,	Rhaglaw Merinwyr.
John Prince,	*Mynwy*,	Arundel Street,	Saer Coed.
Edward Pugh,	*Trefaldwyn*,	Holborn,	Lliain-werthwr.
Ellis Pugh,	*Meirionydd*,	Spring Gardens,	Teganwr.
Evan Pugh,	*Trefaldwyn*,	Bishopsgate Street,	Sebonydd.
Humphrey Pugh,	*Trefaldwyn*,	Spittal Fields,	Lliwydd Ysgarlad.
John Pugh,	*Brecheiniog*,	Fulwood Rents,	Dilladwr.
*Philip Pugh, Esq.,	*Brecheiniog*,	Wales,	Poticari.

R.

| William Rea, | *Trefaldwyn*, | Golden Lane, | Masnachwr Glo. |
| Hopkin Rees, Esq., | *Morganwg*, | Staples Inn, | Cyfreith. ac Ustus Heddwch. |

David Rice,	*Caerfyrddin,*	Ivy Lane,	Poticari.
Morgan Rice,	*Morganwg,*	Thames Street,	Masnachwr Dwfr poeth.
Rev. John Richards, L.L.D.,	*Morganwg,*	Coyty, Wales,	Person Coyty.
Roderick Richards of Penglais, Esq., *Islywydd,*	*Aberteifi,*	Navy Office,	Ustus Heddwch.
Thomas Richards,	*Maesyfed,*	Billiter Lane,	Gwerthwr Brethyn.
Edward Roberts,	*Mwythig,*	Long Lane, Smithfield,	Lledrydd.
Evan Roberts,	*Meirionydd,*	Fore Street, Limehouse,	Siopwr.
Frederick Roberts,	*Dinbych,*	Putney,	Ysgolydd.
John Roberts, (1)	*Dinbych,*	Great Trinity Lane,	Diferwr.
John Roberts, (2)	*Dinbych,*	Holborn,	Gwerthwr Olew.
Robert Roberts,	*Fflint,*	Shoemaker Row, Blackfryars,	Dilladwr.
William Roberts (1)	*Lloegr,*	Staples Inn,	Cyfreithiwr, *Rhieni Cymreig.*
William Roberts (2)	*Caernarfon,*	White Fryars,	Argraphydd.
Evan Rogers,	*Aberteifi*	Saffron Hill,	Saer Coed.
James Rowles,	*Mynwy,*	St. James's Street,	Coffiydd.

S.

Samuel Scott, Esq.,	*Lloegr,*	In the Navy,	Cadpen, *Cymraes ei Wraig.*

T.

John Taylor,	*Morganwg,*	Skinner Street,	Darllawydd.
Charles Thomas,	*Morganwg,*	Temple Bar,	Hosaneuwr.
*David Thomas, (1)	*Fflint,*	Ropemakers Alley, Moorfields,	Hosanwasgwr.
David Thomas of Pwll y Wrach, Esq. (2).	*Morganwg,*	Wales,	Canghell Gynghaws.
Edward Thomas,	*Meirionydd,*	St. Paul's Churchyard,	Gwerthwr Brethyn.
John Thomas, Esq., *Islywydd* (1)	*Caernarfon,*	In the Army,	Cadpen.
John Thomas, (2)	*Morganwg,*	Temple Bar,	Bancwr.
Noah Thomas, M.D.,	*Morganwg,*	Carey Street,	Physygwr.
Richard Thomas,(1)	*Fflint,*	Grub Street,	Hosanwasgwr.
*Richard Thomas,(2)	*Brecheiniog,*	Lowman's Pond,	Sebonydd.
William Thomas,	*Morganwg,*	Wales,	Bonheddig.
James Tomley,	*Trefaldwyn,*	Minories,	Gwerthwr Papur.
Richard Tomley,	*Trefaldwyn,*	Borough Southwark,	Gwerthwr celfi heiyrn.

V.

William Vaughan, of Nannau and Cors y Gedol, Esq., M.P. *Penllywydd,*	*Meirionydd,*	Spring Gardens,	Seneddwr.

Walter Watkin,	*Brecheiniog,*	Exchange Alley,	Llodrydd.
John Wilding,	*Trefaldwyn,*	Pope's Head Alley,	Torrwr Sicrhad.
David Williams,	*Aberteifi,*	Field Lane,	Crydd.
Edward Williams,(1)	*Morganwg,*	Ironmonger Row,	Rhingyll Plwyf St. Luc.
Edward Williams,(2)	*Lloegr,*	Fleet Market,	Trefnwr Claddedig-aethau, *Cymro ei dad.*
Evan Williams,	*Caerfyrddin,*	Hol. Street,	Swyddog y Dollfa.
Francis Williams,	*Trefaldwyn,*	Charles Street, Westminster,	Gloydd.
Henry Williams,	*Morganwg,*	In the Navy,	Pyrswr.
★Hugh Williams, (1)	*Fflint,*	Cheapside,	Hosaneuwr.
Rev. Hugh Williams, (2)	*Caernarfon,*	Anglesey,	Person Aberffraw.
Rev. James Williams, B.D.,	*Caerfyrddin,*	Jesus College, Oxon.,	Hynaf Gyfaill o'r Coleg.
John Williams, (1)	*Caerfyrddin,*	In the Navy,	Pyrswr.
John Williams, (2)	*Caernarfon,*	Gwydyr,	Goruwchwyliwr.
Rice Williams,	*Caerfyrddin,*	Queen's Square, Westminster.	Meddyg.
Robert Williams,	*Mynwy,*	Strand,	Hettydd.
Thomas Williams,	*Brecheiniog,*	Hermitage Bridge,	Saer Cadeiriau, &c.
Walter Williams, Esq.,	*Caerfyrddin,*	Castle Yard,	Cyfreithiwr.
William Williams,	*Caerfyrddin,*	Birchin Lane,	Bonheddig.

Y

William Yates,	*Lloegr,*	Clerkenwell Green,	Ysgolydd, *Cymraes ei Wraig.*

AELODAU GOHEBOL

A.

Rev. Stephen Aldridge,	*Lloegr,*	Clerkenwell,	Person St. John's.
Rice Anwyl,	*Meirionydd,*	Jesus College, Oxon.,	Ysgolaig.
Robert Anwyl,	*Meirionydd,*	Ditto,	Yr un.

B.

Thomas Basnett,	*Mwythig,*	Jesus College, Oxon.,	Ysgolaig.
John Beard, Esq.,	*Lloegr,*	St. Martin's Lane, Westminster,	Cantor.
Sylvanus Bevan, F.R.S.,	*Caerfyrddin,*	Hackney,	Physygwr.
John Bevis, M.D.,	*Lloegr,*	Clerkenwell Close,	Ffilosophydd.

John Bradford, *Bardd*,	*Morganwg*,	Bettws,	Gwehydd.
James Briscoe, Esq.,	*Lloegr*,	Beaumaris,	Cynhullwr y Dollfa, *Cymraes ei Wraig*.

C.

Edward Carne,	*Morganwg*,	Jesus College, Oxon.,	Ysgolhaig.

D.

David Davies,	*Meirionydd*,	Pen y Bont,	Uchelwr.
Griffith Davies, Esq.,	*Penfro*,	Harwich, Essex,	Cynnullwr y Dollfa.
Hugh Davies,	*Meirionydd*,	Jesus College, Oxon.,	Ysgolhaig.
Owen Davies,	*Mon*,	Holyhead,	Golygwr y Dollfa.

E.

Robert Eaton,	*Fflint*,	Jesus College, Oxon.,	Ysgolhaig.
Rev. Edward Edwards, D.D.,	*Meirionydd*,	Jesus College, Oxon.,	Cyfaill o'r Coleg.
Edward Edwards,	*Mon*,	Boston, New England,	Cadpen Llong.
Edward Edwards,	*Mwythig*,	Jesus College, Oxon.,	Ysgolhaig.
Edward Edwards, *Bardd*,	*Fflint*,	All Souls College, Oxon.,	Yr un.
John Edwards of Glyn, Esq.,	*Dinbych*,	Jesus College, Oxon.,	Yr un.
Rev. Richard Edwards,	*Dinbych*,	Ditto,	Cyfaill o'r Coleg.
Timothy Edwards, Esq.,	*Caernarfon*,	In the Navy,	Cadpen.
John Ellis, Esq., F.R.S.,	*Iwerddon*,	Lawrence Lane,	Masnachwr Lliain, *Hil Cymry*.
Rev. John Ellis, LL.B.,	*Caernarfon*,	Bangor,	Archiagon Meirion.
Rev. Thomas Ellis, B.D.,	*Fflint*,	Nutfield, Surrey,	Person Nutfield, ac Ustus Heddwch.
Cadwalader Evans,	America,	Philadelphia,	Physygwr.
Charles Evans, Esq.,	*Caernarfon*,	Trefeilir, Anglesey,	Bonheddig.
David Evans,	*Trefaldwyn*,	Jesus College, Oxon.,	Ysgolhaig.
Rev. Evan Evans, *Bardd*,	*Aberteifi*,	Llanfair Talhaiarn,	Eglwyswr.
Henry Evans,	*Mon*,	Bwlan,	Ffermwr.
Lewis Evans,	*Mon*,	Gwyndy,	Post Feistr.
Michael Evans,	*Mon*,	Llanerchmedd,	Siadellwr.
Rev. Peter Evans,	*Dinbych*,	Harlington, Hants.,	Person Harlington.
Rev. Robert Evans,	*Mon*,	Tre'r Gof,	Person Hen Eglwys.

F.

Rev. David Foulkes,	*Meirionydd*,	Sussex,	Eglwyswr.

G.

Craddock Glascott,	*Morganwg,*	Jesus College, Oxon.,	Ysgolhaig.
Moses Grant,	*Penfro,*	Ditto,	Yr un.
Edmund Griffith, Esq.,	*Caernarfon,*	Guadalupe,	Solicitor General of all the conquered Islands.
Rev. Edward Griffith,	*Fflint,*	Shotteley,	Eglwyswr.
Hugh Griffith, Esq.,	*Caernarfon,*	Guadalupe,	Commissary of Artillery and Stores.
John Griffith, Esq.,	*Mon,*	Garreg-lwyd,	Bonheddig.
John Griffith,	*Meirionydd,*	Jesus College, Oxon.,	Ysgolhaig.
Richard Griffith,	*Caernarfon,*	Bangor,	Athraw yr Ysgol.

H.

Benjamin Hall,	*Penfro,*	Jesus College, Oxon.,	Ysgolhaig.
Joseph Harris, Esq.,	*Brecheiniog,*	Mint, Tower of London,	Prawfwr Bath y Brenhin.
Charles Hennings,	*Trefaldwyn,*	Jesus College, Oxon.,	Ysgolhaig.
Owen Holland, Esq.,	*Caernarfon,*	Conway,	Bonheddig.
Rev. Bulkeley Hughes,	*Mon,*	Tref Iorwerth,	Person Llanllyfni.
Edward Hughes,	*Dinbych,*	Jesus College, Oxon.,	Ysgolhaig.
Hugh Hughes, Esq.,	*Mon,*	Dublin,	Inspector General of the Excise.
Hugh Hughes, *Bardd,*	*Mon,*	Llwydiarth Esgob,	Uchelwr.
Hugh Hughes,	*Mon,*	Jesus College, Oxon.,	Ysgolhaig.
John Hughes,	*Maesyfed,*	Ditto,	Yr un.
Rice Hughes,	*Meirionydd,*	Ditto,	Yr un.

J.

Dr. Jenkins, M.D.,	*Iwerddon,*	Dublin,	Physygwr.
Rev. Owen Jenkins,	*Morganwg,*	Jesus College, Oxon.,	Ysgolhaig.
Rev. Rowland Johnson, M.A.,	*Meirionydd,*	Hemstead, Hertfordshire,	Person Hemstead.
William Johnson, Esq.,	*Lloegr,*	Ditto,	Bonheddig, *Cymro ei Dad.*
Anthony Jones,	*Caerfyrddin,*	Jesus College, Oxon.,	Ysgolhaig.
David Jones, *Bardd,*	*Caernarfon,*	Trefriw,	Clochydd Trefriw.
David Jones,	*Caerfyrddin,*	Jesus College, Oxon.,	Ysgolhaig.
Rev. Hugh Jones,	*Dinbych,*	Bodfari,	Person Bodfari.
Hugh Jones,	*Meirionydd,*	Jesus College, Oxon.,	Ysgolhaig.

Rev. Humphrey Jones,	*Caernarfon*,	Llanfaethlu, Mon,	Person Llanfaethlu.
Humphrey Jones,	*Mon*,	Jesus College, Oxon.,	Ysgolhaig.
Humphrey Jones,	*Dinbych*,	Ditto,	Yr un.
Rev. John Jones, M.A.,	*Aberteifi*,	Welwyn, Hertfordhsire,	Person Boulnhurst, Bedfordshire.
Rev. John Jones, LL.D.,	*Mon*,	Derrynoose, Armagh, Ireland,	Person Derrynoose.
John Jones,	*Mon*,	Jesus College, Oxon.,	Ysgolhaig.
John Jones, Esq.,	*Mon*,	Long Acre,	Haiarnydd.
Morgan Jones,	*Meirionydd*,	Dinas y Mowddwy,	Uchelwr.
Sir Owen Jones, Knt.,	*Mon*,	Long Acre,	Marchog Bonheddig y Brenin.
Rev. Owen Jones,	*Caernarfon*,	Conway,	Bicar Conwy.
Peter Jones,	*Meirionydd*,	Jesus College, Oxon.,	Ysgolhaig.
Rev. Richard Jones,	*Mon*,	Beaumaris,	Eglwyswr.
Robert Jones,	*Dinbych*,	Jesus College, Oxon.,	Ysgolhaig.
Thomas Jones,	*Fflint*,	Ditto,	Yr un.
William Jones,	*Trefaldwyn*,	Ditto,	Yr un.
William Jones,	*Trefaldwyn*,	Ditto,	Yr un.

K.

John Kyffin,	*Meirionydd*,	Jesus College, Oxon.,	Ysgolhaig.
Rev. Uvedale Kyffin, B.D.,	*Lloegr*,	Ditto,	Cyfaill o'r Coleg.

L.

Hugh Lewis,	*Meirionydd*,	Jesus College, Oxon.,	Ysgolhaig.
Rev. John Lewis,	*Caernarfon*,	Ceidio, Anglesey,	Person Llangefni.
John Lewis,	*Mon*,	Jesus College, Oxon.,	Ysgolhaig.
Rev. Robert Lewis, LL.D.,	*Mon*,	Siambr ar Wnna,	Canghellawr Bangor.
William Lewis, Esq.,	*Mon*,	Llanddyfnian.	Bonheddig.
Henry Lucas of Stouthall, Esq.,	*Morganwg*,	Jesus College, Oxon,	Ysgolhaig.
David Lloyd,	*Brecheiniog*,	Ditto,	Yr un.
Evan Lloyd,	*Mon*,	Maes y Porth,	Bonheddig.
Francis Lloyd, Esq.,	*Mon*,	Mynachdy,	Physygwr.
Lewis Lloyd, Esq.,	*Meirionydd*,	Holyhead,	Cynnullwr y Dollfa.
Rev. Pierce Lloyd,	*Meirionydd*,	Ingatestone, Essex,	Eglwyswr.
Rice Lloyd,	*Meirionydd*,	Jesus College, Oxon.,	Ysgolhaig.

Robert Lloyd, Esq.,	*Caernarfon*,	Tregaian, Anglesey.	Ustus Heddwch.
Thomas Lloyd,	*Dinbych*,	Jesus College, Oxon.,	Ysgolhaig.
William Lloyd of Rhiwedog, Esq.,	*Meirionydd*,	Ditto,	Yr un.
Rev. William Lloyd,	*Caernarfon*,	Pen yr Allt,	Person Edern.
Rev. William Lloyd,	*Caernarfon*,	Cowden, Kent,	Person Cowden.
Mr. Lloyd,	*Caerfyrddin*,	Jesus College, Oxon.,	Ysgolhaig.

M.

James Mathews,	*Lloegr*,	Jesus College, Oxon.,	Ysgolhaig.
Owen Meyrick, Esq., M.P.,	*Mon*,	Bodorgan,	Cynghaws, a Seneddwr.
Thomas Meyrick,	*Mon*,	Cefn Coch,	Uchelwr.
David Morgan,	*Aberteifi*,	Gogerddan,	Goruchwyliwr.
Jonathan Morgan,	*Morganwg*,	Jesus College, Oxon.,	Ysgolhaig.
Rev. Tho. Morgan, D.D.,	*Caerfyrddin*,	Byfleet, Surrey,	Person Byfleet.
Right Hon. Harvey, Lord Mount Morres,		Castle Morres,	Barwn.
Hon. Sir William Evans Morres, Bart., M.P.	*Iwerddon* *Hil Cymry*	Ditto,	Marchog urddol, a Seneddwr.
Hon. Redmond Morres, M.P.,		Dublin,	Seneddwr.
Richard Morris,	*Trefaldwyn*,	Rhyd yr Aderyn,	Uchelwr.
William Morris,	*Mon*,	Holyhead,	Cyfarchwyliwr y Dollfa, &c.
William Morris,	*Meirionydd*,	Jesus College, Oxon.,	Ysgolhaig.
William Mostyn of Bryngwyn, Esq.,	*Trefaldwyn*,	Ditto,	Yr un.
William Myddelton, Esq.,	*Fflint*,	Inner Temple,	Cyfreithiwr.

N.

Lewis Nanney, Esq.,	*Meirionydd*,	Llwyn,	Ustus Heddwch.
Mr. Nanney,	*Caernarfon*,	Jesus College, Oxon.,	Ysgolhaig.
John Nicholls, Esq.,	*Lloegr*,	Phœnix Park, Dublin,	Penmeddyg y Llu, *Hil Cymry*.

O.

Edward Owen,	*Meirionydd*,	Jesus College, Oxon.,	Ysgolhaig.
Rev. Humphrey Owen,	*Trefaldwyn*,	Ditto,	Yr un.

John Owen, Esq.,	*Trefaldwyn*,	Ditto,	Yr un.
Rev. Lewis Owen,	*Meirionydd*,	Llanallgo, Anglesey,	Person Llanallgo, &c.
Rev. Nicholas Owen,	*Mon*,	Llandyfrydog,	Person Llanfihang. Tre'r Bardd.
Rowland Owen, *Bardd*,	*Meirionydd*,	Jesus College, Oxon.,	Ysgolhaig.

P.

Paul Panton, Esq.,	*Fflint*,	Plas Gwynn, Anglesey,	Cynghaws.
Rev. Tho. Pardo, D.D.	*Caerfyrddin*,	Jesus College, Oxon.,	Pennaeth y Coleg.
Rev. Tho. Pardo, M.A.,	*Caerfyrddin*,	Ditto,	Ysgolhaig.
Rev. Henry Parry,	*Mon*,	Beaumaris,	Person Llanfadwrn.
John Parry,	*Fflint*,	Jesus College, Oxon.,	Ysgolhaig.
Richard Parry,	*Mon*,	Llanerchmedd,	Ysgolydd.
Joshua Paynter, Esq.,	*Penfro*,	Dale,	Masnachwr.
Thomas Pennant, Esq., F.A.S.,	*Fflint*,	Bychton,	Bonheddig.
Right Rev. Richard Pocock, D.D., F.R.S.,	*Lloegr*,	Offory, Ireland,	Arglwydd Esgob Offory.
Henry Pool,	*Meirionydd*,	Jesus College, Oxon.,	Ysgolhaig.
Hugh Pool,	*Meirionydd*,	Ditto,	Yr un.
Rev. Ellis Price,	*Fflint*,	Holywell,	Eglwyswr.
Rev. John Price,	*Dinbych*,	Llandyfilio,	Person Llandysilio.
Rev. Robert Price,	*Mon*,	Amlwch,	Eglwyswr.
William Price, Esq., F.R.S.,	*Meirionydd*,	Rhiwlas,	Bonheddig.
Owen Prichard, Esq.,	*Mon*,	Preston, Lancashire,	Golygwr y Dollfa.
John Pugh Pryce, Esq., M.P.,	*Aberteifi*,	Gogerddan,	Seneddwr.
James Prosser,	*Maesyfed*,	Jesus College, Oxon.,	Ysgolhaig.
David Pugh,	*Meirionydd*,	Ditto,	Yr un.
Edward Pugh, of Tygwyn yn Ial, Esq., *Bardd*,	*Meirionydd*,	Ditto,	Yr un.
Robert Pugh,	*Maesyfed*,	Ditto,	Yr un.

R.

Edward Richard, *Bardd*,	*Aberteifi*,	Ystrad Meuryg.	Ysgolydd.
George Richards,	*Morganwg*,	Jesus College, Oxon.,	Ysgolhaig.

Rev. Thomas Richards,	*Morganwg*,	Coychurch,	Eglwyswr.
Goodman Roberts,	*Dinbych*,	Jesus College, Oxon.,	Ysgolhaig.
John Roberts,	*Caernarfon*,	Caernarfon,	Poticari.
Lewis Roberts, Esq.,	*Iwerddon*,	Old Connaught, Ireland,	Cynghaws, *Cymro ei Dad.*
Rev. Thomas Roberts,	*Meirionydd*,	Llanrhaiadr,	Person Llanrhaiadr.
John Roch,	*Penfro*,	Jesus College, Oxon.,	Ysgolhaig.

S.

John Salisbury,	*Caernarfon*,	Llanwydden, Creuddyn,	Uchelwr.
Thomas Salmon,	*Lloegr*,	May's Buildings,	Hanefydd.
Francis Savage,	*Fflint*,	Shadwell,	Poticari.
George Scullard, Esq., F.R.S.,	*Lloegr*,	Blechingly, Surrey,	Dadleuwr.
William Seys,	*Mynwy*,	Jesus College, Oxon.,	Ysgolhaig.
Rev. William Stukely, M.D., F.R.S. and F.A.S.,	*Lloegr*,	Queen's Square, Ormond Street,	Person St. George.

T.

Edward Thomas,	*Morganwg*,	Jesus College, Oxon.,	Ysgolhaig.
James Thomas,	*Aberteifi*,	Ditto,	Yr un.
Rev. John Thomas, M.A.,	*Caernarfon*,	Bangor,	Eglwyswr, ac Ysgolydd.
Morgan Thomas, Esq.,	*Caerfyrddin*,	Bristol,	Marsiandwr.
Philip Thomas,	*Lloegr*,	Navy Office,	Bonheddig, *Hil Cymry.*
Edward Tilsley,	*Trefaldwyn*,	Navy Office,	Bonheddig.

V.

Rev. James Vincent,	*Mon*,	Bangor,	Person a Bicar Bangor.

W.

Edward Walters, Esq.,	*Morganwg*,	Brodge End,	Bonheddig.
Evan Williams, *Bardd*,	*Caernarfon*,	Oxford Market,	Telynior, ac Athraw Peroriaeth.
George Williams,	*Caernarfon*,	Dover, Kent,	Meddyg.
Hugh Williams, *Bardd*,	*Caernarfon*,	Gwedyr,	Bonheddig.
John Williams, Esq.,	*Dinbych*,	Jesus College, Oxon.,	Ysgolhaig.
John Williams,	*Meirionydd*,	Jesus College, Oxon.,	Ysgolhaig.
John Williams,	*Caernarfon*,	Ditto,	Yr un.

Rev. Richard Williams,	*Mon,*	Bodafon,	Eglwyswr.
Rev. Robert Williams,	*Caernarfon,*	Ty-newydd,	Person, ac Ustus Heddwch.
Rev. Thomas Williams,	*Morganwg,*	Jesus College, Oxon.,	Cyfaill o'r Coleg.
Thomas Williams,	*Maesyfed,*	Ditto,	Ysgolhaig.
Thomas Williams,	*Maesyfed,*	Ditto,	Yr un.
William Williams,	*Caernarfon,*	Caernarvon,	Poticari.
William Williams,	*Trefaldwyn,*	Jesus College, Oxon,.	Ysgolhaig.
David Wright,	*Lloegr,*	Liverpool,	Masnachwr, *Cymraes ei Fam.*
Howel Wynne,	*Meirionydd,*	Jesus College, Oxon.,	Ysgolhaig.
Lutteral Wynne, B.A.,	*Lloegr,*	Ditto,	Yr un.
		Y.	
John Youde,	*Dinbych,*	Jesus College, Oxon.,	Ysgolhaig.
Thomas Youde,	*Dinbych,*	Ditto,	Yr un.

Nodwch y SAESON, yn y Rhestr yma, a anrhydeddwyd yn Aelodau, am eu Cariad a'u Parodrwydd i wasanaethu, a chymmorth Amcanion da'r Gymdeithas.

YR AELODAU HYN A FUANT FEIRW, ER DECHREUAD Y GYMDEITHAS.

ENWAU.	GENEDIGWLAD.	GALWEDIGAETH.
William Bowling,	*Penfro,*	Cyfreithiwr.
Maurice Davies,	*Meirionydd,*	Ysgolydd.
Robert Evans,	*Trefaldwyn,*	Lliwydd.
William Evans,	*Aberteifi,*	Dilladwr.
Thomas Harris,	*Brecheiniog,*	Yr un.
Francis Howel,	*Morganwg,*	Peirianydd.
Rev. John Hughes,	*Mon,*	Eglwyswr.
Thomas Hughes,	*Aberteifi,*	Ysgolydd,
Capt. Hugh Humphreys,	*Caernarfon,*	Llongwr.
Abel Johnson,	*Lloegr,*	Bonheddig.
John Jones,	*Caernarfon,*	Poticari.
Robert Jones,	*Dinbych,*	Darllawydd.
Howel Lewis,	*Mon,*	Meddyg.
John Lewis,	*Trefaldwyn,*	Cyfferiwr.
Henry Lloyd,	*Trefaldwyn,*	Brethynwerthwr.
David Morgan,	*Caerfyrddin,*	Crydd.
John Owen, *Bardd,*	*Mon,*	Bonheddig.
Robert Peters,	*Caernarfon,*	Masnachwr.
Henry Price,	*Brecheiniog,*	Poticari,
David Reynolds,	*Trefaldwyn,*	Tybacydd.
Rev. Thomas Richards,	*Aberteifi,*	Eglwyswr.

Henry Roberts,	*Caernarfon,*	Suwgr-ferwr.
Rev. John Thomas,	*Meirionydd,*	Eglwyswr.
Gwynn Vaughan, Esq.,	*Penfro,*	Penswyddwr o'r Dollfa.
Daniel Venables,	*Fflint,*	Cyfriydd.
John Warburton, Esq.,	*Lloegr,*	Achwr.
Brown Willis, Esq.,	*Lloegr,*	Hanefydd.
Rev. Wm. Wynne, *Bardd,*	*Meirionydd,*	Eglwyswr.

Lle mae Camgymeriad, neu eisiau Gwybodaeth am Ditl neu Alwedigaeth, &c., neb o'r Aelodau ; yspyser i'r Llywydd, ac fe a'i diwygir ac a'i cyflawnir yn yr Argraphiad nesaf o Enwau'r Gymdeithas.

CRYNODEB

Aberteifi	16
Brecheiniog	8
Caerfyrddin	21
Caernarfon	14
Dinbych	21
Fflint	6
Maesyfed	10
Meirionydd	13
Mon	12
Morganwg	22
Mwythig	4
Mynwy	4
Penfro	5
Trefaldwyn	25
Hiliogaeth Cymry, &c.	17
Aelodau'r Cyfarfod	198
Aelodau Gohebol	183
	381
Buant Feirw	28
Diraddiwyd, am ddrygfoes . . .	1
I gyd . .	410

Swyddogion a ddewisir yn Flynyddol :

Penllywydd	1
Llywydd	1
Islywydd	4
Cynghor	16
Trysorwr	1
Cofiadur	1
Llywodraethwyr	14

Ysgrifennydd : Athraw'r Ysgol Gymreig,
yn oestad 1
Rhingyll 1
Drysawr 1

Cynneddfau Aelodau'r Gymdeithas ydynt y rhai hyn ; sef, bod wedi eu
geni neu eu magu yn Nhywysogaeth Cymru ; neu bod eu Hynafiaid o'r Wlad
honno ; neu eu bod wedi ymgyfathrachu a'r Wlad drwy Briodas ; neu eu
bod yn Berchenogion Tir ynddi : A rhaid iddynt fedru siarad yr Iaith Gymraeg,
neu fod yn ddeisyfus o ddyfod yn gydnabyddus a hi ; a chyhoedd gyfaddef eu
bod yn wir Ewyllyswyr da, a Chynnyddwyr Anrhydedd a Llesiant y Dywysogaeth a'i Thrigolion ; a bod yn un mlwydd ar hugain oed, neu ychwaneg.

Rhaid i'r Sawl a ewyllysio ddyfod yn Aelod o'r Gymdeithas, roi Mis o
Rybedd o'i Fwriad ymlaenllaw, mal y gellir ymofyn ei Hanes, os tybir yn
angenrheidiol : A rhaid iddynt dalu 10 swllt i'r Drysorfa wrth ddyfod i
mewn, a 2s. bob Blwyddyn i Flwch y Tlodion : Ac os bydd pump o'r
Brodyr yn erbyn ei ddewis, ni chaiff ei dderbyn yn Gyfaill.

Gwelwch Lyfr Gosodedigaethau'r Gymdeithas, am gyflawn Hanes o honi.

Dalier Sulw, Na dderbynir un Ceidwad Ty Cwrw yn Aelod o'r Gymdeithas.

LIST OF MEMBERS, 1778

Names.	Places of Abode.	Counties, &c.

A.

| Aldersey, Robert, Esq., | Kings Bench Walks, Temple, | *Montgomery.* |

B.

| Bulkeley, James, Ld. Vis., M.P., | Berkley Square, | *Anglesey.* |
| Beavan, William, | Hatton Garden, | *Radnor.* |

C.

| Christian, James, | Islington, | *Isle of Mann.* |
| Coker, Cadwallader, Esq., | Old Street, | *Welsh Descent.* |

D.

Davies, David,	Islington,	*Caermarthen.*
Davies, Evan,	Carey Street,	*Pembroke.*
Davies, Francis,	Lamb's Conduit Street,	*Pembroke.*
Davies, Matthew,	Long Acre,	*Cardigan.*
Davies, Rice,	Burr Street,	*Cardigan.*
Davies, Thomas, Esq.,	Navy Office,	*Anglesey.*
Davies, Thomas,	New Bond Street,	*Radnor.*
Davies, William,	Lamb's Conduit Street,	*Caernarvon.*
Davies, William,	Ordnance Office,	*Merioneth.*
Dunckerley, Thomas, Esq.,	Hampton Court,	*Welsh Descent.*

E.

Edmunds, Richard, Esq.,	Lincoln's Inn,	*Montgomery.*
Edwards, Arthur, Esq.,	Deptford,	*Welsh Father.*
Edwards, Rev. Edward, D.D.,	Jesus College, Oxon.,	*Merioneth.*
Edwards, Owen,	Bishopsgate Street,	*Merioneth.*
Edwards, Robert,	Doctors Commons,	*Flintshire.*
Edwards, Thomas,	Tottenham Court Road,	*Montgomery.*
Ellis, Griffith,	Moorfields,	*Merioneth.*
Ellis, Rev. Thomas,	Rector of Nutfield, Surrey,	*Flintshire.*
Evans, David,	Fenchurch Street,	*Carmarthen.*
Evans, Edward,	Fleet Street,	*Glamorgan.*
Evans, Henry,	Cateaton Street,	*Montgomery.*
Evans, Rev. John,	Whitehall,	*Caermarthen.*
Evans, John, Esq.,	Oswestry,	*Montgomery,*
Evans, Maurice,	Cheapside,	*Merioneth.*
Evans, Morgan,	Strand,	*Cardigan.*
Evans, Richard,	Lombard Street,	*Brecon.*

Evans, Robert,	Long Acre,	*Welsh Father.*
Evans, Thomas,	Kentish Town,	*Cardigan.*
Evans, Thomas,	Strand,	*Welsh Father.*
Evans, Thomas,	John Street, Minories,	*Glamorgan.*

F.

Fenton, Richard,	Customhouse, London,	*Pembroke.*
Foulkes, Rev. Henry,	Rood Lane,	*Montgomery.*

G.

Griffith, Rev. Jeremiah,	Shadwell,	*Radnor.*
Gunnis, Emmanuel,	Caernarvon,	*Caernarvon.*
Gwynne, Edward,	James Street, Covent Garden,	*Cardigan.*
Gwynne, Richard,	Cold Bath Fields,	*Montgomery.*

H.

Harley, Rt. Hon. Thomas, Alderman of London, M.P.,	Aldersgate Street,	*Welsh Mother.*
Hall, Rev. Benjamin,	Jesus College, Oxon.,	*Pembroke,*
Harris, Rev. Rice, D.D.,	Holborn,	*Caermarthen.*
Herbert, John, Esq.,	Wales,	*Montgomery.*
Hoare, Capt. Dan. Griffiths,	Snow Hill,	*Caermarthen.*
Hudson, George,	Hempstead, Herts.,	*Montgomery.*
Hughes, John,	Hoxton,	*Denbigh.*
Hughes, John,	Piccadilly,	*Montgomery.*
Hughes, Robert,	York Street, Covent Garden,	*Caernarvon.*
Hughes, Robert,	Temple,	*Anglesey.*
Hughes, Robert,	Watling Street,	*Brecon.*
Hughes, Robert,	St. Martin's-le-Grand,	*Montgomery.*
Hughes, Robert,	Wales,	*Denbigh.*
Hughes, William,	Holborn,	*Anglesey.*
Hughes, William,	Temple,	*Anglesey.*
Hughes, William,	St. Paul's Churchyard,	*Flint.*
Humphreys, David,	St. Martin's-le-Grand,	*Montgomery.*

J.

James, John,	Old Bond Street,	*Pembroke.*
Ingram, John,	Custom House, London,	*Montgomery.*
Johnson, Edward, Esq.,	Abington Street,	*Radnor.*
Jones, Andrew,	Tower Street,	*Denbigh.*
Jones, David, Esq.,	Marsham Street,	*Montgomery.*
Jones, David,	Bishopsgate Street,	*Denbigh.*
Jones, David,	Friday Street,	*Denbigh.*
Jones, Evan,	Eyre Street, Holborn,	*Brecon.*
Jones, James,	Grafton Street,	*Cardigan.*
Jones, John Goch, Esq.,	Chiswick,	*Montgomery.*
Jones, John, Esq.,	Temple,	*Anglesey.*

Jones, John,	St. James's Market,	*Denbigh.*
Jones, John,	Artillery Lane,	*Denbigh.*
Jones, Luke Powell,	Carey Street,	*Radnor.*
Jones, Michael,	Hatton Garden,	*Glamorgan.*
Jones, Morris,	St. Giles's,	*Cardigan.*
Jones, Owen,	Duck's-foot Lane,	*Denbigh.*
Jones, Richard,	Howard Street,	*Cardigan.*
Jones, Richard,	Doctors Commons,	*Denbigh.*
Jones, Robert, Esq.,	Customhouse, London,	*Denbigh.*
Jones, Robert,	Bishopsgate Street,	*Merioneth.*
Jones, Rowland,	Ludgate Hill,	*Merioneth.*
Jones, Thomas, Esq.,	Park Street, Westminster,	*Cardigan.*
Jones, Thomas,	Kirby Street,	*Caernarvon.*
Jones, Thomas,	Fenchurch Street,	*Merioneth.*
Jones, Thomas,	Fleet Street,	*Flint.*
Jones, Valentine,	Snow Hill,	*Montgomery.*
Jones, Wheldon,	Shad Thames,	*Anglesey.*
Jones, William, Esq.,	Temple,	*Welsh Father.*
Jones, William,	Lombard Street,	*Caernarvon.*
Jones, William,	Spital Fields,	*Caernarvon.*

K.

Kinsey, Josiah,	Holborn,	*Montgomery.*

L.

Labrow, John,	St. John's Street, Clerkenwell,	*Welsh Wife.*
Langford, William,	St. Thomas Apostle,	*Merioneth.*
Legge, Thomas, Esq.,	Doctors Commons,	*Radnor.*
Lewes, John, Esq.,	Wales,	*Cardigan.*
Lewes, Sir Watkin, Kt. and Alderman,	King's Road,	*Pembroke.*
Lewis, Charles Edward, Esq.,	Staple's Inn,	*Welsh Father.*
Lewis, John, Esq.,	Wales,	*Anglesey.*
Lewis, Rev. John,	In the Navy,	*Cardigan.*
Lewis, John,	Bermondsey Street,	*Anglesey.*
Lewis, Valentine,	Bermondsey Street,	*Brecon.*
Lewis, William,	Bartholomew Lane,	*Welsh Father.*
Lytton, Rev. Warburton, Esq.,	Knebworth, Herts.,	*Welsh Mother.*

Ll.

Llewelyn, Thomas, Esq., LL.D.,	Southampton Street, Bloomsbury,	*Brecon.*
Lloyd, Captain Hugh,	In the Army,	*Caernarvon.*
Lloyd, John, Esq., F.R.S.,	Temple,	*Denbigh.*
Lloyd, John,	Holborn,	*Welsh Father.*
Lloyd, Robert,	Wood Street,	*Merioneth.*
Lloyd, Rev. William,	Cowden, Kent,	*Caernarvon.*
Lloyd, William,	Cornhill,	*Merioneth.*

M.

Mathews, John,	Southampton Buildings,	*Glamorgan.*
Mathews, William,	Fleet Street,	*Glamorgan.*
Meares, George Lloyd, Esq.,	Wales,	*Caermarthen.*
Morgan, Charles,	Fleet Street,,	*Glamorgan.*
Morgan, Philip,	Cripplegate,	*Monmouth.*
Morgan, Thomas,		*Brecon.*
Morris, Hugh,	Downing Street,	*Denbigh.*
Morris, Lewis,	Jamaica,	*Cardigan.*
Morris, Richard, Esq.,	Navy Office,	*Anglesey.*
Morris, Robert,	Doctors Commons,	*Denbigh.*

O.

Owen, Rev. Henry, M.D., F.R.S.,	Rector of Edmonton, Mid.,	*Merioneth.*
Owen, Hugh,	Wales,	*Denbigh.*
Owen, John,	Holborn,	*Caernarvon.*
Owen, Owen,	Holborn,	*Caernarvon.*

P.

Parry, Edward,	Lime Street,	*Montgomery.*
Parry, John, Esq.,	Gray's Inn,	*Montgomery.*
Parry, John,	Rhiwabon,	*Caernarvon.*
Parry, Thomas,	Crutched Friars,	*Welsh Father.*
Paterson, John, Esq.,	New Burlington Street,	*Welsh Mother.*
Paynter, William, Esq.,	Navy Office,	*Denbigh.*
Peake, Thomas, Esq.,	Southampton Buildings,	*Denbigh.*
Philipps, Isaac, Esq.,	Customhouse, London,	*Monmouth.*
Poole, Rev. Henry,	Pancrass,	*Merioneth.*
Powell, Joseph,	Cornhill,	*Denbigh.*
Powell, Thomas, Esq.,	Wales, Nant Eos,	*Cardigan.*
Powell, Rev. William, LL.D.,	Wales, Nant Eos,	*Cardigan.*
Prhys, Clopton, Esq.,	Wales,	*Montgomery.*
Price, Rev. John,	Bodleian Library, Oxon.,	*Denbigh.*
Price, Jonathan, Esq.,	Salters Hall,	*Cardigan.*
Price, Rice,	Fetter Lane,	*Brecon.*
Price, Richard, Esq.,	Knebworth, Herts.,	*Cardigan.*
Price, Thomas,	Strand,	*Denbigh.*
Prichard, Joseph Jones, Esq.,	Prerogative Office,	*Brecon.*
Prichard, Thomas,	Ironmonger Lane,	*Caernarvon.*
Prichard, William, Esq.,	Captain of Marines,	*Anglesey.*
Pryce, Edward, Esq.,	Grays Inn,	*Salop.*
Pryce, Edward,	Bucklers Bury,	*Montgomery.*
Pugh, Rev. Edward Vaughan,	Wales, Ty-gwyn, Jal.,	*Merioneth.*

Pugh, Ellis,	Cockspur Street,	*Merioneth.*
Pugh Evan, Esq., Alderman,	Bishopsgate Street,	*Montgomery.*

R.

Rawlinson, George,	Oxford Street,	*Monmouth.*
Rees, Hopkin, Esq.,	Wales,	*Glamorgan.*
Rice, David,	Islington,	*Caermarthen.*
Rice, Morgan, Esq.,	Tooting,	*Glamorgan.*
Richardes, Roderick, Esq.,	Wales, Penglais,	*Cardigan.*
Richards, Evan,	Gracechurch Street,	*Cardigan.*
Richards, Evan Thomas,	Oxford Street,	*Montgomery.*
Richards, Richard, Esq.,	Temple,	*Merioneth.*
Richards, William,	Mount Street,	*Glamorgan.*
Roberts, Edward,	Long Lane, W. Smithfield,	*Salop.*
Roberts, Edward,	Tavistock Street,	*Montgomery.*
Roberts, John,	St. John's Street,	*Denbigh.*
Roberts, Rice,	Bank Coffee House,	*Anglesey.*
Roberts, Richard,	Houndsditch,	*Denbigh.*
Roberts, Robert,	Shoe Lane, Holborn,	*Denbigh.*
Roberts, Thomas,	Bucks.,	*Denbigh.*
Rogers, John,	Aldersgate Street,	*Monmouth.*
Rutter, John,	Friday Street,	*Denbigh.*

S.

Samuel, John,	Cullum Street,	*Denbigh.*
Sidebotham, Samuel,	Rhiwabon,	*Denbigh.*
Stodhart, William, Esq.,	Gerard Street,	*Welsh Wife.*

T.

Thomas, Charles,	Strand,	*Glamorgan.*
Thomas, David,	Moorfields,	*Flint,*
Thomas, Griffith,	Minories,	*Anglesey.*
Thomas, John,	Welsh School,	*Cardigan.*
Thomas, Joshua,	Wales,	*Brecon,*
Thomas, Sir Noah, Kt., M.D., F.R.S.,	Albemarle Street,	*Glamorgan.*
Thomas William,,	Minories,	*Anglesey.*
Tilsley, William,	Newgate Street,	*Montgomery.*
Troughton, John Ellis, Esq.,	Lieut. in the Navy,	*Anglesey.*

V.

Van, Charles, Esq.,	New Palace Yard,	*Monmouth.*
Vaughan, Charles,	Wales,	*Caermarthen.*
Vaughan, Evan Lloyd, Esq., M.P.	Gloucester Court St. James's,	*Merioneth.*
Vaughan, William,	St. Margaret's Hill,	*Caernarvon.*

Watkins, Rev. William,	Stepney,	*Brecon.*
Whitaker, Rev. John,	Park Street, Westminster,	*Welsh Mother.*
Whittell, Thomas,	Town Clerk's Office, Guildhall,	*Salop.*
Williams, Francis,	Charles Street, Westminster,	*Montgomery.*
Williams, Sir Hugh, Bt., M.P.,	Gerard Street,	*Caernarvon.*
Williams, Rev. Hugh,	Rector of Aberfraw,	*Caernarvon.*
Williams, Rev. James,	Jesus College, Oxon.,	*Caermarthen.*
Williams, John,	Purser in the Navy,	*Caermarthen.*
Williams, John,	Fleet Street,	*England.*
Williams, John,	Cornhill,	*Merioneth.*
Williams, John,	Bengal,	*Pembroke.*
Williams, Rice,	Cornhill,	*Caermarthen.*
Williams, Rice,	Queens Square, Westminster,	*Caermarthen.*
Williams, Richard,	Fleet Street,	*Caernarvon.*
Williams, Robert,	Strand,	*Monmouth.*
Williams, Robert,	Poultry,	*Merioneth.*
Williams, Tobias,	St. Martin's Lane,	*Brecon.*
Williams, Walter, Esq.,	Wales,	*Caermarthen.*
Williams, Walter,	Great Queen Street,	*Salop.*
Williams, Watkin, Esq., M.P.,	Upper Brook Street,	*Denbigh.*
Williams, Rev. William,	Blackheath,	*Cardigan.*
Williams, William,	Mercer's Street, Long Acre,	*Denbigh.*
Wynn, Sir Watkin Williams, Bt., M.P.,	St. James's Square,	*Denbigh.*
Wynne, Robert Watkin, Esq.,	Wales, Henllan,	*Denbigh.*

Y.

Yorke, Philip, Esq., M.P.,	Upper Brook Street,	*Denbigh.*

THE WELSH SCHOOL, CLERKENWELL

THE BANNER
OF THE 1751 SOCIETY

WILLIAM VAUGHAN
(First President)

OWAIN JONES, MYFYR.
Founder of the Gwyneddigion Society, in 1770.
Born 1741. Died 1814.

Published by the Society Jan. 1829.

OWAIN MYFYR

Sir HUGH OWEN

THE CYMMRODORION MEDAL

Sir E. VINCENT EVANS

Rev. Dr. GRIFFITH HARTWELL JONES

LIST

OF

CORRESPONDING MEMBERS

AND

MEMBERS ELECT, NOT YET INITIATED.

NAMES.	PLACES OF ABODE.	COUNTIES, &c.
	A.	
Adams, James,	Excise Office,	Pembroke.
	B.	
Beaufort, His Grace the Duke of,	Grosvenor Square,	Welsh Estates.
Bagot, Sir William, Bt., M.P.,	Upper Brook Street,	Denbigh.
Barrington, Hon. Daines,	Temple,	Welsh Judge.
Bowen, Essex, Esq.,	Lieut. in the Navy,	Pembroke.
Bowen, Rev. Furnival,	Buckenham, Norfolk,	Pembroke.
Bradford, John, Bardd,	Bettws,	Glamorgan.
Brisco, James, Esq.,	Beaumaris,	Welsh Wife.
	C.	
Clough, Richard, Esq.,	Lincoln's Inn,	Denbigh.
Conway, William,	Pettycoat Lane,	Flint.
	D.	
Davies, Griffith, Esq.,	Harwich,	Pembroke.
Davies, James,	Mark Lane,	Radnor.
Davies, William,	Chiswell Street,	Montgomery.
Deere, Reynold Thomas, Esq.,	Temple,	Glamorgan.
Dyer, Rev. John,	Blackman Street,	Caermarthen.
Edwards, David,	Thames Street,	Montgomery.
Edwards, Edward, Bardd,	All Souls College, Oxon.,	Flint.
Edwards, Robert,	Goswell Street,	Flint.
Edwards, Roger,	Jermyn Street,	Caermarthen.
Edwards, Thomas,	Fore Street,	Glamorgan.
Edwards, Timothy, Esq.,	Captain in the Navy,	Caernarvon.

Ellis, Rev. John,	Bangor, Archd. of Merioneth,	*Caernarvon.*
Evans, Charles, Esq.,	Trefellir, Anglesey,	*Caernarvon.*
Evans, Rev. Evan, *Bardd,*	Aberystwyth,	*Cardigan.*
Evans, Rev. Evan,	Hinxsworth, Bedfordshire,	*Cardigan.*
Evans, Rev. Peter,	Rector of Harlington, Hants.,	*Denbigh.*
Evans, Rev. William,	Llandycwyn,	*Merioneth.*

F.

Forssteen, William,	Camberwell,	*Welsh Mother.*

G.

Grosvenor, Rt. Hon. Lord,	Grosvenor Square,	*Welsh Estates,*
Gates, Thomas, Esq.,	Coleman Street,	*Welsh Father.*
Griffith, Holland, Esq.,	Temple,	*Anglesey.*
Griffiths, Rev. Richard,	Bangor,	*Caernarvon.*

H.

Harris, William,	Ordnance Office,	*Glamorgan.*
Hoare, James,	Customhouse, London,	*Pembroke.*
Holland, Owen, Esq.,	Conway,	*Caernarvon.*
Hughes, Rev. David,	Jesus College, Oxon.,	*Denbigh.*
Hughes, James,	Billiter Square,	*Flint*
Hughes, Samuel,	Wales,	*Brecon.*
Hughes, Thomas,	Maiden Lane, Covent Garden,	*Caernarvon.*
Hughes, Thomas,	White Chapel,	*Flint.*
Humphreys, Rev. Hugh,	Rhosgolyn, Anglesey,	*Merioneth.*

J.

Jenkins, Rev. John,		*Cardigan.*
Johnson, William, Esq.,	Clay Hill, Enfield,	*Welsh Father.*
Jones, David, *Bardd,*	Trefriw,	*Denbigh.*
Jones, Griffith, Esq.,	Lieut. in the Navy,	*Montgomery.*
Jones, Herbert, Esq.,	Llynon,	*Anglesey.*
Jones, Rev. Humphrey,	Rector of Llanfaethlu,	*Anglesey.*
Jones, Rev. Humphrey Jones, Junr.,	Rector of Trefriw,	*Anglesey.*
Jones, James,	Leicesterfields,	*Cardigan.*
Jones, Rev. John,	Fellow of Jesus College, Oxon.,	*Denbigh.*
Jones, John,	Gracechurch Street,	*Cardigan.*
Jones, Owen,	Butcher Row,	*Caernarvon.*
Jones, Rice,	Blaenau,	*Merioneth.*
Jones, Richard,	Wyrardsbury, Bucks.,	*Anglesey.*
Jones, Samuel,	Smithfield,	*Denbigh.*
Jones, Thomas,	St. Giles's,	*Montgomery.*
Jones, Valentine, Esq.,	Major General in the Army,	*Cardigan.*

Jones, William,	Minories,	Denbigh.
Jones, William, Esq.,	Temple,	Denbigh.
Jones, William,	Wyrardsbury, Bucks.,	Anglesey.

K.

| Kyffin, Rev. John, | Master of Bangor School, | Merioneth. |

L.

Lanwarn, Thomas,	Abingdon Buildings,	Glamorgan.
Lewis, Hugh,	Cornhill,	Radnor.
Lewis, John,	Excise Office,	Radnor.
Lewis, Miles,	Gough Square,	Radnor.
Lewis, Thomas, Esq.,	Theobald's Road, Middlesex,	Carmarthen.
Lewis, Thomas,	Shacklewell, Middlesex,	Cardigan.
Lewis, William, Esq.,	Llanddyfnan,	Anglesey.
Lewis, William,	Black Fields,	Monmouth.

Ll.

Lloyd, Edward, Esq.,	Temple,	Denbigh.
Lloyd, Lewis, Esq.,	Collector, Customs, Holyhead,	Merioneth.
Lloyd, Thomas, Esq.,	Maesmynan,	Flint.
Lloyd, Thomas, Esq.,	Captain in the Navy.	
Lloyd, Rev. William,	Master of Beaumaris School,	Caernarvon.

M.

Milford, Rt. Hon. Lord, M.P.,	James Street, Westminster,	Caermarthen.
Madocks, John, Esq.,	Bedford Row,	Denbigh.
Meredith, Edward,	Rhiwabon,	Denbigh.
Meyrick, Owen Putland, Esq.,	Old Palace Yard,	Anglesey.
Morgan, Thomas, Esq.,	Cliffords Inn,	Glamorgan.
Morgan, William, Esq.,	Great Queen Street,	Glamorgan.
Morris, Robert, Esq.,	Lincolns Inn,	Glamorgan.
Morris, Valentine, Esq.,	Governor of St. Vincent,	Monmouth.
Mostyn, Sir Roger, Bt., M.P.,	Bruton Street,	Flint.
Myddelton, William, Esq.,	Temple,	Flint.

O.

| Orlton, | Downing Street, | Radnor. |
| Owen, Nathaniel, | Old Street, | Flint. |

P.

Paget, Rt. Hon. Lord,	Saville Row,	Anglesey.
Papps, George,	Abergavenny,	Monmouth.
Parker, Charles,	Holborn.	
Panton, Paul, Esq.,	Plas-gwyn, Anglesey,	Flint.

Parry, Harry,	Mincing Lane,	*Monmouth.*
Parry, Richard,	Exchange Alley,	*Denbigh.*
Parry, Rev. Roger,	Sychdyn,	*Flint.*
Paynter, Joshua, Esq.,	Dale,	*Pembroke.*
Pennant, Tho., Esq., F.R.S.	Downing,	*Flint.*
Phillips, Charles, Esq.,	Grays Inn,	*Monmouth.*
Phillips, Rev. Thomas,	Caerlion,	*Monmouth.*
Price, Daniel,	Victualing Office,	*Pembroke.*
Price, George,	New Street, Covent Garden,	*Brecon.*
Price, Gryffith, Esq.,	Lincolns Inn,	
Price, John,	Post Office,	*Radnor.*
Price, Rice,	Tavistock Street,	*Radnor.*
Price, Richard, Esq.,	Knighton,	*Radnor.*
Price, Thomas, Esq.,	Cleveland Row,	*Monmouth.*
Price, Thomas,	Shadwell,	*Glamorgan.*
Price, Thomas,	Lime Street,	*Denbigh.*
Pryce, Rev. Thomas,	Free School, Norwich.	*Cardigan.*
Pugh, Edward,	Holborn,	*Montgomery.*

R.

Richards, Rev. Thomas,	Coychurch,	*Glamorgan.*
Roberts, John,	Caernarvon,	*Caernarvon.*
Roberts, John,	Tower Street,	*Denbigh.*
Roberts, William,	Trade and Plant. Office,	*Glamorgan.*

S.

Stepney, Sir John, Bt., M.P.,	Fludyer Street,	*Caermarthen.*
Samuel, Rev. John,	Llangar,	*Merioneth.*
Shackerly, William, Esq.,	Captain in the Navy,	*Welsh Descent.*

T.

Territ, John,	Wood Street,	*Welsh Wife.*
Thomas, Rev. Anthony, LL.D.,	Stretham,	*Merioneth.*
Thomas, David,	Pay Office, Whitehall,	*Brecon.*
Thomas, Morgan, Esq.,	Llanonn,	*Caermarthen.*
Thomas, Phillip,	Navy Office,	*Welsh Father.*
Thomas, Rev. Richard,	Penmorfa,	*Caernarvon.*
Totty, William,	Austin Friars,	*Flint.*
Turner, William,	Friday Street,	*Montgomery.*

V.

Vincent, Rev. James,	Vicar of Bangor,	*Anglesey.*

W.

Walters, Edward, Esq.,	Bridgend,	*Glamorgan.*
Walters, Rev. John,	Rector of Landough,	*Glamorgan.*

Walters, John,	Paternoster Row,	*Caermarthen.*
Wilkins, Walter, Esq.,	St. John's	*Brecon.*
Williams, George, Esq.,	Temple,	*Brecon.*
Williams, George,	Surgeon in the Navy,	*Caernarvon.*
Williams, Hugh, *Bardd*,	Gwedyr,	*Caernarvon.*
Williams, John,	Caernarvon,	*Caernarvon.*
Williams, Rev. Richard,	Rector of Llandegfan,	*Anglesey.*
Williams, Thomas,	Whitechapel,	*Denbigh.*
Williams, Thomas,	Broad Street, Soho,	*Brecon.*
Williams, William,	Cateaton Street,	*Radnor.*

Western Mail & Echo Ltd., Cardiff.